Baedeker

Berlin
Potsdam

www.baedeker.com

Verlag Karl Baedeker

SIGHTSEEING HIGHLIGHTS ✶ ✶

The Pergamonmuseum, Potsdamer Platz, the Brandenburg Gate and Unter den Linden are all sights in Berlin that are not to be missed, but there are many other places that are also worth a look.

Brandenburg Gate
Berlin's premier landmark forms the centrepiece of the annual German reunification celebrations

Nefertiti
Berlin's most beautiful woman?

Potsdamer Platz
Indisputably breathtaking, the tent roof of the Sony Center

BAEDEKER'S BEST TIPS

Here is a selection of the hottest tips to be found in this guide. See and experience Berlin at its best.

🄴 Traces of the Wall
There is not much left of the Berlin Wall but there is a place that provides all the information you need about it.
► page 37

The Wall
All you need to know can be learned at the documentation centre on Bernauer Strasse

🄴 The Boros Collection
Berlin's most unusual art collection
► page 50

🄴 In the Captain's Fooststeps
Berlin as seen by the captain of Köpenick
► page 182

🄴 Multimedia guide to the Wall
GPS-supported multimedia tour of 22 places of memorial ► page 192

🄴 World of chocolate
In 1863 Heinrich Fassbender opened a chocolate factory in Mohrenstrasse near Gendarmenmarkt. A newcomer on the opposite side of the square is the first flagship store opened by Ritter Sport.
► page 226

🄴 A Walk to Nikolskoe
A pleasant stroll through the Volkspark Glienicke with plenty of opportunities to stop for a rest ► page 230

🄴 The Mighty Wurlitzer
Cinema sounds from Grandpa's day
► page 246

🄴 Little Vietnam – on a large scale
200 Vietnamese traders in eight halls selling an overwhelming range of goods
► page 256

🄴 A boat trip with sunshine
Glide across Müggelsee without noise or pollution, starting from Köpenick.
► page 265

🄴 Dial A for art
If you would like to have your portrait painted, an agency provides artists who will do it in almost any style.
► page 298

🄴 Florida, nice and cold
The fantastic ice cream from the Florida ice cream parlour is now available not just in Spandau but also in the government quarter. ► page 306

🄴 Berlin Story
A place offering more literature, illustrated books or Berlin kitsch is hard to find.
► page 339

Müggelsee →
...tempting beer gardens in the suburb of Friedrichshagen

Marlene Dietrich – the most
famous Berliner of all?
▶ page 56

PRACTICALITIES

BACKGROUND

Schloss Bellevue is the residence of the German president
► **page 184**

TOURS

BERLIN FROM A TO Z

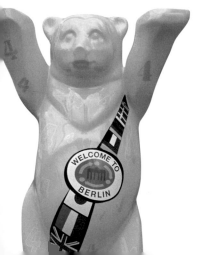

*Friedrich II made his
mark on Potsdam and
Berlin both*
► page 60

POTSDAM
FROM A TO Z

Extremely popular for trips: Pfaueninsel
► page 291

Background

EVERYTHING YOU NEED TO KNOW
ABOUT BERLIN: ITS ECONOMY, ITS
ARCHITECTURE, ITS HISTORY,
AND THE PEOPLE – SUCH AS
THE »CAPTAIN OF KÖPENICK«
WILHELM VOIGT – WHO PLAYED
THEIR PART.

STILL UNDER CONSTRUCTION

The new Berlin is on its way to becoming a proper capital city again since the dismantling of the Wall but will there ever be an end to the sand, dust, stone, glass and steel, the new roofs and towers atop the old walls? A new underground railway line will run beneath the trees lining the avenue of Unter den Linden. Schinkel's Academy of Architecture, a veritable castle in the air, reaches for the sky concealed behind the tiers of stones printed on its tarpaulin sheeting. Cranes cluster around the Ostbahnhof railway station to haul the next building up from the banks of the Spree. This is how the city has been since the start of the century: Berlin is coming into being.

The sky *over Berlin is no longer divided – as if it ever was.*

In this maelstrom of change, visitors to Berlin can be certain of seeing and experiencing new things, be it their first visit or one of many. Architects from all over the world have left startling legacies such as Helmuth Jahn's Sony Center on Potsdamer Platz or Daniel Libeskind's Jüdisches Museum (Jewish Museum) in Kreuzberg. Cultural treasures, crumbling due to the effects of war, lack of money or plain negligence, places like Berlin's Museumsinsel (Museum Island), are now being meticulously restored. Foreign embassies are also adding their own spice to the mix with such contributions as native materials from India or distinctive architecture from Mexico. Yet links to the past are being kept too, not just in terms of architecture but also by the city's 150 museums. They cover German history from Frederick the Great to East Germany under Erich Honecker, including the secrets of the notorious Stasi, as well as the monstrosities perpetrated under the rule of Hitler. Preserved steam boats ply the waterways of the city from historic quays and even underneath the town it is possible to take a guided tour of the old bunkers. Other museums deal with the history of homosexuality or show children how youngsters lived in former times. Antique musical instruments can be heard in concert and one of the most impressive museums of art in the world allows you to admire paintings from all over the western world.

Victoria
The goddess of victory who steers the chariot atop the Brandenburg Gate was originally intended to be Irene, goddess of peace

The Kanzleramt
– the seat of government in Germany. The architecture at the country's political hub dwarfs its visitors

Great names
Do they get the respect they deserve?

Classical and modern
Nike, goddess of triumph, teaches a boy to fight on the Schlossbrücke and has no interest in the Fernsehturm

Art and contemplation
For museum-goers Berlin is a paradise. Some of the world's most evocative treasures are here to be admired

Don't forget
Potsdam has plenty to offer other than palaces and gardens

The City Never Sleeps

A huge selection of entertainment is on offer: opera, theatre, concerts, cabaret and variety, music and dance, readings and art openings are all provided for in spades every day of the week. In Berlin the bars and clubs never close, so that in Kreuzberg, in Schöneberg or around Hackescher Markt there are always night owls about. Every year, some 100,000 young people from all over the world spend time in Berlin, bringing their own influence to bear on the art, culture and fashion of the city and leaving their own indelible mark upon it. The Love Parade, which only a few years ago would attract millions of techno aficionados, is no more, but the Carnival of Cultures, in which people from 80 nations demonstrate their own music, dance and costumes in a festival lasting several days, already looks likely to take its place. Music is everywhere in Berlin, and that has attracted many major companies to the city, looking to make a profit but simultaneously benefiting impoverished parts of the massively indebted metropolis by their money-making presence.

To be a capital city is an expensive affair. Not all of the German ministries have been transferred to Berlin, since some still remain in Bonn, but it is now demonstrably the case that Berlin has become the political epicentre of the republic. It boasts the residence of the president and it is the venue for the meetings of the Bundestag and Bundesrat, the two houses of the national parliament, whose presence here has made for a massive increase in the region's political and media prominence.

Welcome to Berlin!
A city that never closes

Easy Living in Berlin

But Berlin also has its quiet side: green, open spaces with the waters of the Spree lapping against its banks or white sails on the Havel. Even those for whom such places are too far out of town have the numerous parks at their disposal for games, music or open-air cinema in the summer. Then there is always the zoo with its lawns, streams, trees and flowers, boats for hire and, of course, its own beer garden. And only from its steam boats can Berlin be experienced as the Berliners themselves see it. From this vantage point it is plain that there are prettier cities, but are there any as exciting?

Facts

Berlin today: since 1990 Berlin has made huge strides in order to live up to the role of being a capital city, to the extent that the Bonn era is now quite forgotten.

Population · Politics · Economy

The Making of Berlin

Berlin and the march of Brandenburg (Mark Brandenburg) were colonized in the 13th century by people from the lowlands around the Harz mountains and from the Lower Rhine. At the end of the Middle Ages it is estimated that there were 6000 people living in the town. The demographic structure was dramatically influenced by the arrival of some 20,000 **Huguenot** refugees from France, who came to the march after the edict of Potsdam (1685). About 6000 of these »Réfugiés« were settled in Berlin itself and made up around a third of the population at the time. With the expansion of industry after 1800, more and more people flooded into the city. The influx increased even more after Berlin was declared the capital of the German Empire in 1871. By 1943 the population had peaked at around 4.3 million people. Political developments after the Second World War, economic troubles and the building of the Berlin Wall in 1961 all led to a complete upheaval of the demographic and the flow of people. Although the return of evacuees and the arrival of refugees from East Germany initially led to the population of West Berlin steadily rising until 1957, all such growth was dramatically arrested after 13 August 1961. In East Berlin numbers had declined continuously until then, due to defectors fleeing to the West (about 100,000 are estimated to have fled between 1950 and 1960). After 1961, though, the population increased slowly but steadily. Since the fall of the Wall almost a million Berliners have left the city but this exodus has been very nearly matched by a simultaneous influx of newcomers.

A city of outsiders

More than 450,000 of Berlin's population is of foreign extraction, including people from some 183 countries. The largest group of these, almost 30%, is made up of Turks. Many of these are already third-generation Berliners. The main concentrations of Turks are in Kreuzberg and Neukölln. The next largest contingents comprise people from the former Yugoslavia or from Poland.

Foreigners in Berlin

Capital, Federal State, Community

A vote in the German parliament, the Bundestag, on 20 June 1991 established Berlin as the seat of government and parliament in the new united Germany. However, it was not until eight years later that the government and the Bundestag itself finally departed Bonn. Only then could Berlin start to regard itself once again as a fully fledged

Seat of government and parliament

← *The architecture of parliament is cool in style:*
Paul-Löbe-Ufer on the banks of the Spree

Differing ways of life merge together lti-cultural Kreuzberg

capital city. To minimize the consequences to the former West German capital of Bonn, each of the national ministries has a primary and a secondary headquarters, one in each of the two cities. Most of the primary headquarters, though, are on the Spree rather than the Rhine.

Berlin state   The metropolitan district of Berlin also makes up one of Germany's federal states in its own right. The government of the city and of the eponymous state is a senate voted by the elected councillors of the Abgeordetenhaus (House of Representatives) and led by a mayor whose rank is equivalent to that of a prime minister of a state of the federation. This model is the same as that employed in West Berlin from 1950 to 1990. The traditional model involving a municipal government led by a mayor had been retained in East Berlin until that time. The Berlin state legislature, the House of Representatives, is elected every four years and meets in the former Prussian parliament building.

Districts   At the end of 2000/start of 2001 the number of boroughs (»Bezirke«) in Berlin was reduced from 23 to 12. These districts are administered by borough officials led by a local mayor. Two of the newly formed districts (Friedrichshain-Kreuzberg and Mitte = Mitte / Tiergarten / Wedding) cross the former east/west boundaries.

The Shift from Industry to Services

Great industrial   Before the Second World War, Berlin was one of the major centres of
tradition   the German economy. It was home to the country's most important

Berlin City Boroughs

Former route of the Berlin Wall

©Baedeker

I Mitte (city centre)	**V** Spandau	**IX** Treptow-Köpenick
II Friedrichshain-Kreuzberg	**VI** Steglitz-Zehlendorf	**X** Marzahn-Hellersdorf
III Pankow	**VII** Tempelhof-Schöneberg	**XI** Lichtenberg
IV Charlottenburg-Wilmersdorf	**VIII** Neukölln	**XII** Reinickendorf

banks, insurers and syndicates. Companies like Borsig, established in 1837, Siemens & Halske and AEG (Allgemeine Elektrizitätsgesellschaft) also gave Berlin its reputation as Germany's most important centre of industry. After the end of the war, the economy suffered due to the destruction wrought by war, the dismantling of industrial concerns by the Soviets and the blockade of the city: Berlin lost 77% of its pre-war industrial capacity. Nevertheless both sectors of the city developed, in spite of their opposing politico-economic philosophies, into important centres of trade and industry. In spite of its forced isolation, West Berlin became one of the key industrial contributors to the economy of the German Federal Republic. East Berlin took on a similar role in the east and grew to become its primary economic and planning nexus as well as the most important industrial base of the German Democratic Republic.

Facts and Figures Berlin

© Baedeker

Location
▶ North German basin
▶ 52° 31' N
▶ 13° 25' E

Land area
▶ 892 sq km/344 sq mi
▶ North-south axis 38km/24mi
▶ East-west axis 45km/28mi

Highest elevation
▶ Natural: Müggelberge 115m/377ft
▶ Artificial: Rubble mound (Trümmerberg) at Teufelssee 115m/377ft

Population
▶ 3.4 million approx.
▶ Population density: 3804 inhabitants per sq km/1469 per sq mi
▶ Highest population: Pankow 348,000
▶ Highest population density: Friedrichshain-Kreuzberg 12,500 per sq km/ 4800 per sq mi
▶ Inhabitants of foreign origin: 450,900 = 13.5%

Comparisons:
▶ London 7.3 million
▶ Paris 2.1 million
▶ New York 8.1 million

Political status and structure
▶ Federal state
▶ Local mayor equivalent to a prime minister of a German bundesland
▶ 12 districts

Economy
▶ Gross Domestic Product GDP (2008) €87,500 million (8th highest in Germany)
▶ Distribution of employment:
  – 84% services
  – 15.6% industry
  – 0.4% agriculture
▶ Unemployment rate (2008): 13.9%
▶ State debt: €59,100 million

Tourism
▶ 7.9 million visitors in 2008 (most popular destination in Germany, 3rd in Europe)

Transport
▶ Main airport: Tegel (»Otto Lilienthal«), 14.5 million passengers in 2008
▶ 14 regional rail lines (S-Bahn – 331.5km/206mi route mileage)
▶ 10 underground lines (U-Bahn – 144.2km/89.6mi route mileage)
▶ 27 suburban rail lines (Tram – 187.7km/116.6mi route mileage)
▶ 155 bus routes
▶ 1.4 million vehicles
▶ 68.1km/42.3mi inner-city motorway

After the collapse of the Wall, the head-on collision of two such utterly polarized economic systems caused serious problems. Most of the factories in the eastern sector were totally out of date and there was practically no chance that their products would find a market. Many of them were forced to close or to drastically cut staff levels. In the west too, however, the sudden combination of two economic regions had negative effects. The loss of subsidies that had been supporting the isolated city meant that many of its businesses were no longer profitable either. Many companies relocated their business to other regions, especially to parts of the former East Germany but sometimes to what had been East Berlin. The city's status as federal capital, though, meant that many large companies decided to move their headquarters to the new united Berlin. These included Deutsche Bahn AG, Coca Cola, IBM, Daimler-debis and the European arm of Sony.

The merging of the economies

Over 800 industrial enterprises are based in Berlin. The city's leading sector is the electrical industry (the former AEG, Siemens, DeTeWe, Bosch, Osram), followed by mechanical engineering (Rotaprint, ABB, Otis) and motor vehicles (BMW motorcycles, Mercedes Benz, Ford). Further important branches are the paper and printing industry, including the Axel-Springer Verlag, textiles, food (bakeries) and tobacco (Philip Morris). The chemical industry primarily produces consumer goods (Bayer Schering Pharma, Gillette).

Industry

Commerce and service companies have become the driving force behind the Berlin economy. In comparison with other major cities in Germany, Berlin has the second highest rate of growth in the service sector – particularly in entertainment industries. The areas of software, telecommunications, media, music and film are the main engines of growth and there are more than 8000 companies active in these fields. The International Congress Centre (ICC) with its accompanying exhibition and convention grounds has made Berlin an outstanding location for congresses and trade fairs. The most important events include the International Radio Exhibition (Internationale Funkausstellung; IFA), the International Tourism Exchange (Internationale Tourismusbörse, ITB), the International Agricultural Products Exhibition (Grüne Woche) and the International Aerospace Exhibition (Internationale Luft- und Raumfahrt-Ausstellung, Berlin-Brandenburg; ILA). Berlin is Germany's leading destination for city breaks. 723 hotels and other sites make 106,200 beds available for visitors and accommodated 19 million overnight stays in 2009. Almost 40% of the tourists come from abroad, mainly from the United Kingdom, Italy, the Netherlands and Spain. Budget flights have brought the city its very own tourist boom the so-called Easyjetset, mostly young or very young, who come in their thousands every weekend. From Thursday to Sunday they hang out in the techno scene at about half a dozen clubs between Alexanderplatz, Oberbaumbrücke and Ostbahnhof. They have created a subculture that is

Commerce and services

◄ Trade fairs, congresses and exhibitions

◄ Tourism

remarkable in terms of numbers but is hardly noticed by normal Berliners but contributes to Berlin's reputation as the cheap, hip party capital of Europe.

Construction   Berlin experienced an incomparable boom in the construction industry during the 1990s, with huge projects such as the Kanzleramt (Chancellery) and the reconstruction of Potsdamer Platz. Unfortunately Berlin's own construction sector benefited only marginally from this boom as the lion's share of the major projects went to West German and foreign concerns, often using cheap labour from eastern Europe.

Transport   Before the war Berlin was a transport hub to equal any in Europe. In terms of rail traffic in particular, it was a hub between western and eastern Europe with 500 trains a day entering its stations. Its unique situation and the east/west split subsequent to the war meant that the city lost some of that earlier importance. Only very few land routes, road or rail, were left open for traffic to West Berlin and only companies of the western allies offered flights to the city. After the Wall was built, East Berlin was initially closed entirely to westerners and only became accessible to those with passes to visit relatives, then later by means of a one-day visa. Access to the non-urban areas surrounding the city always required a visa. The most controversial of the major projects proposed for Berlin's transport infrastructure in future involves the excavation of tunnels under the government and parliament precinct next to the Spree and Tiergarten for road and rail links.

Berliner Ring ►   Berlin has its own circular motorway ring road, the »Berliner Ring«. Motorways within the inner city include the **Avus** (»Automobil-Verkehrs- und Übungsstrasse«), which was opened as early as 1921 and was the first »dual carriageway with no crossroads, solely for motor vehicles«, i.e. the world's first motorway. Its two parallel straights are both 8.5km/5.3mi long and lead through the Grunewald to the Nikolassee. Nowadays it is designated the A 115. The Avus was even used for the first ever German Grand Prix in 1926. In 1937 Bernd Rosemeyer set a lap record of 276.4kmh / 171.7mph driving an Auto Union car. Rudolf Caracciola set the speed record on the straight, reaching 400kmh / 248.5mph in his Mercedes.

Air traffic ►   Berlin's Tegel airport is the main destination for flights from western Europe and the USA; while Berlin Schönefeld is the primary hub for flights from eastern and southeastern Europe, Asia and the Near East and is particularly important for charter services. The fate of what was formerly the central airport, Berlin Tempelhof in the heart of the city, has been decided: following the failure of a plebiscite, flights came to an end in 2008. Plans for a giant flight terminus to the south of Berlin have been abandoned in favour of expanding the airport at Schönefeld. From 2012 it is planned to be Berlin's sole airport under the name BBI Brandenburg International

An ideal starting point for night owls in the centre of Berlin is the Hackescher Markt S-Bahn station, served by three different lines

Berlin is linked via the Oder-Spree canal, the Teltow canal and the Oder-Havel canal to the European river and canal system. A large proportion of the freight traffic to and from Berlin travels via these canals using the docks at Wedding/Tiergarten in the west and Friedrichshain in the east.

◄ River traffic

With the new **central station**, Europe's largest and most modern rail interchange, Berlin is seeking to regain some of its earlier status as a key transport hub in Europe. The two previous main stations (Bahnhof Zoo in the west, Ostbahnhof in the east) have thus lost their importance for long-distance traffic.

◄ Rail traffic

History of the City

From a trading centre at a ford on the Spree to the capital of the Prussian and finally of the German state. After the defeat of Germany, the city almost faced ruin but since its forced division has been ended, Berlin has begun to sparkle once again.

Germans, Slavs and the House of Ascania

50,000 BC approx.	First signs of settlement
1200–800 BC	Peak of Bronze Age settlement
600	Migration of the West Slavs
1134	Albrecht the Bear becomes first margrave of the northern march of Brandenburg
1237	First documentary evidence of Cölln: founding of the city

Germans

At the time of the Roman empire a German tribe called the Semnon settled alongside the Havel. Locations where villages and homesteads have been found include modern-day Buch (Pankow), Lichterfelde (Steglitz) and what is now the parkland around Schloss Bellevue.

Slavs

In around AD 600 West Slavic tribes entered the region and founded settlements including **Spandau** and **Köpenick**. They maintained independence until 928 when King Heinrich I conquered their Brandenburg fortress. King Otto the Great established the bishoprics of Havelberg and Brandenburg in 948.

Ascanians

Under the Holy Roman Emperor Lothar I the settlements in the northeast came under attack. In 1134 the Ascanian Albrecht the Bear became margrave of the northern march. This encouraged some Ascanian settlers to move to the shores of the Spree from their homelands in the Harz region. People also immigrated from the Rhine and Frankish territories. A trading post was established on the site of what is now Mühlendamm. This became the core of the twin settlements, **Berlin and Cölln**. The towns must have been granted charters in around 1230 by the margraves Johann I and Otto III. However, no documentary mention of Cölln exists until 1237 (and there is no mention of it as a town until 1251). Evidence naming the town of Berlin only exists as of 1244. Nevertheless, 1237 is usually regarded as the official date for the founding of the city. The twin towns profited from the merchants passing through and they were soon able to afford city walls and churches such as the Marienkirche

Memorial to Albrecht the Bear at the Spandau Citadel

← *The Cold War heats up. Soviet and US tanks face each other at Checkpoint Charlie in late October 1961*

(Church of St Mary) and the Nikolaikirche (Church of St Nicholas). In 1280 a mint was established that was the first in the march east of the Elbe. The two towns combined to build a joint town hall in 1307 but with the death of Margrave Waldemar, the last of the Ascanians, that period of peace and prosperity came to an end. Berlin was admitted to the Hanseatic League in 1359 but the twin towns were already caught up in a power struggle between the houses of Luxemburg and Wittelsbach for control of the march. Two major fires in 1376 and 1380 destroyed large parts of the municipality.

Residence of the Elector

1415	Friedrich VI of Hohenzollern becomes elector of Brandenburg
1432	Merging of Berlin and Cölln
1447 –48	The Berlin Indignation
1640–88	The Great Elector

Elevation to electors' residence The struggle for power in the march finally ended when emperor Sigismund appointed the burgrave of Nuremberg, Friedrich VI of Hohenzollern, to take control of the march of Brandenburg in 1411. Friedrich won back both goods and regions that had been stolen by maverick nobles such as the brothers Johann and Dietrich von Quitzow and was rewarded with the title Elector of Brandenburg by the Council of Constance in 1415. Berlin and Cölln were formally amalgamated into a single municipality in 1432. In 1440 Friedrich's son **Friedrich II, »Eisenzahn« (»Irontooth«)**, became elector. He initiated the building of a castle in Cölln in 1443 but his policies, including the separation of the two towns, and the withdrawal of privileges brought him into conflict with the people. The citizens of Cölln and Berlin rose up in revolt in 1447 and 1448 in a rebellion called the »Berlin Indignation« but Friedrich was able to put down the insurrection. Berlin was built up and became the electors' residence with the castle at »Cölln on the Spree« becoming the permanent home of the ruler as of 1470. In 1539 Elector **Joachim II** converted to Protestantism. He invited artists to the city, and among the buildings he built was the Spandau Citadel. Upon his death, however, in 1571 the economy of the march collapsed and Berlin was plunged into serious poverty. In 1600 Berlin still had around 12,000 inhabitants but the Thirty Years' War had a particularly drastic effect on the march of Brandenburg and Berlin's suburbs dwindled.

The Great Elector In 1640 the electorship passed to Friedrich Wilhelm. During his reign the suburbs of Friedrichswerder and Dorotheenstadt came into being, Schloss Köpenick was built, the Lustgarten park was laid out and Berlin was fortified. Construction of the Oder-Spree Canal (Friedrich-Wilhelm Canal) between 1662 and 1668 meant that Berlin became a major transit port between Hamburg and Breslau (Wroclaw). In 1671 the elector authorized the establishment of a Jewish community and his Edict of Potsdam proclaimed in 1685 made it possible for Huguenots being persecuted in France to settle in the march. It is not without reason that Friedrich Wilhelm has gone down in history as »The Great Elector«. His son Friedrich III continued in the same tradition, founding the Akademie der Künste (Academy of Arts) in 1696. A corresponding academy for science was instituted in 1700 by **Gottfried Wilhelm Leibniz**.

Capital of Prussia

1701 – 13	King Friedrich I
1713 – 40	King Friedrich Wilhelm I
1740 – 86	King Friedrich II (Frederick the Great)
1806 – 08	French occupation
1810	Founding of the Friedrich Wilhelm University
1848	March Revolution

Friedrich's own ambitions had a quite different objective, however. In 1701 he made a proclamation in Königsberg declaring himself to be Friedrich I, the first king of Prussia. During his rule the suburb of Friedrichstadt was created and major edifices such as the Zeughaus (arsenal) and **Schloss Charlottenburg** were built. He also founded the Charité University in 1710. At this point Berlin had 56,000 inhabitants, 6000 of whom were French.

Prussia becomes a kingdom

Friedrich I's son, Friedrich Wilhelm I, the »Soldier King«, was the very opposite of his father. He had little time for grandeur. His father had left the state coffers empty and he was forced to make savings. This did not prevent him expanding the army and improving city defences, however, and money was also found for roads, commercial buildings and housing, as well as for the advancement of education. Life was strict and spartan, though, and the Lustgarten park was transformed into a parade ground.

The Soldier King

During the reign of Friedrich II, known as Frederick the Great or even »Old Fritz«, Berlin developed into one of the major cities of Europe. The king managed to persuade **Voltaire**, one of the great thinkers of the age, to join his court and take his place at the head of

Germany's »Capital of the Enlightenment«

an illustrious group of artists and philosophers. They and others such as **Friedrich Nicolai** and **Moses Mendelssohn** made Berlin into Germany's »Capital of Enlightenment«. Frederick ordered the planting of the Unter den Linden boulevard, the construction of Schloss Bellevue and a new wing for Schloss Charlottenburg. Cotton and silk manufacturing also took off, making Berlin the major textile manufacturing centre in Germany. In 1761 the Königliche Porzellan-Manufaktur (Royal Porcelain Factory) was established. By that time, though, Berlin had also seen the flip side of the monarch's politics. The city had come under bombardment from Austrian and Russian forces in 1760 in the course of the Seven Years' War and was occupied for four days. Nevertheless, in the year that Frederick the Great died, Berlin's population was as high as 150,000.

The Prussian royal residence on a copper engraving from 1729

Upon the death of »Old Fritz«, Prussia withdrew from European politics. But by 1800 Berlin had 200,000 inhabitants and was the third-largest city on the continent after London and Paris. It remained the spiritual centre of Prussia and it was a major centre of **German Romanticism**, as epitomized by Schlegel, Tieck, Chamisso and E.T.A. Hoffmann. Even two years of occupation by the French after Napoleon marched into the city on 27 October 1806 was unable to dent the Romantic trend. Subsequently, Berlin developed into a modern city, which by the end of the 19th century was one of the greatest metropolises in the world. The Friedrich-Wilhelm University was established in 1810 by Wilhelm von Humboldt, in 1816 the *Princess Charlotte*, Germany's first steamship, was launched on the Spree, in 1826 the city's first gas works started supplying fuel, the Borsig machine factory opened in 1837, with the first railway line starting operation between Berlin and Potsdam in 1838 followed by the inaugural horse-drawn tram between Alexanderplatz and Potsdamer Platz in 1839. There was a wave of construction, with which the name of **Karl Friedrich Schinkel** is closely associated. This produced such buildings as the Neue Wache, the Schauspielhaus and the Altes Museum. Industrialization had its price, though, with a swathe of social problems arising from the grinding poverty of the working classes.

Demands for free speech and freedom of the press had been growing throughout Europe, and Berlin was no exception. This meant putting an end to an oppressive law called the Karlsbad Resolution. On 18 March 1848 troops opened fire on a crowd gathered before the palace in Berlin. Prince Wilhelm of Prussia, brother of the king, was said to have given the order and was thereafter known as the »Kartätschenprinz« (prince of canister shot). The subsequent riots led to 250 deaths (**»March Martyrs«**). On 19 March the garrison abandoned the city and the king granted freedom of the press, freedom of congregation, coalition and the right to vote. Friedrich Wilhelm IV saw himself as »a romantic on the throne of Prussia« and on 21 March he delivered a proclamation to the German people, declaring that he would seek to lead Germany to the »salvation of the fatherland«. Nevertheless he refused to accept the title of emperor when it was offered to him by the parliament in Frankfurt on 3 April 1849. In 1861 the aforesaid »Kartätschenprinz« succeeded him as Wilhelm I, and a year later Otto von Bismarck was appointed prime minister of Prussia. Berlin became the capital of the North German Confederation and its seat of parliament in 1866.

March Revolution 1848

At the same time, though, Berlin was just as much the centre of Germany's labour movement. The town had hosted the country's first workers' congress as early as August and September of 1848. In April 1862 **Ferdinand Lasalle** published his »programme for workers« and a general labour congress took place in 1868 that resulted in the founding of Germany's first trades unions.

Capital of the German labour movement

Capital of the German Empire

1871	18 January: proclamation of the German Empire
1878	Berlin Congress
1879	World's first electric trams start running in Berlin
1918	Proclamation of the republic
1919	Spartacus revolt
1920	Kapp Putsch; formation of Greater Berlin
1933	30 January: Hitler becomes chancellor 27 February: burning of the Reichstag
1936	XI Olympic Games
1943	18 February: Goebbels declares »total war« in the Sportpalast
1945	8 May: surrender of German forces in Berlin-Karlshorst

Imperial Berlin   On 18 January 1871 in the Hall of Mirrors at Versailles, a German empire (»Deutsches Reich«) was declared with the Prussian Wilhelm I as emperor or »Kaiser«. Berlin was appointed capital and imperial residence. By this time, the city had become home to some 823,000 people. Politics pushed Berlin to the forefront with the Berlin Congress of 1878 and the **Year of the Three Emperors in 1888** when Wilhelm I's successor, Friedrich III, died after reigning for just 99 days to be followed by Wilhelm II. The **resignation of Otto von Bismarck** was soon to follow. In terms of daily life in Berlin, though, it was the technical developments that were of greater importance. In 1879 came the first electric lights and the world's first electric railway ran at the World's Fair in Moabit, in 1881 a telephone service was instituted and electric trams ran for the first time in Lichterfelde, with the tram system opening to the public the following year. In 1902 elevated and underground railways (Zoo – Warschauer Tor) were opened, and 1905 saw the debut of motorized buses on the city streets. The city grew apace. 1.9 million people were resident in Berlin by 1900. Rapid industrialization led to the building of masses of typical barrack-like houses, where working people lived in miserable conditions.

»Donnerwetter!« The impeccable Wilhelm II defined his era

First World War and revolution   Berlin suffered no direct attacks during the First World War, but suffered the deprivations of the conflict in the form of rationing and hunger. Disillusionment with the war was widespread and finally led to revolution. On 9 November 1918, Social Democratic Party leader **Philipp Scheidemann** declared Germany a republic from the window of the Reichstag, the parliament building in Berlin. The intention was to form a socialist republic, as announced by **Karl Liebknecht** from the balcony of the imperial palace on the same day. Kaiser Wilhelm II went straight from the German headquarters at Spa in Belgium into exile in Holland. However wrangles between the government, under the leadership of the social democrats, and the communist party led to the violent outbreak of the Spartacus Revolt in January 1919. In Berlin, particularly around the newspaper publishing district, there was major street fighting. On 15 January **Rosa Luxemburg** and Karl Liebknecht, the leaders of the German communist party, the KPD, were murdered by soldiers of the Freikorps. No sooner was the extreme left dealt with than the right-wing also made a play. During the Kapp Putsch of March 1920, Freikorps militiamen occupied government offices in Berlin and the government itself fled to Stuttgart. It was only the calling of a general strike that pulled the carpet from under the putsch leaders. Berlin itself underwent a boundary reform in the very year that the crisis emerged, its suburbs being divided into 20 boroughs to create a Greater Berlin area that made it the second-biggest city in Europe after London.

During the period of the Weimar Republic, Berlin developed into an economic, political, cultural and social cynosure for all of Europe and Germany's centre for **film, theatre and news publishing**. It was a heady time for the city when names such as Erwin Piscator, Max Reinhardt, Fritz Lang, Elisabeth Bergner, Josephine Baker, Kurt Tucholsky and Bertolt Brecht all came to the fore. In 1923 Germany's first radio broadcast was made from the Vox Haus. Nevertheless, all the glamour could not obscure the political tension beneath. As the National Socialist party gained strength enough for **Joseph Goebbels** to become »Gauleiter« (regional party leader) of Berlin, conflict between left and right grew in intensity. Fights in public places and on the streets were practically daily occurrences as Berlin suffered badly from the depression that had gripped the world.

The »Golden Twenties«

On 30 January 1933 **Adolf Hitler** was appointed chancellor of the German Reich. Nazi stormtroopers celebrated with a torchlight parade through the Brandenburg Gate to the Reichskanzlei (Chancellery). In the midst of it Berlin itself became the headquarters for a reign of terror. A fire that tore through the Reichstag building on 28 February gave the Nazis the chance they needed to eliminate their opponents. By 1 April a boycott of Jewish businesses had begun. On 10 May books by left-wing, democratic and Jewish authors were burned at Opernplatz. In 1936 forced emigration of Jews was instituted. That same year the Olympic games were held in Berlin but the Nazis perverted the event to serve their own propaganda. During the event, a façade of goodwill was presented in which all traces of anti-Semitism were removed from the streets and Jewish athletes were even named in the German Olympic team, while the expulsions continued in the background. In 1937 Hitler appointed Albert Speer to the post of general inspector with the task of redesigning Berlin so that it could be transformed into a pan-Germanic capital to be named »Germania«. Clearly such a design would exclude any Jewish presence and on the night of the 9 and 10 November 1938, **Pogrom**

Berlin under the Nazis

Wilhelmstrasse in 1934: a formation of SS troops stand at ease in front of the Chancellery for the funeral possession of president Paul von Hindenburg

A PLACE IN GERMAN HISTORY

Berlin was the capital of the German Reich from the founding of the country in 1871 until the end of the Nazi era. Its most important ministries, chancelleries and embassies stood along Wilhelmstrasse, which leads southwards from Pariser Platz, and on its side streets.

This part of town is called **Friedrichstadt**, founded in 1688 as a separate community. It was absorbed into the Prussian capital in 1710. In the early 18th century under Friedrich Wilhelm I several mansions were built here for the aristocracy. These were converted into government buildings after the foundation of the German Empire or »Reich« in 1871. As capital of the new state, Berlin underwent considerable development during the latter part of the 19th century and there was a large amount of new building in Friedrichstadt, so that the area was not only **the centre of government**, but also »the most elegant place to live in Berlin«, as Baedeker's Berlin guide of 1878 put it. During the Weimar Republic era the government buildings were kept on unchanged; only when the Nazis came to power did the suburb take on a new look. Their gigantomania brought in the radical new buildings of the »Neue Reichskanzlei« (New Chancellery) on Voßstrasse as well as the air ministry, the Reichsluftfahrt-

ministerium. After the war the East Germans renamed the street between Pariser Platz and Vossstrasse after prime minister Otto Grotewohl and sought to extinguish memories of the past by building a housing estate all along the western side of the road, some 20m/22yd back from where the previous street front had been. Right behind the development was the start of the heavily guarded border strip stretching to Potsdamer Platz.

A look back

With the exception of the former Reichsluftfahrtministerium, nothing remains of the area as it was before the war. The map reproduced to the right shows the buildings that were in existence in 1939.

Right-hand side of Wilhelmstrasse (»Reichsseite«):

No. 70: This had been the British embassy since 1876. Previously it was the city mansion of one Dr. Strousberg. A new British embassy has now been built on the site.

No. 72: Palace of Prince August Wilhelm of Prussia that was used by the agriculture and sustenance ministry during the Third Reich.

No. 73: Built from 1734 to 1737 for Count Schwerin and ministry for the royal house after 1872. Official residence of the German presidents Friedrich Ebert and Paul Von Hindenburg during the Weimar Republic. After Hindenburg's death in 1934 it remained unused until 1939 when it was given over to use as a residence of the foreign minister.

No. 74: Built in 1731 for Privy Councillor von Kellner, as of 1848 it was used initially by the Prussian state ministry but later became the chancellor's office. For a period up until 1919 it became the office of the interior ministry, after which it was combined with no. 75 (formerly belonging to court printers Decker) and no. 76 to make up the headquarters of the foreign ministry.

No. 76: Built for Colonel von Pannwitz in 1735, it served as Bismarck's official residence until 1877.

No. 77: This was built for General von der Schulenberg between 1736 and 1739. It then served as the palace of Count Radziwell from 1795 onwards. It was rebuilt in 1875 / 76 and then served as the palace of the chancellor. It was used by Chancellor Bismarck as his private residence until 1890 and it

■ Buildings in existence before 1933
■ Buildings erected by National Socialists
— Route of the Berlin Wall before demolition

Niederkirchnerstrasse is the former name of Prinz-Albrecht-Strasse (pre 1945). The numbers are the house numbers of the various buildings.

was here that the »Berlin Congress« of 1878 took place.

No. 78: »The new palace of the Count of Pless« was initially used as part of the chancellor's office but this building was demolished in 1927 to be replaced by a new building in 1931 that was then incorporated into the new chancellery.

No. 79: Initially used by the trade ministry and later by the railways directorate.

No. 80: Traffic ministry.

Nos. 82–97: The Reichsluftfahrtministerium or air ministry was built in

The new Reich chancellery building on Vossstrasse. The architecture was intended to be daunting

1935 / 36 on the site of the Prussian war ministry. It is the only building in the area to have survived from the old government precinct. It was used as East Germany's combined »Haus der Ministerien« before becoming the headquarters of the Treuhand privatization trust (it was also renamed »Detlev-Rohwedder-Haus« after the murdered head of that organization). Now it houses the German finance ministry. Around the corner to the left, the building at no.5 Prinz-Albrecht-Strasse was the Prussian Abgeordnetenhaus or parliament. For a period in 1934 / 35 it housed the notorious »Volksgerichtshof« before Goering redefined it as the »Haus der Flieger«. It is now used for Berlin's own council sittings. The building on Leipziger Strasse that adjoins the finance ministry is now home to the Bundesrat (chamber of representatives of the Bundesländer).

No. 102: The Prinz-Albrecht-Palais was constructed in 1737 as a mansion for Baron Vernezobre and was purchased in 1830 by Prince Albrecht of Prussia, the son of Friedrich Wilhelm III. As of 1939, it was the headquarters of the SS. Many other buildings on this stretch of Wilhelmstrasse and Prinz-Albrecht-Strasse were also used by the SS and the Gestapo, making this the epicentre of the »SS state« (▶p. 261).

Left-hand side of Wilhelmstrasse (»Preussenseite«):

No. 65: The justice ministry of Prussia, later of the German Empire.

Nos. 63 and 64: The Prussian state ministry later housed the liaison staff of deputy Führer, Rudolf Hess.

No. 62: Formerly colonial ministry, then ministry for reconstruction of the Weimar Republic era.

No. 61a and Wilhelmplatz 8 – 9: Wilhelmplatz 8 – 9 was built in 1737 for the master of the Knights Hospitallers and was redesigned by Schinkel in 1827 / 28. From 1937 to 1939 it was expanded and formed, along with Wilhelmstrasse 61a, Goebbel's propaganda ministry

Nos. 60 and 61: Originally numbered as Wilhelmplatz 1 and intended for use by the foreign ministry, it eventually became the treasury and finally the finance ministry.

No. 55: Hitler's private chancellery.

Voßstraße

Voßstrasse originally contained many civil service authorities and the Nazi district office at no. 11. The entire northern side was placed by Hitler in the hands of his favourite architect, Albert Speer, for the building of the 430m / 470yd long Neue Reichskanzlei, which was completed in 1939. Only slightly damaged during the war it was blown up in 1949.

Berlin in ruins: a Soviet tank in May 1945 in front of what remained of the Brandenburg Gate

Night (perhaps better known by the Nazis' own euphemism for the event, »Kristallnacht« or »the night of broken glass«), some 80 synagogues in Berlin were destroyed or severely damaged and more than 400 lives are thought to have been lost.

When World War II broke out, Berlin had a population of 4.3 million people including 82,000 Jews (that number had been 160,000 in 1933). The city experienced its first air raid on 25 August 1940; however, such raids were minor in comparison to the first really major attack on 1 March 1943. That is when the »total war« that Goebbels had professed in a notorious speech at the Sportpalast just two weeks earlier on 18 February really hit home. On 20 July 1944 the city also saw the leading officers of a failed conspiracy to assassinate Hitler executed by firing squad in the courtyard of the army high command headquarters on Bendlerstrasse. By April 1945 the Red Army was able to start its assault on Berlin. Hitler committed suicide on 30 April and by 2 May Soviet troops occupied the city. Less than a week later on 8 May, the leaders of Germany's army, the Wehrmacht, signed an unconditional surrender in Berlin-Karlshorst. The population of Berlin at the end of the war was down to 2.8 million and just 7247 Jewish citizens had survived the persecution. 75 million cubic metres/98 million cubic yards of rubble lay in the streets and a fifth of all buildings had been irreparably destroyed, with **75% of the city centre obliterated**.

The Divided City

1946	Forced amalgamation of the KPD (communist party) and SPD (social democrats) to form the SED (Socialist Unity Party)
1948–49	Blockade of Berlin
1949	23 May: establishment of a West German state, the Bundesrepublik Deutschland (Federal Republic of Germany); 7 October: East German state, the Deutsche Demokratische Republik (German Democratic Republic; DDR / GDR) established
1953	17 June: riots in the GDR
1961	13 August: erection of the Berlin Wall
1971	Quadripartite (Four Power) Agreement
1972	Berlin Agreement
1989	9 November: opening of the borders

City of four sectors In June 1945 Berlin became the base for the **Allied Control Council**. British and US troops occupied their sectors on 4 July and on 12 August the French took control of theirs. Berlin was now split into four sectors. It did not take long for cracks in the alliance to become apparent; soon they would lead to the division of the city. Berlin was now the »front« in the Cold War. The Soviet military administration had already permitted the reformation of political parties in their sector in June of 1945. On 21 April 1946 the SPD and KPD were now compelled to amalgamate to form the SED (Sozialistische Einheitspartei Deutchlands) or Socialist Unity Party. Elections to the city council were held on 20 October 1946 under allied supervision. They were the first free elections for 13 years but they would be the last to be held in a united Berlin for another 44. The SPD were the clear victors. On 20 March 1948, the Soviet Union cited the intention of the western allies to create a constitution for their sectors as a reason to leave the Allied Control Council. Three months later on 24 June, the crisis over electoral reform came to a head with the Soviets instituting a **blockade** of all routes to West Berlin. The blockade was not lifted until 12 May 1949, during which time supplies were only maintained to the West Berlin populace by means of the famous **Berlin Airlift**. On 13 October 1948 the properly elected magistracy was forced to move headquarters from East to West Berlin. From then on politics on either side of the city were totally divorced, even though free movement between sectors remained.

Two German states On 23 May 1949 the »Grundgesetz« or fundamental legal structure for the western Federal Republic of Germany (Bundesrepublik Deutschland) was announced. On 7 October, an independent eastern state called the German Democratic Republic was declared in East Berlin. Berlin's new constitution came into force on 1 October, declaring Berlin to be a federal state of the Bundesrepublik Deutschland and claiming to apply to the city as a whole, although it was de facto restricted to West Berlin only. The intervening years before the building of the Berlin Wall were marked by an uprising in the east on 17 June 1953. It was triggered by a strike of **construction workers in Stalinallee** against the excessive raising of work quotas. The revolt was put down with the help of Soviet troops and was utilized for symbolic and propaganda purposes by both sides. These included sessions of the western parliament taking place in the Reichstag, the first of which occurred in October 1955. In the east, Soviet leader **Nikita Khrushchev** delivered his »Berlin Ultimatum«, whereby Berlin would lose its status of occupation by the four powers to become a »free«, demilitarized city. A summit of foreign ministers in Geneva the following year was unable to agree on a solution. The two halves of the town were also drifting apart in economic terms. Whereas West Berlin quickly became one of the key industrial centres of the Federal Republic, development in the east was stagnant. The GDR was also struggling with serious difficulties, not least the number of people fleeing to the west across the still open sector borders.

◄ 17 June 1953

In order to stem the exodus, the East Germans began construction of a wall on 13 August 1961. East Berlin was initially separated from the western sectors by a barbed wire fence and later by a heavily guarded concrete wall. Local rail traffic and underground railways were cut off at the frontier (►Baedeker Special p.190). Berlin was now completely divided. On 26 July 1963, however, there was an unforgettable visit by the American president, **John F. Kennedy**. In a speech in front of the Rathaus in Schöneberg he declared: »All free men, wherever they may live, are citizens of Berlin, and, therefore, as a free man, I take pride in the words ›**Ich bin ein Berliner!**‹«

In the shadow of the Wall

Baedeker TIP

Recalling the Wall

Considering the enormity of the events of 13 August 1961 in the history of the city, it is astonishing how comparatively little is left after 15 years to recall the Wall. The documentation centre in the Berlin Wall Memorial at Bernauer Strasse 11 is the place to look for detailed information on the era when West Berlin was »walled in« (S1, S2 to Nordbahnhof, U8 to Bernauer Strasse; open: April – Oct, Tue – Sun 10am – 6pm, Nov – Mar, closes 5pm).

Quiet diplomacy did lead to some improvement in the situation – **Egon Bahr** coined the phrase »Wandel durch Annäherung« (»change through rapprochement«). Thus in December 1963 an initial **transit permit agreement** was formalized whereby West Berliners were able to visit relatives in the east for the first time in 28 months. In 1971 telephone services that had been broken off in 1952 were reinstituted between the two sectors. On 3 September 1971 the quadripartite or

»Change through rapprochement«

◄ Quadripartite agreement

John F. Kennedy at the Rathaus in Schöneberg: »Ich bin ein Berliner

»four power« agreement over Berlin was signed. It was a milestone in post-war history. The key points were the acknowledgement of the status quo in Berlin, a declaration repudiating violence and the agreement by the Soviet Union to allow traffic to pass between West Berlin and the Federal Republic and not to hinder communications between West Berlin and neighbouring districts, indeed to improve them. For their part, the western allies acknowledged the special status of West Berlin. In 1972 the **Berlin Agreement** once again allowed West Berliners to enter East Germany; and transit between West Germany and Berlin was made much easier. In 1974 West Germany established a **permanent mission in East Berlin**. However, throughout the period of existence of the Berlin Wall many continued to be killed in the attempt to cross it.

Developments in West Berlin

At the end of the 1960s West Berlin and Frankfurt am Main were the hotbeds of the New Left movement and non-parliamentary opposition in West Germany. On 2 June 1967 during a demonstration against a state visit by the shah of Iran, a student called **Benno Ohnesorg** was shot by a policeman. The non-parliamentary opposition grouping or APO (Außerparlamentarische Opposition) organized numerous demonstrations during 1968, primarily against the Vietnam war and the Springer publishers. On 11 April, one of the group's leaders, **Rudi Dutschke**, was seriously injured when he was attacked on the Kurfürstendamm.

Developments in East Berlin

After 1953 there was little in the way of demonstrations in East Berlin. The city was in the grip of the Stasi (**Staatssicherheit / State Security Police**). East German leaders made efforts to give the city back some of its lustre as an international capital. Thus the Palace of the Republic was built on the site of the imperial palace, which had been blown up in 1950. Unter den Linden, the Nikolai Quarter and Gendarmenmarkt (Platz der Akademie) were restored in exemplary fashion and the Fernsehturm (TV Tower) became a striking new landmark. Nevertheless, by the end of the 1980s, as the Soviet Union opened its doors to **perestroika and glasnost**, discontent with the economic and political crisis could no longer be quelled. Major celebrations to mark the 40th anniversary of the GDR did take place on 7 October 1989, but the mood of the country remained unsettled. Soviet communist party leader and head of state **Mikhail Gorbachov** said of the situation in East Germany: »**He who acts too late will be punished by life.**« The reaction of the Politburo was to remove Erich Honecker from his position as party leader and head of state on 18 October 1989, replacing him with Egon Krenz. Unimpressed by this cosmetic action, close to a million people joined a demonstration for democratic reform on 4 November. On 7 November the entire East German government resigned. The government and Politburo reformed the following day with new personnel.

On the evening of 9 November, Politburo-member Günter Schabowski prematurely announced the new government's decision to open the borders to West Berlin and the Federal Republic, without being fully informed of the details and without foreseeing the consequences. Spontaneously, tens of thousands of East German citizens stormed across the border into the west of the city. Over that weekend from 10 to 12 November more than a million people from East Berlin and other parts of the GDR flooded into West Berlin. The opening of the Wall at the Brandenburg Gate on 22 December symbolized the ending of 28 years of division in Berlin. From 24 December there was freedom of passage between the two German states with no need for visas or exchange permits.

The opening of the borders

◄ The fall of the Berlin Wall

The Reunification of Berlin

1990	31 August: reunification agreement 3 October: German reunification	History
1991	20 June: the German parliament, the Bundestag, agrees to re-establish Berlin as the seat of parliament and government in Germany	
1999	Bundestag and government complete the move to Berlin	
2001	The SPD and PDS are in power (re-elected in 2006)	
2008	Closure of Tempelhof Airport. Berlin's Modernist housing estates are declared World Heritage sites.	

Council elections in East Germany on 6 May 1990 led to an SPD-led grand coalition succeeding the former magistracy of East Berlin. The

The path to reunification

10 November 1989 at the Brandenburg Gate: the Wall will divide the city no longer

senate and magistracy of Berlin met in common session for the first time on 12 June. As of 20 June elected officials from Berlin received full voting rights in the German parliament. On 1 July an economic, social and currency union between the two German states came into force. A formal reunification agreement was signed by heads of both states at the Palais Unter den Linden on 31 August 1991. On 12 September a final agreement was signed in Moscow by foreign ministers from the Federal Republic of Germany, the German Democratic Republic, France, Britain, the Soviet Union and the United States of America at the end of the so-called **Two Plus Four Summit**. The agreement declared that the victorious powers of the Second World War would immediately suspend their special rights in Berlin and in Germany as a whole.

Overnight between 2 and 3 October the reunification of Germany was accompanied by massive popular celebrations around the Brandenburg Gate, Unter den Linden and Alexanderplatz. The following day a **combined parliament** comprising all the members of the East German Volkskammer and the West German Bundestag met for the first time in the Reichstag building. On 2 December the first free elections in a united Germany and a united Berlin since 1946 were held. In March of 1993 the Berlin council met for the last time in the Schöneberg Rathaus and in April they moved into a new council

Reunification ▶

German unity ▶

headquarters in the former Prussian Landtag building in the centre of Berlin. During 1990 and 1991 the Berlin Wall was almost completely dismantled. The Lufthansa airline landed its first flight in Berlin since 1945 (at Schönefeld Airport) on 5 August.

The first parliamentary session of the newly elected Bundestag for all Germany took place on 17 January 1991 in the Reichstag building with the aim of ratifying a new constitution. On 20 June a decision was made to move the seat of parliament and government permanently to Berlin. The troops of the western allies held a parade on Strasse des 17. Juni to mark their departure from Berlin. Russian troops held a similar parade in Köpenick.

Berlin – capital of Germany

17 October 1992 saw a state ceremony at the Reichstag in honour of **Willy Brandt**, who had been mayor of Berlin at the time the Wall was being constructed. During the summer of 1995 the **Wrapped Reichstag** project of Christo and Jeanne-Claude attracted art lovers from all over the world to Berlin. The merger of Berlin into Brandenburg was rejected by a popular referendum in May 1996, whilst in February 1998 an era came to an end when the last of the Kreuzberg squatters were evicted. On 19 April 1999 the Bundestag completed its move from Bonn to Berlin and Chancellor Schröder's move into the former Staatsratsgebäude (privy council building) on 23 August marked the official transfer of government itself to the new capital.

◀ Other events during the 1990s

The opening of the Sony Center at the beginning of 2000 marked the virtual completion of building work at Potsdamer Platz. At the turn of the year from 2000 to 2001 the 23 boroughs of Berlin were reorganized into just twelve new districts. The final newly constructed section of railway between Westhafen and Gesundbrunnen was opened in June 2002 to close the local railway loop (S-Bahn ring) for the first time since 1961. The Bundestag voted on 4 July to restore the façade of the historic Stadtschloss palace. In February 2006 work began on the demolition of the Palace of the Republic and in May that year the new central station in the Spreebogen was officially opened.

◀ 2000 – 2007

Tempelhof Airport was closed in October 2008. At the same time in Europe's largest airport construction project began the expansion of Schönefeld to become BBI (Berlin Brandenburg International). Building work continued in the city centre: following the partial opening of the new underground line U 55 (»the Chancellor's subway«), its extension to Alexanderplatz began.After a lengthy construction period, one project has finally been completed: on 16 October 2009 the restored **Neues Museum** opened on Museum Island, which has now been returned to its pre-war condition.

Art and Culture

What was »Prussian Rococo«? Are there still traces of Third Reich architecture in Berlin? Where are the city's finest sculptures? Who has been responsible for the building of the »New Berlin«?

History of Art and Architecture

From the Middle Ages to the 19th Century

There are very few examples of buildings from the Middle Ages in Berlin. The **Nikolaikirche** (Church of St Nicholas), the oldest parish church in the city (from around 1230), has been restored along with the surrounding precinct. The Klosterkirche (Franciscan monastery church), which also dates from the 13th century, has been in ruins since the Second World War. Churches that have been well preserved, albeit having undergone subsequent modifications from their original condition, include the 13th / 14th-century Marienkirche (St Mary's) and the former Heiliggeist-Kapelle (Chapel of the Holy Spirit). The Nikolaikirche in Spandau from the early 15th century is worth mentioning as an example of the late Gothic style. Less well known are the 20 or so former village churches, e.g. in Marienfelde, Mariendorf, Tempelhof, Britz, Buckow, Lichterfelde, Dahlem, Karow, Blankenburg and Stralau, most of which date back to the 13th century. The earliest examples of medieval painting are the murals in the Church of St Anne in Dahlem (14th century) along with the frescoes on the vaults of the village church in Buckow (15th century). The now faded but still famous *Dance of Death* in the Marienkirche (1485) is important mainly for its iconography.

Few traces of the Middle Ages

The lack of locally produced art in Berlin during the Renaissance is evident, specifically in view of the considerable use of outside artists. Joachim I had the headstone for Elector Johann Cicero (1532, in the Berliner Dom) made by Peter Vischer in Nuremberg. The construction of the new palace starting in 1538 was contracted to Caspar Theyss of Saxony, the Italian Count Rochus Guerini of Lynar and Peter Kummer the Elder from Dresden. In addition to the Stadtschloss or city palace, a hunting palace in Grunewald (as of 1542), the Spandauer Citadel (from 1560) and a large number of private buildings were erected, although of the latter only the **Ribbeckhaus** on Breite Strasse remains. The conversion of the ruling house to Calvinism (1613) and the Thirty Years' War led to a hiatus in artistic endeavour. Art in Berlin had its first heyday only in the time of the Great Elector and was heavily influenced by the ruler's own experiences in Holland. Dutch-schooled architects such as Johann Gregor Memhardt (1607 – 78); Johann Arnold Nering (1659 – 95) and Rutger van Langevelt (1635 – 1695), painters like Willem van Honthorst (1594 – 1664) and the sculptors Artus Quellinus and Bartholomew Eggers assumed leading roles at court. One important relic of this era is the palace **Schloss Köpenick** with its chapel.

Imported Renaissance

← *A little piece of the new Berlin: Frank O. Gehry's DZ Bank on Pariser Platz – simple on the outside, simply astonishing on the inside*

Baroque The key instigator of the Baroque movement in Berlin was King Friedrich I. Initially Johann Arnold Nering and Martin Grünberg (1655–1706) continued in the Dutch tradition, but the genius of **Andreas Schlüter** (1659–1714) adopted a vigorous new direction in the form of Italian Baroque. Schlüter was not only the most important artist in northern Germany at the time, he was also a sculptor and architect (having worked on the remodelling of the palace and the Zeughaus). He joined the Berlin court in 1694 and inspired the blossoming of art all over the town. His best-known works are the equestrian statue of the Great Elector that is now on view outside Schloss Charlottenburg, the first such statue to be erected out of doors in Germany, and the 21 heads of dying warriors in the atrium of the Zeughaus. Contemporary to him or slightly later but working in the same vein were such men as the Swede Johann Friedrich Eosander von Göthe (1669–1729) and the Frenchman Jean de Bodt

Germany's first open-air equestrian monument

(1670–1745). The church in Dorotheenstadt (1687), which was destroyed during the Second World War, was the first new Protestant church to be built. It was followed by several more around 1700, including the Parochialkirche and the French and German churches (Französischer Dom and Deutscher Dom) on Gendarmenmarkt, which are particularly noteworthy as examples of buildings with a central ground plan. All this artistic striving gained a focus in 1696 when Schlüter and Dutch painter Augustin Terwesten opened the Academy of Arts. Even though the next king, »the Soldier King« Friedrich Wilhelm I, was less flamboyant, the three large squares Quarré (Pariser Platz), Oktogon (Leipziger Platz) and Rondell (Belle-Alliance-Platz, now called Mehringplatz) were all built during his reign to complete his expansion of the suburbs Dorotheenstadt and Friedrichstadt. He also encouraged the building of homes for the common people according to a standard design and supported the construction of prestigious palaces for the nobility. During his reign, too, the Lustgarten was converted into a parade ground and the palace was completed. The leading architects on the project were Philipp Gerlach (1679–1748) and Schlüter's pupil Martin Böhme (1676–1725). The king also brought in Johann Boumann (1706–76) from Holland.

Under Frederick the Great a distinctive Rococo style grew in importance in Prussia, much influenced by developments in France. This Prussian or Frederician Rococo took on Classical aspects in Prussia and remained inventive there for much longer than elsewhere in Europe. When he was still crown prince, Frederick had already unearthed one of the most talented architects of the age in **Georg Wenzeslaus von Knobelsdorff** (1699–1753), who brilliantly realized the ideas formulated in his sketches in such buildings as Schloss Rheinsberg, Schloss Charlottenburg, in Sanssouci and Potsdam and in particular at the opera house (his masterpiece). As of 1763 he was succeeded by Karl von Gontard (1731–91), who designed the towers of the Französischer Dom and the Deutscher Dom, then by Gontard 's pupils Georg Unger (1743–1812) and Georg Friedrich Boumann (1737–1807 or later), who designed the old library. Frederick the Great's own admiration of French culture was evinced in his attempts to lure large numbers of French artists to Berlin. The only painter to respond to this call was Charles Amédée van Loo, joined by **Antoine Pesne** (1683–1757), who had by now worked for three generations of Prussian royalty, and his most important pupil from the Berlin school, Christian Bernhard Rode (1725–97), best known for his ceiling paintings in the royal palaces. The sculpture studio that the king set up was more successful, attracting such artists as François-Gaspard Adam, Sigisbert-François Michel and Jean Pierre Antoine Tassaert. Their school carried the torch for sculpture in Berlin well into the 19th century. The motifs of painter and engraver **Daniel Chodowiecki** (1726–1801) also introduced a new bourgeois element into art.

»Frederician« (Prussian) Rococo

At the end of the 18th century the burgeoning movement towards Classicism produced some of Berlin's most important monuments. In addition to **Carl Gotthard Langhans** (1732–1808), the director of the court department of works, who created the Brandenburg Gate, Friedrich Wilhelm von Erdmannsdorff (1736–1800) worked in Berlin for a brief period, as did David Gilly (1748–1808), who founded what would become the Bauakademie or Academy of Architecture. The outstanding talent of **Karl Friedrich Schinkel** (1781–1841) from Neuruppin engendered both the consummation of the Classical movement and its denouement in the early 19th century (his legacy includes the Neue Wache, Schauspielhaus, Altes Museum, Schlossbrücke, Friedrichswerdersche Kirche and the Nikolaikirche in Potsdam). His influence on building styles in Berlin endured

Classicism and Romanticism

? DID YOU KNOW …?

■ … that the model for the goddess driving the chariot atop the Brandenburg Gate was the niece of the coppersmith who executed Schadow's design, a man by the name of Jury? The statue actually represents Irene the goddess of peace but after the Battle of Leipzig in 1813 the king ordered Schinkel to add victory laurels to be held in the goddess's hand, so that thereafter the statue was regarded as representing the goddess Victoria.

for more than half the century. The most important sculptors in those first half of the 19th century included **Gottfried Schadow** (1764–1850; responsible for the four-horsed chariot on the Brandenburg Gate, the *Prinzessinnengruppe* in marble (the later Queen Luise and her sister) and his even more influential pupil Christian Daniel Rauch (1777–1857), who sculpted the equestrian statue of Frederick the Great, the generals from the War of Liberation and the sarcophagus of Queen Luise. One of the trailblazers for the Romantic movement was the landscape painter Carl Blechen (1798–1840).

Gottfried Schadow's »Prinzessinnengruppe«

Towards the middle of the 19th century the **historicism** movement sought to instigate a new renaissance in art by harking back to historical art forms. Schinkel's concepts were initially propagated by his pupils Ludwig Persius (1803–45), Friedrich August Stüler (1800–65; designer of the Neues Museum) and Johann Heinrich Strack (1805–80; responsible for the Siegessäule and the Nationalgalerie). The director of the city's planning department, Hermann Blankenstein (1829–1910), heralded the end of the Schinkel tradition with his typical brick buildings including schools, hospitals and market halls. With the more scientific archaeological study of building forms, a plethora of styles emerged that found expression in the major public buildings designed by Friedrich Hitzig (1811–81; Technical College), Hermann Friedrich Waesemann (1813–79; Rotes Rathaus), Paul Wallot (1841–1912; Reichstag), Ernst von Ihne (1848–1917; Neuer Marstall, Staatsbibliothek, Bodemuseum) and Julius Raschdorff (1823–1914; Berliner Dom, Technical College). This diversity is also indicative, however, of the fact that architecture lacked an outstanding leading figure after the death of Schinkel. The same was the case for the Berlin school of sculpture. Artists such as Christian Friedrich Tieck (1776–1851), August Kiss (1802–65), Friedrich Drake (1805–82) and Gustav Bläser (1813–74) remained locked in the tradition of Rauch. Reinhold Begas (1831–1911), though, moved away from Classicism to create a new Baroque style. One of his major works is the monument to Bismarck (now at Grosser Stern). In the world of painting, historical depictions were in fashion and Anton von Werner (1843–1915) dominated art in Berlin for decades with his solemn epic paintings. The one towering figure was **Adolph Menzel** (1815 – 1905), who not only chronicled his own age but also evoked the era of Frederick the Great.

20th Century

Ludwig Hoffmann (1852 – 1932), head of the city planning office, was a guiding figure of the architectural scene of »Wilhelmine Berlin« for many years with his works harking back to the Renaissance and Baroque periods. The Wertheim building (1896 – 1906) created by Alfred Messel (1853 – 1909) instigated a new, practical style for commercial buildings. Peter Behrens (1868 – 1940) similarly opened up a new direction for industrial structures with his AEG turbine hall (1909). Hermann Muthesius (1861 – 1927) was the key figure behind a new style of cottage homes with his housing developments in the suburbs. In the 1920s **Walter Gropius** (1883 – 1969), **Ludwig Mies van der Rohe** (1886 – 1969), Erich Mendelsohn (1887 – 1953), Hans Poelzig (1869 – 1936), Bruno and Max Taut (1880 – 1938 and 1884 – 1967) and **Hans Scharoun** (1893 – 1972) were the men who defined the architectural visage of the city, particularly its housing estates, such as in four major projects including the Hufeisensiedlung (Horseshoe Estate) in Britz (Bruno Taut and Martin Wagner; 1885 – 1957), Onkel Toms Hütte (Uncle Tom's Cabin) in Zehlendorf (Bruno Taut, Hugo Häring and Otto Rudolf Salvisberg; 1882 – 1940), Siemensstadt (Hans Scharoun, Walter Gropius and others) and Weisse Stadt in Reinickendorf (Otto Rudolf Salvisberg, Wilhelm Büning). Other important buildings include the Haus des Rundfunks (Broadcasting House) by Hans Poelzig, the trade fair and exhibition grounds around the Funkturm (radio tower) by Richard Ermisch (1885 – 1960), Tempelhof Airport by Ernst Sagebiel (1892 – 1970) and the Olympic Stadium and Waldbühne designed by Werner March (1894 – 1976). The last two were the first major buildings in Berlin in the spirit of the Nazi era. The plans of Albert Speer (1905 – 81), appointed as inspector general of buildings by Hitler in 1937 and given the task of redesigning Berlin and making it a new capital for the Third Reich to be named Germania, were gargantuan but barely begun. Central to the new concept was construction of a new boulevard 120m / 130yd wide leading from Tempelhof to the Spreebogen (bend in the river Spree), where a gigantic building called the »Volkshalle« 290m / 950ft in height was to be built. What is interesting about this is that the flattening of the Spreebogen area and the district south of it was not caused solely by enemy bombs, but was actually begun by Speer's bulldozers.

Architecture before 1939

Architects from all over the world were involved in creating major landmarks in Berlin after the war. The outstanding edifices in the west include the **Kongresshalle** (1957) by the American Hugh A.

Post-war architecture

Scharoun's Philharmonie building was completed in 1963

Stubbins, the Unité d'Habitation (1957) by Le Corbusier, the Akademie der Künste (Academy of Arts, 1960) by Werner Düttmann, the new **Kaiser-Wilhelm-Gedächtniskirche** (memorial church, 1960/61) by Egon Eiermann, the new Deutsche Oper (German Opera House; 1961) designed by Fritz Bornemann, the Philharmonie (1963) by Hans Scharoun, the Church of Maria Regina Martyrum (1963) by Hans Schädel and Friedrich Ebert, the Neue Nationalgalerie (New National Gallery; 1968) by Ludwig Mies van der Rohe, Tegel Airport (1975) by Meinhard von Gerkan, Volkwin Marg and Klaus Nickels, the Staatsbibliothek (State Library for Prussian Cultural Heritage, 1979) by Hans Scharoun, the Bauhaus-Archiv (1979) by Walter Gropius, the International Congress Centre (ICC; 1979) by Ralf Schüler and Ursulina Schüler-Witte and, in particular, the **Kulturforum at Kemperplatz**, which followed a concept by Hans Scharoun and was only finished after the fall of the Berlin Wall. In East Berlin, too, there was plenty of construction going on, as witnessed by Hermann Henselmann's Stalinallee, the Palast der Republik by Heinz Graffunder (1973–76) or the reconstruction of Friedrichstrasse, although the latter has since been replaced by a new concept (the Galeries Lafayette by Jean Nouvel). First and foremost, though, is the internationally hailed Fernsehturm (TV Tower) by Dieter and Franke. Some very worthwhile buildings were also built for the **International Building Exhibition 1987**, especially in the Kreuzberg and Tiergarten districts. They include Oswald Mathias Ungers' creations at Lützowufer. An amalgamation of many modern ideas can be found in the **Hansaviertel** (1957), which has already claimed its place in the history of architecture. Housing estates at Gropiusstadt (1973) in Berlin-Buckow and the controversial Märkisches Viertel (1974) in northern Berlin, though, exemplify the kind of architecture that was thought to be trailblazing in its day, but which in actual fact has engendered a range of social problems. The prefabricated, late-seventies tower blocks of Marzahn, Hellersdorf and Hohenschönhausen are typical of the communist era.

Reunified Berlin has experienced an unparalleled construction boom. **The new Berlin** Some massive building projects were begun, especially the **Potsdamer Platz** development, the rebuilding of Pariser Platz, and the construction of a new central station on the site of the former Lehrter station, the Kanzleramt (Chancellery) and the parliament precinct, not to mention the renovation of existing buildings, in particular the refurbishment of the Museumsinsel (Museum Island). Although they may be rather overshadowed by all these major efforts, there have also been many smaller projects, including the Jüdisches Museum (Jewish Museum) by Daniel Libeskind, Frank O. Gehry's DZ-Bank on Pariser Platz, where the spectacular architecture only really becomes apparent from within, the Bolle site on the banks of the Spree in Moabit, the Kant

! Baedeker TIP

Chapel of Reconciliation

Helmut Jahn, Renzo Piano, I.M. Pei, Sony Center, Daimler City: the new Berlin is replete with great names and great buildings. Rudolf Reitermann and Peter Sassenroth are known to only a few insiders but their fine creations are attracting fans of architecture from all over the world. Their Kapelle der Versöhnung (Chapel of Reconciliation) on Bernauer Strasse is a wonderfully airy building made of rammed clay sandwiched in wooden laminate walls that replaces the Church of Reconciliation that was blown up by East German border troops in 1985 (S1, S2 to Nordbahnhof, U8 to Bernauer Strasse).

Triangle on Kantstrasse, the new Kranzler Eck on the corner of Kurfürstendamm and Joachimsthaler Strasse, the Trias blocks on Holzgartenstrasse in Friedrichshain or the Mosse centre on Zimmerstrasse in the centre of town. Even on Berlin's outskirts, in Treptow, there were new creations in the form of the 125m / 410ft-tall Treptowers and the even more distinctive Twin Towers.

In 1898 Max Liebermann (1847–1935) and Walter Leistikow **Painting** (1865–1908), the Brandenburg landscape painter, founded the **Secession** grouping that set out entirely new artistic objectives. They were joined by Lovis Corinth (1858–1925), Max Slevogt (1868–1932) and Lesser Ury (1861–1931), who were among the most important names in German Impressionism. Käthe Kollwitz (1867–1945), Hans Baluschek (1870–1935) and **Heinrich Zille** (1858–1929), who popularly depicted Berlin's working-class milieu, all took a stance that was critical of the prevalent society. **Expressionism** had important pioneers and champions such as the art dealer

Berlin's largest sculpture is next to the Spree in Treptow: Jonathan Borofsky's »Molecule Men«

Herwarth Walden (publisher of the periodical *Der Sturm*), Paul Cassirer and Alfred Flechtheim. Max Beckmann (1884–1950), Ludwig Meidner (1884–1966), Ernst Ludwig Kirchner (1880–1938), Emil Nolde (1867–1956), Max Pechstein (1881–1955), Erich Heckel (1883–1970), Karl Schmidt-Rottluff (1884–1976) and Oskar Kokoschka (1886–1980) all assembled in Berlin and developed a their own style. Berlin's own **Dadaist** movement was primarily led by Hannah Höch (1889–1978) and George Grosz (1893–1959) and the **Berlin Realism** school was dominated by painters like Otto Dix (1891–1969) and Rudolf Schlichter (1890–1955). Artists such as Georg Baselitz (born 1938) and Markus Lüpertz (born 1941) carried on Berlin's international reputation as a hotbed for art. In the 1980s, a lot of international acclaim was garnered by the »Junge Wilde« including Salome (born 1945) and Rainer Fetting (born 1949), among whose works is the sculpture of Willy Brandt at the SPD headquarters (►ill. p.57). For clues as to the latest trends in modern art, the studios and galleries of the new Berlin scene, primarily gathered in the Mitte district, are the places to look. The best establishments include the Neuer Berliner Kunstverein, the Kunstwerke studios on Auguststrasse and the Kunst- und Kulturzentrum Tacheles (►p.312).

! **Baedeker TIP**

The Boros Collection

With his Kunstbunker at Reinhardtstr. 20, Christian Boros has created Berlin's most unusual art collection. He converted an above-ground war bunker next to the Deutsches Theater, behind whose palace-like façade the Red Army held war criminals and the GDR stored tropical fruit, into a fascinating space where works by such artists as Anselm Reyles, Santiago Sierra and Tobias Rehberger can be admired against a backdrop of raw concrete and surviving graffiti (tours: Sat, Sun by appointment, www. sammlung-boros.de).

630 galleries, more than in London or New York, present the latest **Galleries** trends to art lovers. Alongside Auguststrasse and Linienstrasse in Mitte more and more new centres of art are springing up: Zimmerstrasse at Checkpoint Charlie, Rudi-Dutschke-Strasse and Lindenstrasse in Kreuzberg, Holzmarkt in Friedrichshain and, since 2008, Heidestrasse behind the Hamburger Bahnhof. The Berlin Biennale (2010, 2012) and Art Forum give impulses to the art market.

In 1987 a »sculpture boulevard« was opened on Kurfürstendamm (▶p.249). This unleashed a flurry of sculpture projects that continue to this day. New buildings and squares have been adorned with sculptures by prominent artists, including Rauschenberg's *Riding Bikes* on Potsdamer Platz and Claes Oldenbourg's *Houseball* on Mauerstrasse. Most prominent of them all, though, is Jonathan Borofsky's aluminium *Molecule Men*, which soars 30m / 100ft over the banks of the Spree in Treptow.

Cultural Life in Berlin

Elector Friedrich III and his wife Sophie Charlotte had the ambition **Akademie der** of creating in Berlin an »excellently appointed academy or school of **Künste** art, but no ordinary painting or sculpture academy of the kind that is already ubiquitous«. Thus in 1696 the Prussian Akademie der Künste (Academy of Arts) was established. Its directors have included Andreas Schlüter, Daniel Chodowiecki and Gottfried Schadow.

The heyday of the academy was in the 1920s under its then president **Max Liebermann**, when the school was supplemented by a section for the literary arts (1926). Its nadir came not long afterwards during the Nazi era, when the academy meekly »cleansed« itself of all those members who were anathema to the National Socialists, including Heinrich Mann, Alfred Döblin and Käthe Kollwitz. The academy's premises on Pariser Platz were destroyed during the war, so that during the Cold War era, two successor establishments were founded. In 1950 the Deutsche Akademie der Künste was founded in East Berlin, claiming to be the true inheritor of the Prussian academy's mantle before being renamed the Akademie der Künste der DDR in 1972. The West Berliners reacted to this by opening their own institution, the West Berlin Akademie der Künste in 1954. The two academies were amalgamated in 1992. The members of the new institute include architects, artists, writers and musicians from Germany and abroad. Its premises at Hanseatenweg 10 and the new building at the old site, Pariser Platz 4, play host to regular symposia, exhibitions, readings, lectures, theatrical presentations and concerts (information under www.adk.de).

A spectacular show is guaranteed at the Volksbühne Theatre on Rosa-Luxemburg-Platz

Festivals Among the most interesting events are the Berlin Festival, a cross section of international art, the International Film Festival, the Berlin Theatre Festival, the Festival of World Culture, the International Summer Festival and the Berlin JazzFest.

Theatre Berlin has been the backdrop for much of the theatrical history of Germany. It is where Gerhart Hauptmann, Henrik Ibsen, August Strindberg and Bertolt Brecht made their breakthroughs and directors such as Max Reinhardt, Erwin Piscator and Gustaf Gründgens also left their legacy. Nowadays Berlin still has an extraordinarily vivid theatre scene. Among what will soon be 100 theatres regularly showing plays, the most important are the Deutsches Theater, the Schaubühne on Lehniner Platz, the Berliner Ensemble and the Volksbühne on Rosa-Luxemburg Platz. In addition there are a large number of independent theatre groups with no regular venue. This makes Berlin the number one theatre destination in German-speaking countries, purely on numbers alone. The Grips-Theater and Rote Grütze mean that Berlin also leads the way in children's and youth theatre.

Music The capital is a veritable magnet for musicians and producers. There are 90 music publishers, more than 130 record labels, 50 recording studios and several hundred groups, making the city the hub of the German music scene. For classical music aficionados there are no less than four opera houses: the Staatsoper Unter den Linden, the Deutsche Oper Berlin, the Komische Oper and the Neuköllner Oper.

There are also numerous orchestras, most prominent of which are the world-famous Berlin Philharmonic Orchestra, founded in 1882 and based in the Philharmonie at the Kulturforum, and the Berlin Symphony Orchestra, who play in the Konzerthaus on Gendarmenmarkt.

Film and television

Before the Second World War, Berlin was the centre of filmmaking in Germany. Its tradition dated back to the very beginnings of art in celluloid. Max Skladanowsky showed the earliest films here in 1895 and Oskar Messter, the early master of the cinema who had made the first cinema projector for normal film in 1896, was born in Berlin. The world's very first sound picture was shown here in 1922 by Vogt, Engl and Masolle. The city is still seeking to rekindle this golden age, although it presently lies in third place for film and television production in Germany after Munich and Cologne. The most important sites are Media City in Adlershof, the Berliner Union film studio in Tempelhof and UFA in Potsdam-Babelsberg. The Berliner Filmhaus including its Mediathek and TV museum and the film museum in the Sony Center on Potsdamer Platz highlight how the public authorities are also supporting the city's claim to be a film centre. These establishments also provide the venues for the Berlin Film Festival. Berlin has appeared as a film location in more and more movies. The best-known examples include *Goodbye, Lenin*, *The Lives of Others*, *The Edukators* and *Run, Lola, Run*.

Literature

Berlin's tradition as a source of literature is well founded, with names such as Friedrich Nicolai, Gotthold Ephraim Lessing, Moses Mendelssohn, E.T.A. Hoffmann, Theodor Fontane, Georg Heym, Gerhart Hauptmann, Kurt Tucholsky, Bertolt Brecht, Alfred Döblin, Heinrich Mann and Anna Seghers. The tradition continues to this day. Berlin still has more living and working authors than any other German city. The only recently deceased Jurek Becker and Stefan Heym join Thomas Brasch, Yaak Karsunke, Christoph Meckel, Elisabeth Plessen, Christa Wolf, Botho Strauss, Jürgen Theobaldy and Peter Paul Zahl among the best known at present. Berlin also has more then 400 publishers, making it second only to Munich in terms of modern German publishing.

Museums

The reconstitution of Berlin's museums is one of the key objectives for the city's culture tsars. As a result of the Second World War, world-famous collections were fragmented in the two halves of the city. A large part of the original inventory was returned to East Berlin from the Soviet Union in 1958. Those parts of the state museums' collections that had been stored in the west were entrusted to the Prussian Cultural Heritage Foundation. The treasures are gathered under the official name **»Staatliche Museen zu Berlin – Preussischer Kulturbesitz« (Berlin State Museums – Prussian Cultural Heritage)** in Germany's largest comprehensive complex of cultural institutes. A

*Prussia's Friedrich-Wilhelm University was renamed
the Humboldt University in 1949*

large number of other museums dotted around the city provide a fitting supplement to the official collections. The most important among them include the Museum für Naturkunde (Natural History Museum), the Deutsches Historisches Museum (Museum of German History), the Deutsches Technikmuseum (German Technology Museum) and the Jüdisches Museum (Jewish Museum) although there are many small and often highly original museums that are equally fascinating (▶Practicalities, Museums).

**Universities,
colleges,
research
institutes**

Berlin has four universities. What is now called the Humboldt University was founded by Wilhelm von Humboldt when King Friedrich Wilhelm III donated to him the palace of Prince Heinrich on Unter den Linden in 1810. Initially the institute was called the Friedrich-Wilhelm University after the king himself, and its teaching staff has included Hegel, Schleiermacher, the Brothers Grimm, Helmholtz, Mommsen, Planck, Einstein, Virchow, Koch and Sauerbruch. It was renamed the Humboldt University only in 1949. The Technische Universität Berlin (TUB; Berlin Technical University) in Charlottenburg was set up in 1946 as successor to a technical college formed by the merger in 1879 of the building academy founded in 1799 and the mercantile academy that came into existence in 1821. The Freie Universität (Free University, FU) of Berlin in Dahlem was created on 4 December 1948 as a result of protests by professors and students against the increasing restriction of academic freedom taking place at the Humboldt University and others in the Soviet sector of Berlin. In 1967 and 1968 the FU, along with the University of Frankfurt, became the focus for non-parliamentary opposition in West Germany thanks to professors like Herbert Marcuse and students such as Rudi Dutschke and was the scene of many student protests. The Hochschule der Künste (College of the Arts) was elevated to university status only in 2001. There are also more than 180 research institutes, some being associated with the universities while others are independent. These include the Hahn-Meitner Institute for Nuclear Research, which was instituted in 1956, the Institute of the Max Planck Society, the Wissenschaftszentrum (Science Centre) Berlin, the Heinrich-Hertz Institute for Communications Technology, the Versuchsanstalt für Wasserbau und Schiffbau (Research Institute for Hydraulic Engineering and Shipbuilding), Berlin's own electron storage ring for the study of synchrotron radiation, the Berliner Elektronenspeicherring für Synchrotronstrahlung (BESSY), the Produktionstechnische Zentrum Berlin, which studies industrial production techniques, and the Wissenschafts- und Wirtschaftsstandort Adlershof (WISTA), established for scientific and economic studies.

Famous People

What peak did Alexander von Humboldt conquer? Who created »Nante«, the loafer on the corner? Who sang: »Wer schmeisst denn da mit Lehm?« (Who's that chucking the mud around?) Here are some miniature memorials to some of Berlin's key figures.

Willy Brandt (1913 – 92)

In Berlin's darkest hour since the war, 13 August 1961, the day the building of the Wall began, the serving mayor Willy Brandt gave a spontaneous speech to an agitated crowd, in which he eloquently expressed his bitterness over the events, yet still managed to calm the explosive mood of his listeners. His ability to see the reality yet continue in hope was one of his outstanding attributes.

Chancellor

Willy Brandt was born on 18 December 1913 in Lübeck under the name Herbert Frahm. His membership of Germany's socialist workers' party meant that he was forced to flee to Norway in 1933, where he adopted the name »Willy Brandt« to conceal his identity from the Nazis. In 1938 he became a citizen of Norway. He arrived in Berlin after the war as the Norwegian press attaché, but soon re-adopted German nationality and joined the SPD in 1947. By 1949 he was a member of the first Bundestag. In 1957 he was elected mayor of Berlin, a post he was to keep until 1966. Throughout this period, he was already displaying the guiding focus of his politics, a recognition of and a pragmatic interaction with reality. He became leader of the SPD in 1964 and in

Sculpture of Willy Brandt by Rainer Fetting at the SPD headquarters in Kreuzberg

1966 he accepted the posts of foreign minister and deputy chancellor in a grand coalition of the parties. In 1969 he accomplished an historic »shift of power«, becoming federal Germany's first social democratic chancellor in a coalition with the FDP (Free Democratic Party). With his slogan »mehr Demokratie wagen« (»risk greater democracy«) he sought to incorporate the political underswell of the 1968 generation into mainstream society. His policies towards the east were his greatest historical triumph as he succeeded in reconciling with the countries of eastern Europe that had been invaded by Hitler's Germany. His most unforgettable gesture was when he got to his knees before the monument to the victims of the Warsaw Ghetto in 1971. Only in Germany itself was he disparaged as a »denial politician« or »betrayer of the Fatherland«. He had already become the first West German chancellor to visit the GDR in 1970 and in 1973 he was a signatory to the new »basis agreement« between the two German states. The exposure of the Guillaume spy affair caused Brandt to resign in 1974. In 1976 he took on the leadership of the

← *One international star from Berlin: Marlene Dietrich*

Socialist International grouping. For Willy Brandt, Berlin was a symbol for the division of Europe and it was only right and proper that, although he was no longer in any political office, he should make a speech to the people in front of the Schöneberg Rathaus in November 1989. He died in Unkel near Bonn on 8 October 1992.

Bertolt Brecht (1898 – 1956)

Dramatist Brecht was born in Augsburg on 10 February 1898 but lived in Berlin from 1924 onwards, occasionally directing for Max Reinhardt at the Deutsches Theater. In 1933 he took flight from the Nazis via Denmark and Moscow, then moving on to the USA in 1941. He returned from there in 1947 and settled in Zurich. A year later he founded the Berliner Ensemble in East Berlin, which was then managed by his wife, the actress Helene Weigel. Both their names are inextricably associated with the building in Schiffbauerdamm. Brecht's dramas are often structured as parables and polemics. He developed a method that he described with the term »epic theatre«, in which he sought not to divert and entertain the public, but to tell a story that would make a clear statement. His best known works include the *Threepenny Opera* written in conjunction with Kurt Weill as well as *Mother Courage and Her Children*, *The Good Person of Szechwan* and *The Caucasian Chalk Circle*. Brecht died in East Berlin on 14 August 1956.

Marlene Dietrich (1901 – 92)

Actress and singer The daughter of an officer from Schöneberg had already played in 17 silent films before she made her breakthrough in 1930 as the seedy Lola opposite Emil Jannings as Professor Unrat in *The Blue Angel*. This cemented her reputation as the eternal femme fatale. That same year Paramount Studios offered a contract to take her and Josef von Sternberg, the director of *The Blue Angel*, to Hollywood. She made six more films with him there, including *Morocco* with Gary Cooper. But though Sternberg's career thereafter faded away, hers was only beginning to take off. The most renowned directors – Lubitsch, Hitchcock, Orson Welles – used her in films alongside some of Hollywood's greatest stars. After the Second World War – during which she maintained committed opposition to Hitler and did much work entertaining US troops – she gradually retired from film work, although roles in *Judgement at Nuremberg* and *Witness for the Prosecution* brought her further successes. She retained a high profile even outside the film world, and performed as a singer on the world's premier stages, further cementing her image as a diva and a vamp. She had numerous affairs, of which the one with Jean Gabin was probably the most intense. Nevertheless she never divorced from her husband Rudolf Sieber, whom she had married in 1924. In 1974 a fall on stage caused her to give up her singing career. She lived the rest of her life as a total recluse in Paris.

Rudi Dutschke (1940 – 79)

In the late sixties, German students responded to the call to »shake **Student leader** the dust of a thousand years from the caps and gowns of your peers« and conceived a new kind of non-parliamentary opposition under the charismatic leadership of Rudi Dutschke. Dutschke was born in Schönefeld near Lucken-walde on 7 March 1940. He arrived in West Berlin shortly before the building of the Wall to study sociology at the Free University. He became an active member of the SDS, the Sozialistische Deutsche Studentenbund (Socialist Union of German Students), and he was soon to be seen leading protests against the war in Vietnam. His political objective was the non-violent refashioning of what he believed to be the repressive society of West Germany. He summed this up in his credo of »the long march through the institutions«. Rudi Dutschke was the symbol of the APO (non-parliamentary) movement and its

»A long march through the institutions«

era. Some saw him as a visionary of clear-minded sociological analysis while others regarded him as the embodiment of a violent enemy of society. On 11 April 1968 he was shot in broad daylight by a 23-year-old worker on Kurfürstendamm and suffered serious head injuries. After his recovery he left the country and died of an epileptic fit related to the attack on Christmas Eve in 1979.

Even long after his death Rudi Dutschke once again caused a furore in Berlin: in 2008, and only after a plebiscite on the subject, the section of Kochstrasse between Friedrichstrasse and Axel Springer Strasse was named after him – the street that passes right by the office building of the Springer-Verlag.

Theodor Fontane (1819 – 98)

Theodor Fontane was born on 30 December 1819. He initially **Writer** worked as an apprentice apothecary before taking up writing full time, chronicling 19th-century Berlin and its environs. Country landscapes and cityscapes play a major role in his greatest novels. In his *Travels Through the March of Brandenburg* (1862 – 82) he wrote in loving detail and with dutiful attention to historical truth about the founding and the significance of Havelland, Oderland, Spreeland and their interactions with Berlin. His most important works include the novels *A Man of Honour* (1883) and *Effi Briest* (1895).

Friedrich II, Frederick the Great (1712 – 86)

The third king of Prussia was born on 24 January 1712. His father **King of Prussia** Friedrich Wilhelm I (1688 – 1740), the »Soldier King«, had been a

strict and pragmatic individual with a liking for military matters. As crown prince, Frederick was more inclined towards music and was open to the new ideas of the Enlightenment. He corresponded with Voltaire, whom he later invited to join his court. The antagonism with his father apparently got so bad that in 1730 he unsuccessfully tried to flee to England with his friend Lieutenant von Katte and was put on trial for treason by his father. Katte was condemned to death and by order of King Friedrich Wilhelm he was executed at the castle of Küstrin before the eyes of the prince. Only when Frederick was engaged to Elisabeth Christine of Brunswick-Beveren in 1732 there reconciliation between him and his father. Frederick lived at the Palace of Rheinsberg, where he wrote down his concept of the king as »prime servant of the state« in his treatise *Anti-Machiavell*. In 1740 he ascended to the throne. His deeds as the Prussian monarch are characterized by the expansion of Prussian lands in the Silesian Wars (1740 – 42 and 1744) and the Seven Years' War (1756 – 63), by the end of which Prussia had become a power on a par with the mightiest in Europe. He also continued the internal stabilization of Prussia that had been begun by his father, organizing the state along strictly corporate lines. The latter years of the king's reign were characterized by personal isolation and mistrust. His nickname »Old Fritz« typifies the ambivalence of his personality, reflecting both the many anecdotes of his fatherly rule as well as what he finally became, a reclusive and cynical Prussian king with no issue.

Adolf Glassbrenner (1810 – 76)

Writer The popular »Berlin people's poet« was born on 27 March 1810. Initially a merchant's apprentice, he emerged as a writer and liberal journalist using the pseudonym »Brennglas« after 1830. In 1841 he was working in Neustrelitz, where he was leader of the Democratic Party at the time of the 1848 revolution. Five years later he was deported as a result of discontent with his political attitude. He spent this period outside Prussia, in Hamburg, but returned to Berlin in 1858 to become an editor. His poems and prose using the local dialect and accent really captured the opinions of the man on the street. His works were issued in massively popular booklets and their scenes from everyday life made them hugely successful. His most popular editions were called *Berlin as it is – and drinks* (1832 – 50) and his *Komischen Volkskalender* (Peculiar Calendar for the People; 1846 – 67). His character »Nante, the loafer on the corner« was famous all over Germany. Glassbrenner died on 25 September 1876.

E.T.A. Hoffmann (1776 – 1822)

Writer Ernst Theodor Amadeus Hoffmann was born on 24 January 1776 in Königsberg. He was one of the most idiosyncratic and bizarre poets of the German Romantic era. He studied law in his home town from

1792 to 1795 before heading for Berlin in 1798 to take up a post as clerk to the Court of Justice. Two years later he became an assessor in Posen. He spent time in various other towns in Prussia before returning to Berlin to earn his living as a musician, draughtsman, man of letters and newspaper editor. In 1808 he took up a post as a music teacher, producer, decorative painter and orchestra director in Bamberg. From 1813 to 1814 he directed orchestras in Leipzig and Dresden and then in 1816 he was appointed councillor to Berlin's Court of Justice. He set up a round table of the Serapion Fraternity at the famous Lutter & Wegner wine lodge on Gendarmenmarkt and counted many actors and poets among his friends, including Ludwig Devrient, the Brentanos, Adelbert von Chamisso and Friedrich de la Motte-Fouqué. Hoffmann was considered among the most amusing and witty of individuals in the Berlin salon scene, but was also one of its thirstiest. His often rather peculiar behaviour caused some alarm but he nevertheless gained both esteem and popularity, particularly thanks to his artistic fairy tales. He died on 25 June 1822.

The Humboldt Brothers

Brothers Alexander and Wilhelm von Humboldt were widely travelled and entertaining wits who were very popular figures in Berlin's society and literary circles as well as at the Prussian court.

? DID YOU KNOW ...?

- ... that Alexander von Humboldt was a world record mountaineer? On 23 June 1802 he climbed Mount Chimborazo in Ecuador, at 6310m / 20,700ft the highest known peak in the world at the time, to a height of 5878m / 19,285ft equipped with no warmer clothing than a frock coat, poncho and jackboots. It was the highest that anyone would reach for another thirty years.

Alexander von Humboldt is considered the originator of agricultural economics, meteorology, marine geography and plant geography. He was born in Berlin on 14 September 1769. He initially studied law along with his brother Wilhelm in Frankfurt an der Oder, but later went to the mountaineering academy in Freiberg, Saxony. In 1790 he travelled throughout Europe, then from 1792 to 1797 he was a mountain assessor and expert in Franconia. Along with French botanist A. Bonpland he spent the years from 1799 to 1804 on an extensive expedition to South and Central America. After his return he was based for most of the period between 1807 and 1827 in Paris, where he assimilated the results of his South American studies. He returned to Berlin in 1827 and gave lectures at the Friedrich-Wilhelm University before undertaking another expedition in 1829, this

Alexander von Humboldt (1769 – 1859), scientist

time to the Asian regions of Russia. His principal work *Cosmos* was published in four volumes between 1845 and 1858 (with a fragment of a fifth appearing posthumously in 1862). He died on 6 May 1859.

Wilhelm von Humboldt (1767 – 1835) Prussian civil servant

Wilhelm Freiherr von Humboldt was born in Potsdam on 22 June 1767. He studied law in Frankfurt an der Oder and in Göttingen. Between 1802 and 1808 he was the diplomatic representative of Prussia in Rome until he was named as head of the Prussian culture and education board at the interior ministry in Berlin in 1809. It was in this role that he founded and built the Berlin University (now the Friedrich-Wilhelm University) with the sponsorship of Friedrich Wilhelm III. In 1819 he became a member of the state ministry. Upon retiring from state service later that year he undertook linguistic studies in his mansion next to Lake Tegel. He died there on 8 April 1835.

August Wilhelm Iffland (1759 – 1814)

Actor

The actor and dramatist was born on 19 April 1759 to wealthy parents in Hanover. It was originally intended that he study theology but in 1777 he dropped out and took to the stage, initially at the court theatre in Gotha, then later in Mannheim. He was usually cast as the comedian or sentimental hero but he made a tremendous impression as the villain »Franz von Moor« in Schiller's *Die Räuber*. In 1796 he was appointed director of the Royal National Theatre of Prussia in Berlin, becoming director-general of royal plays in 1811. He himself wrote sentimental, middle-class plays but his key productions were works by Shakespeare, Schiller and Zacharias Werner. Iffland was a patriotic fighter, particularly during the French occupation, when he artfully wriggled out of all his obligations. He died on 22 September 1814. His name lives on thanks to the Iffland Ring, which is now the highest acting award in German speaking countries and is passed from each of its winners to a successor of his or her own nomination.

Friedrich Ludwig Jahn (1778 – 1852)

»Father of gymnastics«

Jahn, born on 11 August 1778 in Freyburg an der Unstrut, was to become famous as the father of gymnastics. In 1811 he set up his first gymnasium at the Hasenheide fields in Berlin and sought to toughen up young people by means of spartan living and exercise. His patriotism was initially directed in its entirety against Napoleon and during the wars of liberation he commanded one of the Lützow battalions. With the restoration of the Prussian state though, his brusque speeches and outspokenness brought him into conflict with the authorities. In 1819, his gymnastic facilities were closed down and he was put on trial. He received a pardon, however, in 1825, although he remained under police observation until 1840. During the German national assembly of 1848, his ideas on the monarchy were rejected and he sullenly retired from public life. He died on 15 October 1852 and there is a memorial to him at the northeastern corner of Hasenheide park.

Hildegard Knef (1925 – 2002)

Berlin, dein Gesicht hat Sommersprossen (Berlin, you have freckles) or *Ich hab' noch einen Koffer in Berlin* (I still have a suitcase in Berlin) were among the chansons sung in the breathy tones of Hildegard Knef that gave musical expression to a way of life in the isolated West Berlin of the 1960s and made her the very epitome of Berlin itself. In fact she was not actually a Berliner and even her singing voice was something of a late discovery. Hildegard Knef was born in Ulm on 28 December 1925 but grew up in Berlin, taking acting lessons in

Actress, singer and writer

1942. Her first leading role was in the first film to be made in post-war Germany, *Die Mörder sind unter uns* (*The Murderers Are Among Us*) directed by Wolfgang Staudte in 1946. In 1948 she received the Best Actress award at the Locarno Film Festival for her role in *Film ohne Titel* (*Film Without A Title*). There was, however, absolute furore at her brief nude appearance in *Die Sünderin* (*The Sinner*; 1951). She made her ultimate breakthrough in the USA, where she appeared on Broadway 675 times as Ninotchka in the Cole Porter musical *Silk Stockings*. This led to roles in Hollywood. It was not until 1963 that she started her new career as a singer of chansons. Her unusual style led Ella Fitzgerald to dub her »the best singer without a voice«. In 1970 her autobiography *Der geschenkte Gaul* (*The Gift Horse*) brought her huge success as a writer. The last three decades of her life were scarred by illness, against which she struggled indomitably. Her

Hildegard Knef in »The Sinner«

strength and youthful vitality were exhibited once more in 1995 when she appeared on stage with the German new-wave band »Extrabreit«, who had released a version of Knef's *Für mich soll's rote Rosen regnen* (For me it should rain red roses). Even then she effortlessly outshone her young co-performers. She died on 1 February 2002 in Berlin.

Käthe Kollwitz (1867 – 1945)

The graphic artist and painter was born Käthe Schmidt on 8 July 1867 in Königsberg. She studied in Berlin, Königsberg and Munich, marrying the doctor Karl Kollwitz from Berlin in 1891. She lived in the capital until her studio was destroyed in 1943. In 1919 she was appointed as a professor at the Berlin Akademie der Künste, but was forced to give up the distinction in 1933. Käthe Kollwitz completely

Artist

dedicated her work to the impoverished sufferings of the capital's proletariat. At times her creations – particularly her wood cuts – were akin to expressionism. She died on 22 April 1945 in Moritzburg near Dresden.

Max Liebermann (1847 – 1935)

Painter Painter and graphic artist Max Liebermann, one of the great masters of impressionism in Germany, came from a wealthy family of Berlin merchants and joined the Berliner Akademie in 1898. In 1899 he combined with Walter Leistikow and Max Slevogt to found the Berlin Secession group. From 1920 to 1932 he served as president of the Akademie der Künste but in 1933 he was prohibited from exhibiting as a dedicated opponent of National Socialism. His response to the stormtroopers' march to the Kanzleramt through the Brandenburg Gate on 30 January 1933 has become famous: »I can't eat enough to be as sick as I want to be.« Many of his works are on display in the Nationalgalerie.

Paul Lincke (1866 – 1946)

Composer The most famous operetta by Paul Lincke, *Frau Luna*, describes a balloon ride to the moon by a handful of Berliners and includes the march *Das ist die Berliner Luft, Luft, Luft* (That's the Berlin air), which has become the anthem of Berlin. Born 7 November 1866 in Berlin he led his first orchestra at just 18, mostly conducting for the popular stage. After a while he left for Paris before returning to make his career in Berlin. He died on 3 September 1946.

Adolph Menzel (1815 – 1905)

Painter Among the most important painters and graphic artists of the German realism movement, Adolph Menzel was born on 8 December 1815 in Breslau and was trained by his own father in lithography. He inherited his parent's workshop in 1832 and in 1842 he produced his first major work, the illustrations for *The Life of Frederick the Great* by Franz Kugler. During the 1840s and 1850s he mainly produced paintings, many of which anticipated the later impressionist movement. One of the most famous of these pictures, *Frederick the Great with Friends at Table in Sanssouci* was probably destroyed during the Second World War.

Adolph Menzel was soon highly in demand – for portraits too – and was given all kinds of public awards. He was even elevated to the aristocracy, became a member of the Akademie and was invested with several orders. His diligence was famous. Wherever he went, wherever he stood, he would sketch the scene around him. Although he was unusually small with an impressive bald pate, he was a veritable institution in both Berlin's cafés and its mansions. However, his own personal fate was to be quite tragic. Due to his short stature, he was playfully dubbed the »Little Excellency«, which rendered him mistrustful and brusque with people. He died on 9 February 1905. An excellent collection of his works can be seen at the Alte National-galerie (►Museumsinsel).

Wolfgang Neuss (1923 – 89)

He was called the »Mann mit der Pauke« (man with the drum) and made sharp commentaries on the politics of the early 1960s. Wolf-

Cabaret performer

gang Neuss was born on 3 December 1923 in Bres-lau and became famous as a cabaret performer and actor. After his matriculation examination, he spent five years as a soldier until he deliberately shot off his own left index finger and thus avoided service at the front. After the war ended he started his new career in cabaret in Düsseldorf, appearing in popular films, mostly in comic but subtle roles. His key sphere however was film and stage satire, working as author, producer and leading actor along with his genial compadre Wolfgang Müller in shows such as *Wir Kellerkinder* (We Children of the Cellar) and *Genosse Münchhausen* (Comrade Münchhausen) and exhibiting a decidedly contrary way of thinking laterally. In 1962 he even went as far as giving away in the *Bild* newspaper the care-fully guarded name of the murderer in *Das Hal-stuch*, a serialized German television version of Francis Durbridge's mystery, *The Scarf*. His greatest successes came in West Berlin in the years follow-ing 1963 where he had his own cabaret revue *Das jüngste Gerücht* (The Latest Rumour). He was a sympathizer of left-wing political groups and was one of the founder members of the Republican

The Man with the Drum

Club. As of the early 1970s, Wolfgang Neuss faded from public view. He spoke of little else other than his increasing drug consumption and he went badly to seed. He died on 5 May 1989.

Ernst Reuter (1889 – 1953)

Ernst Reuter was born on 29 July 1889 in Apenrade, Denmark. He joined the SPD in Germany in 1912 and was elected to the Berlin Magistracy in 1926. He was also appointed to organize the Berlin transport company (BVG), became mayor of Magdeburg in 1931 and was elected to the Reichstag in 1932. 1933, though, saw him em-igrate from Germany and he was not to return until after the war, when he re-entered politics and was elected mayor of Berlin in 1947, although a Soviet veto prevented him from taking office in 1948. He

Elected mayor

was returned as mayor of West Berlin from 1950 until he died on 29 September 1953 and his incumbency saw the events of the Berlin blockade and the Berlin Airlift. His fame was cemented with the appeal he made before the Reichstag during a demonstration against the blockade on 9 September 1948:

»Peoples of the world, look upon this city!«

»If we call the world to this city today, then we shall do so because we know that the strength of our people is in the very earth where we grew up and shall continue to grow until the powers of darkness are broken and smashed. We shall experience this day in front of our old Reichstag with its proud inscription ›for the German people‹; and we will celebrate with assurance that in our trouble and need, our cares and misery, we have brought this about with steadfastness and stamina... You peoples of the world! You peoples in America, in England, France and Italy! Look upon this city and see that you must not betray this city and its people, you cannot betray it. There is only one chance for all of us: to hold together every one of us until this struggle has been won, until the struggle has finally been crowned with victory over the enemy, victory over the powers of darkness. The people of Berlin have spoken. We have done our duty and we will continue to do our duty. Peoples of the world, look upon Berlin and the people of Berlin and be assured of them that this fight, this fight they are seeking, this fight we shall win!«

Hans Rosenthal (1925 – 87)

Compère Hans Rosenthal was born on 2 April 1925. A dyed in the wool Berliner, he became one of the most popular comperes of German radio and television. He was the son of a Jewish bank clerk, killed in 1937. His mother and his brother were both murdered at a concentration camp in Riga in 1941. Between 1940 and 1943 he was compelled to perform forced labour, including as a gravedigger, until he succeeded in escaping. For two years he managed to remain concealed in an allotment with the aid of two Berlin women. After the war he started as a cub reporter at Berliner Rundfunk, swapping to the broadcaster RIAS in 1948. There his career took off and he became an editor, director, ideas man and most memorably a quizmaster. His best known shows included *Allein gegen alle* (Alone Against the World). In 1967 he took his first steps in the world of television, where he took control of the ZDF quiz *Dalli-Dalli* from 1971. This assured him of his greatest success until 1986. Behind the smiling face of the TV star, though, there was a man of substance. Until 1980 he was a member of the directorate of Germany's central council of Jews and as chairman at the conference of representatives for the Jewish community in Berlin, he actively worked for reconciliation between Germans and Jews. Hans Rosenthal died on 10 February 1987 in Berlin.

Ernst Ferdinand Sauerbruch (1875 – 1951)

The famous surgeon was born on 3 July 1875 in Barmen. As of 1928 he worked in Berlin as director of the Charité University's surgical clinic. His key medicinal legacy was in the areas of lung and heart surgery. It should not be denied, however, that Sauerbruch – along with more than 900 other leading doctors – put his name to a letter declaring devotion to Hitler shortly after the National Socialists seized power in 1933. Sauerbruch died on 2 July 1951.

Surgeon

Kurt Tucholsky (1890 – 1935)

Born on 9 January 1890, the writer initially studied law but between 1924 and 1929 worked as a journalist and foreign correspondent (primarily in Paris, later in Sweden). In 1926 he briefly acted as publisher of the *Weltbühne* magazine, for which he had been working since 1913. Tucholsky also published under pseudonyms such as Theobald Tiger, Peter Panter, Ignaz Wrobel and Kaspar Hauser. A satirist and critic of his times, he created, along with Erich Kästner and Walter Mehring, the modern urban chansons and made many imaginative contributions to the Berliner Kabarett. He also produced tales such as *Rheinsberg* and *Schloss Gripsholm*. He fled from the Nazis in 1933 and, in despair at the political regime in Germany, he took his own life in Hindås in Sweden on 21 December 1935.

Writer

Wilhelm Voigt (1849 – 1922)

Wilhelm Voigt was born on 13 February 1849 at Tilsit in eastern Prussia. He got into trouble with the authorities at a very early age and was sentenced to 12 years' imprisonment for counterfeiting deeds at the age of 18. After his release he spent some years leading a more respectable existence as a cobbler, but he fell into unemployment and began to pursue one crime after another. He sought to leave Prussia but was denied a passport. This was an object lesson to him in how intransigent civil servants could be, but it also enlightened him as to how much they were in thrall to anyone in uniform. This fact and his own criminal modus operandi, favouring money stored in legal and council institutions, may have led him to devise his slick caper. On 16 October 1906, Wilhelm Voigt apprehended the mayor of the then independent Köpenick dressed in a captain's uniform that he had assembled from flea markets and junk shops and »confiscated« the city funds. When the mayor asked the reason for the arrest, Voigt simply pointed to the fixed bayonets of the soldiers

»Captain of Köpenick«

behind him (who he had gathered from a public street simply by ordering them to accompany him in a suitably commanding tone) and declared that resistance would be useless, stating: »Orders are orders. You can make your complaints afterwards.« The heist was greeted with amusement throughout Germany. Wilhelm Voigt was soon caught and sentenced to four years in prison, although he was released after just two. He chose to leave the country and moved to Luxemburg in May 1909, although he actually planned to emigrate to Canada. In 1910 he did indeed travel overseas, although it was only a short trip to the USA, where he appeared in Barnum & Bailey's circus as the »Captain of Köpenick«. He returned to Luxemburg that same year, and he died there on 3 January 1922.

»Who's chucking the mud around? Shame on 'em!!«

Claire Waldoff (1884 – 1957)

Claire Waldoff was born on 21 October 1884 and worked as an actress, but she became better known for her cabaret appearances and her »Schnauze« (big mouth), epitomizing the Berlin version of the »chanson« musical form with lines like »Wer schmeißt denn da mit Lehm? Der sollte sich was schäm'« (Who's chucking the mud around? Shame on them!). Her cheeky but thoughtful couplets told of the city, its »Zillemilljöh« (Zille's milieu), and the joys and troubles of ordinary people. Her perky number *Röhre* was recorded on plenty of discs, and her red hair and chubby little frame were trademarks of Berlin's poster painters. When she died on 22 January 1957, Germany lost a true original. She is buried in Stuttgart.

Heinrich Zille (1858 – 1929)

Draughtsman Heinrich Zille was born in Radeburg, Saxony on 10 January 1858. Famous as the chronicler of Berlin's »Milljöh« or backstreet lifestyle, he himself came from humble beginnings. He was a pupil of the

The Rat.
»How did it die, then?«
»Our house is too
damp for it!«

popular painter Theodor Hosemann and started out as a lithographer. He worked for the periodicals *Simplicissimus*, *Jugend* and *Lustige Blätter* before joining the Prussian Academy Of Arts. Zille made his name with drawings laced with social critique depicting the poverty of Berlin's backstreets and yards. Zille's humour, based on caricature, his brilliant hand and sharp eye for funny situations often led people astray from the artist's own view of himself as a critic of social deprivation, seeking not to cheer people with joviality but to challenge those seeing his work, to evoke pity, and to recognize the reality of poverty and need. He died on 9 August 1929.

Practicalities

HOW DO YOU FIND WHAT YOU ARE LOOKING FOR IN BERLIN? WHERE ARE THE BEST RESTAURANTS? WHAT IS THE BEST WAY TO SPEND AN EVENING? A VISIT TO VARIETÉ CHAMÄLEON PERHAPS, WHERE THINGS CAN GET REALLY WILD!

Accommodation

Hotels   Berlin's hotel industry now provides 106,200 beds at more than 720 addresses, and more are under construction – both budget and luxury hotels. A new feature is the increasing number of holiday apartments, especially in Mitte. Accommodation is available for four people for € 40 per day, for example in Friedrichshain, Neukölln and Wedding. A hotel listing can be obtained from the Berlin Hotline (tel. 030 / 25 00 25, and tourist information, ▶ Information). **Online bookings** can be made under www.visitberlin.de and www.ehotel.de; holiday homes and private rooms can be found at www.ferienwohnungen-berlin.de.

Prices ▶   The prices given here are average prices for a double room. Usually breakfast is included but, especially in the higher echelon of hotels, it may be that breakfast is charged separately. In many hotels it is worth asking about discounted group and weekend deals.

Hotel and rooms listing ▶

▶ RECOMMENDED HOTELS

▶ ① **See maps on pages 74 – 77**
No number: not in the area covered by the maps

LUXURY: from €200

▶ ① **Adlon Kempinski Berlin**
Unter den Linden 77 (Mitte)
D-10117 Berlin
Tel. 22 61-0, fax 22 61 22 22
www.hotel-adlon.de
401 rooms and 78 suites, wellness studio. S-Bahn: Unter den Linden
Legendary hotel where Enrico Caruso, Tsar Nicholas, Albert Einstein and Thomas Alva Edison all stayed. Restaurant/bistro, Club Bar, American Bar, smoker's lounge and lifestyle shop.

▶ **Alma Berlin**
Schlosshotel im Grunewald
Brahmsstr. 10 (Grunewald)
D-14193 Berlin
Tel. 89 58 40, fax 89 58 48 00
www.schlosshotelberlin.com
54 rooms, restaurant, bars, gym
Top location in Grunewald, rooms

by Karl Lagerfeld with plush decor and stucco.

▶ ⑯ **Brandenburger Hof**
Eislebener Str. 14 (Wilmersd.)
D-10789 Berlin
Tel. 21 40 50, fax 21 40 51 00
www.brandenburger-hof.com
62 rooms, restaurants, bar, wellness studio.
U-Bahn: Augsburger Str. (U 1)
Not far from the Gedächtniskirche in a splendid city mansion. Rooms are furnished in Bauhaus style.

▶ ⑱ **Grand Hotel Esplanade**
Lützowufer 15 (Tiergarten)
D-10785 Berlin
Tel. 2 54 78 82 55, fax 2 43 78 82 22
www.esplanade.de
390 rooms, 38 suites, restaurants, bar, wellness. Bus: 129
Luxury hotel in simple but elegant designer style. Ellipse Lounge with Asian cuisine, homely pub.
Harry's New York Bar is a popular meeting place.

Hotel Adlon lobby

▶ ⑲ **Grand Hyatt Berlin**
Marlene-Dietrich-Platz 2 (Daimler Precinct/Tiergarten)
D-10785 Berlin
Tel. 25 53 12 34, fax 25 53 12 35
http://berlin.grand.hyatt.com S-Bahn/U-Bahn: Potsdamer Platz
342 rooms. Super-modern luxury hotel on the new Potsdamer Platz with every conceivable luxury; Vox top restaurant.

▶ ⑮ **Kempinski Hotel Bristol**
Kurfürstendamm 27
(Charlottenburg.)
D-10719 Berlin
Tel. 8 84 34-0, fax 8 83 60 75
www.kempinskiberlin.de
301 rooms, restaurants, bar, wellness studio.
U-Bahn: Uhlandstr. (U 15)
Hotel with a long tradition that has played host to John Wayne, Peter Ustinov, Kirk Douglas, Theodor Heuss and Willy Brandt among others.

▶ ⑥ **Sofitel Berlin Gendarmenmarkt**
Charlottenstr. 50 – 52 (Mitte)
D-10117 Berlin
Tel. 20 37 50, fax 20 37 51 00
www.accorhotels.com
92 rooms, restaurant, wellness.
U-Bahn: Stadtmitte (U 6)
Modern luxury in Berlin's top location on Gendarmenmarkt.

MID-RANGE: €100–200

▶ ⑦ **Alexander Plaza**
Rosenstr. 1 (Mitte)
D-10178 Berlin
Tel. 24 00 10, fax 24 00 17 77
www.alexander-plaza.com
92 rooms, restaurant, bar, fitness studio.
S-Bahn: Hackescher Markt
The Alexander was built from 1897 to 1900 for fur trader Siegfried Abrahamson as a commercial building. Unbeatable location opposite the Hackesche Höfe.

Berlin Hotels, Restaurants, Going Out & Cafés

Where to stay
1. Adlon
2. Jolly Hotel Vivaldi
3. Arte Luise Kunsthotel
4. Honigmond
5. Mittes Backpacker
6. Sofitel Berlin Gendarmenmarkt
7. Alexander Plaza
8. art'hotel ermelerhaus
9. Myer's Hotel

Entertainment
1. Ballhaus Berlin
2. Reingold
3. Clärchens Ballhaus
4. Dice Club
5. b-flat
6. Kaffee Burger
7. Roter Salon
8. Ständige Vertretung
9. Oxymoron
10. CSR-Bar
11. Berghain
12. Cueva Buena Vista
13. Felix

Where to eat
1. Rutz
2. Las Cucarachas
3. Botequim Carioca
4. Kasbah
5. Sophieneck
6. Margaux
7. Samâdhi
8. Lutter & Wegner
9. Borchardt
10. Guy
11. Vau
12. Entrecôte
13. Cantamaggio
14. Susuru
15. Georgbräu
16. Zur letzten Instanz

Café
1. Kaffekombinat
2. Barcomi's
3. Café Orange
4. Berliner Republik
5. Telecafé
6. Die Eins
7. Café Einstein
8. Operncafé

250 m
750 ft
© Baedeker

Former route of the Berlin Wall

Berlin Hotels, Restaurants, Going Out & Cafés

Where to stay

10 Artemisia
11 Dittberner
12 Bogotà
13 Bleibtreu
14 Fasanenhaus
15 Kempinski Bristol
16 Brandenburger Hof
17 Sorat Ambassador
18 Grand Hotel Esplanade
19 Grand Hyatt
29 Paris Bar
30 Ess-Klasse
31 Diekmann
32 Quadriga
33 Moritz
34 Daitokai
35 First Floor
36 Hugos
37 Zollpackhof
38 Facil
39 Tony Roma's
40 Hakuin
41 Tuk Tuk

Where to eat

17 Moustache
18 Capt'n Schillow
19 Schleusenkrug
20 Café am Neuen See
21 Good Friends
22 El Borriquito
23 Angora
24 Marjellchen
25 Calcutta
26 Franz Diener
27 Terzo Mondo
28 Dicke Wirtin

Entertainment

14 Wilhelm Hoeck
15 A Trane
16 Zwiebelfisch
17 Quasimodo
18 Baccara Berlin
19 Maxxim
20 Irish Harp Pub

21 Universum Lounge
22 Zur weißen Maus
23 Harry's New York Bar
24 Bar am Lützowplatz
25 Trompete
26 40 Seconds
27 Green Door
28 Leydicke
29 Yorck-Schlösschen
30 Ballhaus Walzerlinksgestrickt

Café

10 Kleine Orangerie
11 Buchwald
12 Berliner Kaffeerösterei
13 Schwarzes Café
14 Literaturhaus
15 Kranzler
16 Einstein
17 Liebermans
18 Tomasa
19 Blisse 14

▶ ③ **Arte Luise Kunsthotel**
Luisenstr. 19 (Mitte)
D-10117 Berlin
Tel. 2 84 48-0,
Fax 2 84 48-4 48
www.luise-berlin.com
49 rooms.
S-/U-Bahn: Friedrichstr.
Original and very pleasant building right in the government precinct, where every room plus the lobby and stairwell have been decorated by a different artist.

▶ ⑧ **art'hotel ermelerhaus Berlin**
Wallstr. 70–73 (Mitte)
D-10179 Berlin
Tel. 24 06 20
Fax 24 06 22 22
www.artotels.de; 109 rooms
U-Bahn: Spittelmarkt (U 2)
Old town house linked to a modern building in the Nikolaiviertel with interior design by Baselitz.

▶ ⑬ **Bleibtreu**
Bleibtreustr. 31
(Charlottenbg.), D-10707 Berlin
Tel. 8 84 74-0, fax 8 84 74-444
www.bleibtreu.com
60 rooms, restaurant, wellness
S-Bahn: Savignyplatz
Hotel in a large town house that seeks to be environmentally friendly in terms of both fittings and cuisine.

▶ **Estrel Hotel Berlin**
Sonnenallee 225 (Neukölln)
D-12057 Berlin
Tel. 6 83 12 25 22
Fax 68 31 23 45
www.estrel.com, 1125 rooms
S-Bahn: Sonnenallee
Europe's biggest hotel is a bit off the beaten track. It is an ultra-modern building with all the

facilities for congresses, fitness studios, five restaurants, a bar – and a live show »Stars in Concert«.

▶ ④ **Honigmond**
Tieckstr. 11 (Mitte)
D-10115 Berlin
Tel. 2 84 45 50
Fax 28 44 55 11
www.honigmond.de; 36 rooms
U-Bahn: Zinnowitzer Str. (U 6)
Very charming and beautifully appointed hotel right in the centre of town but still with its lovely garden.

▶ ② **Jolly Hotel Vivaldi**
Friedrichstr. 96 (Mitte)
D-10117 Berlin
Tel. 20 62 66-0
Fax 2 06 26 69 99
www.nh-hotels.de; 292 rooms
S-Bahn/U-Bahn: Friedrichstrasse
New hotel in a marvellously central location with an Italian touch to the service in the Vivaldi restaurant, the bistro and the wine bar.

▶ ⑨ **Myer's Hotel**
Metzstr. 26 (Prenzlauer Berg)
D-10405 Berlin
Tel. 4 40 14-0
Fax 4 40 14-104
www.myershotel.de; 41 rooms, lobby bar
U-Bahn: Senefelder Platz (U 2)
Stylish accommodation in an excellent place for going out in the evening.

▶ ⑰ **Sorat Ambassador**
Bayreuther Str. 42 (Schöneberg)
D-10787 Berlin
Tel. 21 90 20
Fax 21 90 23 80
www.sorat-hotels.com
U-Bahn: Wittenbergplatz (U 1)

218 rooms. Retro design from four different decades, lounge bar with a courtyard terrace.

BUDGET: €50–100

► ⑫ **Bogotà**
Schlüterstr.45 (Charlottenbg.)
D-10707 Berlin
Tel. 8 81 50 01
Fax 8 83 58 87
www.hotelbogotaberlin.com
123 rooms. S-Bahn: Savignyplatz
Comfy but slightly aged looking hotel, which is well priced for its location around the corner from Ku'damm.

► ⑪ **Dittberner**
Wielandstr. 26 (Charlottenbg.)
D-10707 Berlin
Tel. 884695-0
Fax 8854046, 20 rooms
Bus: 119, 129, 219
www.hotel-dittberner.de
Budget guesthouse in a large and convoluted town house, very friendly service.

► ⑭ **Fasanenhaus**
Fasanenstr. 73 (Charlottenbg.)
D-10719 Berlin
Tel. 8 81 67 13, fax 8 82 39 47, 25 rooms U-Bahn: Uhlandstr. (U 15)
www.fasanenhaus.de
Low-price guesthouse.

► ⑩ **Frauenhotel Artemisia**
Brandenburgische Str. 18 (Wilmersdorf)
D-10707 Berlin
Tel. 8 73 89 05, fax 8 61 86 53
www.frauenhotel-berlin.de
12 rooms, roof terrace.
U-Bahn: Konstanzer Str. (U 7)
4th and 5th floors are reserved solely for female guests. Exhibitions by contemporary female artists.

IN POTSDAM
(See map p.352 / 353)

► ① **Hotel am Luisenplatz**
Zeppelinstr. 136
D-14471 Potsdam
Tel. (03 31) 97 19 00
Fax 99 71 90 19
www.hotel-luisenplatz.de; 38 rooms
Town mansion from the 19th century with stylish furnishings. The B & B Hotel next door is cheaper.

► **Filmhotel Lili Marleen**
Grossbeerenstr. 75
D-14482 Potsdam (Babelsberg)
Tel. (03 31) 74 32 00, fax 7 43 20 18
www.filmhotel.potsdam.de.
65 rooms; ideal place for film fans because its neighbour is the Filmstadt Babelsberg.

HOSTELS FOR BACKPACKERS (up to €50)

► **BaxPax Backpacker's Hostel**
Skalitzer Str. 104 (Kreuzberg)
D-10997 Berlin
Tel. 69 51 83 22
Fax 69 51 83 72
www.baxpax.de/kreuzberg; 59 beds
With kitchen for self-catering.
U-Bahn: Kottbuser Tor (U 1, U 15, U 12, U 8).

► **Jetpack Downtown**
Pariser Str. 58 (Wilmersdorf)
D-10719 Berlin
Tel. 7 84 43 60, www.jetpak.de
Awarded best hostel prize in 2006
U-Bahn: Spichernstr. (U 3, U 9)

► **Die Fabrik. Hostel Kreuzberg**
Schlesische Str. 18
D-10997 Berlin
Tel. 6 11 71 16, fax 6 18 29 74
www.diefabrik.com

45 rooms, bathrooms on floor.
U-Bahn: Schlesisches Tor (U 1,
U 15, U 12)
In a converted factory building.
Meals are provided in Café Eisen-
waren

▶ ⑤ **Mittes Backpacker Hostel**
Chausseestr. 102
D-10115 Berlin (Mitte)
Tel. 28 39 09 65
Fax 28 39 09 35
www.backpacker.de; 59 beds
U-Bahn: Zinnowitzer Str. (U 6)
Very simple but very cheap with
self-catering

ASSOCIATION YOUTH HOSTELS

▶ **Deutsches Jugendherbergs-
werk Berlin-Brandenburg**
Tempelhofer Ufer 32
D-10963 Berlin
Tel. 26 49 52-0
Fax 2 62 04 37
www.djh-Berlin-Brandenburg.de

▶ **Jugendgästehaus Berlin Int.**
Kluckstr. 3 (Schöneberg)
D-10785 Berlin
Tel. 2 61 10 98 Fax 2 65 03 83
www.jh-berlin-international.de

▶ **Jugendherberge Ernst Reuter**
Hermsdorfer Damm 48–50
(Tegel/Hermsdorf)
D-13467 Berlin
Tel. 4 04 16 10
Fax 4 04 59 72
www.jh-ernst-reuter.de

▶ **Jugendgästehaus Am Wannsee**
Badeweg 1 (Grunewald)
D-14129 Berlin
Tel. 8 03 20 34
Fax 8 03 59 08
www.berlin-wannsee-
jugendherberge.de

OTHER ACCOMMODATION FOR YOUNG PEOPLE

▶ **CVJM-Haus**
Einemstr. 10 (Schöneberg)
D-10787 Berlin
Tel. 26 491088
www.cvjm-berlin.de

▶ **Jugendgästehaus**
Antwerpener Str. 40
(Wedding), D-13353 Berlin
Tel. 45 31 03 36, fax 45 31 03 37
www.jgh-berlin.de

▶ **Jugendgästehaus am Zoo**
Hardenbergstr. 9a
(Charlottenburg)
D-10623 Berlin
Tel. 3 12 94 10, fax 3 12 54 30
www.jgh-zoo.de

▶ **Jugendgästehaus Central**
Nikolsburger Str. 2–4
(Wilmersd.), D-10717 Berlin
Tel. 8 73 01 88, fax 8 61 34 85
www.jugendgaestehaus-central.de

▶ **Hostel am Flussbad**
Gartenstr. 50 (Köpenick)
D-12557 Berlin
Tel. 65 88 00 94, fax 65880093
www.der-coepenicker.de/hostel

▶ **Jugendgästehaus Nordufer**
Nordufer 28 (Wedding)
D-13351 Berlin, tel. 4 51 70 30
www.nordufer.de

▶ **Jugendgästehaus
St.-Michaels-Heim**
Bismarckallee 23 (Wilmersdorf)
D-14193 Berlin, Tel. 8 96 88-0

▶ **Jugendgästehaus Tegel**
Ziekowstr. 161
D-13509 Berlin
Tel. 4 33 30 46
Fax 4 34 50 63

▶ **Jugendgästehaus
Vier Jahreszeiten**
Bundesallee 31a (Wilmersdorf)
D-10717 Berlin, tel. 8 73 20 14

BED & BREAKFAST

▶ **Bernd Rother**
City office: Ahlbecker Str. 3
D-10437 Berlin
Tel. 44 05 05 82, fax 44 05 05 83
Mon–Fri 9am–6pm
bedbreakfa@aol.com

▶ **bed and breakfast Berlin**
Feilnerstr. 1
D-10969 Berlin
Tel. 78 91 39 71 Fax 78 91 39 72
www.bed-and-breakfast.de

SHARED ACCOMMODATION AGENCIES

▶ **Agentur Wohnwitz**
Holsteinische Str. 55
(Wilmersdorf)
D-10717 Berlin
Tel. 8 61 82 22
Fax 8 61 82 72
www.wohnwitz.com

▶ **City Mitwohnzentrale GmbH**
Hardenbergplatz 14
(Charlottenburg)
D-10623 Berlin
Tel. 1 94 30, Fax 2 16 94 01
www.city-wohnen.de

▶ **Erste Mitwohnzentrale**
Sybelstr. 52, D-10629 Berlin
Tel. 3 24 30 31
Fax 3 24 99 77
www.mitwohn.com

▶ **HomeCompanyBerlin**
Joachimstaler Str. 17
(Charlottenburg)
D-10623 Berlin
Tel. 1 94 45, fax 8 82 66 94
www.wohnpool.de

▶ **Wohnagentur
am Mehringdamm**
Mehringdamm 66 (Kreuzberg)
D-10961 Berlin
Tel. 7 86 20 03
Fax 7 85 06 14
www.mitwohnzentrale-
berlin.de

CAMPING

▶ **Deutscher Camping Club (DCC)**
Kladower Damm 113 – 117
D-14089 Berlin
Tel. 2 18 60 71
Fax 2 13 44 16
www.dcc-berlin.de

▶ **Bürgerablage (BCC)**
Niederneuendorfer Alle 60 (
Spandau)
D-13587 Berlin
Tel./fax 3 35 45 84
April – Sep. With beach and pier
for swimming on the river Havel.

▶ **DCC-Campingplatz Gatow**
Kladower Damm 113 – 117
(Spandau), D 14039 Berlin
Tel. 3654340
Fax 36808492
Open all year round.

▶ **DCC-Campingplatz Kladow**
Krampnitzer Weg 111 – 117
(Spandau)
D-14089 Berlin
Tel. 3652797
Ffax 3651245
Open all year round.

▶ **DCC-Campingplatz
Am Krossinsee**
Wernsdorfer Str. 38
(Treptow-Köpenick)
D-12527 Berlin
Tel. 6758687
Fax 6759150
Open all year round.

Arrival · Before the Journey

By car Berlin is nearly 1100km / 700mi from London, but most of the journey can be made on motorways and the German Autobahn. The journey is likely to take eleven or twelve hours. Those coming from northern France having taken the ferry from Dover will pass through Belgium and then Holland, entering Germany near Venlo. Taking the A 40 towards Cologne, join the A 3 close to Duisburg, and then the A 2 near Oberhausen. The A 2 now leads most of the remaining 500km / 300mi to Berlin. All the major roads and motorways leading to Berlin open out onto its ring road, the Berliner Autobahnring (A 10), from which side roads lead off to the various suburbs and the

Environmental zone ► city centre. The part of the city within the inner S-Bahn (local rail) circle has been declared an environmental zone, which only vehicles that have a yellow or green sticker certifying their emission level may enter.

Crossing the Channel There are car ferry services from Dover or Folkestone to Calais. Alternatively, those wishing to take their car through the tunnel can travel on the Eurotunnel Shuttle Service, a rail link between Folkstone and Calais.

By bus or coach Eurolines operate a daily service from London Victoria to Berlin. The trip takes 19 hours. Coaches run regularly from many towns and cities in Germany to Berlin's central bus station, Zentrale Omnibusbahnhof (ZOB), located near the International Congress Centre (ICC) in Charlottenburg. Within Germany and elsewhere, travel agents offer cheap coach trips, weekend breaks and fixed-price deals.

By train It is possible to travel from London St Pancras to Berlin quite comfortably. The Eurostar from London reaches Brussels in 2.5 hours; the high-speed Thalys train continues on to Cologne in a little more

Tegel Airport is still as busy as ever
That transfer of flights to Schönefeld in 2007 didn't happen

USEFUL ADDRESSES

RAIL TRAVEL

► **In London**
Rail Europe Travel Centre
1 Lower Regent Street
London SW1Y 4XT
Tel. 0844 8 48 40 64,
www.raileurope.co.uk
www.raileurope.co.uk

► **In Berlin**
DB Reiseauskunft:

Tel. (0 18 0) 5 99 66 33 (24 hours)
Rail information for Berlin:
Tel. (0 800) 1 50 70 90
www.bahn.de

BUS

► **Eurolines**
Bookings online and in UK
through Eurolines
Tel. 087 17 81 81 81
www.eurolines.co.uk

than 2 hours. From Cologne there is a regular ICE (inter-city express) service to Berlin, taking 4.5 hours. Travellers can also take an early evening Eurostar from London to Paris or Brussels and then the overnight sleeper train to Berlin.

Berlin is incorporated in the German railways' ICE/IC/EC network. The main inter-city stations are the **Hauptbahnhof** in Berlin-Mitte, Gesundbrunnenstation in the north and a southerly interchange now called Südkreuz at the former Papestrasse station, both of which connect to the S-Bahn stations on the ring that encircles the city centre. No trains run any longer from Ostbahnhof to the north or south of Germany but there are still services to Frankfurt/Main and Hanover. Zoologischer Garten station is only frequented by night trains to Munich and Zurich nowadays, but there are new regional stations at Jungfernheide, Gesundbrunnen, Potsdamer Platz, Südkreuz and Lichterfelde Ost.

Rail connections

Plenty of airlines fly to the three airports in Berlin. Direct flights are available from all the most important towns in Germany as well as cities in the rest of Europe, though with many airlines there is a change of planes when flying out of London. Those offering direct flights from the UK include British Airways and BMI (Heathrow to Tegel), Air Berlin (Stansted to Tegel) and Ryanair (Stansted to Schönefeld). Continental fly direct from New York Newark to Tegel, while other carriers stop off in Frankfurt or Düsseldorf. Qantas and British Airways both offer a service from Sydney to Berlin via London Heathrow; Qantas also fly out of Melbourne. Those travelling to Berlin from Canada generally need to change planes in New York.

By air

Berlin has two major airports: Berlin Tegel (Flughafen Otto Lilienthal) in the northwest and Berlin-Schönefeld in the south of the city. Tegel is the terminus for flights within Germany or for international

◄ Airports

⏵ HOW TO GET THERE

RAILWAY STATIONS

► Hauptbahnhof
Tiergarten
S-Bahn: S 3, S 5, S 7, S 75, S 9
U-Bahn: U 55
Bus
M 41 (Potsdamer Platz), TXL (Tegel or Alexanderplatz), M 85
(Steglitz), 245 (Bahnhof Zoo)

► Bahnhof Zoologischer Garten
Hardenbergplatz
S-Bahn: S 3, S 5, S 7, S 75, S 9
U-Bahn: U 2, U 9

► Ostbahnhof
Friedrichshain
S-Bahn: S 3, S 5, S 7, S 75, S 9

► Bahnhof Gesundbrunnen
Wedding
S-Bahn: S 1, S 2, S 41, S 42
U-Bahn: U 2, U 9

► Bahnhof Südkreuz
Schöneberg
S-Bahn: S 2, S 26, S 41, S 42

AIRPORTS

► Berlin Tegel (TXL)
Location: 10km / 6mi northwest of
Mitte
Bus: Jet Express bus TXL to
Hauptbahnhof, government precinct and Potsdamer Platz (20
minute journey); Express bus X 9
to Zoologischer Garten station
(approx. 20 minute journey); 109
bus to Zoologischer Garten station
via Charlottenburg S-Bahn and
Jakob-Kaiser-Platz U-Bahn (approx. 30 minute journey); 128 bus
via Kurt-Schumacher-Platz U-Bahn and Franz-Neumann-Platz
U-Bahn to Osloer Strasse U-Bahn
(approx. 25 minute journey).

All services run at ten minute
intervals on weekdays as a rule,
and every 20 minutes at weekends.

► Berlin-Schönefeld (SXF)
Location: 20km/12mi southeast of
city centre
Rail: regional rail services RB 14
and RE 7 to Alexanderplatz station
and Bahnhof Zoo, travel time 30
mins.
S-Bahn: S 9 and S 45 from
Schönefeld station.
Bus: SXF 1 from terminal A.

► Airport information
For all three airports
Tel. (0 18 05) 00 01 86

AIRLINES

► Air Berlin
Tel. (0 18 05) 737 800
Tel. (UK) 0871 5000 737
www.airberlin.com

► British Airways
Tel. (0 18 05) 266 522
Tel. (UK) 0870 850 9850
www.britishairways.com

► Continental
Tel. (0 18 0) 321 2610
Tel. (US) 800 231 0856
www.continental.com

► Lufthansa
Tel. (0 18 03) 803 803
Tel. (UK) 0871 945 9747
www.lufthansa.com

► Qantas Airways
Tel. (0 18 05) 250 620
Tel. (Australia) 13 13 13
www.qantas.com

links to western Europe and the USA, while Schönefeld mainly handles traffic from east and southeast Europe, the Near East and Asia. Schönefeld is also an important hub for charter flights. The old central airport, Berlin-Tempelhof in the heart of the city, is now closed. Tegel too is set for closure when the expansion of Schönefeld to Berlin Brandenburg International has been completed.

Immigration and Customs Regulations

The identity cards and passports of EU citizens are often no longer checked. However, since random inspections are carried out at the border and identification is required at airports, all visitors should be able to show their **passports** when they enter the country. Children under 16 years of age must carry a children's passport or be entered in the parent's passport.

Travel documents

Always carry your driving licence, the motor vehicle registration and the international green insurance card when driving in Germany. Motor vehicles must have the oval sticker showing nationality unless they have a Euro licence plate. If your travel papers are lost or stolen, contact your diplomatic representation in Germany, but first go to the police to obtain a **report of theft**. It is easier to obtain replacement documents if you have **photocopies of the originals** or can download them from your electronic mailbox.

Car documents

◄ *Loss or theft*

Those who wish to bring pets (dogs, cats) to Germany require a **pet pass**. It contains an official veterinary statement of health (no more than 30 days old), a rabies vaccination certificate that is at least 20 days and no more than eleven months old, and a passport photo. In addition, the animal must have a microchip or tattoo. A muzzle and leash are required at all times for dogs.

Pets and travel

The European Union member states (including Germany) form a common economic area within which the movement of goods for private purposes is largely duty-free. There are merely certain maximum quantities which apply (for example 800 cigarettes, 10 litres of spirits and 90 litres of wine per person). During random inspections customs officers must be convinced that the wares are actually intended for private use.

Customs regulations for EU citizens

For travellers from outside the EU, the following duty-free quantities apply: 200 cigarettes or 100 cigarillos or 50 cigars or 250g of tobacco; also 2 litres of wine and 2 litres of sparkling wine or 1 litre of spirits with an alcohol content of more than 22% vol.; 500g of coffee or 200g of coffee extract, 100g of tea or 40g of tea extract, 50ml of perfume or 0.25 litres of eau de toilette. Gifts up to a value of €175 are also duty-free.

Customs regulations for non-EU citizens

Travel Insurance

Health insurance Citizens of EU countries are entitled to treatment in Germany under the local regulations in case of illness on production of their **European health insurance card**. Even with this card, in most cases some of the costs for medical care and prescribed medication must be paid by the patient. Upon presentation of receipts the health insurance at home covers the costs – but not for all treatments. Citizens of non-EU countries must pay for medical treatment and medicine themselves and should take out private health insurance.

Private travel insurance Since some of the costs for medical treatment and medication typically have to be covered by the patient, and the costs for return transportation may not be covered by the normal health insurance, additional travel insurance is recommended.

Children in Berlin

It should be impossible for children to get bored in Berlin. Many areas of Berlin have special leisure facilities for children so that fun and excitement are always available. Using public transport to get there is free for any child of six and under and there is a child discount for any children who have not yet reached their 15th birthday (▸ transport). In the state museums (Staatliche Museen Berlin), children up to 16 years of age pay no admission. Many museums offer guided tours and courses for children as part of the »Jugend im Museum« programme. Theatrical performances for children and

 BERLIN FOR CHILDREN

SWIMMING POOLS

▸ **Kinderbad Monbijou (children's swimming pool)**
Oranienburger Str. 78 (Mitte)
Tel. 2828652 May–July Mon–Fri
11am–7pm, Sat, Sun
10am–7pm; Aug daily
10am–7pm S-Bahn: Hackescher
Markt opposite the Museumsinsel

▸ **Strandbad Wansee**
Wannseebadweg 25 (Zehlendorf)
Tel. 70 71 38 33 Mon–Fri
10am–7pm, Sat, Sun 8am–8pm
S-Bahn: Nikolasssee, then by 118
or 318 bus to Badeweg and 218
bus to Wannseebadweg

LEISURE CENTRES

▸ **Britzer Garten**
Sangerhauser Weg 1 (Neukölln)
Tel. 70 09 09-0
Fax 70 09 06-70
www.britzer-garten.de
▸Neukölln, Britz

▸ **FEZ Wuhlheide leisure and recreation centre**
An der Wuhlheide 197 (Köpenick)
Tel. 53 07 12 81

www.fez-berlin.de
Tue – Fri 11am – 6pm (summer
holidays till 6pm only), Sat 1pm to
6pm, Sun 10am – 6pm
20 minutes from the city centre by
S-Bahn (S 3): creative work on
your own (including puppet
shows, pottery, modelmaking,
computer courses), theatricals,
concerts, ceinema, swimming and
sports hall, open-air plays, lakes to
bathe in, sports facilities and
playing fields plus park railway.

► **Kinderinsel**
Eichendorffstr. 17 (Mitte)
Tel. 41 71 69 28, fax 41 71 69 48
www.kinderinsel.de
Parties for children, experience
tours, child-oriented sightseeing,
excursions and join-in theatre,
language courses, family breakfast

MUSEUMS FOR CHILDREN

► **Jugendmuseum Schöneberg
(Museum of Youth)**
Hauptstr. 40/42
Tel. 78 76 21 76, Wed – Thu 3pm
to 6pm, Sun from 2pm
Historical household items, books,
toys and clothes, to rummage
through and admire.

► **Kinder- und Jugendmuseum
Prenzlauer Berg (Museum for
Children and Youth)**
Senefelder Str. 5, tel. 74 77 82 00
www.b.shuttle.de/museum
Tue – Son 10am – 6pm
Learning with play, involving such
topics as environmental protection
or the history of the city suburb.

► **Labyrinth Kindermuseum**
Osloer Str. 12 (Wedding)
Tel. (0800) 93 11 50
www.kindermuseum-labyrinth.de
Fri, Sat 1pm – 6pm, Sun

11am – 6pm, longer hours in
school holidays
Annually rotating interactive
exhibition project.

► **Machmit! Museum für Kinder**
Senefelder Str. 5 (Prenzlauer Berg)
Tel. 74778200
www.machmitmuseum.de
Play for six to twelve year olds in a
former church

► **Museum Kindheit und Jugend
(Childhood and Youth
Museum)**
Wallstr. 32 (Mitte), tel. 2 75 03 83
www.stadtmuseum.de
Tue – Fri 9am – 5pm
The history of schooling in Ger-
many, items from the lives of
children and youngsters over the
last hundred years or so.

► **Puppentheater-Museum Berlin
(Puppetry Museum)**
Karl-Marx-Str. 135 (Neukölln)
Tel. and fax 6 87 81 32
www.puppentheater-
museum.de
Mon – Fri 9am – 4pm, Sun
11am – 4.30pm
Story of puppetry in theatres with
puppets to touch and play with
and puppet show performances.

► **Science Center Spectrum**
in the Deutsches Technikmuseum
Scientific phenomena demonstrated specially for children, (►p.212)

► **Waldmuseum mit Waldschule
(Forestry Museum and School)**
Jagdschloss Grunewald
(Zehlendorf)
Tel. 8 13 34 42
www.waldmuseum-waldschule.de
Tue – Fri 10am – 3pm, Sun
1pm – 6pm

Fun in the Labyrinth Kinder-museum (children's museum)

Everything about life in the woods, with many dioramas, guessing games and the chance of a look through a microscope.

THEATRE FOR CHILDREN

► **Berliner Kindertheater (Children's Theatre)**
Summer: open-air stage at Zita-delle Spandau; winter: Fontane-Haus in the Märkisches Viertel, Wilhelmsruher Damm 142c
Tel. 62 70 59 26
www.berliner-kindertheater.de

► **Theater an der Parkaue**
Parkaue 29 (Lichtenberg)
Tel. 55 77 52 52,fax 5 53 34 95
www.parkaue.de
Germany's largest children's thea-tre, founded in the GDR in 1950, for children aged 5 and over

► **Fliegendes Theater**
Urbanstr. 100 (Kreuzberg)
Tel. 6 92 21 00
Fax 6 92 16 54
www.fliegendes-theater.de

► **Figurentheater Grashüpfer (puppet theatre)**
Puschkinallee 16a (Treptow)
Tel. 53 69 51 50

Fax 53 69 51 51
www.theater-grashuepfer.de

► **Grips Theater**
Altonaer Str. 22 (Tiergarten) and Klosterstr. 68 (Mitte)
Tel. 39 74 74 77
www.grips-theater.de

► **Zaubertheater Igor Jedlin (magical theatre)**
Roscherstr. 7 (Charlottenburg)
Tel. 3 23 37 77
www.zaubertheater.de

CHILDREN'S CINEMA

► **`Spatzenkino**
Tel. 449 47 50
www.spatzenkino.de
This project organizes children's films in various cinemas, with time to play between the films.

INDOOR PLAY AREAS

► **Jolos Kinderwelt**
Am Tempelhofer Berg 7d (Kreuzberg)
Tel. 61 20 27 98, Mon – Fri 2pm – 7pm, Sat, Sun 11am – 7pm climbing frames, bouncy castles, miniature railway

► **Legoland**
Sony Center (Tiergarten)
Tel. 3030400
www.legolanddiscoverycentre.com
Europe's first indoor Legoland (adults €14, children €11!)

OTHERS

► **Charlottenchen**
Droysenstr. 1 (Charlottenburg)
Tel. 324 47 17
www.charlottchen-berlin.de
Playground and restaurant. At weekends theatre for children, music or cabaret for parents.

youngsters include a varied programme of plays and a trip on the Spree is fun for young and old alike. Those who love water are well catered for in Berlin anyway since the range of lakes and swimming pools is huge. Two zoos have an exciting selection of exotic animals for kids from one to ninety-one (▶Tierpark Friedrichsfelde, ▶Zoologischer Garten). One very special attraction – even for grown-ups – is the **sweet factory** at Oranienburger Str. 32. Most hotels will also help out with babysitters.

Electricity

The German mains grid generally supplies 230-volt electricity at 50Hz. Due to the variety of sockets all visitors, especially who are not from mainland Europe, are advised to take an **adapter**.

Emergency

▶ **Fire brigade, paramedics**
Tel. 112

▶ **Police**
Tel. 110

▶ **Emergency medical service**
Tel. 31 00 31

▶ **Emergency dental service**
Tel. 89 00 4333

▶ **Child emergency service**
Tel. 61 00 61

▶ **Drugs emergency service**
Tel. 1 92 37

▶ **Poison emergency service**
Tel. 1 92 40

▶ **Counselling hotline**
Tel. 08 00–1 11 01 11
Tel. 08 00–1 11 02 22

Entertainment

Berlin's nightlife is, as it ever was, the wildest in the republic. The city literally never sleeps so those who have stamina enough can party through the night: you will always find something going on till dawn. The scene is highly dynamic and constantly changing – see Baedeker Special p.92).

Open all hours

ENTERTAINMENT: see maps on pages 74 – 77

CLUBS

► ㉖ **40 Seconds**
Potsdamer Str. 4 (Tiergarten)
Tel. 89 06 420
U-Bahn: Kurfürstenstr. (U 1)
Penthouse with three roof terraces.
Chic people enjoy a sensational
view, dance music and house.

► ⑱ **Baccara Berlin**
Meineckestr. 20 (Charlottenburg)
Tel. 88 71 85 56
U/S-Bahn: Bahnhof Zoo (U 2, U 9)
The stylish, laid-back party scene
makes its comeback in the west of
the city with classics, house, soul
and funk.

► ⑪ **Berghain**
Am Wriezener Bahnhof
(Friedrichshain)
S-Bahn: Ostbahnhof
The British DJ Mag voted Berg-
hain »best techno club 2009« for
its live acts by top DJs.

► ⑬ **Felix**
Behrenstr. 72 (Mitte)
Tel. 2 06 28 60
U-Bahn: Französische Str. (U 6)
Exclusive place to be, at the back
of Hotel Adlon

► **Knaack Klub**
Greifswalder Str. 224
(Prenzlauer Berg)
Tel. 4 42 70 61
U-Bahn: Eberswalder Str. (U 2)
Disco and rock concerts

► **Maria am Ostbahnhof**
An der Schilingbrücke
(Friedrichshain), tel. 21 23 81 90
S-Bahn: Ostbahnhof
Leading venue for techno and hip
hop for many years

► **Matrix**
Warschauer Platz 18
(Friedrichshain), tel. 29 49 10 47
Massive club under Warschauer
Strasse S-Bahn station

► ⑲ **Maxxim**
Joachimstaler Str. 15 (Charl.)
Tel. 41 76 62 40
U-Bahn: Kurfürstendamm
(U 1, U 9)
The west's excellent answer to the
scene in the east

► ⑦ **Roter Salon in der
Volksbühne**
Rosa-Luxemburg-Platz (Mitte)
Tel. 28 59 89 36
U-Bahn: Rosa-Luxemburg-Platz
(U 2)
Disco, pop concerts, but mainly
tango dancing in a plush atmos-
phere, salsa on Wednesdays

► ④ **Dice Club**
Voltairestr. 5 (Mitte)
www.dice-club.de
U-Bahn: Jannowitzbrücke (U 8)
Party scene Fri and Sat from
midnight in a former power
transformer station, now equipped
with the finest lighting and sound
installations. Next door are the
event location Volt and a concert
hall.

► **Watergate**
Falckensteinstr. 49
(Kreuzberg)
No tel., www.water-gate.de
S-Bahn: Ostbahnhof
Berlin's nicest club in a warehouse
by the river bank with views of the
Spree and the Oberbaumbrücke,
with terrace, occasionally guest DJ
stars from UK

DANCE

▶ ① **Ballhaus Berlin**
Chausseestr. 102 (Mitte)
Tel. 2 82 75 75
www.ballhaus-berlin.de
U-Bahn: Zinnowitzer Str. (U 6)
Bar and live music every day for
young and old alike, tables linked
to the bar by telephone

▶ ③ **Clärchens Ballhaus**
Auguststr. 24 (Mitte)
Tel. 2 82 92 95
S-Bahn: Hackescher Markt
Nostalgic and classic Berlin ballroom but no longer just a place for
senior citizens: now it has been
refurbished, afternoons can be
spent in its garden until the
youngsters start dancing in the
evening.

▶ ㉚ **Ballhaus
Walzerlinksgestrickt**
Am Tempelhofer Berg 7
(Kreuzberg)
Tel. 69 50 50 00
www.walzerlinksgestrickt.de
U-Bahn: Pl. der Luftbrücke (U 6)
The place to go for the free dance
scene.

MUSIC VENUES

▶ ⑮ **A Trane Jazzclub**
Bleibtreustr. 1
(Charlottenburg)
Tel. 3 13 25 50
wwww.a-trane.de
S-Bahn: Savignyplatz
Modern jazz, late night jam ses-
sions for connoisseurs

▶ ⑤ **b-flat Jazzclub**
Rosenthaler Str. 13 (Mitte)
Tel. 2 83 31 23
S-Bahn: Hackescher Markt
Small jazz bar that hosts concerts
by major acts

▶ **Parkhaus Treptow**
Puschkinallee 5 (Treptow)
Tel. 5 33 79 52
S-Bahn: Treptower Park
Well-established jazz cellar

▶ ⑰ **Quasimodo**
Kantstr. 12a
(Charlottenburg)
Tel. 3 12 80 86
S-/U-Bahn: Zoologischer Garten
The classic place in the west for
jazz, blues, folk, funk and soul.

TRENDY BARS,
COOL PUBS

▶ **An einem Sonntag im August**
Kastanienallee 103
(Prenzlauer Berg)
Tel. 44 05 12 28
U-Bahn: Eberswalder Str. (U 2)
Popular bar with a highly recom-
mended buffet

▶ **Ankerklause**
Kottbusser Damm 104/
Maybachufer (Kreuzberg)
Tel. 6 93 56 49
U-Bahn: Kottbusser Tor
(U 1, U 15, U 12, U 8)
Classic venue by the Landwehr
canal.

▶ **Astro Bar**
Simon-Dach-Str. 40
(Friedrichshain), tel. 29 66 15
U-Bahn: Frankfurter Tor (U 5)
Funk, soul, beat, 2 step

▶ **Badeschiff Arena**
Eichenstr. 4 (Treptow)
Tel. 5 33 20 30
U-Bahn: Schlesisches Tor (U1)
800 places for sunbathing and
swimming in summer from 8am

▶ ㉔ **Bar am Lützowplatz**
Lützowplatz 7 (Tiergarten)

»Früher Donnerstag«: Thursday early doors at »Trompete«

WELCOME TO THE CLUB, BUT WHICH ONE?

It all used to be so much easier. It was always clear who, what or where represented the hottest thing in Berlin, be it West or East: it was always Prenzlauer Berg on one side of the wall and Kreuzberg and Schöneberg on the other. The cool scene was avant garde, but that was before the Wall came down.

When the Wall disappeared, nightlife moved to the centre of the city and on the fringes moved down into cellars or up into domestic flats and attic studios. It penetrated into Spandauer Vorstadt, occupied whole lengths of streets with clubs and galleries, vibrant bars and unusual shops. The atmosphere was almost that of a gold rush with a large dose of flirtatiousness. But what is happening now? It looks like the centre of the action, the centre of the city itself, is being lost. Young people dressed in black and sporting ponytails hold negotiations over a quick »coffee to go« and plan future events amid the whirl of business. The centre of Berlin, which along with Spandauer Vorstadt once acted as a magnet to creative people from all kinds of fields and from all kinds of countries, is becoming establishment. What used to be an underground scene is now slumbering in designer lounges on leather sofas, cocktail in hand. So where has the underground gone now?

The scene is everywhere

If you can tell minimalist house from home-made, electronically flavoured indie rock and soul-tinged retro rock, then you are certainly hip to the scene. So are those who know that techno, tekkno and the old love parade scene have long since given way to pop and even the luminaries of the machine-age are fashioning music with melody. Songwriting and a retro-scene like the current passion for the

1980s are in. With that in mind, it is probably no surprise that the denizens of Berlin night life are once again turning to Kreuzberg and Schöneberg, Prenzlauer Burg and Friedrichshain for the hippest parties. Even Charlottenburg makes it onto the party radar with its Universum Lounge. From Marzahn in the east (Springpfuhlhaus) to Spandau in the west (J.W.D.) the modern scene is taking root in places that were previously known only to people from the so-called Berlin Kiez. Even Potsdam is included (Waschhaus). The off-beat is no longer far away from your door, wherever you are.

Mythology and classics

Some places that have been going for decades now only attract the uninitiated, although others still staunchly guard their reputations, such as Big Eden on Kurfürstendamm where anyone is welcome. Small town visitors will not feel out of place there, with the wood panelling, billiard tables and chart music. There is much more secretiveness, and thereby more appeal, surrounding the illegal clubs, named after days of the week that you won't see on any posters or flyers. Somewhere, in the centre of town maybe, you may encounter a damp cellar on a Wednesday, then an invitation, hand-written of course, will mention some other mysterious event that takes place in an attic in Friedrichshain on a Friday. This is the mythology of the new Berlin. The Club der Visionäre is to be found at an idyllic spot under weeping willows along the Spree's flood culverts. People relax in the open air with their feet in the water, the air full of the latest sounds. What could be nicer? Perhaps standing on white sand or relaxing in a hammock with a cocktail but with the Oberbaumbrücke and the Fernsehturm in view, then diving into the 325 sq m/3500 sq ft swimming pool of the pool boat on the Spree. Its water is as warm as 24°C/75°F and in the winter it is ringed by saunas. A few legends of the Berlin nightlife had to make way for the new building work, and few of them then managed to recover their place among the popular night spots, a feat that the Maria am Ostbahnhof pulled off when it moved to Schillingbrücke. Immigrants and expatriates, though, can be astonishingly faithful to their clubs: check out the Francophiles that frequent Sternradio on Alexanderplatz, the Scandinavians at the Mudd Club and the Brazilians at Kreuzberg's Muvuca. The Goa scene that was driven out of its base in Pfefferberg due to renovation work has found a new home at the Altes Kaufhaus on Oranienplatz in Kreuzberg. Right nearby on Oranienstrasse, SO 36 has been tempting denizens of the subculture onto its dance floor for years and is always open on Wednesdays for the »Hungrige Herzen« gay parties. Kiez bingo is played on Tuesdays for good causes like a women's crisis hotline. The gay scene, long since an established tourist magnet, is firmly anchored around Nollenbergplatz and Motzstrasse in Schöneberg, plus a few places in Prenzlauer Berg.

The cramped Ankerklause bar at Kottbusser Tor, once a haunt only of those in the know, has now become a classic spot. Much the same seems to be happening to Kaffee Burger on Torstrasse, where the Russian decor and disco are the talk of the town. If it gets too busy there, the neighbouring »Club der polnischen Versager« is able to handle the overflow. No music is played and nobody dances when the young writers of the Heimbühne Volk und Welt are in occupation, and as they even draw serious literary critics into the dance dives, it might be thought that some degree of mockery might ensue on account of the look of the venues alone. In Kreuzberg and Friedrichshain, though, night owls are not put off by run-down surroundings and are even happy to drink an uncooled pilsner or listen to kitsch old pop hits as long as the atmosphere, or rather the location, is right. NASA knickknacks and crumpled sofas in the Astro Bar are just as acceptable as the fine cocktails in the still unbeatable Green Door in Schöneberg. Being on the Partytrain is for many the greatest feeling there is: the special rail service that runs to Werder an der Havel (near Potsdam) features a bar, DJs and music to accompany the trip – the 50,000 watt PA system pumps out the beats as soon as you board.

You don't need a party to party

Partying doesn't need to involve an actual conventional party, or what used to be called a disco. An einem Sonntag im August is the name of a spot on Kastanienallee where an event called »Kellner lesen für Gäste« or "Waiters read to the guests« takes place on Sundays. Of course there is food and drink to be had as well as music and dancing. But what if you don't know how to dance?

Well, then there are places where you can learn, whether salsa for beginners at the Cueva Buena Vista or Latino Hip Hop. After-work parties haven't really caught on except for the »Frühen Donnerstag« evenings at Ben Becker's Trompete bar (from 6pm onwards). People can meet in a lounge as early as the afternoon but a club with dancing and music might only take off after midnight and even then you might be too early. The Berlin scene is, like anywhere else, ever young. Looking through the numerous listings, though, it is still possible to find a few events for over-30s: sometimes they even have free entry.

Clothes are important

Nevertheless, you might find yourself a bit lost finding an outfit to go out in. There are plenty of shops with vivid clothes on offer because creative young people design the latest fashions themselves. The number of fashion labels from Berlin is growing. What they create is »to die for«, at least according to one popular shop in the city centre. There are already whole rows of springing up in its wake in Prenzlauer Berg, and Boxhagener Strasse and Simon-Dach-Strasse in Friedrichshain have even been creeping up on the outside to overtake. Nowhere in the inner city, around the now fading new centre, is as trashy as here. The first bars, though, are already looking like they once did on Oranienburger Strasse, with orange walls and either sparse or cult furniture, which can even have its own trashy chic nowadays.

Tel. 2 62 68 07
U-Bahn: Nollendorfplatz
(U 1, U 12, U 15, U 4)
Outstanding cocktails from one
one of the longest bars in the city

▶ ⑫ **Cueva Buena Vista**
Andreasstr. 66 (Friedrichshain)
Tel. 24 08 59 51
S-Bahn: Ostbahnhof
Cuban bar for lovers of salsa

▶ ⑩ **CSR-Bar**
Karl-Marx-Allee 96
(Friedrichshain)
Tel. 29 04 47 41
U-Bahn: Weberwiese (U 5)
Pure nostalgia for the East in the
former head office of the Czech
airline, Ceskoslovensko Aeroline

▶ **Frannz**
Schönhauser Allee 36
(Prenzlauer Berg)
Tel. 72627930
U-Bahn: Eberswalder Str. (U2)
Formerly a key nexus of the East
Berlin scene that now welcomes
anybody

▶ ㉗ **Green Door**
Winterfeldtstr. 50
(Schöneberg)
Tel. 2 15 25 15
U-Bahn: Nollendorfplatz
(U 1, U 12, U 15, U 4)
Everything is green and the cock-
tail menu is endless.

▶ ㉓ **Harry's New York Bar**
Lützowufer 15, in Grand Hotel
Esplanade (Tiergarten)
Tel. 2 54 78-0
U-Bahn: Nollendorfplatz
(U 1, U 12, U 15, U 4)
Live piano music and excellent
cocktails from a long bar made of
black granite

▶ ⑳ **Irish Harp Pub**
Giesebrechtstr. 15
(Charlottenburg), tel. 8 82 77 39
Pub with a never-ending bar and
nostalgic plush decor

▶ ⑥ **Kaffee Burger**
Torstr. 60 (Mitte)
Tel. 28 04 64 96
www.kaffeeburger.de
U-Bahn: Rosenthaler Pl. (U 2)
Gypsy jazz, grooves, electronic
sounds, Russian disco, book read-
ings

▶ ㉘ **Leydicke**
Mansteinr. 4 (Schöneberg)
Tel. 2 16 29 73
www.leydicke.de
S-Bahn/U-Bahn: Yorck-/
Grossgörschenstrasse
Berlin institution: berry wines
with a kick, nostalgic decor

▶ **Metzer Eck**
Metzer Str. 33 13
(Prenzlauer Berg)
Tel. 4427656
U-Bahn: Senefelderplatz. (U 2)
Well established Berlin pub dating
back to 1913 with delicious Berlin
cuisine

▶ **Orient Lounge**
Oranienstr. 13 (Kreuzberg)
Tel. 69 56 67 62
U-Bahn: Görlitzer Bahnhof
(U 1, U 8)
Above the Rote Harfe you can
retreat to a secluded booth.

▶ ⑨ **Oxymoron**
Rosenthaler Str. 40/41 (Mitte)
Tel. 28 39 18 85
www.oxymoron-berlin.de
S-Bahn: Hackescher Markt
The place to go in the Hackesche
Höfe: plush salon, café, bar

► ② **Reingold**
Novalisstr. 11 (Mitte)
Tel. 28 38 76 76
U-Bahn: Oranienburger Tor (U 6)
Chic cocktail bar in thirties style
with someone checking faces
when the doorbell rings

► ⑧ **Ständige Vertretung**
Schiffbauerdamm 8 (Mitte)
Tel. 2 82 39 65
S/U-Bahn: Friedrichstrasse
Rhineland fare including Kölsch
beer and Sauerbraten run by
converted Berlin hater and ex-
celebrity bar owner from Bonn,
Friedel Drautzburg; a magnet for
tourists

► **Stars in Concert**
Estrel Festival Center
Sonnenallee 225 (Neukölln)
Tel. 68316831
S-Bahn: Sonnenallee
The best mega-star doppelgangers

► ㉕ **Trompete**
Lützowplatz 9 (Tiergarten)
Tel. 23 00 47 94
U-Bahn: Nollendorfplatz
After work lounge, Thursdays
from 6pm with funk, soul, rock
and disco

► ㉑ **Universum Lounge**
Kurfürstendamm 153,
in Schaubühne (Charlottenburg)
Tel. 89 06 49 94
U-Bahn: Adenauerplatz (U 7)
Space-age bar in seventies style

► ⑭ **Wilhelm Hoeck**
Wilmersdorfer Str. 149
(Charlottenburg), tel. 3 41 31 10
U-Bahn: Richard-Wagner-Platz
(U 7)
A real Berlin pub that has hardly
changed since 1892

► **Würgeengel**
Dresdener Str. 122 (Kreuzberg)
Tel. 6 15 55 60
U-Bahn: Kottbusser Tor
(U 1, U 15, U 12, U 8)
Stylish cocktail bar with jazz

► ㉙ **Yorckschlösschen**
Yorckstr. 15 (Kreuzberg)
Tel. 2 15 80 70
S-/U-Bahn: Yorck-/
Grossgörschenstrasse
Kreuzberg institution, with jazz
brunch on Sundays

► ㉗ **Zur weissen Maus**
Ludwigkirchplatz 12
(Wilmersdorf), tel. 8 82 22 64
U-Bahn: Hohenzollernplatz (U 1)
Cocktails and laid-back music

► ⑯ **Zwiebelfisch**
Savignyplatz 7
(Charlottenburg)
Tel. 3 12 73 63
S-Bahn: Savignyplatz
Keeps its 1968 revolutionary tra-
dition alive, but the air is no
longer thick with smoke

CASINO

► **Spielbank Berlin**
Marlene-Dietrich-Platz 1 (Mitte)
Tel. 2 55 99-0
www.spielbank-berlin.de
S-/U-Bahn: Potsdamer Platz
11.30am – 5pm (18 and over)

CINEMAS

Most of the cinemas are located
around Kurfürstendamm, in Mitte
or in Friedrichshain-Kreuzberg.
Ever year in February the *Berlin
International Film Festival (Berlinale)* takes place with movies
competing for the Golden Bear
awards, a children's film festival
and the »Perspektive Deutsches

Kino« platform for new German film productions. The films are mostly shown in the cinemas at Potsdamer Platz or the Filmzentrum Zoo-Palast.

▶ **Programme information**
Tel. (01 90) 11 50 30
www.kino-berlin.de
www.kinokompendium.de
www.freiluftkino-berlin.de

▶ **Astor Film Lounge**
Kurfürstendamm 225
(Charlottenburg)
Tel. 883 55 51
Luxurious cinema for those who are prepared to pay more for a doorman and valet parking, comfortable seats and waiter service for food and drinks.

▶ **Babylon**
Rosa-Luxemburg-Str. 30 (Mitte)
Tel. 2 42 59 69
The only cinema that has remained in its original condition since silent movie days. Built in 1928 to a design by expressionist architect Hans Poelzig. Retrospec-

tives include examples from the former East German film archive.

▶ **Filmkunst 66**
Bleibtreustr. 12
(Charlottenburg)
Tel. 8 82 17 53
Current movies, special series, retrospectives and cult films

▶ **Hackesche Höfe**
Rosenthaler Str. 40 / 41 (Mitte)
Tel. 2 83 46 03
Films in English, documentaries

▶ **IMAX**
Potsdamer Str. 4,
Sony Center (Tiergarten)
Tel. 26 06 64 00
U- / S-Bahn: Potsdamer Platz
The world's largest screen for 3D films, 25,000 watt sound system

▶ **Open-air cinema**
Sommerkino Potsdamer Platz
www.yorck.de
Open-air Charlottenburg
www.openaircharlottenburg.de
Freilichtbühne am Weissensee
www.kinoundkonzerte.de

Etiquette and Customs

Berliner Schnauze

Germans in general favour straightforwardness, and will be direct to the point of bluntness. Accordingly, Berliners tend not to waste time with unnecessary niceties when it comes to expressing an opinion or making a request. There is a temptation for outsiders to interpret this as rudeness, but Berlin bluntness (known in Germany as the »Berliner Schnauze«) is better viewed as an endearing local quirk. In Berlin, as in Yorkshire, there is no need to beat about the bush.

Rules and regulations

Germany is heavily regulated and extremely bureaucratic, and Germans tend to follow rules to the letter and often display more deference to those in authority than other nationalities. It is an offence (albeit a minor one) for example to step out into the road at a crossing if the pedestrian signal shows red, even if there is no vehicle in sight – visitors may be surprised to see large groups of people patiently waiting for the figure of the green »Ampelmännchen« to illuminate and indicate that they may now cross the empty road. Moreover, there will be disapproving looks – and possibly verbal reprimands – for those who break this rule (not to mention a fine should a police officer spot the guilty party). It is arguable however that Berlin, less conservative than other German cities and with its diverse influences, does not quite fit this German cliché: in Berlin, perhaps, the rulebook is still being written.

German efficiency is of course world renowned, and though it will be regularly encountered in banks, hotels, and even government offices, the visitor may at times also come across instances of clanking bureaucracy. Here, Berlin is no exception. Those who lock horns with the city's bureaucratic machinery should prepare to have their patience well tested.

Efficiency versus bureaucracy

Since 1 January 2008 smoking has been prohibited in all public buildings in Germany, including cafés, bars, restaurants and nightclubs. A smoking area is permitted, but smokers are only served in non-smoking areas (in order to protect staff from the effects of passive smoking). Individuals breaking this law are liable to a fine of €100; a €2000 penalty applies to the proprietor of the offending establishment.

No smoking

In restaurants and cafés it is usual to tip about 10% of the amount on the bill. If you pay cash, tell the waiter the amount you wish to pay (normally a rounded up figure) as you hand over the money, or say »Stimmt so« if you don't expect any change at all. If you pay by cheque or credit card, leave the tip in cash on the table or on the plate provided. Taxi drivers, city guides, toilet attendants and room service personnel are also pleased to receive a tip.

Tipping

Many Germans do not feel comfortable discussing the events of the Second World War: while the period is fascinating it is for obvious reasons regarded as a subject for serious discussion and private thought only, and the somewhat gung ho, flag-waving approach taken in the UK and other places is anathema in Germany. Unless you intend to engage in learned discourse, it is best to follow the famous advice – and not mention the war. In contrast the communist era is viewed with affectionate nostalgia and even romanticized by many, and is celebrated in films and shops selling Eastern bloc memorabilia.

Discussing Berlin's history

The accepted way to greet somebody in Berlin is to shake hands; men and women who know each other better will kiss each other on both cheeks, like in France; established friends, men included, will even hug one another.

Greeting Berliners

Festivals and Events

 DATES FOR THE CALENDAR

JANUARY

▶ **Berliner Neujahrslauf (New Year's Day Fun Run)**
Start: 1 January, noon from the Brandenburg Gate, 4km/2.5mi. www.berlin-marathon.com

▶ **International Green Week**
Trade fair dealing with food and agriculture – with any number of stalls where visitors can sample produce for themselves. www.messe-berlin.de

▶ **Berliner Motorradtage (International Motorcycle Show)**
www.messe-berlin.de

▶ **Sechs-Tage-Rennen (Berlin Six Day Race)**
Cycle racing in the Velodrom Landsberger Allee www.sechstagerennen-berlin.de

FEBRUARY

▶ **International Film Festival**
Glamour in Berlin with the competition for the Golden Bear awards. www.berlinale.de

MARCH

▶ **Internationale Tourismus-Börse**
The largest tourism fair in the world; www.messe-berlin.de

▶ **Musik-Biennale**
Biennial (2009, 2011 etc.) festival for contemporary music. www.berlinerfestspiele.de

▶ **Berliner Frühlingsfest**
Berlin's spring festival on the central festival grounds in front of Tegel Airport. www.berliner-festplatz.de

APRIL

▶ **Berlin Half-Marathon**
20,000 participants, an international event

▶ **Festtage**
Opera and concerts in the Deutsche Staatsoper on Unter den Linden. www.staatsoper-berlin.de

▶ **Britzer Baumblüte**
Colourful spring festival.

MAY

▶ **Karneval der Kulturen**
Colourful multi-cultural spectacular in Kreuzberg; www.karneval-berlin.de.

▶ **Theatertreffen**
Selected performances of German plays. www.berlinerfestspiele.de

▶ **Internationale Luft- und Raumfahrtausstellung ILA (International Aerospace Exhibition)**
At Schönefeld Airport. www.ila-berlin.de

▶ **German football cup final**
In the Olympic stadium.

JUNE

▶ **Deutsch-Französisches Volksfest (German-French Festival)**
The largest of Berlin's public

festivals takes place between mid-June and mid-July on the central festival grounds. www.schausteller verband-berlin.de

► **Christopher Street Day**
Wild parade for gays and lesbians. www.csd-berlin.de

► **Fête de la Musique**
Berlin turns itself into one big open-air stage on 21 June. www.fetedelamusique.de

► **Brandenburgische Sommerkonzerte**
»Classics in the country« from late June to early September. www.brandenburgische-sommerkonzerte.de

► **Musikfestspiele Potsdam (Potsdam Music Festival)**
Classical music in palaces and gardens
www.musikfestspiele-potsdam.de

JULY

► **Classic Open Air**
Classical music played before the magical backdrop of Gendarmenmarkt. www.classicopenair.de

► **Fashion Week**
Berlin designers show their mettle.

► **Babelsberger Filmparknacht**
Night-time ventures in the Babelsberg film park – with all kinds of special events.

AUGUST

► **Deutsch-Amerikanisches Volksfest (German-American Festival)**
In Dahlem.
www.deutsch-amerikanisches-volksfest.de

► **Derby-Woche**
A week of races at the trap-racing circuit in Mariendorf. www.berlintrab.de

► **Internationales Tanzfest Berlin (Berlin International Dance Festival)**
www.tanzfest.de

► **Internationale Funkausstellung Berlin (International Radio Exhibition)**
Biennial (2007, 2009 etc.) exhibition covering everything to do with the media and media technology. www.ifa-berlin.de

► **Lange Nacht der Museen (Museum Night)**
More than 50 of Berlin's museums open all night, also held in late January or early February. www.lange-nacht-der-museen.de

► **Potsdamer Schlössernacht**
Nights of music, dance, theatre shows and food and drink with Potsdam's parks and palaces illuminated.

SEPTEMBER

► **Internationales Stadionfest der Leichtathleten ISTAF (Berlin Athletics Meeting)**
The world's best athletes at the Olympic stadium. www.istaf.de

► **Berliner Festwochen (Berlin Festival Weeks)**
Exhibitions, concerts, literature, films, meetings. www.berlinerfestspiele.de

► **Wannsee in Flammen**
Parade of boats with fireworks on Wannsee lake.

▶ **Art Forum Berlin**
Renowned fair for contemporary art. www.art-forum-berlin.de

▶ **Berlin Marathon**
www.berlin-marathon.de

OCTOBER

▶ **Deutschlandfest**
Big festival in front of the Reichstag and Brandenburg Gate to coincide with the anniversary of German reunification on 3 October.

▶ **aaa avus automobile akzente**
Biennial exhibition (2008, 2010 etc.) covering all aspects of automobiles.

▶ **Berliner Volksfest (Berlin People's Festival)**
Kurt-Schumacher-Damm
www.berliner-oktoberfest.de

▶ **Festival of Lights**
For ten days about 50 buildings and landmarks are made into artworks in light.

▶ **JazzFest Berlin**
Lasts until early November.
www.berlinerfestspiele.de

NOVEMBER

▶ **Jüdische Kulturtage (Jewish Culture Days)**
Exhibitions, films, theatre plays, music, readings.
www.juedische-kulturtage.org

DECEMBER

▶ **Christmas markets**
Markets take place in all parts of Berlin. The ones around the Gedächtniskirche and at the Opernpalais on Unter den Linden are particularly nice.

▶ **Berliner Silvesterlauf (New Year's Eve Pancake Race)**
A fun race through the Grunewald over the Teufelsberg and Drachfliegerberg, some participants in costume.

Food and Drink

Restaurants Berlin is certainly on a par with any capital city when it comes to restaurants, as can be seen from the sheer number of celebrated establishments. The city now boasts ten chefs with a Michelin star. Japanese, crossover and, increasingly, French cuisine are in vogue. Even for those of more modest means, though, there are plenty of good restaurants. And if Eisbein with sauerkraut, curry sausage and Spree gherkins do not appeal, there is always plenty of ethnic cuisine in Berlin.

Traditional Berlin cuisine Berlin's traditional fare is not especially sophisticated; it is primarily good plain cooking. The problem is more that it has become hard to find. The best-known recipes are for Buletten (rissoles) and Eisbein

The classic Berlin meal: rissole, potato salad and a cool beer

(boiled knuckle of pork), the latter usually being served with sauerkraut and mushy peas. Other basic Berlin dishes include Berliner Schlachteplatte, which literally translated means »slaughter plate« and consists of various meat items including Blutwurst (black pudding), Leberwurst (liver sausage), Wellfleisch (fatty belly of pork) and pork kidneys, roast liver with apple rings, and Bollenfleisch (Bollen = onions; this is chunks of lamb or mutton and onions); the celebrated Teltower Rübchen (oxtail with turnips) are now a rarity. For dessert Rote Grütze (a compote of red berries) with custard or cream is often served. Doughnuts filled with jam are popular in Berlin – in fact, they are known as Berliners in the rest of Germany.

Plenty of corner pubs over Berlin offer snacks to enjoy alongside a beer: rollmops (pickled herring), Bratheringe (fried herring) and cold Buletten rissoles with mustard, pickled gherkins and pickled eggs. At snack bars, though, (Germans call a snack bar at which you can eat in or take away an »Imbiss«) the popular meals are Currywurst and Turkish döner kebab. ◄ Snacks

The Havel river and the lakes around the city used to be a fine source of fish, but most fresh water fish nowadays are imported from Poland. Well-known Berlin fish dishes include Aal grün or Hecht grün (eel or pike in parsley sauce) with cucumber salad. ◄ Fish

»Beer is best for our climate«, claimed Prussia's Soldier King, Friedrich Wilhelm I, who when taking pipe tobacco with friends, drank nothing but beer and had his son, the future Frederick the Great, learn the art of brewing. Berlin's two main breweries (Schultheiss and Berliner Kindl) mainly brew fine hoppy pils lagers. Czech beer (Pilsener Urquell, Budweiser, Krusovice) are often on tap. One particular speciality is Berlin's Weisse beer, a mild wheat beer that matures in the bottle. It is either drunk straight from large bowls (although it tastes a bit ordinary like that), or more often »mit Schuss«, i.e. with some raspberry or woodruff syrup, in which case it is drunk through a straw. Berliner Weisse is a particularly tasty refreshment for the summer months. **Drinks** ◄ Beer ◄ Berliner Weisse

RECOMMENDED RESTAURANTS

▶ ① etc. see maps on
pages 74 – 77
No number: not in the area
covered by the maps

▶ **Price categories**
Expensive (category I):
more than €30
Moderate (category II): €15 – €30
Inexpensive (category III):
€10 – €15

TOP RESTAURANTS

▶ ㉟ **First Floor (cat. I)**
Hotel Palace, Budapester Str. 45
(Charlottenburg)
Tel. 25 02-0
S-Bahn/U-Bahn: Zoologischer
Garten
Among the best restaurants in
Berlin for many years

▶ ㊱ **Hugos (cat. I)**
Hotel Intercontinental, Budapester
Str. 2 (Charlottenburg)
Tel. 26 02 12 62
S-Bahn/U-Bahn: Zoologischer
Garten
Culinary jaunts through the
French Mediterranean in laid-back
atmosphere

▶ ⑥ **Margaux (cat. I)**
Unter den Linden 78 (Mitte)
Tel. 22 65 26 11
S-Bahn: Unter den Linden
(S 2, S 25)
The very best, according to many
critics – fantastic wine list with
over 900 to choose from

*900 wines on
the list in
Margaux*

▶ ㉜ **Die Quadriga (cat. I)**
Hotel Brandenburger Hof
Eislebener Str. 14 (Wilmersdorf)
Tel 21 40 56 51
U-Bahn: Kurfürstendamm
(U 9, U 15)
The highly praised cuisine delights
even connoisseurs.

▶ ⑪ **Vau (cat. I)**
Jägerstr. 54 – 55 (Mitte)
Tel. 2 02 97 30
U-Bahn: Französische Str. (U 6)
Kolja Kleeberg guarantees utmost
quality.

**GERMAN AND
INTERNATIONAL CUISINE**

▶ **Bieberbau (cat. II)**
Durlacher Str. 15 (Wilmersdorf)
Tel. 8 53 23 90
S-Bahn/U-Bahn: Bundesplatz
Original but perfected German
cuisine in the former home of
stucco master Bieber

▶ ⑨ **Borchardt (cat. II)**
Französische Str. 45 (Mitte)
Tel. 20 38 71 10
U-Bahn: Französische Str. (U 6)
The famous clientele is perhaps
better known than the cuisine at
this celebrity meeting place on
Gendarmenmarkt.

▶ ㉛ **Diekmann (cat II)**
Meinickestr. 7 (Charlottenburg)
Tel. 8 83 33 21
U-Bahn: Kurfürstendamm
(U 9, U15)
Bistro cuisine in an atmosphere
reminiscent of a colonial shop

▶ ㉚ **Ess-Klasse (cat. II)**
Kurfürstendamm 28
(Charlottenburg)

Tel. 39 01 19 68
U-Bahn: Kurfürstendamm
(U 9, U 15)
High quality Swabian fare in a car
showroom

▶ ㊳ **Facil (cat. I)**
Potsdamer Str. 3 (Tiergarten)
Tel. 5 90 05 12 34
S-Bahn/U-Bahn: Potsdamer Platz
Brand new restaurant in the
Mandala hotel that has quickly
gained a ranking with the best

▶ ㉈ **Guy (cat. II)**
Jägerstr. 59 – 60 (Mitte)
Tel. 20 94 26 00
U-Bahn: Französischer Str. (U 6)
Lovely restaurant with seasonal
Mediterranean cuisine

▶ **Hartmanns (cat. II)**
Fichtestr. 31 (Kreuzberg)
Tel. 61 20 10 03
U-Bahn: Südstern (U 6)
This straightforward gourmet res-
taurant run by a young chef is an
astonishing thing to find in
Kreuzberg.

▶ ⑧ **Lutter & Wegner (cat. II)**
Charlottenstr. 59 – 60 (Mitte)
Tel. 20 29 54 10
U-Bahn: Stadtmitte (U 6)
Austrian and German cuisine.
E.T.A. Hoffmann was a regular
guest at this wine lodge on Gen-
darmenplatz. There is another nice
branch in Charlottenburg at
Schlüterstr. 55.

▶ ㉙ **Paris Bar (cat. II)**
Kantstr. 152 (Charlottenburg)
Tel. 3 13 80 60
S-Bahn: Savigny Platz
An institution and a meeting place
for journalists and media celebri-
ties. Bistro cuisine

▶ ① **Rutz (cat. II)**
Chausseestr. 8 (Mitte)
Tel. 24 62 87 60
U-Bahn: Oranienburger Tor (U 6)
Superlative wine list and bistro
cuisine

▶ ⑬ **Horvath (cat. II)**
Paul-Lincke-Ufer 44a (Kreuzberg)
Tel. 61 28 99 92
U-Bahn: Kottbusser Tor (U 1, U 8)
High-class cooking on the Landwehrkanal, ranging from Bresse
chicken to Nantaise duck. Amuse-
bouche menu with five to ten
courses.

BERLIN CUISINE

▶ ⑨ **Brauhaus Georgbräu
(cat. III)**
Spreeufer 4 (city centre)
Tel. 2 42 42 44
S-Bahn/U-Bahn: Alexanderplatz
Hearty Berlin fare and beer
brewed on site attract diners to the
Nikolaiviertel.

▶ ㉘ **Dicke Wirtin (cat. III)**
Carmerstr. 9 (Charlottenburg)
Tel. 3 12 49 52
S-Bahn: Savigny Platz
Tasty soups in a Berlin pub
atmosphere. An institution.

▶ **Henne (cat. II)**
Leuschnerdamm 25 (Kreuzberg)
Tel. 6 14 77 30
U-Bahn: Kottbusser Tor (U 1)
Classic, practically cult chicken
restaurant serving only half
chickens from the spit

▶ ㉖ **Franz Diener (cat. II)**
Grolmanstr. 47 (Charlottenburg)
Tel. 8 81 53 29
S-Bahn: Savignyplatz
Established at Savignyplatz for 40
years.

Café am Neuen See in Tiergarten park

▶ ⑤ **Sophieneck (cat. III)**
Grosse Hamburger Str. 37 (Mitte)
Tel. 2 82 40 50
S-Bahn: Hackescher Markt
Try the potato soup and the cake.

▶ ⑯ **Zur letzten Instanz (cat. II)**
Waisenstr. 14 – 16 (Mitte)
Tel. 2 42 55 48
U-Bahn: Klosterstr. (U 2)
The proximity to the city courts
has also influenced the menu at
Berlin's oldest tavern (est. 1621). If
you like beef olive, then order
»Justizirrtum«.

BEER GARDENS

▶ **Alter Dorfkrug Lübars (cat. III)**
Alt-Lübars 8 (Reinickendorf)
Tel. 92 21 02 20
222 bus from Waidmannlust
S-Bahn station

▶ ㊲ **Zollpackhof (cat. III)**
Alt Moabit 143 – 145 (city centre)
Tel. 33 09 97 20
S-Bahn Hauptbahnhof
Under old-growth trees on the
banks of the Spree with a view of
the Reichstag and the central
station

▶ **Blockhaus Nikolskoe
(cat. III)**
Wannsee (Zehlendorf)
Nikolkoer Weg
Tel. 8 05 29 14
316 bus from Wannsee S-Bahn
station
Very nice garden pub overlooking
the Wannsee lake

▶ ⑳ **Café am Neuen See
(cat. III)**
Lichtenstein Allee (Tiergarten)
Tel. 2 54 49 30
S-Bahn: Tiergarten
One of the most popular beer
gardens in the city

▶ **Café am Ufer (cat. III)**
Paul Lincke Ufer 42 (Kreuzberg)
Tel. 61 62 92 00
U-Bahn: Kottbusser Toer
(U 1, U 8)

▶ ⑱ **Capt'n Schillow
(cat. III)**
Strasse des 17. Juli/
Charlottenberger Brücke
(Tiergarten)
Tel. 31 50 50 15
By the Landwehrkanal

► ㊲ **Schleusenkrug (cat. III)**
Müller-Breslau-Str. (Tiergarten)
Tel. 3 13 99 09
S-Bahn: Tiergarten

► **Schrörs (cat. III)**
Josef-Nawrocki-Str. 16 (Köpenick)
Tel. 64 09 58 80
60/61 tram from Friedrichshagen
S-Bahn station
Right on the Müggelsee

► **Klipper (cat. III)**
Bulgarische Str. (Treptow)
Tel. 53 21 64 90
S-Bahn: Treptower park
By the Spree

► **Wirtshaus Moorlake (cat. III)**
Moorlake 1 (Zehlendorf)
Tel. 8 05 58 09
Bus: 316 from Wannsee S-Bahn
station

► **Zenner (cat. III)**
Alt Treptow 14 – 17 (Treptow)
Tel. 5 33 73 70
S-Bahn: Treptower park
Traditional place to go in Trep-
tower Park

AMERICAN

► ㊸ **Tony Roma's (cat. III)**
Marlene-Dietrich-Platz. 3
(Tiergarten)
Tel. 25 29 58 30
S-Bahn/U-Bahn: Potsdamer Platz
(U1, U 15, U12, U8)
Chicken and in particular varia-
tions on spare ribs

AUSTRIAN

► **Austria (cat. III)**
Bergmannsttr. 2 (Kreuzberg)
Tel. 6 94 44 40
U-Bahn: Gneisenau Str. (U 7)
The big wiener schnitzels are
particularly popular.

𝑖 Worth a visit

- Lutter and Wegner on Schluterstrasse: fine foods from Austria
- Diekmann: simply excellent
- Henne: for anyone who likes chicken
- Schleusenkrug: beer garden with Berlin food
- Good Friends: authentic Chinese dishes
- Suriya: Indian food at reasonable prices
- Hartmanns: a young chef just starting out
- Cantamaggio: Sardinian Italians

BOHEMIAN

► **Prager Café Slavia (cat. III)**
Wiesbadener Str. (Wilmersdorf)
Tel. 82 70 31 20
U-Bahn: Rüdesheimer Platz (U 1)
Straightforward Bohemian fare
with a Prague-style, Art Nouveau
ambience

BRAZILIAN

► ③ **Botequim Carioca (cat. III)**
Linienstr. 160 (Mitte)
Tel. 694 22 55
S-Bahn: Oranienburger Str.
U-Bahn: Rosenthaler Platz (U 8)
A Brazilian bar with reasonably
priced snacks, main courses that
change daily and of course cai-
pirinha

CHINESE

► ㉑ **Good Friends (cat. III)**
Kantstr. 30 (Charlottenburg)
Tel. 3 13 26 59
S-Bahn: Savigny Platz
Rather spartan furnishing but
certainly authentic Cantonese
food. Make a reservation before-
hand.

► **Ostwind (cat. III)**
Husemannstr. 13
(Prenzlauer Berg)
Tel. 4 41 59 51

U-Bahn: Senefelder Platz. (U 2)
Real Peking cuisine

EAST PRUSSIAN

▶ ㉔ **Marjellchen (cat. III)**
Mommsenstr. 9 (Charlottenburg)
Tel. 8 83 26 76
S-Bahn: Savigny Platz
Succulent East Prussian food for
aficionados

FRENCH

▶ ⑫ **Entrecôte (cat. II)**
Schützenstr. 5 (Mitte)
Tel. 20 16 54 96
U-Bahn: Kochstr. (U 6)
Classic French cuisine in a cosy
atmosphere.

▶ **Le Cochon Bourgeois (cat. II)**
Fichtestr. 24 (Kreuzberg)
Tel. 693 01 01
U-Bahn: Südstern
(U 7)
Bus: M 41
Pleasanter than the revolutionary
name suggest: simple, excellent
quality, proper napkins, candle-
light and piano music.

▶ ⑰ **Moustache (cat. II)**
Galvanistr. 12 (Charlottenburg)
Tel. 3 42 30 94
U-Bahn: Richard-Wagner-Platz
(U 7)
Specialities from various regions of
France

GREEK

▶ ㉗ **Terzo Mondo (cat. III)**
Grolmanstr. 28 (Charlottenburg)
Tel. 8 81 52 61
S-Bahn: Savigny Platz
The owner, Pannoaitis, is well-
known in Germany from the
Lindenstrasse TV soap opera.
Otherwise the Greek fare is un-
spectacular.

INDIAN

▶ ㉕ **Calcutta (cat. III)**
Bleibtreustr. 17 (Charlottenburg)
Tel. 38 83 62 93
S-Bahn: Savigny Platz
Original Tandoori cuisine for
connoisseurs with a large selection
of vegetarian dishes

▶ ㉕ **Suriya Kanthi (cat. III)**
Knaackstr. 22 (Prenzl. Berg)
Tel. 442 53 01
U-Bahn: Senefelder Platz (U 2)
Wonderful curries with organic
ingredients

INDONESIAN

▶ **Tuk Tuk (cat. III)**
Grosgörschenstr. 2 (Schöneberg)
Tel. 7 81 15 88
S-Bahn/U-Bahn: Yorck-
Grosgörschenstr
Authentic cuisine from the islands

ITALIAN

▶ **Ana e Bruno (cat. I)**
Sophie-Charlotten-Str. 101
(Charlottenburg)
Tel. 3 25 71 10
S-Bahn: Westend
Not only the best Italian restaurant
in Berlin but one of the best
restaurants of any kind in the city

▶ ⑬ **Cantamaggio (cat. III)**
Alte Schönhauser Str. 4 (Mitte)
Tel. 2 83 18 95
S-Bahn: Hackescher Markt
Sardinian cooking in the Scheu-
nenviertel

▶ **Il pane e le rose (cat. III)**
Am Friedrichshain 6
(Prenzlauer Berg)
Tel. 4 23 19 16
Tram/Metro: 2, 4 from Alexan-
derplatz
Restaurant, bar and café

JAPANESE

► ㉞ **Daitokai (cat. II)**
Tauentzianstr. 9 – 12
Europa Center (Charlottenburg)
Tel. 2 61 80 90
U-Bahn: Eberswalder Str.
Berlin's finest Japanese reastaurant, expensive but very good

► **Sasaya (cat. III)**
Lychener Str. 50
(Prenzlauer Berg)
Tel. 44 71 77 21
U-Bahn: Eberswalder Str.
Not so much effort in the presentation but much more traditional Japanese cookery

► ㉝ **Susuru (cat. III)**
Rosa-Luxemburg-Str. 17 (Mitte)
Tel. 2 11 11 82
S-Bahn/U-Bahn: Alexanderplatz
Absolutely wonderful bar for noodle soup

MEXICAN

► ② **Las Cucarachas (cat. III)**
Oranienburger Str. 2 (Mitte)
Tel. 2 82 20 44
S-Bahn: Oranienburger Str.
Atmospheric ambience for outstanding specialities

► **Viva Mexico (cat. III)**
Chausseestr. 36 (Mitte)
Tel. 2 80 78 65
U-Bahn: Zinnowitzer Str. (U 6)
Small but wow! Authentic stuff for those in the know

MOROCCAN

► ④ **Kasbah (cat. III)**
Gipsstr. 2 (Mitte)
Tel. 27 59 43 61
U-Bahn: Weinmeisterstr. (U 8)
S-Bahn: Hackescher Markt
Seating in an oriental-style courtyard

RUSSIAN

► **Pasternak (cat. III)**
Knaackstr. 22 – 24
(Prenzlauer Berg)
Tel. 4 41 33 99
U-Bahn: Eberswalder Str. (U 2)
Fashionable place for Russians or fans of Russian food

Classic destination in Prenzlauer Berg: Pasternak

SPANISH

► ㉒ **El Borriquito (cat. III)**
Wielandstr. 6 (Charlottenburg)
Tel. 3 12 99 29
S-Bahn: Savigny Platz
Very tasty food but correspondingly busy

SWISS

► ㉝ **Moritz (cat. II)**
Regensburgerstr. 7
(Wilmersdorf)
Tel. 2 18 42 82
U-Bahn: Spichern Str. (U 1, U 9)
Fine Swiss cuisine in the former Bamberger Reiter

REGISTERED TRADE MARK 721 319

»If you're feeling down, you need something to chew on, a currywurst«. That is more or less the sense of a song by Herbert Grönemeyer, who actually comes from Germany's Ruhr valley but would surely feel quite at home with his classic German snack in Berlin, as this is where the currywurst was invented.

It is even known precisely where and when the currywurst came into existence and who created it. It was 4 September 1949 at a sausage stall, sadly no longer in existence, on Stuttgarter Platz. The perpetrator of the deed was one Hertha Heuwer, who died in 1999. The creation would make her into a legend. The lady's husband had been a prisoner of war under the Americans and had fallen in love with spare ribs with ketchup during that time. He was constantly sounding off about them to his wife. In post-war Berlin, though, there was no way under the sun that anyone was going to come by spare ribs; there were plenty of Brühwurst sausages, though. Hertha decided to start a series of experiments. She mixed up various trial versions of a gooey tomato sauce containing all kinds of spices until she and her husband were happy with the taste. When they poured it over a sausage, the currywurst was born. The couple even registered the name as trade mark no. 721 319 as the dish took Germany by storm. At the peak of the boom Hertha Heuwer was selling up to 10,000 of them per week and coined the slogan »often copied but never

Serving snacks since 1930: Konnopke by the U-Bahn station at Eberswalder Strasse

surpassed«. They soon left behind such traditional recipes as fried herring, cold rissoles, pickled eggs, pickled gherkins and bockwurst from the »Wurst-Maxe« sausage stand.

A true art

It may seem hard to believe that the currywurst, one of Germany's classic everyday products, may have its secrets. Nevertheless, early connoisseurs noted the difference between the versions boiled in the skin or smoked without skin. Of course, the piquancy is in the sauce. Be wary of establishments that simply pour a tasteless, ready-made product over the sausages. A true currywurst chef will brew up the sauce according to a house

recipe. Artists of the frituriers' art can be found at places like the stall at Amtsgerichtsplatz on the corner of Suarezstrasse and Kantstrasse, in Curry 36 at Mehringendamm 36 in Kreuzberg, at Wilhelmstrasse 104, where Berlin's taxi drivers come for a snack, or in the legendary Konnopke Imbiss at Eberswalder Strasse underground station in Prenzlauer Berg, which is renowned as Berlin's oldest snack establishment. The finest in Berlin café fare has been sold here since 1930 and the founder's daughter Waltraud Ziervogel still remains to ensure the reputation is maintained. Even the East German government was unable to harness the Konnopke family to its communist yoke. The shop remained private and nowadays, apart from selling what is said to be the finest currywurst in Berlin, it also offers such traditional Berlin specialities as bockwurst with potato salad and solyanka.

Alternatives

However, just as the currywurst once triumphed over pickled gherkins and pickled eggs, it was later to face its

Will the future of fast food in Berlin be the Sushi bar? They said something similar about the döner kebab – but the Currywurst still lives on.

own nemesis. The döner kebab was to provide stiff competition. While there is a difference of opinion as to whether the first Berlin döner turned on its spit in 1969 or 1973, the place where it was introduced is undisputed. It was at Ahmet Ucarkus' shop on Kottbusser Damm in Kreuzberg. Turkish kebab served in flat pancake bread is now sold in greater numbers in Berlin than even the poor sausage in its spicy ketchup. This is hardly surprising, as the finest kebab shops are to be found in Berlin, in Kreuzberg as ever around Kotbusser Tor U-Bahn station, on Oranienstrasse and on Bergmannstrasse. Döner butchers even submitted to their own purity law in 1991, since some black sheep were endeavouring to reduce the actual meat content of their kebabs down to practically zero. Nowadays kebab spits are even exported from

Berlin to Turkey itself. However, for those whose taste buds fail to be tickled by either dish, why not try out one of the many Chinese or Thai restaurants, or go for sushi or any of the multi-cultural offerings, or even drop into a soup café (such as Soup Kultur on the corner of Kurfürstendamm/Meineckestrasse). There are vegetarian options too: the Lebanese diner at Yorckstrasse 14, the snack bar at Schlesisches Tor U-Bahn station and Habibi on Winterfeldtplatz (Goltzstr. 24) are all good places for falafel. Tasty vegetable dishes are also offer in Fresco at Oranienburger Str. 48 in Spandauer Vorstadt.

Multi-cultural

There is now a rich set of options for assuaging your hunger in Berlin. It could be Arabic food one day, Chinese the next, then Polish, no problem. But the quintessentially German spicy sausage is not likely to die out any time soon. On the contrary, it is even winning back lost territory little by little: many a döner shop also has sausages sizzling away alongside the kebab spit. Anyone for currywurst?

TURKISH

► ㉓ **Angora (cat. II)**
Schlüterstr. 29 (Charlottenburg)
Tel. 3 23 70 96
S-Bahn: Savigny Platz
No döner kebabs here, only the
finest in Turkish cuisine

VEGETARIAN

► ㊵ **Hakuin (cat. II)**
Martin-Luther-Str. 1 (Schöneberg)
Tel. 2 18 20 27
U-Bahn: Viktoria-Luise-Platz
(U 4)
Creative and quiet in typically
Japanese fashion

► ㊵ **Samadhi (cat. II)**
Wilhelmstr. 77 (Mitte)
Tel. 22 48 88 50
U-Bahn: Mohrenstr. (U 2)
Dishes from various southeast
Asian countries

IN POTSDAM
(see map p.352/353)

► ① **Speckers Landhaus (cat. II)**
Jägerallee 13
Tel. (0331) 2 80 43 11
Imaginative gourmet food in what
was once the quarters of the Ulan
guards. Three rooms for overnight
stay

► ② **Drachenhaus (cat. II)**
Maulbeerallee in Sanssouci Park
Tel. (03 31) 505 38 08
Regional and international dishes
in the »Dragon House«, built in
1770

► ③ **Meierhaus im neuen Garten
(cat. III)**
Im neuen Garten 10
Tel. (0331) 7 04 32 11
Cosy brewery pub with hearty
food under arches or in a nice beer
garden

► ④ **Zum Fliegenden Holländer
(cat. III)**
Benkertstr. 5
Tel. (0331) 27 50 30
Traditional tavern dating from
1869 with straightforward dishes

CAFÉS (IN MITTE)

► ② **Barcomi's**
Sophienstr. 21
Tel. 28 59 83 63
S-Bahn: Hackescher Markt
American breakfast with bagel
sandwiches and aromatized coffee.
There is another affiliate in
Kreuzberg at Bergmannstr. 21.

*Freshly
roasted
coffee at
Barcomi's*

► ⑥ **Die Eins**
In the ARD Hauptstadtstudio
Reichstagsufer
Tel. 22 48 98 88
S-Bahn/U-Bahn: Friedrichstrasse
Breakfast from 9am to midnight
with a view of the Spree and the
Reichstag alongside the occasional
celebrities from the ARD TV
station.

► ⑦ **Café Einstein**
Unter den Linden 42
Tel. 2 04 36 32
S-Bahn: Unter den Linden
Unlike the regular haunt in the
Tiergarten, this café more resem-
bles a French brasserie or a coffee
house from the 1930s. A meeting
place for celebrities

▶ ① **KaffeKombinat**
Chausseestr. 5
Tel. 28 09 41 00
U-Bahn: Oranienburger Tor (U 6)
The name and logo evoke an
earlier period although the reality
looks more modern American
with bagels, muffins, etc.

▶ ⑧ **Operncafé**
Unter den Linden 5, tel. 20 26 83
S-Bahn: Oranienburger Tor (U 6)
Popular meeting place for cake
fans. 50 of the finest sorts of cakes
as well as other fare

▶ ③ **Café Restaurant Orange**
Oranienburger Strasse 42
Tel. 28 38 52 42
S-Bahn: Oranienburger Strasse
Low-key, pleasant place for
breakfast and tasty dishes

▶ ④ **Die Berliner Republik**
Schiffbauerdamm 8
Tel. 30 87 22 93
S-Bahn/U-Bahn: Friedrichstr.
Members of parliament and civil
servants mix with tourists in the
government precinct

▶ ⑤ **Telecafé**
In the Fernsehturn on
Alexanderplatz
Tel. 2 42 33 33
S-Bahn/U-Bahn: Alexanderplatz
The telecafé is situated at a height
of 207m/680ft and turns on its axis
twice every hour. It gets partic-
ularly busy in the evenings.

**... IN CHARLOTTENBURG
AND WILMERSDORF**

▶ ⑲ **Blisse 14**
Blissestr. 14
Tel. 8 21 20 79
U-Bahn: Blissestr. (U 1)
The garden is open in the summer

and also serves salads and warm
food. Jazz brunch on Sundays

▶ ⑮ **Kranzler**
Kurfürstendamm 18
Tel. 8 87 13 90
U-Bahn: Kurfürstendamm. (U 1,
U 9)
The red and white awning is still
there and on the 2nd floor a room
remaining from the famous old
café.

▶ ⑭ **Café im Literaturhaus**
Fasanenstr. 23
Tel. 8 82 54 14
U-Bahn: Uhlandstr. (U 15)
A stylish coffee house atmosphere
with a wonderful breakfast menu
is combined with literary ambi-
ence. A garden café

▶ ⑩ **Kleine Orangerie**
Schloss Charlottenburg
Soandauer Damm 20
Tel. 3 22 20 21
U-Bahn: Richard-Wagner-Platz
(U 7)
Café with a large garden on an
historic site

▶ ⑬ **Schwarzes Café**
Kantstr. 148, tel. 3 13 80 38
S-Bahn: Savigny Platz
A contrasting atmosphere: a beat-
up, run down look but with the
feel of home. A popular breakfast
café for old political radicals and
students

▶ ⑫ **Berliner Kaffeerösterei**
Uhlandstr. 173/174
Tel. 88 67 79 20
U-Bahn: Uhlandstr. (U 1)
Arabica beans roasted on site plus
self-made drinking chocolate and
confectionery along with tea and
snacks

... IN SCHÖNEBERG

► ⑱ **Tomasa**
Motzstr. 60
Tel. 2 13 23 45
U-Bahn: Viktoria-Luise-Platz.
(U 4)
Popular place for breakfast in
Schönenberg

... IN KREUZBERG

► ⑧ **Kuchenkaiser**
Am Oranienplatz 11–13
Tel. 61 40 26 97
U-Bahn: Kottbusser Tor (U 1, U 8)
Legendary café in turbulent SO 36

► **Café am Ufer**
Paul-Lincke-Ufer 42/43
Tel. 61 62 92 00
U-Bahn: Kottbusser Tor (U 1/U 8)
Classic Kreuzberg café with front
garden and a view of the Land-
wehrkanal

► ⑰ **Liebermanns**
Lindenstr. 9 – 14
(in the Jewish Museum)
Tel. 25 93 97 60
U-Bahn: Hallesches Tor (U 6)
Upper echelon bistro with modern
Jewish cuisine

... IN PRENZLAUER BERG

► **Sowohlalsauch**
Kollwitzstr. 88
Tel. 4 42 93 11
U-Bahn: Senefelderplatz. (U 2)
Espresso, tea and milk creations
with home-made cakes

... IN TIERGARTEN

► ⑪ **Café Buchwald**
Bartningallee. 29
S-Bahn: Bellevue
A tradition since 1852, and the
ultimate place to go for Baum-
kuchen.

► ⑯ **Café Einstein**
Kurfürstenstr. 58 (Tiergarten)
Tel. 2 61 50 96
An institution situated in a splen-
did city mansion. Viennese café
with early 20th century charm.

... IN POTSDAM

► ⑨ **Café Heider**
Friedrich-Ebert-Str. 29
Tel. (0331) 270 55 96
Supplier of the royal court in
imperial days, a trendy rendezvous
in GDR days, now a coffee house
and restaurant

Health

Germany's healthcare system is excellent. Berlin's doctors and den-
tists are listed in the »Gelbe Seiten« (Yellow Pages) under »Ärzte«
and »Zahnärzte« respectively. The US and UK consulates can point
you in the direction of medical practitioners who speak English.

**Medical
help**

► **Medical emergency service**
Tel. 112

► **Medical emergencies for
Berlin visitors**
Tel. 01804 / 22 55 23 62

Pharmacies (Apotheken) are generally open Mon–Sat 9.30am–8pm.
They are closed on Sundays. Every pharmacy displays in the window
or door a list of pharmacies which are open at night and on holidays.

Information

 USEFUL ADDRESSES

FOR BERLIN

► **Berlin-Tourismus Marketing**
BTM Berlin Tourismus Marketing
GmbH
Am Karlsbad 11, D-10785 Berlin
Tel. (030) 25 00 25, www.btm.de
Fax 25 00 24 24, www.btm.de
From abroad:
Tel. 00 49 (18 05) 75 40 40

► **Berlin Infostores:**
Central station
(North entrance, Europaplatz 1)
open daily 8am–10pm
Neues Kranzlereck
Kurfürstendamm 21, Passage
Mon–Sat 10am–8pm, Sun
10am–6pm
Brandenburg Gate (south wing)
April–Oct 9.30am–6pm daily,
10am–6pm at other times
Pavillon am Reichstagsgebäude
April–Oct 8.30am–8pm daily,
10am–6pm at other times
Alexa Shopping Centre
Gruner Str. 20 / Alexanderplatz
Mon–Sat 10am–8pm

FOR POTSDAM

► **Potsdam Tourist Service**
Brandenburger Str. 3
D-14467 Potsdam
Tel. (03 31) 275 580
Fax 275 5829
www.potsdamtourismus.de

► **Tourist Information Centres**
Brandenburger Tor
Brandenburger Str. 3
April–Oct Mon–Fri 9.30am–8pm,
Sat and Sun until 4pm; Nov–
March Mon–Fri 10am–6pm, Sat
and Sun 9.30am–2pm
Potsdam Main Station
Mon–Fri 9.30am–8pm, Sat
9am–8pm, Sun 9.30am–2pm
Fax 275 5829
www.potsdamtourismus.de

EMBASSIES IN BERLIN

► **Australian embassy**
Wallstrasse 76–79, Mitte
Tel. 880 0880
www.australian-embassy.de

► **British embassy**
Wilhelmstrasse 70, Mitte
Tel. 204 570

► **Canadian embassy**
Leipziger Platz 17, Tiergarten
Tel. 203 120, www.kanada-info.de

► **Embassy of the
Republic of Ireland**
Jägerstr. 51, Mitte
Tel. 220 720
www.embassyofireland.de

► **New Zealand embassy**
Friedrichstrasse 60, Mitte
Tel. 206 210, www.nzembassy.com

► **United States embassy**
Clayallee 170
Tel. 832 9233
www.us-botschaft.de

INTERNET

► **www.berlin.de**
Official page for the Berlin federal
state, also combined with
www.berlinonline.de: well-struc-
tured, fast and extensive source of
information.

► **www.berlin-info.de**
Private and commercial information from and about Berlin, also
covering sightseeing, hotels and
leisure options. English version of
the site.

► **www.berlinonline.de**
Practical information on everything from cinema and theatre
programmes to chemists' hours,
cultural venues and cash machines. German only.

► **www.visitberlin.de**
Home page of Berlin Tourismus
Marketing GmbH, a good place to
start amid the flood of informa-
tion and able to handle bookings.
Also available in English.

► **www.berlinfo.com**
An extensive overview of the city,
with information on art and
culture, theatre and film, clubs and
restaurants.

► **www.bundestag.de**
Parliament and its activities; good
English version.

► **www.friedrichstrasse.de**
All you need to know about the
shopping street of Friedrichstrasse, in a variety of languages.

Also available for the shopping
centre, Shoppingzentrum im
Westen:
www.kurfuerstendamm.de.

► **www.hackesche-hoefe.com**
Website about Germany's biggest
enclosed estate, featuring flats,
culture, art and business in equal
proportions. German only.

► **www.007-berlin.de**
Website with events for the Russian community in Berlin –
everything from Russian discos to
cockroach racing. German and
Russian only.

► **www.art-in-berlin.de**
Online magazine with up-to-date
information on exhibitions, art,
literature and architecture, in
German only.

► **www.berlin-hidden-places.de**
Featuring hidden places, parks,
back yards and many other spots
in Berlin that you might never
find if it were not for this website,
which is in both German and
English.

► **www.kulturnetz.de/
berlin.htm**
Everything Berlin has to offer in
terms of culture is assembled here.

► **www.smb.spk-berlin.de**
Covers the museums belonging to
the Prussian Cultural Heritage
Trust, in comprehensive and well-
presented fashion – and in
English.

► **www.spsg.de**
Information about Potsdam's
palaces and gardens; much of it
also in English.

INTERNET CAFÉS

▶ **Cyberbar Zoo**
Joachimsthaler Str. 5–6 (Charlottenburg)

▶ **c-fox Inte**
Ostbahnhof main concourse (Friedrichshain)

▶ **Internetcafé Webpearl**
Bergmannstr. 97 (Kreuzberg)

▶ **Netlounge**
Auguststr. 98 (Mitte)
Tel. 24 34 25 97
www.netlounge-berlin.de

Language

GERMAN

General

Yes / No	Ja / Nein
Perhaps. / Maybe.	Vielleicht.
Please.	Bitte.
Thank you. / Thank you very much.	Danke. / Vielen Dank!
You're welcome.	Gern geschehen.
Excuse me!	Entschuldigung!
Pardon?	Wie bitte?
I don't understand.	Ich verstehe Sie / Dich nicht.
I only speak a bit of ...	Ich spreche nur wenig ...
Can you help me, please?	Können Sie mir bitte helfen?
I'd like ...	Ich möchte ...
I (don't) like this.	Das gefällt mir (nicht).
Do you have ...?	Haben Sie ...?
How much is this?	Wieviel kostet es?
What time is it?	Wieviel Uhr ist es?
What is this called?	Wie heißt dies hier?

Getting acquainted

Good morning!	Guten Morgen!
Good afternoon!	Guten Tag!
Good evening!	Guten Abend!
Hello! / Hi!	Hallo! Grüß Dich!
My name is ...	Mein Name ist ...
What's your name?	Wie ist Ihr / Dein Name?
How are you?	Wie geht es Ihnen / Dir?
Fine thanks. And you?	Danke. Und Ihnen / Dir?

Goodbye! / Bye-bye!	Auf Wiedersehen!
Good night!	Gute Nacht!
See you! / Bye!	Tschüss!

Travelling

left / right	links / rechts
straight ahead	geradeaus
near / far	nah / weit
Excuse me, where's ..., please?	Bitte, wo ist ...?
... the train station	... der Bahnhof
... the bus stop	... die Bushaltestelle
... the harbour	... der Hafen
... the airport	... der Flughafen
How far is it?	Wie weit ist das?
I'd like to rent a car.	Ich möchte ein Auto mieten.
How long?	Wie lange?

Traffic

My car's broken down.	Ich habe eine Panne.
Is there a service station nearby?	Gibt es hier in der Nähe eine Werkstatt?
Where's the nearest gas station?	Wo ist die nächste Tankstelle?
I want	Ich möchte ...
... liters / gallons of ...	Liter / Gallonen (3,8 l) ...
... regular/premium	.... Normalbenzin/Super
... diesel.	... Diesel.
... unleaded	... bleifrei.
Full, please.	Volltanken, bitte.
Help!	Hilfe!
Attention!/Look out!	Achtung!/Vorsicht!
Please call ...	Rufen Sie bitte ...
... an ambulance.	... einen Krankenwagen.
... the police.	... die Polizei.
It was my fault.	Es war meine Schuld.
It was your fault.	Es war Ihre Schuld.
Please give me your name and address.	Geben Sie mir bitte Namen und Anschrift.
Beware of ...	Vorsicht vor ...
Bypass (with road number)	Ortsumgehung (mit Straßennummer)
Bypass (Byp)	Umgehungsstraße
Causeway	Brücke, Pontonbrücke
Construction	Bauarbeiten
Crossing (Xing)	Kreuzung, Überweg

Dead End	Sackgasse
Detour	Umleitung
Divided Highway	Straße mit Mittelstreifen
Do not enter	Einfahrt verboten
Exit	Ausfahrt
Hill	Steigung / Gefälle/unübersichtlich (Überholverbot)
Handicapped Parking	Behindertenparkplatz
Junction (Jct)	Kreuzung, Abzweigung, Einmündung
Keep off ...	Abstand halten ...
Loading Zone	Ladezone
Merge (Merging Traffic)	Einmündender Verkehr
Narrow Bridge	Schmale Brücke
No Parking	Parken verboten
No Passing	Überholen verboten
No Turn on Red	Rechtsabbiegen bei Rot verboten
U Turn	Wenden erlaubt
No U Turn	Wenden verboten
One Way	Einbahnstraße
Passenger Loading Zone	Ein- und Aussteigen erlaubt
Ped Xing	Fußgängerüberweg
Restricted Parking Zone	Zeitlich begrenztes Parken erlaubt
Right of Way	Vorfahrt
Road Construction	Straßenbauarbeiten
Slippery when wet	Schleudergefahr bei Nässe
Slow	Langsam fahren
Soft Shoulders	Straßenbankette nicht befestigt
Speed Limit	Geschwindigkeitsbegrenzung
Toll	Benutzungsgebühr, Maut
Tow away Zone	Absolutes Parkverbot, Abschleppzone
Xing (Crossing)	Kreuzung, Überweg
Yield	Vorfahrt beachten

Shopping

Where can I find a ...?	Wo finde ich ... eine / ein ..?
... pharmacy	... Apotheke
... bakery	... Bäckerei
... department store	... Kaufhaus
... food store	... Lebensmittelgeschäft
... supermarket	... Supermarkt

Accommodation

Could you recommend ... ?	Können Sie mir ... empfehlen?

... a hotel / motel	... ein Hotel / Motel
... a bed & breakfast	... eine Frühstückspension
Do you have ...?	Haben Sie noch ...?
... a room for one	... ein Einzelzimmer
... a room for two	... ein Doppelzimmer
... with a shower / bath	... mit Dusche / Bad
... for one night	... für eine Nacht
... for a week	... für eine Woche
I've reserved a room.	Ich habe ein Zimmer reserviert.
How much is the room	Was kostet das Zimmer
... with breakfast?	... mit Frühstück?

Doctor

Can you recommend a good doctor?	Können Sie mir einen guten Arzt empfehlen?
I need a dentist.	Ich brauche einen Zahnarzt.
I feel some pain here.	Ich habe hier Schmerzen.
I've got a temperature.	Ich habe Fieber.
Prescription	Rezept
Injection / shot	Spritze

Bank / Post

Where's the nearest bank?	Wo ist hier bitte eine Bank?
ATM (Automated Teller Machine)	Geldautomat
I'd like to change dollars/pounds into euros.	Ich möchte Dollars/Pfund in Euro wechseln.
How much is ...	Was kostet ...
... a letter ...	... ein Brief ...
... a postcard ...	... eine Postkarte ...
to Europe?	nach Europa?

Numbers

1	eins	2	zwei
3	drei	4	vier
5	fünf	6	sechs
7	sieben	8	acht
9	neun	10	zehn
11	elf	12	zwölf
13	dreizehn	14	vierzehn
15	fünfzehn	16	sechzehn
17	siebzehn	18	achtzehn
19	neunzehn	20	zwanzig

21	einundzwanzig	30	dreißig
40	vierzig	50	fünfzig
60	sechzig	70	siebzig
80	achtzig	90	neunzig
100	(ein-)hundert	1000	(ein-)tausend
1/2	ein Halb	1/3	ein Drittel
1/4	ein Viertel		

Restaurant

Is there a good restaurant here?	Gibt es hier ein gutes Restaurant?
Would you reserve us a table for this evening, please?	Reservieren Sie uns bitte für heute Abend einen Tisch!
The menu please!	Die Speisekarte bitte!
Cheers!	Auf Ihr Wohl!
Could I have the check, please?	Bezahlen, bitte.
Where is the restroom, please?	Wo ist bitte die Toilette?

Frühstück / Breakfast

Kaffee (mit Sahne / Milch)	coffee (with cream / milk)
koffeinfreier Kaffee	decaffeinated coffee
heiße Schokolade	hot chocolate
Tee (mit Milch / Zitrone)	tea (with milk / lemon)
Rührei	scrambled eggs
pochierte Eier	poached eggs
Eier mit Speck	bacon and eggs
Spiegeleier	Fried eggs
harte / weiche Eier	hard-boiled / soft-boiled eggs
(Käse- / Champignon-) Omelett	(cheese / mushroom) omelette
Pfannkuchen	pancake
Brot / Brötchen / Toast	bread / rolls / toast
Butter	butter
Zucker	sugar
Honig	honey
Marmelade / Orangenmarmelade	jam / marmalade
Joghurt	yoghurt
Obst	fruit

Vorspeisen und Suppen / Starters and Soups

Fleischbrühe	broth / consommé
Hühnercremesuppe	cream of chicken soup
Tomatensuppe	cream of tomato soup
gemischter Salat	mixed salad

grüner Salat . . . . green salad
frittierte Zwiebelringe . . . . onion rings
Meeresfrüchtesalat . . . . seafood salad
Garnelen- / Krabbencocktail . . . . shrimp / prawn cocktail
Räucherlachs . . . . smoked salmon
Gemüsesuppe . . . . vegetable soup

Fisch und Meeresfrüchte / Fish and Seafood

Kabeljau . . . . cod
Krebs . . . . crab
Aal . . . . eel
Schellfisch . . . . haddock
Hering . . . . herring
Hummer . . . . lobster
Muscheln . . . . mussels
Austern . . . . oysters
Barsch . . . . perch
Scholle . . . . plaice
Lachs . . . . salmon
Jakobsmuscheln . . . . scallops
Seezunge . . . . sole
Tintenfisch . . . . squid
Forelle . . . . trout
Tunfisch . . . . tuna

Fleisch und Geflügel / Meat and Poultry

gegrillte Schweinerippchen . . . . barbecued spare ribs
Rindfleisch . . . . beef
Hähnchen . . . . chicken
Geflügel . . . . poultry
Kotelett . . . . chop / cutlet
Filetsteak . . . . fillet
(junge) Ente . . . . duck(ling)
Schinkensteak . . . . gammon
Fleischsoße . . . . gravy
Hackfleisch vom Rind . . . . ground beef
gekochter Schinken . . . . ham
Nieren . . . . kidneys
Lamm . . . . lamb
Leber . . . . liver
Schweinefleisch . . . . pork
Würstchen . . . . sausages
Lendenstück vom Rind, Steak . . . . sirloin steak
Truthahn . . . . turkey

Kalbfleisch	veal
Reh oder Hirsch	venison

Nachspeise und Käse / Dessert and Cheese

gedeckter Apfelkuchen	apple pie
Schokoladenplätzchen	brownies
Hüttenkäse	cottage cheese
Sahne	cream
Vanillesoße	custard
Obstsalat	fruit salad
Ziegenkäse	goat's cheese
Eiscreme	ice cream
Gebäck	pastries

Gemüse und Salat / Vegetables and Salad

gebackene Kartoffeln in der Schale	baked potatoes
Pommes frites	french fries
Bratkartoffeln	hash browns
Kartoffelpüree	mashed potatoes
gebackene Bohnen in Tomatensoße	baked beans
Kohl	cabbage
Karotten	carrots
Blumenkohl	cauliflower
Tomaten	tomatoes
Gurke	cucumber
Knoblauch	garlic
Lauch	leek
Kopfsalat	lettuce
Pilze	mushrooms
Zwiebeln	onions
Erbsen	peas
Paprika	peppers
Kürbis	pumpkin
Spinat	spinach
Mais	sweet corn
Maiskolben	corn-on-the-cob

Obst / Fruit

Äpfel	apples	Birnen	pears
Aprikosen	apricots	Orange	orange
Brombeeren	blackberries	Pfirsiche	peaches
Kirschen	cherries	Ananas	pineapple

Weintrauben	grapes	Pflaumen	plums
Grapefruit	grapefruit	Himbeeren	raspberries
Zitrone	lemon	Erdbeeren	strawberries
Preiselbeeren	cranberries		

Getränke / Beverages

Bier (vom Fass)	beer (on tap)
Apfelwein	cider
Rotwein / Weißwein	red wine / white wine
trocken / lieblich	dry / sweet
Sekt, Schaumwein	sparkling wine
alkoholfreie Getränke	soft drinks
Fruchtsaft	fruit juice
gesüßter Zitronensaft	lemonade
Milch	milk
Mineralwasser	mineral water / spring water

Literature

Alfred Döblin: *Berlin Alexanderplatz: The Story of Franz Biberkopf*. Continuum International Publishing Group Ltd. (2004). In the Berlin of the 1920s Franz Biberkopf tries to re-enter normal life after a spell in gaol and fails, not least because of the city itself.

Novels and journalism

Joseph Roth: *What I Saw: Reports from Berlin 1920-33*. Granta Books (2004). Novelist Roth (*The Radetzky March*) describes both the exciting cosmopolitanism and the sinister cruelty of Berlin in the early years of the Weimar republic.

Theodor Fontane: *Delusions, Confusions and the Poggenpuhl Family*. Continuum International Publishing Group Ltd. (1997). Story of an illicit and doomed love affair in imperial Berlin.

Anna Funder: *Stasiland: Stories from Behind the Berlin Wall*. Granta Books 2004. A brilliant and sometimes amusing account of life under a dictatorship. London's *Evening Standard* made it a book of the year.

Judith Hermann: *The Summer House, Latery*. Flamingo 2002. Set principally in Germany's modern capital, Hermann's short stories revolve around the contemporary concerns of thirty-something Berliners.

History **Helga Schneider**: *The Bonfire of Berlin: A Lost Childhood in Wartime Germany*. Vintage 2006. Schneider gives a shocking account of the horrors of wartime Berlin, which she experienced as a child abandoned by her parents.

Anonymous; Philip Boehm (Translator): *A Woman in Berlin: Diary 20 April 1945 to 22 June 1945*. Virago Press Ltd 2006. First-hand account of the events in Berlin immediately after the end of the War, when the Russians moved in, written from a woman's point of view. Sometimes harrowing, very popular with the critics.

Frederick Taylor: *The Berlin Wall: 13 August 1961 - 9 November 1989*. Bloomsbury Publishing PLC 2007. The story of the post-war political conflict which was symbolized by the Wall; a mix of history, archive research and personal accounts.

i **Berlin on film**

- *The Spy Who Came in from the Cold*: the cold war on both sides of the Wall
- *One Two Three*: witty comedy by Billy Wilder
- *Der Himmel über Berlin* (*Wings of Desire*): an angel comes to Berlin
- *Run Lola Run*: thriller, love story, race against time

Michael S. Cullen: *The Reichstag: German parliament between monarchy and federalism*. Bebra/VAH, Berlin 1999. The most detailed book about the building by far, including its varied history, the spectacular art project that wrapped it up in 1995 and its rebuilding for the new German parliament.

Lost Property

▶ **Zentrales Fundbüro (central lost property office)**
Platz der Luftbrücke 6
D-12101 Berlin
Tel. 75 603101

▶ **Berliner Verkehrsbetriebe (public transport authority)**
Holzmarktstr. 15
Tel. 19449

▶ **Deutsche Bahn AG**
Enquire about lost property at the »ServicePoints« in the stations or call the Lost Property hotline:
tel. (0900) 199 05 99

Money

Since 2002 the euro has been the official currency of Germany.   Euro

Citizens of EU members countries may import to and export from Germany unlimited amounts in euros.   Currency regulations

At Schönefeld Airport (in Terminal A) and Tegel (on the main concourse) there are various banks and bureaux de change with long opening hours. Cash dispensers operated by various banks are dotted all over the city and money can be obtained without problems round the clock by using credit and debit cards with a PIN.
Loss of a card must be reported immediately.   Bureaux de change and cash dispensers

i Exchange rates

- 1 € = 1.30 US$
- 1 US$ = 0.77 €
- 1 £ = 1.20 €
- 1 € = 0.83 £

Most international **credit cards** are accepted by hotels, restaurants, car rentals and many shops. Credit cards have limits.

If bank cards or cheque and credit cards should get lost, you should call your own bank or credit card organization to make sure they are immediately stopped. It is a good idea to make a note of the telephone number on the back of the card.   Loss of bank cards and credit cards

CONTACT DETAILS FOR POPULAR CARDS

In the event of lost bank or credit cards you can either contact the following offices in Germany or the number given by the bank in your home country:

► **Eurocard/MasterCard**
Tel. 069 / 7933 1910

► **Visa**
Tel. 0800 / 814 9100

► **American Express**
Tel. 069 / 97 97 0

► **Diners Club**
Tel. 05921 / 86 12 34
Have the bank sort code, account number and card number as well as the expiry date ready.

Museums and Galleries

 BERLIN'S MUSEUMS

INFORMATION

► **Kulturprojekte Berlin**
Networks, support and communication for cultural projects
www.kulturprojekte-berlin.de

► **Internet**
www.berlin.de/orte/museum
www.smb.spk-berlin.de

ARCHITECTURE/DESIGN

► **Bauhaus Archive Berlin**
(Museum für Gestaltung – Design Museum)
Klingelhöferstr. 14 (Tiergarten)
www.bauhaus.de
U-Bahn: Nollendorfplatz (U 2)
Bus: M 29, 100, 106, 187
Wed – Mon 10am – 5pm

► **Museum der Dinge
(Museum of Objects)**
(Werkbund Archive)
Oranienstr. 25 (Kreuzberg)
U-Bahn: Kottbusser Tor (U 1, U 8)
www.museumderdinge.de
Fri – Mon noon – 7pm

GALLERIES

► **Galerie Carlier / Gebauer**
Holzmarktstr. 15–18 (Mitte)
Tel. 240 08 63-0
U/S-Bahn: Jannowitzbrücke (U 8)
Large rooms above the Spree,
Berlin and international artists

► **Eigen + Art**
Auguststr. 26 (Mitte)
Tel. 280 66 05
U-Bahn: Weinmeisterstr. (U 8)
Gerd Harry Lybke is famous for

his ability to spot new talent. His gallery represents stars from Leipzig such as Neo Rauch, Tim Eitel and David Schnell.

► **Galerie Neu**
Philippstr. 13 (Mitte)
Tel. 285 75 50
U-Bahn: Zinnowitzer Str. (U 6)
Represents the free club and project scene in what was once the stables of the Charité veterinary institute.

► **Galerie Nordenhake**
Lindenstr. 34 (Kreuzberg)
Tel. 821 18 92
U-Bahn: Kochstr. (U 6)
This classic gallery from Malmö has set up shop in the art quarter around Checkpoint Charlie with lots of space in a former department store. Artists from Poland, Slovenia and elsewhere.

► **Galerie Max Hetzler**
Oudenaarder Str. 16–20 (Wedding)
Tel. 229 24 37
U-Bahn: Nauener Platz (U 9)
Big names such as Jeff Coons and Ernesto Neto

► **DAAD-Galerie**
Zimmerstr. 91–99 (Mitte)
Tel. 261 36 40
U-Bahn: Kochstr. (U 6)
Cross the courtyard of the gallery centre to see what guests of the German academic exchange service have produced.

► Halle am Wasser
Invalidenstr. 50 (Mitte)
S-Bahn: Hauptbahnhof
New premises behind the Hamburger Bahnhof for several galleries and the Berlin collector Harald Frisch

► IFA-Galerie
Linienstr. 139 (Mitte)
Tel. 22 67 96 16
U-Bahn: Oranienburger Tor (U 6)
Contemporary art from Latin America, Central Asia, Arab countries and eastern Europe

► Kunstwerke Berlin
Auguststr. 69 (Mitte)
Tel. 24 34 59-0
S-Bahn: Oranienburger Str.
(S 1, S 25)
Epicentre of Berlin's contemporary art scene, showing extraordinary exhibitions. Organiser of the Berlin-Biennale.

HISTORY/HISTORY OF CIVILIZATION

► Alliierten-Museum (Allies' Museum)
►p.181

► Anne Frank Zentrum
Rosenthaler Str. 39 (Mitte)
S-Bahn: Hackescher Markt (S 5, S 7, S 9, S 75)
May – Sept Tue – Sun 10am – 8pm, Oct – April until 6pm
Exhibition about the diary and life of Anne Frank

► Anti-Kriegs-Museum (Anti-War Museum)
Brüsseler Str. 21 (Mitte)
U-Bahn: Amrumer Str. (U 9)
4pm – 8pm daily
Documents and photographs from both world wars.

► Schloss Cecilienhof
►Potsdam, Neuer Garten

► Deutsches Historisches Museum (German History Museum)
►Unter den Linden, Zeughaus

► Deutsch-Russisches Museum (German-Russian Museum) Berlin-Karlshorst
►Lichtenberg

► DDR-Museum (Museum of the East German Republic)
►Berliner Dom

► Erinnerungsstätte Notaufnahmelager Marienfelde (Memorial at the former refugee camp in Marienfelde)
Marienfelder Allee 66 – 80 (Tempelhof), www.enm-berlin.de
S-Bahn: Marienfelde (S 2)
Tue – Sun 10am – 6pm
Tours: Wed and Sun only at 3pm
Documentation about the arrival of refugees from East Germany at the former refugee camp.

► Forschungs- und Gedenkstätte Normannenstrasse (Stasi research centre and memorial)
►Lichtenberg

► Gedenkstätte Berliner Mauer (Berlin Wall memorial)
►Baedeker Special p.193

► Gedenkstätte Berlin-Hohenschönhausen (Hohenschönhausen memorial)
Genslerstr. 66, www.stiftung-hsh.de
Tram/Metro: M 6, 7, 17
Tours: Mon – Fri 11am, 1pm and 3pm, Sat and Sun hourly from 9am – 4pm
Former Stasi interrogation cells

▶ **Gedenkstätte Deutscher Widerstand (Memorial to German resistance)**
►p.224

▶ **Gedenkstätte Haus der Wannsee-Konferenz (Wannsee conference memorial)**
►Wannsee

▶ **Gedenkstätte Köpenicker Blutwoche Juni 1933**
Puchanstr. 12
www.heimatmuseum-koepenick.de
S-Bahn: Köpenick (S 3)
Thu 10am – 6pm
Memorial to the victims of Nazi stormtroopers in a week of bloodshed that took place in June 1933 in Köpenick.

▶ **Gedenkstätte Plötzensee**
►p.225

▶ **Hauptmann von Köpenick (the captain of Köpenick)**
►Alt-Köpenick

▶ **Haus der brandenburgisch-preussischen Geschichte (House of Brandenburg and Prussian History)**
►Potsdam, city centre

▶ **Hugenottenmuseum**
►Gendarmenmarkt

▶ **Informations- und Dokumen-tationszentrum der Bundes-beauftragten für die Stasi Unterlagen (Information and documentation centre run by the national body in charge of Stasi documents)**
Mauerstr. 38 (Mitte)
U-Bahn: Mohrenstr. (U 2)
Mon – Sat 10am – 6pm

How the Stasi arranged its network of spies

▶ **Jüdisches Museum (Jewish Museum)**
►p.235

▶ **Knoblauchhaus**
►Nikolaiviertel

▶ **Landesarchiv Berlin (Berlin's regional archives)**
Eichborndamm 115 – 121 (Reinickendorf)
S-Bahn: Eichborndamm (S 25);
bus: 221, 322
Tue – Thu 9am – 6pm, Fri 9am – 3pm

▶ **Märkisches Museum**
►Märkisches Ufer

▶ **Mauermuseum (Haus am Checkpoint Charlie – Museum for the Berlin Wall)**
►Friedrichstrasse

▶ **Museum für Kommunikation (Museum for Communication)**
►Leipziger Strasse

▶ **Museum für Vor- und Frühgeschichte (Museum of Early History and Prehistory)**
►Museumsinsel: Neues Museum

▶ **Museum im Gutshaus Dahlem**
►Dahlem

▶ **Museum gegen politische Gewalt (Museum opposing Political Violence)**
►Potsdam, city centre

▶ **Museumsdorf Düppel (museum village)**
Clauertstr. 11 (Zehlendorf)
S-Bahn: Mexikoplatz (S 1), then by

115, 118, 269 bus
April – mid-Oct Thu 3pm – 7pm,
Sun and holidays 10am – 5pm
Open-air museum village on the
site of an original archaeological
dig at Machnower Fenn. A reconstruction of how the village must
have looked at the beginning of
the 13th century with smithy,
cobbler, potter, beekeeper. Regular
demonstrations by craftsmen.

► **Polizeihistorische Sammlung
(Police History Collection)**
Platz der Luftbrücke 6
(Tempelhof)
U-Bahn: Platz der Luftbrücke
(U 6); bus: 104, 119, 184, 341
Mon – Wed 9am – 3pm, Thu / Fri
for groups by appointment
The history of Berlin's police force
from the 19th century to the
present day.

► **Potsdam Museum**
►Potsdam, town centre

► **Preussenmuseum
(Prussian Museum)**
►Potsdam, town centre

► **Rotkreuz-Museum Berlin
(Red Cross Museum)**
Bachestr. 11 (Steglitz)
S-Bahn: Bundesplatz (S 45, S 46)
U-Bahn: Friedrich-Wilhelm-Platz
(U 9)
Wed 5pm – 7pm
The Red Cross and its history in
Berlin.

► **Sammlung Kindheit und
Jugend (Collection on
Childhood and Youth)**
Wallstr. 32 (Mitte)
U-Bahn: Märkisches Museum
(U 2)
Mon – Fri 9am – 5pm

► **Spandovia Sacra**
►Spandau

► **Stadtgeschichtliches Museum
Spandau (history of the
town of Spandau)**
►Spandau

► **The Kennedys**
Pariser Platz 4a (Mitte)
S-Bahn. Unter den Linden
10am – 6pm daily
300 photographs, documents and
JFK's briefcase

► **The Story of Berlin**
►Kurfürstendamm

► **Topografie des Terrors**
►Kreuzberg

► **Wege – Irrwege – Umwege
(ways, lost ways and
diversions)**
►Gendarmenmarkt

ART AND ANTIQUITIES

► **Abgusssammlung antiker
Plastik (casts of ancient
statues)**
Schlossstr. 69 b
(Charlottenburg)
Bus: M 45, 109, 309
Thu – Sun 2pm – 5pm
Copies of ancient masterpieces at
Schloss Charlottenburg.

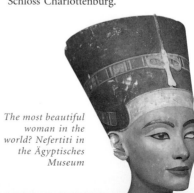

*The most beautiful
woman in the
world? Nefertiti in
the Ägyptisches
Museum*

▶ **Ägyptisches Museum und Papyrussammlung (Egyptian Museum and Papyrus Collection)**
▶Museumsinsel, Neues Museum

▶ **Alte Nationalgalerie**
▶Museumsinsel

▶ **Altes Museum**
▶Museumsinsel

▶ **Antikensammlung (Collection of Antiquities)**
▶Museumsinsel: Altes Museum, Pergamonmuseum

▶ **Berlinische Galerie**
▶Jüdisches Museum (Jewish Museum)

▶ **Bildergalerie (Picture Gallery)**
▶Potsdam, Sanssouci

▶ **Bodemuseum**
▶Museumsinsel

▶ **Bröhan Museum**
▶ S. 196

▶ **Brücke Museum**
▶Dahlem

▶ **Dahlem Museums**
▶Dahlem

! **Baedeker** TIP

Night at the museum
The »Lange Nacht der Museen« (Long Night of Museums) usually takes place every two years. Between 6pm and 2pm, visitors have the choice of visiting more than 80 museums. A bus shuttle service runs between the various sites and a combined ticket includes the use of public transport and admission to the participating museums.

▶ **Deutsche Guggenheim**
▶Unter den Linden

▶ **Ephraim Palais**
▶Nikolaiviertel

▶ **Helmut Newton Trust**
▶Kurfürstendamm

▶ **Gemäldegalerie (Picture Gallery)**
▶Kulturforum

▶ **Georg Kolbe Museum**
Sensburger Allee 25
(Charlottenburg)
www.georg-kolbe-museum.de
S-Bahn: Heerstr. (S 5, S 75)
Bus: M 45
Tue – Sun 10am – 6pm
Rotating exhibitions of works by sculptor Georg Kolbe exhibited in his studio

▶ **Gipsformerei der Staatlichen Museen zu Berlin (plaster casting department for Berlin's city museums)**
Sophie-Charlotte-Str. 17 – 18
(Charlottenburg)
Tel. 3 26 76 90; U-Bahn: Richard-Wagner-Pl. (U 7);
bus: M 45, 309
Mon – Fri 9am – 4pm, Wed closes 6pm
Casts of antique statues
Close to Schloss Charlottenburg

▶ **Gutshaus Steglitz**
(Wrangelschlösschen)
Schlossstr. 48
Tel. 7 97 39 86
S-Bahn and U-Bahn: Rathaus Steglitz (S 1, U 9)
Tue – Sun 2pm – 7pm
Built in 1800 according to plans by David Gilly; early classical building; rotating exhibitions

▶ **Käthe Kollwitz Museum Berlin**
▶Kurfürstendamm

▶ **Keramik-Museum Berlin (Pottery Museum)**
Schustehrusstr. 13 (Charl.)
U-Bahn: Richard-Wagner-Platz
(U7); Sun – Mon 1pm – 5pm

▶ **Kunstbibliothek (Art Library)**
▶Kulturforum

▶ **Kupferstichkabinett (Engraving Museum)**
▶Kulturforum

▶ **Kunstgewerbemuseum (Museum of Applied Art)**
▶Köpenick ▶Kulturforum

▶ **Kunstsammlung Süd-, Südost- und Zentralasiens (Art of South, Southeast and Central Asia)**
▶Dahlem, Dahlem museums

▶ **Martin-Gropius-Bau**
▶p.260

▶ **Museum für Fotografie (Photography Museum)**
▶Kurfürstendamm

▶ **Museum Berggruen**
▶p.266

▶ **Museum für Asiatische Kunst (Museum of Asian Art)**
▶Dahlem: Dahlem museums

▶ **Museum für Gegenwart (Museum of the Present Day)**
▶Hamburger Bahnhof

▶ **Museum für Islamische Kunst (Museum of Islamic Art)**
▶Museumsinsel, Pergamon-museum

▶ **Museum für Ostasiatische Kunst (Museum of Far Eastern Art)**
▶Dahlem, Dahlem museums

▶ **Museum für Spätantike und Byzantinische Kunst (Museum of Late Antiquity and Byzantine Art)**
▶Museumsinsel, Bodemuseum

▶ **Neue Nationalgalerie (New National Gallery)**
Kulturforum

▶ **Neues Museum (New Museum)**
▶Museumsinsel

▶ **Porcelain collection at the Belvedere**
▶Schloss Charlottenburg

▶ **Porcelain collection in the Chinese House**
▶Potsdam, Sanssouci

▶ **Pergamonmuseum**
▶Museumsinsel

▶ **Roman baths**
▶Potsdam, Sanssouci

▶ **Hoffmann collection**
▶Spandauer Vorstadt

▶ **Scharf/Gerstenberg collection**
▶Museum Berggruen

▶ **Schinkel Museum**
▶Schlossplatz, Werderscher Markt

▶ **Schinkel Pavilion**
▶Schloss Charlottenburg

▶ **Sculpture collection**
▶Museumsinsel, Bodemuseum

The Marlene Dietrich Collection in the Filmmuseum on Potsdamer Platz has all the makings of a pilgrimage site.

▶ **Das Stille Museum (The Silent Museum)**
Linienstr. 154a (Mitte)
www.das-stille-museum.de
S-Bahn: Oranienburger Strasse (S 1, S 2)
U-Bahn: Oranienburger Tor (U 6); for admission tel. 28 04 71 29
Meditative art experience

▶ **Das Verborgene Museum (The Hidden Museum)**
Schlüterstr. 70 (Charlottenburg)
S-Bahn: Savignyplatz (S 3, S 5, S 7, S 9, S 75); bus: 149
Thu, Fri 3pm – 7pm, Sat, Sun noon – 4pm
Women's art

▶ **Vorderasiatisches Museum (Museum of the Near East)**
▶Museumsinsel, Pergamonmuseum

LITERATURE, THEATRE AND FILM

▶ **Anna-Seghers-Gedenkstätte / Memorial**
Anna-Seghers-Str. 81 (Treptow)
S-Bahn: Adlershof (S 6, S 8, S 9, S 45, S 46); Tue, Thu 10am – 4pm
The home of the writer

▶ **Brecht-Weigel-Gedenkstätte / Memorial**
Chausseestr. 125 (Mitte)
U-Bahn: Zinnowitzer Str. (U 6)
Tram/Metro: M6, 8; bus: 240, 245

Tours: Tue, Sat 10am – 3pm, Wed and Fri 11.30am, Thu 10am – 6.30pm, Sun 11am – 6pm
Home of Bertolt Brecht and Helene Weigel

▶ **Filmmuseum Potsdam**
▶Potsdam, town centre

▶ **Mori-Ogai-Gedenkstätte (Mori Ogai memorial)**
Luisenstr. 39 (Mitte)
S-Bahn and U-Bahn: Friedrichstrasse (S 1, S 2, S 25, S 5, S 7, S 9, S 75, U 6); bus: 147, 157
Mon – Fri 10am – 2pm
Memorial room for the Japanese poet and physician Mori Ogai

▶ **Museum für Film und Fernsehen/Deutsche Kinemathek (Museum of Film and TV)**
▶Potsdamer Platz

NATURE AND TECHNOLOGY

▶ **Arboretum at the Humboldt University in Berlin**
Späthstr. 80/81 (Treptow)
S-Bahn: Baumschulenweg (S 8, S 9, S 45, S 46, S 47, S 85), then by 260 or 170 bus
U-Bahn: Blaschkoallee (U 7), then by 270 bus
Early April – late Oct Wed, Thu, Sat, Sun and holidays 10am – 6pm
1200 types of trees and herbs

▶ **Archenhold-Sternwarte and Himmelskundliches Museum (Observatory and Museum of the Night Sky)**
▶Treptow

▶ **Berliner Medizinhistorisches Museum (History of Medicine Museum)**
▶Friedrichstrasse, Charité

▶ **Berliner S-Bahn Museum**
Rudolf-Breitscheid-Str. 203 (S-Bahn depot Griebnitzsee)
D-14482 Potsdam
www.s-bahn-museum.de
S-Bahn: Griebnitzsee (S 7)
April – Nov every other weekend 11am – 5pm

▶ **Berliner U-Bahn Museum**
Rossitterplatz 1 (Charlottenburg)
(S-Bahn depot Griebnitzsee)
U-Bahn: Olympiastadion (U 2)
Second Sat in each month 10.30am – 4pm
A century of the underground railway. Includes the Olympiastadion signal and control centre, commissioned in 1931

▶ **Botanisches Museum (Botanical Museum)**
▶Dahlem

▶ **Deutsches Technikmuseum (German Museum of Technology)**
▶p.212

▶ **Dampfmaschinenhaus (mosque)**
Steam engine house, now the mosque in ▶Potsdam city centre

▶ **Feuerwehrmuseum
(Fire Brigade Museum)**
Berliner Str. 16
(Tegel fire station)
U-Bahn: Alt-Tegel (U 6)
Bus: 133
Sun – Thu 9am – noon, Wed
4pm – 7pm
Historical fire equipment demon-
strating the development of fire
fighting

▶ **Historischer Hafen
(Historic docks)**
▶Märkisches Ufer

▶ **Jagdmuseum
(Hunting Musuem)**
▶Grunewald

▶ **Medizinhistorisches Museum
(Museum of Medical History)**
▶Friedrichstrasse, Charité

▶ **Museum für Kommunikation
(Museum of Communication)**
▶Leipziger Strasse

▶ **Museum für Naturkunde
(Natural History Museum)**
▶S. 267

▶ **Robert Koch Museum**
Dorotheenstr. 96 (Mitte)
S-Bahn: Unter den Linden (S 1,
S 2, S 25)
U-Bahn: Friedrichstrasse (U 6);
bus: 100, 147, 200
By appointment (tel. 45 0 52 40 02)
Life and work of doctor and
bacteriologist Robert Koch

▶ **Scheringianum**
Fennstr. 10 (Wedding)
U-Bahn: Wedding, Reinickendor-
fer Strasse (U 6)
Mon – Fri 10am – noon
Schering factory museum

▶ **Wasserwerk Friedrichshagen
(Friedrichshagen water works)**
▶Müggelsee

▶ **Wilhelm-Foerster-Sternwarte
(Observatory)**
Munsterdamm 90 (Steglitz)
S-Bahn: Priesterweg (S 2)
Information: tel. 79 00 93-0

▶ **Zucker-Museum im Institut für
Lebensmitteltechnologie
(Museum of Sugar at the
food science institute)**
Amrumer Str. 32 (Wedding)
U-Bahn: Amrumer Strasse (U 9),
Seestrasse (U 6);
Tram: M 13, 50; Bus: 106, 221
Mon – Thu 9am – 4.30pm, Sun
11am – 6pm; tours: Sun 11.30am
and 2.30pm
Everything about sugar producing
plants and the production of sugar

LOCAL MUSEUMS

Almost every borough of the city
has its own local museum. The
following are of particular interest
for the history of Berlin.

▶ **Museum Charlottenburg-
Wilmersdorf**
Schlossstr. 69, U-Bahn: Sophie-
Charlotte-Platz (U 2); bus: M 45,
109, 309; Tue – Fri 10am – 5pm,
Sun 11am – 5pm

▶ **Kreuzberg Museum für
Stadtentwicklung und
Sozialgeschichte (Kreuzberg
Museum of City Development
and Social History)**
Adalbertstr. 95 A
U-Bahn: Kottbusser Tor (U 1,
U 8); bus: M – 29, 140
Tue – Fri 11am – 4pm

► **Mitte Museum am Festungsgraben**
Am Festungsgraben 1
S/U-Bahn: Friedrichstrasse (S 1, S 2, S 25, S 5, S 7, S 75, S 9, U 6)
Wed, Fri, Sat, Sun 1pm – 5pm

FOLK CULTURE AND CRAFTS

► **Ethnologisches Museum (Ethnological Museum)**
►Dahlem, Dahlem museums

► **Gründerzeitmuseum (Museum of the Early Imperial Period)**
►Marzahn

► **Museum Europäischer Kulturen (Museum of European Cultures)**
►Dahlem

► **Museum der unerhörten Dinge (Museum of Unheard-of Things)**
Crellestr. 5-6 (Schöneberg)
S-Bahn: Julius-Leber-Brücke (S 1)
Wed – Fri 3pm – 7pm
Fantastical, »unheard-of« finds

OTHER MUSEUMS

► **Berliner Unterwelten-Museum (Berlin Underground Museum)**
Brunnenstr. 108a (Mitte)
U-Bahn: Gesundbrunnen (U 8)
Tours Thu – Mon 11am – 4pm
The history and development of Berlin as seen from underground in the former air raid bunker, Luftschutzbunker B.

► **Blindenmuseum (Museum of the Blind)**
Rothenburgstr. 14 (Steglitz)
U-Bahn: Rathaus Steglitz (U 9)
Wed 3pm – 6pm

► **Deutsches Currywurst-Museum**
►Friedrichstrasse

► **Deutsches Fußballmuseum**
Anton-Saefkow-Platz 13 (Lichtenberg)
S-Bahn: Storkower Str. (S 41, S 42)

► **Erotik-Museum Beate Uhse**
Kantstrasse corner Joachimstaler Strasse (Charlottenburg)
S-/U-Bahn: Zool. Garten (S 1, S 2, S 3, S 5, S 7, S 75, S 9, U 1, U 12, U 9)
Mon – Sat 11am – midnight, from 18 years of age
Everything you need to know about »eroticism« in a museum run by the Beate Uhse company.

► **Grünauer Wassersportmuseum (Museum of Water Sports)**
Regattastr. 141
S-Bahn: Grünau (S 6, S 8, S 46), then by 68 tram
Tue Wed 9am – noon and 2pm to 4.30pm, Sat 2pm – 4.30pm

► **Hanfmuseum (Hemp Museum)**
►Nikolaiviertel

► **Hofgärtnermuseum (Court Gardening Museum)**
►Glienicke

► **Gaslaternen-Freilichtmuseum (Open-air Museum of Gas Lamps)**
►Baedeker tip p.323

► **Jugendmuseum Schöneberg (Childhood Museum)**
►Children in Berlin

► **Kinder- und Jugendmuseum Prenzlauer Berg (Museum of Childhood and Youth)**
►Children in Berlin

► **KPM-Welt**
►Tiergarten

► **Labyrinth Kindermuseum**
►Children in Berlin

► **Luftwaffenmuseum der Bundeswehr (German Air Force Museum)**
►Spandau

► **Museum Kindheit und Jugend (Museum of Childhood and Youth)**
►Children in Berlin

► **Musikinstrumenten-Museum**
►Kulturforum

► **Puppentheater-Museum**
►Children in Berlin

► **Schwules Museum (Museum of Homosexuality)**
Mehringdamm 61 (Kreuzberg)

www.schwulesmuseum.de
U-Bahn: Mehringdamm (U 6, U 7);
bus: 119, 140, 219
Wed – Mon
2pm – 6pm, Sat
closes 7pm

► **Sportmuseum Berlin**
Haus des Deutschen Sports
Hanns-Braun-Str.
(Charl.) U-Bahn:
Olympia-Stadion
(U 2)
Mon – Fri
10am – 2pm
Special exhibitions only

Newspapers and Magazines

Newspapers   Several major newspapers are published in Berlin. The range covers *taz* and *Neues Deutschland* on the alternative or left wing to the tabloid *BZ*. Between the two poles are papers like *Tagesspiegel*, *Berliner Zeitung*, the *Welt* and the *Berliner Morgenpost*.

City magazines   The two city and events magazines *zitty* and *tip* both appear fortnightly while *Berlin-Programm* comes out once a month.

English-language newspapers   Most of the main British and American newspapers can be purchased at any of the main stations or the International Presse newsagents. Kiosks in areas especially frequented by tourists, such as Checkpoint Charlie and the Europa Center, are also good places to find English language press. The British Bookshop is excellent for British and London newspapers while bookshops like Hugendubel and Dussman also stock international titles.

Berlin-based monthly in English   The *Exberliner* is an English-language monthly magazine with articles, commentaries, reviews and a what's-on guide, as well as classified ads.

Post and Communications

Post offices tend to be open 9am–6pm Mon–Fri, 9am–1pm Sat   Post
(closed Sun). The large, central post offices have longer opening
hours: eg 9am–8pm at Joachimstrasse 7 (Zoologischer Garten).
Postage stamps for letters up to 20g/0.7oz within Germany cost
€0.55, to other European countries €0.70, and elsewhere €1.70. Postcards are a little cheaper: €0.65 (Europe) or €1.00 (elsewhere).

Public telephones accept coins (€0.10, 0.20, 0.50) and/or Deutsche   Telephone>
Telekom phonecards, available in 5, 10 and 20-euro denominations
from post offices and newsagents. International calling cards offer
more competitive rates (www.comfi.com). A large number of call
shops or »Telefon-Cafés« offer cheap rates for calls abroad.
The German **mobile networks** function with providers such as T-
Mobile, Vodafone, E-Plus, Base and O2. It is worth checking on
roaming tariffs, which can be pricey, before you leave.

► TELEPHONE NUMBERS

DIALLING CODES

► **Dialling codes to Berlin**
from Germany: tel. 030
from the UK and Republic of
Ireland: Tel. 00 49 30
from the USA, Canada and Australia: tel. 00 11 49 30
It is not necessary to dial the 030
area code for local calls within
Berlin.

► **Dialling codes from Berlin**
to the UK: tel. 00 44
to the Rep. of Ireland: tel. 00 353

to the USA and Canada: tel. 00 1
to Australia: tel. 00 61
The 0 that precedes the subsequent local area code is omitted.

DIRECTORY ENQUIRIES

► **National**
Tel. 11 833

► **International**
Tel. 11 834

► **Enquiries in English**
Tel. 11 837

Prices and Discounts

A WelcomeCard allows you to travel free on all buses and trains as   WelcomeCard
well as offering discounts of up to 50% at more than 130 places of
interest for tourists, such as museums, theatres, city tours, bars,
pubs, restaurants, and sights. Cards are valid for either 48 or 72

WHAT DOES IT COST?

Beer (0.5l)
from €3.50

Simple meal
from €5

Simple double room
from €60

Espresso
from €2

hours and apply to the inner Berlin fare zone (zones AB) or for Berlin and Potsdam (zones ABC). They are valid for adults accompanied by up to three children under 14. Cards are available online (www.visitberlin.de/welcomecard) at Infostores, in hotels, at airports, service counters of public transport concerns (► Public Transport) and their ticket machines or from Potsdam Information (► Information).

SchauLust
Museen Berlin

This is a card valid for for three days costing €19 and allowing entry to more than 70 museums, including those run by the Staatliche Museen Berlin. They are available only from Infostores or online (►Information).

Shopping

Shopping streets
and centres

Charlottenburg-Wilmersdorf remains one of the classic places to shop in Berlin: Kurfürstendamm and its side streets such as Savignyplatz, Joachimsthaler Strasse, Kantstrasse and Wilmersdorfer Strasse, Bleibtreustrasse and Mommsenstrasse or Breitscheidplatz and Tauentzienstrasse. The best known shopping centres in the region are the Europa Center next to the Gedächtniskirche, which has more than 90 shops and is open 24 hours a day. Not to be missed, of course, is the **KaDeWe** on Wittenbergplatz, one of Germany's most famous stores, a temple of luxury and indeed excess, particularly with regard to the delicatessen section on the sixth floor (► Sights from A to Z, KaDeWe).

Its counterpart in the east is, meanwhile, **Friedrichstrasse** with shopping arcades at 205 (mainly fashion), 206 (highly exclusive and dear with shows, cosmetics, fashion, accessories and designer goods) and 207, where Galeries Lafayette is based, the first German branch of the famous Parisian store with creations and accessories by famous designers plus leather goods and French delicatessen. Books, music and software are available in KulturKaufhaus Dussmann at Friedrichstr. 90. The arcades at **Potsdamer Platz** have more than 100 shops focussing on fashion and textiles: they are making a great effort to keep up with the major players. Berlin's second-largest shopping mall is Alexa on Alexanderplatz with 180 stores.

It should not be forgotten, though, that it is always worth shopping off the beaten track, particularly because it is away from the designer mainstream that really unusual items may be found. Have a look around Spandauer Vorstadt – Auguststrasse, Hackesche Höfe, Mulackstrasse, Weinmeisterstrasse (which has become a high-class street of fashion designers) – and check out Simon-Dach-Strasse in Friedrichshain, Kastanienallee in Prenzlauer Berg, Winterfeldtplatz and its environs, Maassenstrasse in Schöneberg and Kreuzberg's Bergmannstrasse.

The classic souvenir is the Berlin bear, be it a cuddly toy, cast metal model, or a picture on any other kind of item. Almost as popular are models of the Brandenburg Gate, the Funkturm or the Reichstag. There are also souvenirs nowadays related to »reunification«, things like the famous East German traffic light figures or »Ampelmännchen«, (real?) pieces of the Berlin Wall, and all kinds of medals and uniform trappings from the East German or Soviet army. Many museums also have copies of their most popular exhibits for sale.

Souvenirs

► WHERE TO SHOP

COMICS

► **Grober Unfug**
Weinmeisterstr. 9 (Mitte) and Zossener Str. 32 – 33 (Kreuzb.)
Comics, especially Manga and Anime, CDs, DVDs, and exhibitions.

DELICATESSEN

► **Erich Hamann, chocolate shop and factory**
Brandenburgische Str. 17 (Wilmersdorf)
The speciality for those with a sweet tooth is the bitter chocolate. Everything made by the small family business is available here, including full-cream milk chocolate pralines that taste bitter because they have so much cocoa in them.

► **Fassbender & Rausch**
Charlottenstr. 60 (Mitte)
Europe's largest chocolate shop

► **Galeries Lafayette**
Friedrichstr. Quartier 207 (Mitte)
Delicatessen with products from all over the world

► **KaDeWe**
Tauentzienstr. 21 – 24, 6th floor (Schöneberg)
A temple to consumption with the biggest delicatessen section in Europe, including 1300 cheeses alone, plus 1200 types of sausage and ham, 2400 wines – and many counters where shoppers can sample the produce

► **Kadó**
Graefestr. 75 (Kreuzberg)
400 kinds of liquorice with unbelievable flavours, sourced from Lapland to Sicily. The house flavour is ginger liquorice.

► **Königsberger Marzipan**
Pestalozzistr. 54a (Charlottenburg)
Marzipan from Lübeck is famous
– but tea candy from Königsberg?

DESIGN AND FITTINGS

► **Art + Industry**
Bleibtreustr. 40 (Charlottenb.)
Furniture, lamps, and arts and
crafts of the 20th century

► **Berlinomat**
Frankfurter Allee 89
(Friedrichshain)
About 125 Berlin designers exhibit
their fashion, furniture, jewellery
and product design creations here.
Everything from postcards to so-
fas, all made in Berlin

► **Gipsformerei**
Sophie-Charlotte-Str. 17 – 18
(Charlottenburg)
6500 plaster castings and replicas
mainly of objects from the Berlin
museums are exhibited for sale

► **Leinenkontor**
Tucholskystr. 22 (Mitte)
Finest linen, not just for tailors but
also for tablecloths, walls and floors

► **Linkshänderr**
Schmargendorfer Str. 34 (Steglitz)
Everything for left-handers: scis-
sors, writing implements, musical
instruments, kitchen utensils ...

► **Make Design**
Hackesche Höfe, Hof V (Mitte)
Everything to do with the legen-
dary East German traffic light
Ampelmännchen

► **Russische Samoware H. Amann**
Marburger Str. 5 (Charlottenburg)
Real Russian samovars, antique
and new

► **Stilwerk**
Kantstr. 17 (Charlottenburg)
57 shops on five floors displaying
layouts and designs for rich tastes
and well-stocked wallets

FASHION AND ACCESSORIES

► **Betty Bund**
Oderberger Str.53 (Pankow) and
Hackesche Höfe (Hof 3, Mitte)
Futuristic fashion

► **Berliner Klamotten**
Hackesche Höfe (Mitte)
The work of Berlin designers in a
raw factory atmosphere

► **Department Store 206**
Friedrichstr. 71 (Mitte)
Fashion plus other fine and expensive items, but it's OK just to
look and admire

► **Falbala Antikmode**
Knaackstr. 43 (Prenzl. Berg)
Fashion from 1860 to 1970

► **Filippa K**
Alte Schönhauser Str. 11 (Mitte)
Filippa Knutsson from Stockholm
presents understated Scandinavian
fashion with a remarkable attention to detail in her flagship store

► **Firma**
Mulackstr. 1 (Mitte)
One of Berlin's most successful
labels, originally for men, now for
women too

► **Hautnah**
Uhlandstr. 170 (Charlottenburg)
Underwear for the lady and the
gentleman, including exclusive
and daring items

► **Herr von Eden**
Alte Schönhauser Str. 14 (Mitte)

The door bell says it all: this is not a place for casual browsing. High-class modern fashion for men in the tradition of British gentlemen's outfitters

► Hut up
Oranienburger Str. 32 (Mitte)
From a selection of trilbies to the extremes of the fashion spectrum. Attractive and unusual hats at unusually high prices

► Ic!Berlin
Oranienburger Str. 32 (Mitte)
Internationally successful designers of eye-glasses work and sell in Berlin. Celebrities worldwide go for the spectacle hinge system used here – and the cool sunglasses

► Just for the Boys
Raumerstr. 28 (Prenzl. Berg)
Exclusive second-hand shop for suit-wearers

► Kaufhaus Schrill
Bleibtreustr. 46 (Charlottenburg)
Its name effectively conveys the vivid nature nature of its wares. from wigs to socks and sunglasses, it purveys anything that looks wild and kooky.

► Kleidzeitlos
Rosenthaler Str. 37 (Mitte)
The finest materials, reserved colours and soft contours are the distinctive features of this label.

► Lala Berlin
Mulackstr. 7 (Mitte)
Delicate colours, soft textiles, pullovers, shirts, dresses, silk, Egyptian cotton, mohair

► Maassenzehn
Maassenstr. 10

Branded jeans with minor faults in Schöneberg

► Melrose
Walter-Benjamin-Platz 1 (Charlottenburg)
Luxury brands from all round the world – second-hand

► Respectmen
Neue Schönhauser Str. 14 (Mitte)
Designer label that is both chic and suitable for business wear. Other labels are also represented in the shop. Not far away are two other shops called Respectwomen and Respectless.

► Stoffwechsel
Oranienstr. 32 (Kreuzberg)
Chic streetwear

► to die for
Neue Schönhauser Str. 10 (Mitte)
Beautiful fashions »to die for« from a Berliner label

JEWELLERY

► Perlenatelier
Pariser Str. 44 (Wilmersdorf)
Farmed pearls competing with glittering jewellery

► Rio
Bleibtreustr. 52 (Charlottenburg)
Well-known fashion jewellery by designer Barbara Kranz

► Schmuckwerk
Hackesche Höfe, Hof 4 (Mitte)
Fine materials for modern jewellery design

► Schwermetall
Winterfeldtstr. 50 (Schöneberg)
Astrid Stenzel is famous for designing the gay and lesbian film prize, but she can do much more,

making jewellery that is both playful and austere.

▶ **Up-Arts**
Goltzstr. 12 (Schöneberg)
Ethnic jewellery and tribal arts from Asia und Oceania

▶ **Zeitmesser 2000**
Gabriel-Max-Str. 20 (Friedrichshain)
From dignified outfits to futuristic wardrobes across the ages

KITCHEN UTENSILS

▶ **Küchenladen**
Knesebeckstr. 26 (Charlottenburg)
Kitchen implements for both professional and hobby cooks

SHOES

▶ **Barfuss oder Lackschuh**
Oranienburger Str. 89 (Mitte)
Trendy footwear for the brand-aware

▶ **Bleibgrün**
Bleibtreustr. 29 (Charlottenburg)
From evening wear to kooky stuff, almost too good to actually wear

▶ **New Shoes im Steinbruch**
Kurfürstendamm 237 (Charlottenburg)
Includes platform soles nearly 30cm/1ft high as well as other off-beat footwear for partygoers

▶ **Luccico**
Neue Schönhauser Str. 18 (Mitte)
Classical or bold, this Italian shoemaker guarantees »shoes for a lifetime«.

▶ **Riccardo Cartillone**
Savignyplatz 5 (Charlottenburg)
Italian shoes, classically elegant and smart

▶ **Zeha Flagship Store**
Kurfürstendamm 188 – 189 (Charlottenburg)
A GDR brand of sports shoes that has been revived

▶ **Trippen**
Hackesche Höfe, Hof 4 (Mitte)
Hand-made and off-beat

FLEA MARKETS

▶ **Flohmarkt am Arkonaplatz**
(Prenzlauer Berg)
U-Bahn: Eberswalder Str. (U 2)
Sat and Sun 10am – 4pm
Family atmosphere

▶ **Hallentrödelmarkt**
Eichenstr. 4, entered via Puschkinallee (Treptow)
S-Bahn: Treptower Park
Sat and Sun 10am – 6pm
For the bargain hunter

▶ **Kunst- und Flohmarkt am 17. Juni**
Art fair and flea market on Strasse des 17. Juni, near to Tiergarten S-Bahn station
Sat and Sun 11am – 5pm
Well established but sometimes high prices

▶ **Kunst- und Nostalgiemarkt**
Art fair and nostalgia market on the corner of Am Kupfergraben and Georgenstr. In front of the Museumsinsel (Mitte)
S-Bahn: Hackescher Markt
Sat and Sun 11am – 5pm
Includes Berlin's biggest book market

▶ **Nordberliner Antik-, Kunst und Sammlermarkt**
Buddestr. 2 – 4, in what was formerly a French military railway station

U-Bahn: Alt-Tegel (U 6)
Sat and Sun 10am – 5pm
High-priced art and antiques

▶ **Trendmafia Kreativmarkt**
Revaler Str. 99 (Hall 40 on the
RAW site; Friedrichshain)
S/U-Bahn: Warschauer Str. (S 3,
S 5, S 75, S 9, U 6)
First Saturday in the month
Fashion, jewellery, design by new
talents

MARKET HALLS

▶ **Arminius-Markthalle**
Arminiusstr. 2 (Moabit)
Mon – Fri 7.30am – 7pm,
Sat closes 2pm
U-Bahn: Turmstr. (U 9)
The market hall, built in 1891 and
now a listed building, houses a
rich selection from foodstuffs to
bootlaces.

▶ **Eisenbahn-Markthalle**
Eisenbahnstr. 42 – 43
(Kreuzberg)
Mon – Fri 7.30am 7pm,
Sat closes 2pm
U-Bahn: Görlitzer Bahnhof
(U 1, U 15, U 12)
Also opened in 1891

▶ **Marheineke-Markthalle**
Marheinekeplatz 15 (Kreuzberg)
Mon – Fri 7.30am – 7pm, Sat
closes 2pm;
U-Bahn: Gneisenaustr. (U 7)

The newest of Berlin's old market
halls opened in 1892.

MARKETS

▶ **Kennedyplatz**
(Schöneberg)
U-Bahn: Rath. Schöneberg (U 4)
Tue and Fri 8am – 1pm
Fresh fruit and vegetables, meat –
and books as well

▶ **Kollwitzplatz**
(Prenzlauer Berg)
U-Bahn: Senefelder Platz (U2)
Thu 12 noon – 7pm, Sat 9am – 4pm
Berlin's nicest, finest, but most
expensive market with a guaranteed
organic market to boot

▶ **Winterfeldtplatz**
(Schöneberg)
U-Bahn: Nollendorfplatz
(U 1, U 15, U 12, U 4)
Wed 7am – 1.30pm, Sat 8am – 2pm
The largest weekly market in
Berlin is also a popular place to
meet as it is surrounded by nice
shops and inviting cafés.

▶ **»Türkenmarkt«**
Maybachufer (Neukölln)
U-Bahn: Kottbuser Tor:
(U 1, U 15, U 12, U 8)
Tue and Fri 9am – 6.30pm
Exotic delights and aromatic spices
create an oriental atmosphere at
the Turkish market by the
Landwehrkanal.

Sports and Outdoors

The sporting highlights in the city are the Six Day Race in January,   Spectator sports
the German cup final in May, a long distance regatta in the autumn
and the Berlin marathon in September.

▶ SPORTS

BASKETBALL

▶ O2-World
Am Ostbahnhof (Friedrichshain)
Tel. (0 18 05) 57 00 11
www.albaberlin.de
S-Bahn: Ostbahnhof (S 3, S 5, S 7,
S 75, S 9)
New arena at the Ostbahnhof
station for the ALBA Berlin club

CLIMBING

▶ Magic Mountain
Böttgerstr. 20–26 (Wedding)
U-Bahn: Gesundbrunnen (U 8)
www.magicmountain.de
Europe's biggest climbing arena,
with 200 routes of different levels
of difficulty, 60 top ropes, spa area

CYCLING

▶ Berlin Arena (Velodrom)
Am Falkplatz
(Prenzlauer Berg)
Tel. 44 30 45
www.velodrom.de
S-Bahn: Landsberger Allee
(S 8, S 10, S 85, S 86)

FOOTBALL/ATHLETICS

▶ Olympic Stadium
Olympischer Platz 3
(Charlottenburg)
Ticket service:
Tel. (0 18 05) 43 78 42
S-/U-Bahn: Olympiastadion
(S 5, S 75, U 2)
Home of the Hertha BSC football
club

▶ Friedrich-Ludwig-Jahn-Sportpark
Cantianstr. 24 (Prenzlauer Berg)
Tel. 44 30 37 00
U-Bahn: Eberswalder Str. (U 2)
Association football, American
football, athletics

▶ Mommsenstadion
Waldschulallee 34
(Charlottenburg)
Tel. 34 30 65 20
S-Bahn: Messe Süd (S 5, S 75)
Association football, American
football, athletics

▶ Stadion Alte Försterei
Hämmerlingstr. 80 – 88
(Köpenick)
Ticket service: tel. 65 66 88-0
S-Bahn: Köpenick (S 3)
Home ground for the 1. FC Union
football club

GOLF

▶ Golfverband Berlin-Brandenburg
Forststr. 34 (Steglitz)
D-12163 Berlin, tel. 8 23 66 09
www.gvbb.de

▶ Berliner Golfclub Gatow
Kladower Damm 182 – 288
(Spandau)
Tel. 3 65 00 06

▶ Golf- u. Landclub Berlin-Wannsee
Golfweg 22,
Tel. 8 06 70 60
(Zehlendorf)
www.glcbw.de

HORSE RACING

▶ Trabrennbahn Mariendorf
Mariendorfer Damm 222 – 298
(Tempelhof)
Tel. 7 40 12 12
U-Bahn: Alt-Mariendorf (U 6),
then by 176 or 179 bus

▶ Trabrennbahn Karlshorst (trap racing circuit)
Treskowallee 129 (Köpenick)

At the races in Mariendorf. Who's that coming up on the inside?

Tel. 50 01 71 21
S-Bahn: Karlshorst (S 3)

▶ **Galopprennbahn Hoppegarten
(horse racing circuit)**
Goetheallee 1
(Dahlwitz-Hoppegarten)
Tel. (0 33 42) 389 30
www.galopprennbahn-
hoppegarten.de
S-Bahn: Hoppegarten (S 5)

ICE HOCKEY/
FIGURE SKATING

▶ **O2-World**
Address and transport as above
Ticket service: tel. 97 18 40 40
www.eisbaeren.de

SWIMMING

▶ **Badeschiff**
Eichenstr. 4

(on the grounds of the arena in
Treptow)
U-Bahn: Schlesisches Tor (U1)
Spree swimming resort in summer
months with beach on the river
bank; spartan sauna in winter with
a small terrace outside
10am – midnight daily

▶ **Lakes for bathing**
Dahme, Grosser Müggelsee,
Grunewaldsee, Halensee, Havel,
Krumme Lanke, Langer See, Or-
ankesee, Plötzensee, Schlachtensee, Tegeler See, Wannsee,
Weissensee and Ziegeleisee
The Wannsee and Müggelsee
bathing beaches are particularly
popular. Practically every suburb
has its own outdoor or indoor
swimming pools and the following
are especially nice:

▶ Stadtbad Charlottenburg
Alte Halle
Krumme Str. 10
Tel. 34 38 38 60
U-Bahn: Deutsche Oper (U 2),
Richard-Wagner-Platz (U 7)
Marvellous Art Nouveau building

▶ Stadtbad Mitte
Gartenstr. 5
Tel. 30 88 09 10
S-Bahn: Nordbahnhof (S 1, S 2)
Unique glass architecture

▶ Stadtbad Neukölln
Ganghoferstr. 5
Tel. 68 24 98 12
U-Bahn: Rath. Neukölln (U 7)
Nostalgic swimming pool built in
1914

SKATEBOARDING/ INLINE SKATING

Alongside the conventional Berlin
Marathon in September, a skate
marathon is also held. There is
also a skaters' half-marathon in
April. Practically every suburb has
its own facilities for skateboarding
or inline skating. The following
are among the examples:

▶ fo(u)r wheels
Saarbrücker Str. 36 – 38
(Prenzlauer Berg)

Tel. 2 64 45 00
U-Bahn: Senefelder Platz (U 2)

▶ Kickstone
Rosenthaler Str. 51 (Mitte)
Tel. 28 09 52 91
S-Bahn: Hackescher Markt (S 3,
S 5, S 9, S 75)

▶ Kronprinzessinnenweg
Zehlendorf
S-Bahn: Nikolassee
Only walkers and joggers, no cars
on a length of almost 4km/2.5mi

▶ Skate In
Schichauweg
(Lichtenrade)
Tel. 7 21 50 70
S-Bahn: Schichauweg (S 2)

TENNIS/SQUASH

▶ Squash 2000
Persiusstr. 7a
(Friedrichshain)
Tel. 2 91 29 11
S-Bahn: Ostkreuz (S 3, S 5, S 7)

▶ Tennisclub LTTC Rot-Weiss e.V.
Gottfried-von-Cramm- Weg
47 – 55
(Grunewald)
Tel. 8 95 75 50
Also promotes the Women's German Open tournament

Theatre · Music · Concerts

Berlin's theatres   Directors and playwrights like Erwin Piscator, Max Reinhardt and
Bertolt Brecht made Berlin's reputation as a place for modern, experimental theatre. Nowadays the theatre scene comprises renowned
state-run theatres alongside many private establishments that often
have a very good reputation of their own, as well as numerous small
theatre groups away from the mainstream.

⊙ INFORMATION AND ADDRESSES

TICKETS IN ADVANCE

► **Berliner Theater und Konzertkasse BTK**
Spreeufer 6, Nikolaiviertel
Tel. 2 41 46 87
www.btk-berlin.de

► **Galeria Kaufhof**
Theaterkasse
Alexanderplatz
Tel. 24 74 33 27

► **Hekticket am Zoo/ am Alex**
Hardenbergstr. 29d
(in the Foyer of the Deutsche Bank)
Tel. 2 30 99 30
Alexanderplatz 8 at Articket
Tel. 24 31 24 31
www.hekticket.de
Sometimes tickets for shows the same day can be obtained here at half price.

► **Kartenservice Velomax**
Am Falkplatz (Max-Schmeling-Halle), tel. 44 30 44 30
www.velomax.de

► **Showtime GmbH**
Free hotline
Tel. 80 60 29 29
www.showtimetickets.de
Seven branches in department stores for information and ticket collection, including in KaDeWe, Karstadt in Tegel and Wertheim Kurfürstendamm and Steglitz

► **Theater- und Konzertkasse**
S-Bahnhof Alexanderplatz
Tel. 24 72 16

BERLIN THEATRES

► **Berliner Ensemble**
Theater am Schiffbauerdamm
Bertolt-Brecht-Platz 1 (Mitte)
Tel. 2 84 08-1 55 (tickets)
Tel. -1 53 (information, tours)
www.berliner-ensemble.de
S-Bahn/U-Bahn: Friedrichstrasse
Modern plays, contemporary and historical theatre pieces and works by Brecht

► **Berliner Kriminaltheater**
Palisadenstr. 48 (Friedrichshain)
Tel. 47997488
www.kriminaltheater.de
U-Bahn: Weberwiese (U 5)

► **Deutsches Theater und Kammerspiele**
Schumannstr. 13a (Mitte)
Tel. 2 84 41-3 47
www.deutschestheater.de
Ticket office for the Deutsches Theater, tel. 2 25
Ticket office for the Kammerspiele, tel. -2 26
www.deutsches-theater.berlin.net;
U-Bahn: Oranienburger Tor (U 6)
Classical and modern plays

► **F40-English Theatre Berlin**
Fidicinstr. 40 (Kreuzberg)
Tel. 6 91 12 11
www.thefriends.de
U-Bahn: Platz der Luftbrücke (U 6)
English-speaking theatre

► **HAU 1 (Hebbel am Ufer)**
Stresemannstr. 29 (Kreuzberg)
Tel. 25 90 04 27
www.hebbel-theater.de
U-Bahn: Hallesches Tor (U 1, U 15, U 12, U 6)
Theatre, dance, music

▶ **HAU 2**
Hallesches Ufer 32 (Kreuzberg)
Tel. see above
U-Bahn: Möckernbrücke
(U 1, U 7)

▶ **HAU 3**
Tempelhofer Ufer 32 (Kreuzberg)
Tel. see above
U-Bahn: Möckernbrücke
(U 1, U 7)

▶ **Kleines Theater**
Südwestkorso 64 (Wilmersdorf)
Tel. 8 21 20 21
www.kleines-theater.de
U-Bahn: Friedrich-Wilhelm-Platz
(U 9)
Modern comedy, cabaret

▶ **Maxim-Gorki-Theater and Gorki-Studio**
Am Festungsgraben 2 or behind
Giesshaus (Mitte)
Tel. 20 22 11 15
www.gorki.de
S-Bahn: Hackescher Markt
Contemporary drama.

▶ **Ratibortheater**
Cuvrystr. 20 (Kreuzberg)
Tel. 6 18 61 99
www.ratibortheater.de
U-Bahn: Schlesisches Tor
(U 1)
Programme includes improvizational theatre.

▶ **Renaissance-Theater**
Knesebeckstr. 100
(Charlottenburg)
Tel. 3 12 42 02
www.renaissance-theater.de
S-Bahn: Savignyplatz
Plays and comedy

▶ **Schaubühne am Lehniner Platz**
Kurfürstendamm 153
(Charlottenburg)
Tel. 89 00 23
www.schaubuehne.de
U-Bahn: Adenauerplatz (U 7)
Modern plays and classical drama

▶ **Schlossparktheater**
Schlossstr. 48 (Steglitz)
U-Bahn: Rathaus Steglitz (U 9)
Tel. 78 95 66 71 00
www.schlossparktheater.de
After years of neglect the theatre
has come to life again under the
direction of a popular German
comedian, Dieter Hallervorden –
serious drama is staged with
renowned actors in addition to
comedy.

▶ **Sophiensäle**
Sophienstr. 18 (Mitte)
Tel. 2835266
S-Bahn: Hackescher Markt
www.sophiensaele.com
Venue for avant garde theatre
performances

▶ **Theater 89**
Torstr. 216 (Mitte)
Tel. 2 82 46 56
www.theater89.de
U-Bahn: Rosa-Luxemburg-Platz
(U 2)
Independent theatre founded in
1989

▶ **Tribüne**
Otto-Suhr-Allee 18
(Charlottenburg)
Tel. 3 41 26 00
www.tribuene-berlin.de
U-Bahn: Ernst-Reuter-Platz (U 2)
Contemporary works, people's
theatre, musical plays

▶ **Vaganten-Bühne**
Kantstr. 12a
(Charlottenburg)

Provocative works on stage: the Volksbühne

Tel. 3 12 45 29; S-/U-Bahn:
Zoologischer Garten
Modern theatre

▶ **Volksbühne am
Rosa-Luxemburg-Platz**
Rosa-Luxemburg-Platz (Mitte)
Tel. 2 40 65-777
www.volksbuehne-berlin.de
U Bahn: Rosa-Luxemburg-Platz
(U 2)
Provocative works

EVENT VENUES

▶ **Admiralspalast**
Friedrichstr. 101-102
(Mitte)
Tel. 47997499
www.admiralspalast.de
S-/U-Bahn: Friedrichstr.
Theatre, concerts, cabaret

▶ **Arena**
Eichenstr. 4
(Treptow)
Tel. 5 33 73 33
www.arena-berlin.de;
S-Bahn: Treptower Park
Theatre, concerts, dance and cin-
ema events in a former bus depot

▶ **Columbiahalle**
Columbiadamm 9-11
(Tempelhof)
Tel. 69812828
U-Bahn: Platz der Luftbrücke
(U 6)

▶ **Deutschlandhalle**
Messedamm 26
(Charlottenburg)
Tel. 30 38-0
www.deutschlandhalle.de
S-Bahn: Messe Süd

▶ **Haus der Kulturen der Welt**
John-Foster-Dulles-Allee 10
(Tiergarten)
Tel. 3 97 87-0
www.hkw.de
Bus: 100
Theatre and concerts, exhibitions,
lecture series; open-air festivals in
summer

▶ **Kulturbrauerei**
Sredzkistr. 35
(Prenzlauer. Berg)
Tel. 4 43 15-1 00
www.kulturbrauerei.de

In the Kulturbrauerei

U-Bahn: Eberswalder Str. (U 2)
Top address for readings, exhibitions, music and theatre

► **Max-Schmeling-Halle**
Am Falkplatz (Prenzlauer Berg)
Tel. 44304430 S-Bahn:
Schönhauser Allee

► **O2 World**
Am Ostbahnhof (Friedrichshain)
Tel. (0 18 03) 20 60 70
www.o2world.de
S/U-Bahn: Warschauer Str. (S 3,
S 5, S 7, S 75 ,U 1)
All kinds of big events

► **Radialsystem V**
Holzmarktstr. 33
(Friedrichshain)
Tel. 288788588
www.radialsystem.de
S-Bahn: Ostbahnhof
Contemporary dance, old music,
classical music and pop in a
former pumping hall

► **Tacheles**
International art venue
Oranienburger Str. 54 – 56
(Mitte)
Tel. 28 09 68 85
U-Bahn: Oranienburger Tor (U 6)
Events and productions in all

spheres of art

► **Tempodrom**
Möckernstr. 10
(Kreuzberg)
Tel. 69 53 3885
www.tempodrom.de
S-Bahn: Anhalter Bahnhof
Legendary venue that has been
resurrected at Anhalter Bahnhof.
Classical and rock concerts, musicals and circus performances;
part of the »Heimatklänge« summer festival

► **Tipi**
Marquee on Grosse Querallee next
to the Kanzleramt (Mitte)
Tel. 0180/3279358
www.tipi-da-zelt.de
Pleasant, sizeable subsidiary of Bar
jeder Vernunft

► **UFA-Fabrik**
Viktoriastr. 10 – 18
(Tempelhof)
Tel. 75 50 30
www.ufafabrik.de
U-Bahn: Ullsteinstrasse (U 6)
Variety, cabaret, music, circus;
culture centre

► **Waldbühne**
Glockenturmstr. 1

(Charlottenburg)
Tel. 23 08 82 30
S-Bahn: Pichelsberg

**CHILDREN´S AND
YOUTH THEATRE**
►p.88

CABARET

► **BKA – Berliner Kabarett
Anstalt**
Mehringdamm 34 (Kreuzberg)
U-Bahn: Mehringdamm and
Luftschloss, Schlossplatz (Mitte)
S-Bahn: Hackescher Markt
Tel. 2 02 20 07
www.bka-theater.de
Cabaret, chansons, tango

► **Distel**
Friedrichstr. 101 (Mitte)
Tel. 2 04 47 04
www.distel-berlin.de S-/U-Bahn:
Friedrichstrasse

► **Kabarett Kartoon**
Kochstr. (Axel-Springer-Passage,
Kreuzberg)
Tel. 25 89 87 20
www.kabarettkartoon.de
U-Bahn: Kochstr. (U 6)

► **Mehringhoftheater**
Gneisenaustr. 2a
(Kreuzberg)
Tel. 6 91 50 99
www.mehringhoftheater.de
U-Bahn: Gneisenaustrasse (U 7)

► **Quatsch Comedy Club**
Friedrichstadtpalast, basement
(Mitte)
Tel. 53026262
www.quatschcomedyclub.de

► **Die Stachelschweine**
Europa-Center
(Charlottenburg)

Tel. 2 61 47 95
www.die-stachelschweine.de
S-/U-Bahn: Zoolog. Garten

► **Die Wühlmäuse**
Pommernallee 2 – 4
(Charlottenburg)
Tel. 306730-11
www.wuehlmaeuse.de
U-Bahn: Theodor-Heuss-Platz
(U 2)

PUPPET THEATRE

► **Puppentheater
für Kinder**
►Children in Berlin

► **Ostendtheater**
Boxhagener Str. 99
(Friedrichshain)
Tel. 70 71 96 56
www.ostendtheater.de
U-Bahn: Frankfurter Tor (U 5)

► **Puppentheater auf der
Zitadelle**
Zitadelle Spandau
Tel. 3 35 37 94
www.puppentheater-zitadelle.de
U-Bahn: Zitadelle (U 7)

► **Die Schaubude**
Greifswalder Str. 81 – 84
(Prenzlauer Berg)
Tel. 4 23 43 14
www.schaubude-berlin.de
S-Bahn: Greifswalder Strasse

REVUE/VARIETY

► **Bar jeder Vernunft**
Schaperstr. 24
(Wilmersdorf)
Tel. 8 83 15 82
www.bar-jeder-vernunft.de
U-Bahn: Spichernstr. (U 1, U 7)
Cabaret and chanson under a tent-
like mirror-glass roof

► Bluemax Theater
Marlene-Dietrich-Platz 4
(Tiergarten)
Tel. 018054444
www.bluemangroup.de
U-/S-Bahn: Potsdamer Platz

► Chamäleon Varieté
Rosenthaler Str. 40/41 (Mitte)
Tel. 4 00 05 90
www.chamaeleonberlin.de
S-Bahn: Hackescher Markt

► Chez Nous
Marburger Str. 14
(Charlottenburg)
Tel. 2 13 18 10
U-Bahn: Kurfürstendamm
(U 9, U 15)
Drag acts

► Friedrichstadtpalast
Friedrichstr. 107 (Mitte)
Tel. 23 26 23 26
www.friedrichstadtpalast.de
S-/U-Bahn: Friedrichstrasse
Europe's biggest revue theatre has
classical large-scale revue shows
just like in the good old days, with
men in evening dress and long-
legged dancing girls

► Scheinbar
Monumentenstr. 9 (Schöneberg)
Tel. 7 84 55 39
www.scheinbar.de
S-Bahn/U-Bahn: Yorck-/
Grossgörschenstrasse
From Wednesdays to Saturdays the
public can join in

► La Vie en Rose
In the US training centre at Tempelhof Airport (to the left of the
main entrance)
Tel. 69 51 30 00;
www.lavieenrose-berlin.de
U-Bahn: Pl. der Luftbrücke (U 6)

► Zaubertheater Igor Jedlin
Roscherstr. 7 (Charl.)
Tel. 3 23 37 77
www.zaubertheater.de
S-Bahn: Charlottenburg

OPERA/OPERETTA/BALLET

► Deutsche Oper Berlin
Bismarckstr. 35 (Charlottenburg)
Tel. 0700 67 37 23 75 46
Kartenansagedienst:
Tel. 3 41 02 49
www.deutscheoperberlin.de
U-Bahn: Deutsche Oper (U 2)

► Staatsoper Unter den Linden
Unter den Linden 5-7
(Mitte)
Tel. 2 03 54-5 55, fax -4 83
S-Bahn: Hackescher Markt
www.staatsoper-berlin.de
Closed for refurbishment since
2010, performances are held in
Haus der Festspiele, Bismarck-
strasse

► Hebbel am Ufer (HAU)
Along with the Berliner Kammer-
oper and the Zeitgenössischer
Oper Berlin (contemporary opera
house; dance and music theatre)
►Theatre

► Komische Oper Berlin
Behrenstr. 55 – 57
(Mitte)
Tel. 47997400
www.komische-oper-berlin.de
U-Bahn: Französ. Str. (U 6)

► Neuköllner Oper
Karl-Marx-Str. 131 – 133
(Neukölln)
Tel. 68 89 07-77, fax -89
Station: Karl-Marx-Str. (U 7)
Experimental productions

MUSICALS/REVUES/DANCE

► Friedrichstadtpalast
Friedrichstr. 107 (Mitte)
Information: tel. 23 26 22 03
Tickets: tel. 23 26 23 26
Fax 23 26 23 23
www.friedrichstadtpalast.de
S-/U-Bahn: Friedrichstrasse

► Theater am Potsdamer Platz
Marlene-Dietrich-Platz 1
(Tiergarten)
Tel. 25 92 90
www.stage.de
S-/U-Bahn: Potsdamer Platz

► Tanzfabrik Berlin
Möckernstr. 68 (Kreuzberg)
Tel. 7 86 58 61
Fax 78 89 53 42
www.tanzfabrik-berlin.de
U-Bahn: Möckernbrücke
(U 1, U 15, U 7)

► Theater des Westens
Kantstr. 12 (Charlottenburg)
Tel. 3 19 03-0, Fax -107
Ticket hotline: 01805 4444
www.theater-des-westens.de
S-Bahn/U Bahn: Zoolog. Garten

CONCERTS (classical)

► Akademie der Künste
Haus 1: Hanseatenweg 10
(Mitte)
Tel. 200571000
www.akd.de
S-Bahn: Bellevue

► Grosser Sendesaal des SFB
Haus des Rundfunks
Masurenallee 8 – 14
(Charlottenburg)
Tel. 30 31-0
U-Bahn: Kaiserdamm (U 2)
Main auditorium of the Berlin
public broadcasting company

► Herrenhaus Domäne Dahlem
Königin-Luise-Str. 49
(Zehlendorf)
Tel. 8 32 50 00
Fax 8 31 63 82
www.domaene-dahlem.de
U-Bahn: Dahlem-Dorf (U 1)

► Konzerthaus Berlin
Gendarmenmarkt (Mitte)
Tel. 2 03 09-21 01/21 02
www.konzerthaus.de
U-Bahn: Französ. Str. (U 6)

► Philharmonie
Herbert-von-Karajan-Str. 1
(Tiergarten)
Tel. 2 54 88-0
www.berliner-philharmoniker.de
S-Bahn/U-Bahn: Potsdamer Platz

► Schloss Friedrichsfelde
Am Tierpark 125 (Lichtenberg)
Tel. 5 13 81 42
U-Bahn: Tierpark (U 5)

► Urania Berlin
Kleiststr. 13 (Schöneberg)
Tel. 2 18 90 91;
U-Bahn: Wittenbergplatz
(U 1, U 15)

CHURCH CONCERTS

► Berliner Dom
Am Lustgarten (Mitte)
Konzertkasse: Portal 9
Tel. 2 02 69-136
www.berlinerdom.de
S-Bahn: Hackescher Markt
Small organ recitals on weekdays at
noon and 6pm, concerts Sat 6pm

► Choir and organ recitals in St Hedwig's Cathedral
St Hedwig's Cathedral (Mitte)
Tel. 2 03 48 26
www.hedwigschor-berlin.de
S-Bahn: Hackescher Markt

Time

Berlin is in the central European time zone (CET), one hour ahead of Greenwich Mean Time. For the summer months from the end of March to the end of October European summer time is used (CEST = CET+1 hour).

Tours and Guides

Bus tours
BVG services 100,
200 ►

One of the cheapest ways of seeing the city is to catch its major sights by bus on services 100 or 200 run by the local bus authority, the BVG, between Bahnhof Zoo and Alexanderplatz or Prenzlauer Berg – although there is no tour guide of course. One very popular service also provided by the BVG is the Zille Express, an hourly tour bus (German and English) with nine stops, where it is possible to get on and off. The vehicle is a faithful co-py of a »Robert-Kaufmann-Wagen« (open-topped double-decker bus), such as plied routes in Berlin from 1916 to 1928. The guides and dri-vers wear historic uniforms. Main stop: Marlene-Dietrich-Platz; from May to September daily between 10am und 5pm every 45 minutes, also in the six months of winter on Sat, Sun and holidays. A tour on one of the BVG's bright red Top-

> ! *Baedeker* TIP
>
> **Berlin from the back door**
> Admittedly, this is only for people with time and a penchant for public transport, but a trip around Berlin on the S-Bahn ring services S 41 or S 42 slowly opens up a hidden world with a view into many of Berlin's backyards.

Tour buses with their open top deck lasts about two and a half hours in all, although you can get on and off at any stop. Main stop: Kur-fürstendamm 18 (next to the former Café Kranzler); from Easter un-til end of October, between 10am and 5pm daily, every 30 to 60 minutes.

CityCircle-
Sightseeing

The bus companies BBS, Berolina, BVB and Severin + Kühn have all got together to provide a joint service called CityCircle-Sightseeing, a two-hour guided tour of the key sights with 14 stops. This also al-lows for getting on and off at any stop, so that the journey can be broken and later resumed at any time. Buses run every 15 minutes (April to October) or 30 minutes (November to March) from any stop between 10am and 4pm. Tickets can be obtained on board the bus, from the bus companies or in hotels.

Boat trips

Boat trips are an excellent and relaxing way to see Berlin from a completely different angle. Most operators offer historic trips mostly lasting an hour as well as so-called moonlight or dance trips.

SIGHTSEEING

BUS TOURS/S-BAHN

► BVG Berliner Verkehrsbetriebe
Departure: Kurfürstendamm 18
(Café Kranzler)
Tel. 25 62 65 70
It is possible to spend all day on
one of the red open-top double-
deckers or maybe to break the
journey to visit a museum or go
for a coffee. Live guide, not a
recorded commentary

► BBS Berliner Bären Stadtrundfahrt
Office: Seeburger Str. 19b
Departure: Rankestr. 35 (opposite
the Gedächtniskirche)
Tel. 35 19 52-70, fax -90

► Berolina
Office: Meinekestr. 3
Departure: Kurfürstendamm/
Corner of Meinekestrasse, Alex-
anderplatz/Forum Hotel
Tel. 88 56 80 30, fax 8 82 41 28

► BVB Bus-Verkehr-Berlin
Office: Kurfürstendamm 229
Departure: Kurfürstendamm 225
Tel. 6 83 89 10
Fax 68 38 91 50
CityCircle-Tour:
Tel. 88 68 37 11

► Severin + Kühn Berliner Stadtrundfahrt
Office and departure point:
Kurfürstendamm 216
Tel. 8 80 41 90, fax 8 82 56 18

► Kaibel and Erdmann
Berlin tours
Stubenrauchstr. 23A
Tel. 6 61 01 27, fax 6 62 98 98
kaibel-berlin@t-online.de

► Klaus Schölzel
Lübecker Str. 25
Tel. 3 95 97 99
Fax 3 95 94 52
Individual trips and guided tours
in Berlin and Potsdam

► Panorama S-Bahn
S-Bahn Berlin GmbH
Invalidenstr. 19
Tel. 29 74 38 62
www.s-bahn-berlin.de
On Saturdays and Sundays a one-
hour journey on the Panorama
S-Bahn from Ostbahnhof offers
some fascinating views.

► Skip
Uhlandstr. 162
Tel. 69 04 11-25, fax -24
www.skip-berlin.de
Tours to order, multiple foreign
languages

► Stadtrundfahrtbüro Berlin
Europa-Center, 15th floor
Tel. 2 61 20 01, fax 2 61 20 22
www.stadtrundfahrtbuero-
berlin.de
Bus, boat and combined trips

CYCLE TOURS

► Fahrradstation
Cycle routes through Berlin, also

featuring rickshaw rental (with driver of course) ►Transport

THEMED TOURS

► **art: berlin**
Oranienburger Str. 32
Tel. 28 09 63 90
Fax 28 09 63 91
artberlin@berlin.de
Art, culture and architecture

► **Frauentouren (women's tours)**
Sophienstr. 32, tel. 2 81 03 08
From Prussian queens to Berlin washerwomen

► **Gangart Berlin-Erkundungen**
Callandrellistr. 19
Tel. 32 70 37 83
www.berlinstreet.de/tipps/gangart
Tours of city districts

► **Go Art!**
Halle am Wasser, Invalidenstr. 50–51
Tel. 30 87 36 26, www.goart-berlin.de
Tours for art and fashion

► **Kultur Büro Berlin**
Malmöer Str. 6
Tel. 4 44 09 36, fax 4 44 09 39
www.stadtverfuehrung.de
Various and widespread topics

► **Alter Fritz (Frederick the Great)**
Tel. 45023874
www.koenig-friedrich.de
Guide Dr. Kappelt wears the garb of »Old Fritz«, Easter to Oct daily 2pm, 4pm, 6pm, 8pm from the Brandenburg Gate

► **Schöne Künste Exkursionen**
Dr. Susanne Oschmann
Grossgörschenstr. 18
Tel. 7 82 12 02

Trips through Berlin's music and theatre world

► **StattReisen Berlin**
Malplaquetstr. 5
Tel. 4 55 30 28, fax 45 80 00 03
www.stattreisen.berlin.de
Broad range of topics including the Berlin Wall

► **Unterwegs**
Samoastr. 7
Tel. 4 53 53 04
Jewish life in Berlin

BOAT TRIPS

► **Berliner Geschichtswerkstatt – Dampfergruppe (historic steamboats)**
Goltzstr. 49
Tel. 2 15 44 50, fax 2 15 44 12
www.berliner-geschichtswerkstatt.de
Departure: Märkisches Ufer at the Historic Docks

► **City-Schifffahrt H.G. Gabriel**
Dovestr. 1b
Tel. 3 45 77 83
www.cityschifffahrt.de
Departure: Karl-Liebknecht-Brücke (opposite Berlin Cathedral)

► **Reederei Dieter Hadynski**
Niederkirchnerstr. 35
Tel. 4 24 84 06
www.reederei-hadynski.de
Departure: south of the Friedrichsbrücke, diagonally opposite Berlin Cathedral

► **Reederei Riedel**
Tel. 693 46 46
www.reederei-riedel.de
Departs from Haus der Kulturen der Welt, Jannowitzbrücke, Alte Börse, Potsdamer Brück

► **Reederei Triebler**
Johannastr. 24
Tel. 3 31 54 14
www.reederei-triebler.de
Departure: Wannsee, Spandau-
Lindenufer

► **Reederei Bruno Winkler**
Mierendorffstr. 16
Tel. 3 49 95 95
www.reedereiwinkler.de
Departure: Schlossbrücke (next to
Schloss Charlottenburg), Haus der
Kulturen der Welt, Fried-
richsbrücke (Reichstagsufer)

► **Stern- und Kreisschifffahrt**
Puschkinallee 15
Tel. 5 36 36 00
www.sternundkreis.de
Departure: u.a. Jannowitzbrücke,
Nikolaiviertel, Schlossbrücke (next
to Schloss Charlottenburg)

► **In Potsdam:**
Weisse Flotte Potsdam
Tel. (03 31) 2 75 92-10, -20
Fax 29 10 90
Abfahrt: Lustgarten

► **Havel Dampfschifffahrt GmbH**
Tel. (03 31) 2 75 92 33
Fax 2 70 62 29
Departure: Lustgarten

AIR TOURS

► **Air Service Berlin CFH GmbH**
Schönefeld Airport
Tel. 53 21 53 21 (Tickethotline)
www.air-service-berlin.de
By sea plane from Treptow
Hy-Flyer from Zimmer-/
Wilhelmstr.

► **Airship Air Service**
Schönefeld Airport
Tel. 60 91 38 00
www.airship.de

Transport

Regional public transport in Berlin is very well organized so that most of the places to see are easily reached by such means. The Berliner Verkehrsbetriebe (BVG), Deutsche Bahn AG (DB), S-Bahn Berlin GmbH, Verkehrsbetriebe Potsdam GmbH (ViP) and various smaller transport companies from Berlin and its environs have been merged into the Verkehrsgemeinschaft Berlin-Brandenburg (VBB). The most important carriers of passengers are the S-Bahn, U-Bahn, trams or Metro services and buses.

Verkehrsgemeinschaft Berlin-Brandenburg (VBB)

There are three tariff zones: A is the innermost part of Berlin, enclosed by the S-Bahn ring. Zone B ends at the city limits of Berlin, while zone C includes the regions thereabouts. Normally an AB ticket will suffice for visitors to Berlin; but Schönefeld Airport is in zone C.

Tariff zones

Individual tickets and period tickets are available from most U-Bahn and S-Bahn stations, from ticket machines, on buses and trams, in tobacconists and drug stores.

Ticket sales

Tickets

Ordinary tickets are valid for two hours and only in one direction of travel (i.e. not valid for the return journey). Anyone making a journey of 3 stations or less on the S-Bahn or up to six stations on the U-Bahn or stops on the bus can buy a short journey ticket or »Kurzstreckenkarte«. Children travel free until their 7th birthday while between the ages of 7 and 14 they travel at a discount rate. There are tickets valid for 1 day, tourist offers for 48 and 72 hours as well as a transferrable ticket called an »Umweltkarte« (environment ticket), which is valid for one month.

Period tickets ►

R-Bahn

A total of 26 lines are operated by the DB as R-Bahn services along with 8 RegionalExpress lines that connect Berlin with outlying towns in Brandenburg.

S-Bahn

15 S-Bahn lines serve the city, some of them running 24 hours. Now that the inner city ring is in service, S-Bahn trains are once again a major public transport carrier.

U-Bahn

Nine U-Bahn lines operate on working days between 4am in the morning and 2am at night. At the weekends (Fri–Sun) they run around the clock (except for the U 4 service where there is a night bus replacement). Some U-Bahn stations have been beautifully restored. Among the nicest are the Art Nouveau stop at Wittenbergplatz (U 1, U 2, U 15) and the stations at Hausvogteiplatz, Märkisches Museum (U 2) and Brandenburger Tor (U 55).

Buses and trams

Trams run almost exclusively in the eastern part of Berlin. Countless bus services serve areas where no rail or tram access is available. The Zentrale Omnibusbahnhof, the central bus station for long-distance coaches, is located near the Funkturm, Messedamm 19. Most of the major routes with no U-bahn or S-Bahn link are served by trams and buses under the Metro-Linien banner that run for 20 hours a day, seven days a week at regular intervals. Metro line services are indicated by an **»M« in front of the service number**.

Metro lines ►

Cycle hire

Berlin offers no particular hindrance to cyclists and there are cycle paths alongside all the main roads. There are many cycle hire companies. A list of places from which bikes can be rented is available from the Allgemeiner Deutscher Fahrrad-Club (ADFC) of Berlin. 1700 socalled **Call Bikes** belonging to the Deutsche Bahn railway company are available in the city. They can be rented by telephone (phone number on the wheels). Payment is made by means of a credit card – no cash is needed.

Car rental

Branches of the major car rental companies are mostly found at the airports (► Airports) and there are some at the Hauptbahnhof and Ostbahnhof. Apart from the major firms, there is of course a wide range of smaller rental companies.

TRANSPORT INFORMATION

BVG

► **BVG price and route information**
Tel. 1 94 49 (24-hour service))
www.bvg.de
Pavilion at Bahnhof Zoo
Hardenbergplatz
6am – 10pm

► **Customer centres**
in the following stations: Alexanderplatz, Hauptbahnhof, Friedrichstrasse, Lichtenberg, Zoologischer Garten, Spandau, Potsdam Hauptbahnhof

► **Alexanderplatz Station**
5.30am – 8.30pm daily

► **S-Bahn Berlin**
Tel. 29 74 33 33
www.s-bahn-berlin.de

► **VBB**
Hardenbergplatz 2
Tel. 25 41 4141
www.vbbonline.de

► **Zentraler Omnibusbahnhof Berlin (central bus station)**
Messedamm 19
Tickets: Masurenallee 4 – 6
Tel. 3 02 53 61 (national),
3 11 02 21 (Europe)
www.zob-berlin.de

CYCLE HIRE

► **ADFC Landesverband Berlin**
Brunnenstr. 28,
D-10119 Berlin
Tel. 4 48 47 24, fax 44 34 05 20

► **DB Call Bikes**
1700 bicycles are available for hire in the city (phone numbers on the wheels, non-cash payment).

► **Fahrradstation**
(also including tours of the city and rickshaw taxis)
Leipziger Str. 56 (Mitte)
D-10117 Berlin
Tel. (0 18 05) 10 80 00
www.fahrradstation.de
Branches:
Auguststr. 29 (Mitte)
Tel. 22 50 80 70
Bergmannstr. 9 (Kreuzberg)
Tel. 2 15 15 66
Dorotheenstr. 30 (Mitte)
Tel. 28 38 48 48
Goethestr. 46 (Charlottenburg)
Tel. 93 95 27 57
Kollwitzstr. 56 (Prenzl. Berg)
Tel. 93 95 81 30
Leipziger Str. 56 (Mitte)
Tel. 66 64 91 80

► **Pedalpower Berlin**
Pfarrstr. 116 (Lichtenberg)
Tel. 5 55 80 98
Grossbeerenstr. 53 (Kreuzberg)
Tel. 78 99 19 39
www.pedalpower.de

► **City Rad Potsdam**
Bicycle rank at Potsdam station
D-14473 Potsdam
Tel. (03 31) 61 90 52 (May – Sept)

CAR RENTAL

► **AVIS**
Tel. (0 18 05) 55 77 55

► **Budget**
Tel. (0 18 05) 24 43 88

► **Europcar**
Tel. (0 18 05) 80 00

► **Hertz**
Tel. (0 18 05) 33 35 35

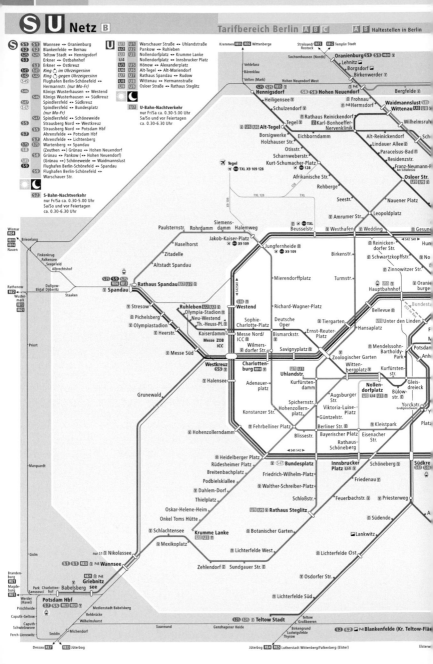

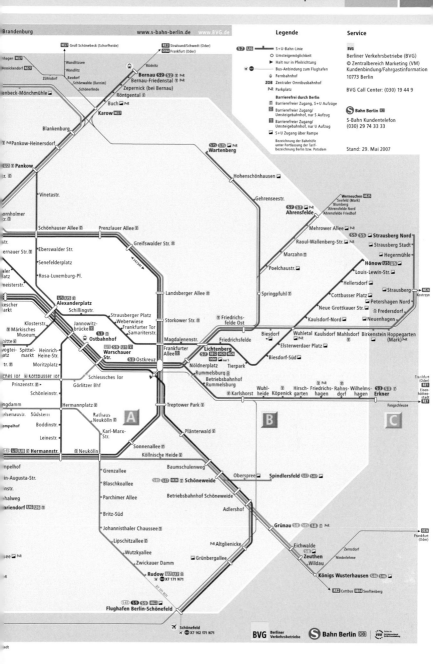

Brandenburg   www.s-bahn-berlin.de   www.BVG.de

Legende

S+U-Bahn-Linie
○ Umsteigemöglichkeit
► Halt nur in Pfeilrichtung
Bus-Anbindung zum Flughafen
Fernbahnhof
ZOB Zentraler Omnibusbahnhof
P+R Parkplatz

Barrierefrei durch Berlin
Barrierefreier Zugang, S+U Aufzüge
Barrierefreier Zugang/ Umsteigebahnhof, nur S Aufzug
Barrierefreier Zugang/ Umsteigebahnhof, nur U Aufzug
S+U Zugang über Rampe

Bezeichnung der Bahnhöfe unter Fortlassung der Tarifbezeichnung Berlin bzw. Potsdam

Service

BVG
Berliner Verkehrsbetriebe (BVG)
© Zentralbereich Marketing (VM)
Kundenbindung/Fahrgastinformation
10773 Berlin

BVG Call Center: (030) 19 44 9

S Bahn Berlin
S-Bahn Kundentelefon
(030) 29 74 33 33

Stand: 29. Mai 2007

► **Sixt**
Tel. (0 18 05) 25 25 25

AUTOMOBILE CLUBS

► **ADAC**
Bundesallee 29/30
D-10717 Berlin
Tel. 86 86-0
Fax 8 68 68 11
Taubenstr. 20–22
D-70117 Berlin
Tel. 20 39 37 11
Fax 20 39 37 23
ADAC Information Service
Tel. (0 18 05) 10 11 12
www.adac.de

► **AvD**
Friedrichstr. 204
D-10117 Berlin
Tel. 22 48 73 73
Fax 22 48 73 74 www.avd.de

► **VCD**
Yorckstr. 48, D-10965 Berlin
Tel. 4 46 36 64
www.vcd.org/berlin

BREAKDOWN SERVICES

► **ADAC-Pannenhilfe**
Tel. (0 18 02) 22 22 22

► **ACE-Pannenleitstelle**
Tel. (0 18 02) 34 35 36

► **AvD-Verkehrshilfsdienst**
Tel. (08 00) 9 90 99 09

TAXI SERVICES

If you only need to go a short distance (up to 2km/1.2mi or 5 min.) and wave down a taxi, there is a so-called wave-down charge of €4 to be paid.

City-Funk: Tel. 21 02 02
Funk-Taxi Berlin: Tel. 0800261026
Go Taxi: Tel. 01801113322
Taxi-Funk: Tel. 69022
TaxiFunk: Tel. 443322
Würfelfunk: Tel. 21 01 01

Travellers with Disabilities

▶ SUPPORT FOR THE DISABLED IN BERLIN

► **Berliner Behindertenverband (disabled society)**
Jägerstr. 63 D, D-10117 Berlin
Tel. 2 04 38 47 Fax 20 45 00 67
www.bbv-ev.de

► **BBV activity group (Beschäftigungswerk)**
Bizetstr. 51–55, D-13088 Berlin
Tel. 5 45 87 00 Fax 5 45 87 99
www.beschaeftigungswerk.de

► **Movado e.V.**
Langhansstr. 64, D-13086 Berlin
Tel. 4 71 51 45, fax 4 73 11 11
www.movado.de

► **Tourism for All**
c/o Vitalise, Shap Road Industrial Estate, Shap Road, Kendal
Cumbria LA9 6NZ
Tel. 08 45 124 99 71
www.tourismforall.org.uk

► **In USA: SATH (Society for Accessible Travel and Hospitality)**
347 5th Ave., no. 610
New York, NY 10016

Tel. (21) 4 47 72 84
www.sath.org

Weights and Measures

IMPERIAL/
METRIC MEASURES

1 inch = 2.54 centimetres
1 centimetre = 0.39 inches
1 foot = 0.3 metres
1 metre = 3.3 feet
1 mile = 1.61 kilometres
1 kilometre = 0.62 miles
1 kilogram = 2.2 pounds
1 pound = 0.45 kilograms

1 gallon = 4.54 litres
1 litre = 0.22 gallons

The metric system is used in Germany. Visitors should keep in mind that a comma is used for decimals (2,5 not 2.5) and a point indicates thousands (2.500 instead of 2,500).

When to Go

There is always something going on in a city like Berlin. Those who choose to visit in winter should be aware that temperatures are likely to hover just above or below freezing. In spring it is worth planning a trip to the Baumblüte (tree blossom festival) festival in Werder, 12km/8mi west of Potsdam: Erich Kästner once wrote that »Berlin's spring took place in Werder«. Summer is of course the season of open-air festivals and drinking in beer gardens, for which there are plenty of opportunities in Berlin.

Tours

WHY NOT BE CHAUFFEURED AROUND BERLIN IN A RICKSHAW BIKE? SIMPLY GIVE YOUR DRIVER ONE OF OUR TOUR ROUTES!

Getting Around in Berlin

Getting around in Berlin is no problem. With S-Bahn (urban railway), U-Bahn (underground railway) and bus links, it is easy to get to any of the interesting places in the city. It is worth buying a ticket valid for the whole period of your stay for any journey. The only remaining question, then, is what part of town to make your base. Night owls should seek out the city centre, Kreuzberg or Prenzlauer Berg, and either side of Kurfürstendamm there is still plenty on offer, too. After all, who wants to go to bed early in Berlin?

Tour 1 The Heart of Berlin

Start and finish: Alexanderplatz to the Brandenburg Gate   **Duration:** 3 hours

This tour covers some of the most impressive parts of Berlin from the Nikolaiviertel, the oldest part of the city, along Unter den Linden in the footsteps of the Prussian kings and German emperors, to the Brandenburg Gate, the most evocative landmark of the city.

The starting point for this walk is ❶**Alexanderplatz**, with the ❷✱ **Fernsehturm** in the middle, offering a fantastic view of the whole city. Head towards the Marienkirche and past the Rotes Rathaus into the ❸✱ **Nikolaiviertel**, where there will be time for a brief pause. Even if much of the historic legacy of the quarter has gone, it still remains the kernel of the city. A little bit further along the Spree and over the Rathausbrücke is ❹✱ **Schlossplatz**, where the East German Palast der Republik stood until its demolition in 2007. Straight ahead is the Berliner Dom, Berlin's main Protestant church, plus the Lustgarten park with the Altes Museum behind it. Across the Schlossbrücke is the prestige boulevard of Unter den Linden with the ❺✱ **Zeughaus**, one of the finest buildings in old Berlin, on the right. Opposite is the Kronprinzenpalais and a little further on stand the ❻✱ **Neue Wache** (central war memorial) on the right, the ❼✱ **Staatsoper** (opera house) on the left and then Bebelplatz with an ❽✱ **equestrian statue of Frederick the Great** in front of Humboldt University and the state library. After that it is just a short diversion along Charlottenstrasse to ❾✱✱ **Gendarmenmarkt** and the finest assemblage of buildings in the city, including the Schauspielhaus and the French and German churches. The square is ideal for a break since there are plenty of cafés and restaurants in the locality. This is the ideal point to stop off for some shopping, since the route to ✱ **Friedrichstrasse** goes through the malls of the Friedrichstadtpassagen. Alternatively it might simply be enough to take a look at Fassbender & Rausch, the chocolate purveyors on the corner of

Gendarmenmarkt: Berlin's prettiest square

Charlottenstrasse and Mohrenstrasse. The route then proceeds along Friedrichstrasse back onto Unter den Linden and left towards the ❿ ✹ ✹ **Brandenburg Gate** itself.

Tour 2 Scheunenviertel and the Museumsinsel

Start and finish: Friedrichstrasse station   **Duration:** 3 hours, not including museum visits

This walk concentrates on culture in the broadest sense of the word: the established art of the Museumsinsel (Museum Island), the vibrant scene of the Scheunenviertel, memories of Jewish Berlin. There are some lovely shops, too.

Start out at ❶ **Friedrichstrasse station**, then head along the bank of the Spree to ❷ **Schiffbauerdamm**, famous as the address of the Berliner Ensemble, which can be seen on the left-hand side of the road. A bronze statue in front of the building represents the theatre's founder Bertolt Brecht. The next leg leads to **Friedrichstrasse** before turning off right beyond the Friedrichstadtpalast along ❸ **Oranienburger Strasse**. Formerly a stronghold of the alternative scene, the area is now an established attraction for both its pubs and its galleries. The Tacheles culture centre is just a few steps ahead; then come the

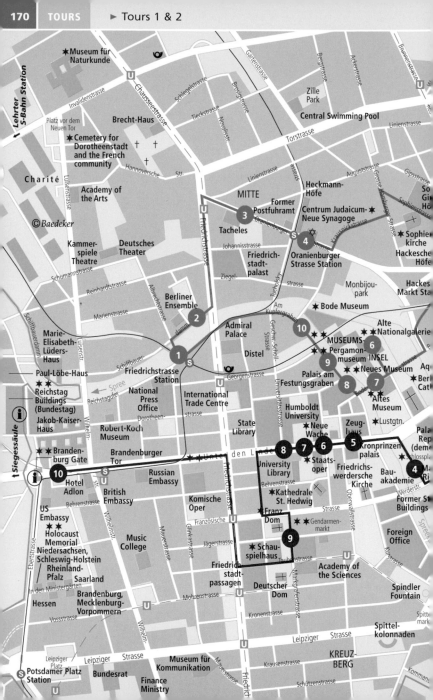

★ Museum für Naturkunde

Zille Park

Central Swimming Pool

Lehrter S-Bahn Station

Platz vor dem Neuen Tor

Brecht-Haus

★ Cemetery for Dorotheenstadt and the French community

Charité

© Baedeker

Academy of the Arts

Heckmann-Höfe

MITTE

Former Postfuhramt

★ Centrum Judaicum-Neue Synagoge

★ Sophien-kirche

Hackesche Höfe

Kammer-spiele Theatre

Deutsches Theater

Tacheles

Friedrich-stadt-palast

Oranienburger Strasse Station

Monbijou-park

Hackes Markt Sta

★ Bode Museum

Berliner Ensemble

Admiral Palace

Distel

Alte Nationalgalerie

MUSEUMS-INSEL

★ Pergamon-museum

★ Neues Museum

Altes Museum

Friedrichstrasse Station

Marie-Elisabeth-Lüders-Haus

Paul-Löbe-Haus

★★ Reichstag Buildings (Bundestag)

Jakob-Kaiser-Haus

National Press Office

International Trade Centre

Palais am Festungsgraben

Lustgtn.

Robert-Koch Museum

★★ Brandenburg Gate

Brandenburger Tor

State Library

Humboldt University

Neue Wache

Zeug-haus

Kronprinzen-palais

Bau-akademie

Pala Rep (dem Schlosspl.

★ Unter den Linden

University Library

Staats-oper

Friedrichs-werdersche Kirche

Former S Buildings

Hotel Adlon

Russian Embassy

Komische Oper

★ Kathedrale St. Hedwig

Gendarmen-markt

Foreign Office

British Embassy

Franz Dom

US Embassy

★★ Holocaust Memorial

Music College

★ Schau-spielhaus

Academy of the Sciences

Spindler Fountain

Niedersachsen, Schleswig-Holstein

Rheinland-Pfalz

Saarland

Friedrich-stadt-passagen

Deutscher Dom

KREUZ-BERG

Spittel-kolonnaden

Brandenburg, Mecklenburg-Vorpommern

Hessen

Leipziger Platz

Potsdamer Platz Station

Bundesrat

Museum für Kommunikation

Finance Ministry

TOURS IN BERLIN

Two walks through Berlin's central borough, Mitte, show the entire spectrum of the city – imposing, magnificent and just a little off-the-wall.

━━━ **TOUR 1**   **The Heart of Berlin**
Berlin's imposing architecture from Alexanderplatz to the Brandenburg Gate.   ► **page 168**

━━━ **TOUR 2**   **Scheunenviertel and the Museumsinsel**
Culture, the in-scene and
lovely shops   ► **page 169**

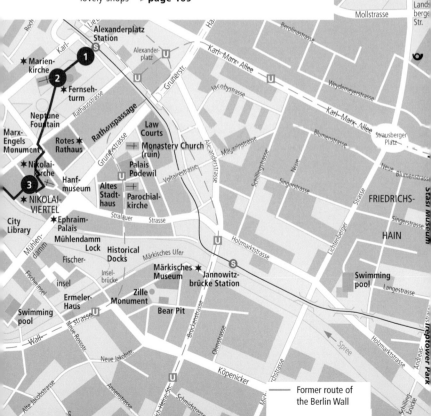

Former route of
the Berlin Wall

Heckmannhöfe arcades. There is another kind of scene here, too, at least during the night, when prostitution still lingers in its old haunts. Nevertheless the magnificence of the ❹ ✱ **Neue Synagoge**, now as before the nexus of the Jewish community in Berlin, is what really dominates the area. Continuing, take a left into Krausnickstrasse, where some remnants of the earliest Jewish cemetery in Berlin still remain. Next, go a short way down Grosse Hamburger Strasse before turning right into Sophienstrasse, with its restored architecture in 19th-century style. Just before this meets Rosenthaler Strasse, look out carefully for the entrance to the courtyards known as the ❺ ✱ **Hackesche Höfe** on the right. Entering from this side means that the finest of these courtyards is the last to be encountered. Now it is time for a stop, either in the Hackesche Höfe themselves or in one of the bars underneath the Hackescher Markt S-Bahn station. What comes next is an official World Heritage Site. Under the railway, head right towards Burgstrasse and then across the Spree to walk right into the middle of the ✱✱ **Museumsinsel (Museum Island)**. This is culture distilled: paintings in the ❻ ✱✱ **Alte Nationalgalerie**, antique sculpture in the ❼ ✱✱ **Altes Museum**, Egyptian remains including the famous head of Nefertiti in the reopened ❽ ✱✱ **Neues Museum**, great monuments from the ancient Middle East in the ❾ ✱✱ **Pergamonmuseum** and more sculptures and coins in the ❿ ✱ **Bodemuseum**. This is right at the tip of the Museumsinsel. Those who enjoyed Oranienburger Strasse can cross the bridge, the Monbijoubrücke, back there and perhaps finish the tour in Café Orange, while others may prefer to follow the Spree back to the station at Friedrichstrasse.

Tour 3 Kantstrasse and Kurfürstendamm

Start and finish: Bahnhof Zoo   **Duration:** 2–3 hours

The western part of central Berlin has had to face stiff competition from Unter den Linden and Friedrichstrasse since the fall of the Berlin Wall. Nevertheless Kurfürstendamm, often shortened to Ku'-damm, still exudes the cosmopolitan flair of one of the world's finest city boulevards.

The tour starts at ❶**Zoologischer Garten station** (Bahnhof Zoo), follows Joachimstaler Strasse for a short stretch and turns right into Kanstrasse, passing the ❷**Theater des Westens** and making a short detour into Fasanenstrasse to the ❸**Jüdisches Gemeindehaus**, the Jewish community centre. Back on Kantstrasse turn left again and walk past the Paris-Bar and Stilwerk to reach busy ❹**Savignyplatz**, an almost unaltered piece of old-time Charlottenburg. This is the ideal place to gather strength in one of the pubs. Then take Knesebeckstrasse and walk under the S-Bahn arches to Kurfürstendamm. Head east along Ku'damm to Breitscheidplatz, site of the Europa-Center and the ❺ ✶ **Kaiser-Wilhelm-Gedächtniskirche** (Kaiser Wilhelm memorial church), which is not to be missed.. On the north side of Breitscheidplatz , on Budapester Strasse, you pass the Elephant Gate of the ✶✶ **zoological gardens** themselves; it is worth taking time out for a proper visit there later on. The tour concludes via Tauen-tzienstrasse at the famous store ❻**Kaufhaus des Westens**, KaDeWe for short, where the biggest attraction for most people is the delica-tessen department on the top floor, a wonderful place to relax and take refreshments.

Tour 4 Diplomacy, Art and Politics

Start and finish: Grosser Stern   **Duration:** 4–5 hours

This tour leads through and around part of the Tiergarten and then runs past the Kulturforum and Potsdamer Platz to the parliament and government precincts.

Start at the Siegessäule (victory column) at ❶**Grosser Stern** (which you can reach by bus), then head southwest along Fasanerieallee through the park to Grosser Weg. Go left along there as far as Klingelhöferstrasse. Anyone interested in modern architecture might like to take a look at the ❷**Tiergartendreieck**, which includes the Nordic embassy, the Mexican embassy and the headquarters of the CDU, the conservative Christian Democratic Party. From here go along vonder-Heydt-Strasse and Reichpietschufer to Stauffenbergstrasse, which leads to the ❸**Gedenkstätte Deutscher Widerstand** (memorial to the German resistance) and, in the direction of the St.-Matthäuskirche (St Matthew's Church) as far as the ❹✶✶ **Kulturforum**, a shop window for modern architecture that is also the site of some of the finest museums: the ✶✶ **Gemäldegalerie (Painting Gallery)**, ✶✶ **Kunstgewerbemuseum (Museum of Decorative Arts)**, ✶ **Kupferstichkabinett (Museum of Prints and Drawings)**, ✶✶ **Neue Nationalgalerie (New National Gallery)**, the ✶ **Musikinstrumenten-Museum (Museum of Musical Instruments)** and the ✶ **Philharmonie** and Staatsbibliothek (State Library). Towering behind them are the ❺✶✶ **Potsdamer Platz** buildings, a pleasant place to take a rest. Here you have the choice between two alternatives: either take Ebertstrasse along the Tiergarten to pass the ❻**Holocaust Memorial** or cross Kemperplatz and stroll through a section of the Tiergarten. Both routes end at Pariser Platz and Berlin's best-known landmark, the world-famous ❼✶✶ **Brandenburg Gate**.

Schloss-garten
Gustav-Adolf-Kirche
Tegeler Weg
Kaiserin- Augusta- Allee
Neues Ufer
Goslarer
Huttenstr.
Tegel Airport ↑
Beusselstr.
St. Paulus ✝
Turmstrasse
Heilandskirche ✝
Town hall

Mierendorffpl.
Quedlinburger Str.
Ufer
Am Spreebord
Spree
Sömmeringstrasse
Schuler
Einsteinufer
Production Centre
Helmholtzstrasse
Franklinstrasse
Landwehrkanal
Alt
Moabit
strasse
Levetzowstrasse
Bundesratufer

Schloss ✱ ✱ Charlottenburg
Spandauer Damm
Otto-Suhr-Allee
Town hall
Lietzow-kirche
Cauerstrasse
Guericke str.
Fraunhoferstr.
Marchstr.
Royal Porcelain Factory (KPM)
Bachstrasse
Klopstockstr.
Am
HA
VI
Kaiser-F Ged.-kir
Neuer

CHARLOTTENBURG
★ Berggruen Collection
Schlossstr.
Zillestr.
Zillestr.
Ernst-Reuter-Platz
Technical University
Tiergarten Station
Strasse des 17.Juni

Bismarckstrasse
Deutsche Oper Berlin
Schiller-Theater
Schillerstrasse
Wilmersdorfer str.
Hardenbergstrasse
Technical University
TU
★★ Zoological Gardens

Law Chambers
Schillerstrasse
Suarezstr.
Pestalozzistr.
Goethestrasse
Trinitatskirche
Leibnizstrasse
Goethestrasse
Pestalozzistr.
Stein-platz
High Court
Zoologischer Garten Station
Buda

Kantstrasse
Stuttgarter-Platz
Savignyplatz Station
Savigny-platz
Theater des Westens
①
★ Kais.-Wilh. Ged.-kirche
Breitscheid-platz

Olympic Stadium, Radio tower; Exhibition halls, Congress Centre →
Charlottenburg Station
Röntgenstr.
Gervinusstr.
Sybel
Mommsenstr.
Leibnizstrasse
④
Kant str.
③ Jewish Comm. Centre
②
ⓘ
▼
⑤
Euro
Cen
Augsburger Strasse
Wit
KaD

Grunewald
Damaschkestr.
Kurfürstendamm
strasse
Pariser Str.
Düsseldorfer Strasse
Kurfürstendamm
Ku'-Damm-Karree
Theatre
Fasanenstr.
Lietzenburger Strasse
Lietzenburger Str.
Nürnberger Platz
Geisbergstrasse
Regensburger Str.
Vik
Lui
Pla

Westfälische Str.
Paulsborner
Nestorstr.
Brandenburgische strasse
Str.
Bayerische
Straße
Württemberger
Strasse
Ludwigs-kirche
Uhlandstrasse
Pariser Str.
Bundesallee
Regensburger Str.
Hohenstaufenstr.
Motzstr.

WILMERSDORF
500 m
1500 ft
© Baedeker
Konstanzer Str.
Fehrbelliner Platz
Hohenzollerndamm
Sächsische
Uhlandstrasse
Bundes
Bamberger
Bayer. Platz
Barbarossastr.

Zehlendorf →
-zollern-
Hohenzollern-damm Station
Town hall
Eisenacher
Berliner Strasse
Berliner
Straße

TOURS IN BERLIN

wo routes through the west of the city – along slightly
wanky »Ku'damm« and through the centre of power

— TOUR 3   Along Kurfürstendamm
»Ku'damm« still exudes a little
cosmopolitanism. ► **page 172**

— TOUR 4   Diplomacy, Art and Politics
The business of government takes place here.
And there's no shortage of green open
spaces either. ► **page 173**

Former route of
the Berlin Wall

Between the steles of the Holocaust Memorial

This is where the last leg through the parliament and government precinct begins: past the **8** ✶ ✶ **Reichstag building** along Paul-Löbe-Allee to the **9** ✶ **Bundeskanzleramt** (office of the federal chancellor), then down the banks of the Spree on John-Foster-Dulles-Allee and across Paulstrasse to **10** **Schloss Bellevue**, the residence of the German president. From there it is not far back to Grosser Stern. If it is summer and you still have time and energy, there is a lovely beer garden alongside the lake in the Tiergarten. Alternatively a taxi or a bus will take you to the Mitte district to relax.

Other Attractions

Berlin's museums

There is such a wide range of museums in Berlin that it is a good idea to decide in advance which ones to visit. It may even be possible to incorporate them into one of the suggested walks. Antiquity and archaeology are splendidly presented, primarily by the world-famous ✶ ✶ **Pergamonmuseum** with its famous Pergamon altar among its collection of antiquities. Painting aficionados may have to divide their time between the ✶ ✶ **Alte Nationalgalerie** and the Kulturforum, where the ✶ ✶ **Gemäldegalerie** and the ✶ ✶ **Neue Nationalgalerie** are situated. For students of anthropology can spend at least a day in the collections of ethnology, Far Eastern art, Indian art and European culture in the ✶ ✶ **museums of Dahlem**. For a rest in the midst of all this, consider the ✶ **Botanical Gardens**. The ✶ **Märkisches Museum (Museum of the Brandenburg March)** is the premier historical museum, but practically all suburbs have their own local museum. The ✶ **Jüdisches Museum** tends to get a bit full: it is not

Highlights in the Outer Boroughs Map

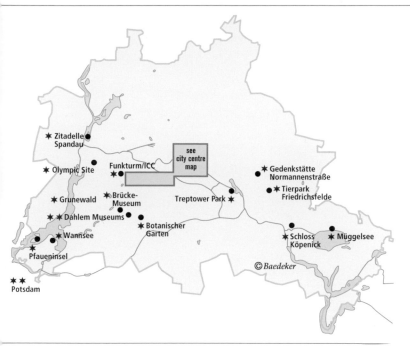

only a place of pilgrimage for Jews but also for fans of architecture. Those interested in technology will be attracted to the ✳ **Deutsches Technikmuseum (German Technology Museum)**, and to see the world's largest dinosaur skeleton go to the ✳ **Museum für Naturkunde (Natural History Museum)**. Obviously this list is by no means complete, and museums to match any taste can be found in the chapter of this guide entitled »Practicalities from A to Z«.

Zoos

If neither art nor antiquity appeal, there is still one major alternative for a day out in Berlin: firstly a visit to the ✳✳ **Zoologischer Garten** and then, for the sake of comparison, a walk through ✳✳ **Tierpark Friedrichsfelde** in the eastern part of the city.

Parks and gardens

If the noise of the city gets too much to bear, take a trip to the suburbs. In the west the place to go is the ✳ **Wannsee**, which can easily be combined with a trip to ✳ **Pfaueninsel (Peacock Island)**. In the east the alternative is a trip through **Köpenick** to the ✳ **Müggelsee**. If gardens are more to your liking, visit the park at ✳✳ **Schloss Charlottenburg**, the gardens and palaces of **Potsdam** (►from p.344), or the ✳ **Botanical Gardens**.

Sights
from A to Z

FROM HIGH UP ON THE
SIEGESSÄULE, »GOLDELSE«
SURVEYS BERLIN'S ATTRACTIONS:
UNTER DEN LINDEN, THE TIERGARTEN,
THE GOVERNMENT PRECINCT,
POTSDAMER PLATZ... THERE IS
MUCH TO DISCOVER.

Ägyptisches Museum

▶Museumsinsel, Altes Museum

Alexanderplatz

K 17/18

Location: Mitte
City centre map: B 14/15

S-Bahn and U-Bahn: Alexanderplatz
(S 3, S 5, S 7, S 75, S 9, U 2, U 5, U 8)

Alexanderplatz has always struggled to belong to a prestigious capital city. Its characteristic scent is rather that of the simple man, as embodied in literature by Franz Biberkopf in Alfred Döblin's novel *Berlin Alexanderplatz*.

The home of Franz Biberkopf

The East German government, however, sought to make the square the focal point of East Berlin, rebuilding it according to socialist architectural concepts that transformed the former lively vigour of the old »Alex« into what is now, architecturally speaking, a rather bleak concrete plain. Plans for restructuring the site have been in discussion for years, but they don't really offer much hope of an improvement. Alexanderplatz has existed since the creation of the Georgsspital (St George's Hospital) in front of the Oderberg Gate at the end of the 13th century. In about 1700 a cattle market grew up around the site, which was joined by a wool market in the middle of the 18th century. After the elector Friedrich III entered Berlin by the gate then called the Georgentor, having declared himself Friedrich I, »King in Prussia«, the gate was renamed the Königstor (King's Gate). As of 1777, at the instigation of Friedrich II, the prestigious Königsbrücke (King's Bridge) stood here. It passed over a channel leading off the Spree that was still visible at the time. A row of colonnades to lead up to the bridge was designed by Karl von Gontard, but they are now situated at the Kleist Park in front of the former headquarters of the Allied Control Council. In 1805 the name of the square was changed from »Ochsenplatz« to its present name in honour of Tsar Alexander I. Its history is depicted in **eight porcelain bas-reliefs in the pedestrian subway** next to the Hochhaus hotel. From left to right they show the Königstor in around 1730, the cattle market on Contre Escarpe in 1780, the Königsbrücke in 1785, the wool market in 1830,

? DID YOU KNOW ...?

■ He is called Alex, of course. He is healthy and in no way dangerous. The official of the Berlin Senate who is responsible for wild animals has confirmed this, and so the raccoon that lives in a multi-storey car park on Alexanderplatz can stay at this high-class address. Alex lives on the fruit, vegetables and burgers that he finds there, supplementing this diet with rats and mice. Between 100 and 120 raccoon families live in Berlin.

Alexanderplatz as it was around 1900 and 1930, the ruins of the square in 1945 and finally the rebuilt development at the end of 1968.

Buildings

Among the buildings of the old site – the colossal statue of Berolina, sculpted by Emil Hundrieser in 1895, and the Berlin police headquarters were its greatest landmarks – only the Berolinahaus and the Alexanderhaus to the south remain. Both were erected according to plans drawn up by Peter Behrens between 1928 and 1931. The rest of the area is dominated by modern buildings, the 30-storey Forum Hotel (now Park Inn) built from 1967 to 1970 and rising to 120m/ 394ft, the Centrum-Warenhaus building (now Kaufhof), the shallow dome of the Kongresshalle, the 18-storey Haus des Reisens (Travel House) and the red **shopping mall Alexa**. The assault of colour outside gives way to a surprise within: Berlin's second-largest shopping centre with 180 stores is an attractive complex with curved passageways, wood and mosaics. Within this mainstream retail offering the miniature world of Loxx appeals to railway fans of all ages: it is one of the world's largest digital model railways, in H 0 gauge, and mainly shows Berlin scenes (daily 10am–7pm). The Brunnen der Völkerfreundschaft (Fountain of Friendship between Peoples) was created by Walter Womacka in 1969, the same year that the Weltzeituhr (World Time Clock) was built by Erich John. Underneath Alexanderplatz's regional and S-Bahn station there is an extensive labyrinth of passages that make up the U-Bahn station.

Alliierten-Museum (Allies' Museum)

Q 10

Location: Clayallee 135, Zehlendorf   **U-Bahn:** Dahlem-Dorf (U 1), then by X 83 bus

The subject of the Allies' Museum in the southwestern suburb of Zehlendorf is the period when West Berlin, at the forefront of the Cold War, was the remotest outpost of western freedom.

The former US Army cinema is used to show the film *Outpost* about the period between 1945 and 1949 and the museum recalls the period from 1950 to 1994 from the point of view of the western allies, the USA, Britain and France, in the building next door. The US military government and the high command of the Berlin Brigade was based on the opposite side of Clayallee. The museum covers topics such as the major politics of the age, the Airlift, the Allied Control Council and the war crimes prison in Spandau, as well as the lives of soldiers and West Berliners and the interaction between them. Documents and original artefacts call to mind a time when West Berlin was seen as an island of freedom amid the »Evil Empire«. Exhibits

⊙
Opening hours:
Daily except Sat
10am – 6pm

include a British »Hastings« transport plane as used in the Berlin Airlift, a carriage from a French interzone train, a US jeep, an American spy tunnel and the museum's prized possession, the original guard hut from Checkpoint Charlie.

Alt-Köpenick

South east N 20

Location: Köpenick

S-Bahn: Köpenick (S 3), then by tram 60, 62

The suburb of Köpenick, known for the famous story of the Captain of Köpenick (►Famous People, Wilhelm Voigt), is greener and has more lakes than any other district of Berlin.

The greenest district of Berlin This is where the Dahme or Wendish Spree flows into the Spree itself and there are plenty of opportunities for day trippers to spend a summer's day perhaps swimming in the ► Müggelsee lake, taking a boat trip on the Müggelspree river or the lake, or rambling in the Müggelberg hills. The core of Köpenick, which is an ancient settlement like Cölln and Spandau, was the Koppenik fortress built for the ruler Jaczo de Copnic on what is now called the Schlossinsel (Castle Island). The first recorded mention of the fort is from 1240. In the 19th century the large number of establishments taking in washing led to Köpenick being dubbed **»Berlin's laundry«**. After the empire was established, it attracted more and more factories, elevating Köpenick to one of Berlin's major centres of industry, as witnessed by the industrial sites in Oberschöneweide. The site of the modern Peter Behrens building of the Samsung electronics company was where the National Automobile Company (NAG) manufactured its vehicles until 1933; it then became the AEG-Telefunken factory and during the GDR era it was a factory producing electronics for televisions. Köpenick became a part of Greater Berlin in 1920.

Old town The first steps through the Altstadt naturally lead to the Rathaus or city hall, designed by Hans Schütte and built between 1901 and

! *Baedeker* TIP

In the Captain's footsteps
The Berlin Treptow Tourist Association provides tours through the centre of Berlin and out to Köpenick in the footsteps of the famous Captain of Köpenick. Tel. 65 48 43 40 to book.

The magnificent stucco decoration in the Arms Hall at Schloss Köpenick

1904. On its steps there is a monument to »Köpenick's most famous son«, the Captain of Köpenick, who at the time of his caper in 1906 was a 57-year-old cobbler from Tilsit called Wilhelm Voigt (► Famous People). Wearing a second-hand captain's uniform he had put together from various sources, he issued orders to 12 grenadiers from the Plötzensee military swimming baths and led them to Köpenick, where they arrested the mayor, confiscated the municipal funds and in the process exposed the absurd thrall in which a man in uniform was held in Prussia at that time. A small exhibition in the Rathaus (to the right on the ground floor; opening hours: 10am – 6pm daily) covers details of the heist and the rest of Wilhelm Voigt's life. Alt-Köpenick itself, the old part of the suburb, mainly spreads out between Kietzer Strasse, Kirchstrasse, Rosenstrasse and Schüsslerplatz. The Köpenicker Heimat- und Fischereimuseum (Köpenick Local Museum and Fishing Museum) to the east (Alter Markt 1) covers Köpenick's history.

Fischerkietz

Something of the idyll of a bygone age is still apparent in the fishing village of Kietz, which was incorporated into Köpenick in 1898. The village had been granted fishing rights as early as 1451. Its prettiest street is Strasse Kietz with its single-storey fishermen's cottages.

★
Schloss Köpenick

In the mid-16th century the elector Joachim II ordered the building of a palatial, Renaissance-style hunting lodge on the site of the Slav's Wasserburg fort on the Schlossinsel. During the Thirty Years' War, Gustav Adolf of Sweden was also quartered there. At the end of the 17th century the Great Elector had the palace remodelled into its current form by Rutger van Langerfeldt. Among the rooms that were built at the time is the magnificent Hall of Heraldry, in which the court martial of Crown Prince Friedrich (later to become Friedrich II) and his friend Lieutenant Hans Hermann von Katte took place from 22–28 October 1730 upon the orders of King Friedrich Wilhelm I. Katte had assisted the crown prince in an attempt to flee the country, for which he was condemned to death and executed before Friedrich's very eyes at Küstrin. Since 1963 the palace has housed part of the collection from the Kunstgewerbemuseum or Museum of Decorative Arts, which was established in 1867. After a renovation project lasting ten years it reopened in the middle of 2004 as a subbranch of the museum based at the ▶ Kulturforum. Its 29 »epoch chambers« display art from the Renaissance, Baroque and Rococo periods, the highlight being the **Silver Buffet** from the Berlin Stadtschloss (City Palace). The palace chapel designed by Johann Arnold Nering (1680–1690) is also part of the museum (opening hours: Tue–Sun 10am–6pm).

◀ Kunstgewerbemuseum ▶

⏱

Schloss Bellevue

L 14

Location: Spreeweg 1, Tiergarten
City centre map: A 7

S-Bahn: Bellevue (S 3, S 5, S 75, S 9)
Bus: 100, 187

Schloss Bellevue, situated to the north of the Grosser Stern intersection within the ▶Tiergarten, has been the official office and residence of the German president since 1994. It was built in 1785 as a summer palace for Prince August Ferdinand, the youngest brother of Frederick the Great, but was totally destroyed during the Second World War. The building, including its oval ballroom, has been faithfully rebuilt according to plans made in 1791 by Carl Gotthard Langhans. The western section of the park surrounding the palace (20ha/50ac) has been laid out in the style of an English country park and is open to the public. The car park, which has a thatched roof, also hosts exhibitions and concerts. The **Bundespräsidialamt** (president's office) is located in the park alongside the palace to the southwest. Its elliptical design faced with black granite was created by Frankfurt architects Martin Gruber and Helmut Kleine-Kraneburg.

Schloss Bellevue, residence of the German president

✱ Berliner Dom (Berlin Cathedral)

K 17

Location: Lustgarten, Mitte
S-Bahn: Hackescher Markt (S 3, S 5, S 75, S 9)

City centre map: B 13
Bus: 100, 200

Berlin Cathedral, the Berliner Dom, was built on the instructions of Kaiser Wilhelm II as the foremost Protestant church in Prussia and house the graves of the Hohenzollern royal family.

It was constructed between 1894 and 1905 according to a design by Julius Carl Raschdorff and replaced a church dating back to the time of Frederick the Great (1747 – 1750, designed by Johann Boumann the Elder). The building with its central ground plan and neo-Baroque historicist elements was originally organized into three main sections. In the north was the now demolished memorial church, in the south the nuptial church for christenings and weddings, and in the middle the main parish church, which seats 2000. The building is 116m/381ft high and 114m/125yd long. The dome is covered with mosaics designed by Anton von Werner and its apex is 74.8m/245.5ft high. The oldest of the cathedral's bells dates from 1532. The building was badly damaged during the war but was renovated between

⏲
Opening hours:
Apr – Sept
Mon – Sat
9am – 8pm,
Sun and holidays
noon – 8pm;
Oct – Mar closes
7pm

The Berliner Dom has a fine reputation for sacred music

1974 and 1982. Renovation of the interior was completed in the summer of 1993. It was reopened with a mass and a dedication ceremony for the massive Sauer's organ (built in 1904, it has 113 stops and 7200 pipes). Its most valuable possessions include a baptismal font by Christian Daniel Rauch and Karl Friedrich Schinkel's altar with the 12 apostles, but its prized possessions are the sarcophagi of the Great Elector and his wife Dorothea (designed by Johann Arnold Nering), Elector Johann Cicero, the magnificent tomb of the first Prussian royal couple Friedrich I and Sophie Charlotte (designed by Andreas Schlüter) and the headstone of Kaiser Friedrich III (by Reinhold Begas). Their actual remains, though, are kept in the **Hohenzollern crypt**, where 94 coffins, dating from the 16th to the 20th centuries, hold the mortal remains of Hohenzollern family members.

Imperial staircase ▶
The crypt is open to the public (opening hours: Mon – Sat 9am – 8pm, Sundays and holidays noon – 8pm). The imperial staircase was for the exclusive use of the royal family. It is decorated with bronzed capitals and 13 tempera paintings created by the landscape painter Albert Hertel (1905). The imperial box offers a splendid view of the cathedral interior. Further up the stairs is the Dom-Museum, which catalogues the architectural history of the edifice.

Dome ▶
A maze of stairs and passages leads away from the imperial staircase into the cathedral dome. From the gallery around the dome, 50m/ 164ft above the ground, it is possible to see the whole of Berlin (last admission 5pm in summer, 4pm in winter).

Lustgarten
The Lustgarten park, situated between the Dom and the Altes Museum (▶Museumsinsel) is at the very heart of old Berlin. It was initially created as a kitchen garden in 1573 but was transformed into a decorative garden in 1643. Its design and uses have been altered many times since. Under Friedrich Wilhelm I it became a parade ground, and trees were first planted from 1830 onwards. During the Weimar Republic it was a favoured venue for political gatherings, but under the Nazis it was concreted over and used for marches. It has now been made into a green park once more. The large granite bowl in front of the old museum was polished up between 1827 and 1830 by Christian Gottlieb Cantian using an erratic block that was found in the Brandenburg March. It is 6.9m/23ft in diameter, weighs 75 tons and is nicknamed **»Berlin's biggest soup dish«**.

? DID YOU KNOW ...?

■ ... that the first potatoes in Prussia were planted in the Lustgarten in 1649?

Dom Aquarée
Dom Aquarée is a new hotel and office development on the other side of the Liebknecht bridge and has three popular attractions: **Sealife** features 30 pools filled with native freshwater and salt-water creatures; **Aquadom** is the world's largest aquarium with a height of 26m/85ft and a diameter of 11.5m/38ft and is remarkable in that it is

viewed from a lift that runs through its centre; and the DDR Museum on the ground floor, which seeks to exhibit »the life and times of the former state in a unique hands-on experience«. The museum includes a complete living room and kitchen from the GDR era, and shows film documentaries which can be enjoyed from an authentic East German cinema seat (opening hours: 10am – 8pm daily, closes 10pm on Sundays).

◄ DDR Museum

⊙

Brandenburg Gate · Pariser Platz

L 15

Location: Pariser Platz, Mitte

City centre map: B 10

S/U-Bahn: Brandenburger Tor (S 1, S 2, S 25, U 55)

Bus: 100, 157, 348

The monumental Brandenburg Gate is Berlin's defining landmark and has come to symbolize the ending of the division in Germany.

It was built on the instructions of King Friedrich Wilhelm II between 1788 and 1791 using a design by **Carl Gotthard Langhans the Elder**, who took the propylaea of the Acropolis in Athens as his inspiration. It was intended to provide a suitable conclusion to the western end of the Unter den Linden boulevard. Its classical sandstone construction, unique at the time in Berlin, is 26m/85ft high (including the Quadriga statue), 65.5m/215ft wide and 11m/36ft across. On both sides of the gate, front and back, are six Doric columns, between which are five passages for traffic. The central opening is 5.6m/18ft wide and was originally for the exclusive use of the royal family's carriages while the other four side passages (each 3.8m/12.5ft wide) were open to general traffic. The wings built to the north and south, with the façades of Doric temples, were given over to the city's toll collectors and guards. On 6 August 1791 the Brandenburg Gate was opened as a public thoroughfare with no great ceremony in the absence of the king. New passages were made between the gate and its side buildings by Johann Heinrich Strack between 1861 and 1868, during which time he also added open galleries of columns to the gatehouses. The statues of Mars and Minerva were also moved. The gate was very badly damaged during the Second World War and it was not until 1958 that all the damage was repaired. Corrosion and damage caused during the New Year's celebrations of 1989 / 90 resulted in another major renovation and yet more harm was done when traffic was diverted through the gate after the fall of the Wall. The gate is now only open to pedestrians.

Berlin's definitive landmark

The Brandenburg Gate's artistic adornments, particularly the Quadriga, the four horse chariot on top of the building, is primarily the work of **Johann Gottfried Schadow**. His plans were carried out by a

Quadriga

Potsdam coppersmith by the name of Jury, whose niece Ulrike acted as the model for the statue of the chariot's driver, Irene, goddess of peace, although the statue would later be regarded as representing the goddess of victory, Victoria, after victory laurels were placed in her hands. The Quadriga was lifted onto the top of the gate in 1793, although it was moved to Paris after Napoleon conquered the city in 1806. It was only after the French defeat at the Battle of Leipzig in 1813 that Marshall Blücher was able to arrange for the statue to be returned. It was put back in its rightful place on 14 August 1814 to joyous celebration among the Berliners. By order of the king, Karl Friedrich Schinkel was commanded to give the goddess of peace a new trophy, a wreath of oak laurels wrapped around the iron cross and crowned with the eagle of Prussia. With this trophy the statue took on a new meaning and was thereby transformed into the goddess Victoria. Along with the laurels there were initially other trophies in the form of a helmet on a spear, a breastplate and two shields. The Quadriga was destroyed during the Second World War, leaving nothing but the head of one horse, now on display in the Märkisches Museum (► Märkisches Ufer). Thanks to plaster casts made in 1942 it was possible for the Noack casting company in Friedenau to fashion a new Quadriga, which was hoisted into place in September 1958. Shortly afterwards though, the iron cross and the Prussian eagle were removed by order of the East German government.

! **Baedeker TIP**

Take a breather

If your tour of Berlin is starting to take it out of you, or you just need a short rest, the »Raum der Stille« (Room of Silence) in the Brandenburg Gate's northern gatehouse is the ideal place to grab a little peace and quiet among the mayhem.

Witnesses to history   Since the entry of the French in 1806 the Brandenburg Gate has witnessed any number of musters and victory parades, including the return of the Prussian troops from Denmark in 1864, in 1866 after the campaign against the Austrians, the victors over France in 1871 and the establishment of the German Reich. At the start of the First World War the Berlin garrison marched through it, and Nazi stormtroopers paraded by torchlight to Wilhelmstrasse on 30 January 1933 in celebration of Hitler's takeover. When the Wall went up on 13 August 1961 the Brandenburg Gate became the symbol of the city's division – the wall ran right next to the western side of it. It was only a few weeks after the opening of the borders on 9 November 1989, though, that the Brandenburg Gate could once again celebrate its official reopening on 22 December.

Pariser Platz   Under Friedrich Wilhelm I, Pariser Platz was one of three large squares, the Oktogon (Leipziger Platz), the Rondell (Mehringplatz) and Quarré, Pariser Platz itself. It gained its present name in 1814

Every year fireworks over the Brandenburg Gate mark Germany's Unity Day

and until the Second World War it was a heavily built-up area. It was the site of the French and British embassies, and the home of Max Liebermann and the legendary Hotel Adlon. The new construction at the site has sought to hark back to this era. Thus both Haus Liebermann (to the north with J. P. Kleihues as the architect) and Haus Sommer (Commerzbank) have appeared either side of the gate. The northern side of the square is now graced by the Palais am Pariser Platz (Winking/Froh), the Dresdner Bank (Gerkan & Partner), the French embassy (Christian de Portzamparc) and finally a new building for the AGB property company The US embassy by More, Rubel, Yndell at the southwest corner opened on 4 July 2008 to devastating reviews from the architecture critics. In contrast next door the cuboid DZ Bank building has a quiet exterior that belies the fantastic »architectural sculpture« by Frank O. Gehry (▶ ill. p.42) inside. Next to that, the glass structure of the Akademie der Künste (Academy of Arts) (Behnisch/Durth) rather disrupts the historical recreation intended by the senate, intentions that are fully realized by the new Hotel Adlon. Around the corner from Adlon on Wilhelmstrasse, however, the British embassy by Michael Wilford is a bolder modern creation.

✱
◀ DZ Bank

To the south of the Brandenburg Gate there is now a memorial to the Jews murdered in Europe during the Holocaust. Peter Eisenman's design features 2711 concrete blocks of varying size to make up a structure that can be perceived differently from any place within it as you walk through. According to Eisenman himself, he made this radical departure from conventional memorial architecture because »the extent and scale of the Holocaust mean that any attempt to represent it by conventional means is doomed to fail hopelessly. Our memorial is attempting to create a new concept of reminiscence that is quite

✱ ✱
Holocaust Memorial
(▶ ill. p.176)

»No one intends to build a wall...«

NO ONE INTENDS TO BUILD A WALL

»If I understand your question, there are people in West Germany who wish us to mobilize the building workers of the German Democratic Republic to erect a wall. I am not aware that any such intent exists. The builders in our city are chiefly concerned with building homes for our people (...) No one intends to build a wall.«

The leader of the East German state council and general secretary of the SED party, **Walter Ulbricht**, reacted with furious indignation to a journalist who questioned him on 15 June 1961 about certain rumours that had been circulating for quite some time. Less than two months later, around 2am on the night of 12 to 13 August 1961, units from the police, union pickets and the East German army shut off the border to the Eastern part of Berlin along the perimeter of the Soviet sector for the purposes of »reliable monitoring and effective control of the state borders«. They started erecting road blocks and rolling out barbed wire and mesh fencing. In a matter of hours, the official responsible for the action, one **Erich Honecker**, declared the operation complete.

»Anti-Fascist protective wall«

For years the constant exodus of refugees across the sector boundaries in Berlin had been causing the East German government serious headaches. Since 1952, when the border between East and West Germany had been closed, Berlin had turned into **the only gap in the Iron Curtain,** as the agreement between the four allied powers guaranteed freedom of movement. Between 1952 and the building of the Wall, some 2.7 million people had taken this opportunity to flee. East Germany was threatened with losing its population and the SED believed that their final option was to fence its people in. Obviously this was never officially admitted. Instead the Wall was justified as a method of ensuring peace and as protection against »constant provocation from the West Berlin side of the border«. The propaganda phrase that was spawned called it an »anti-Fascist protective wall«.

Berlin walled in

As soon as the first fences went up, the number of crossing points was reduced: first from 81 to twelve, then shortly afterwards to seven. Cross-border S-Bahn and U-Bahn services

17 August 1962: GDR border guards retrieve the body of 17-year-old Peter Fechter, who was shot while trying to escape and lay bleeding for an hour in no-man's land in the border strip

were halted except for an interchange at Friedrichstrasse and those lines that passed under East Berlin territory would pass through ghost stations guarded by members of the East German police. As early as 15 August, the first road blocks and barbed wire fences were already being replaced by pre-fabricated concrete walls. Any buildings that were right on the boundaries, like those on **Bernauer Strasse**, were evacuated as of 19 August and all the doors and windows facing the west were bricked up. Many got away at the last minute by leaping out to the windows into West Berlin where passers-by, policemen and firemen were waiting to catch them. On 24 August the first person to be shot while escaping was fired on while trying to swim across the Humboldthafen. Suddenly Berlin was literally a divided city. The Wall through the inner-city split western boroughs like Reinickendorf, Wedding, Tiergarten, Kreuzberg and Neukölln from eastern

Berlin city boundary
Boundary between east and west sectors
Sector boundaries in West Berlin
Borough boundaries

! *Baedeker* TIP

Multimedia guide to the Wall

The official Berlin Wall guide takes in 22 places of memorial. The multimedia device, equipped with GPS, contains films and commentaries in English. It can be rented from kiosks at the Brandenburg Gate, in Bernauer Strasse, at Checkpoint Charlie, in Niederkirchnerstrasse and at the East Side Gallery (information and sample download at www.mauerguide.com).

suburbs like Pankow, Prenzlauer Berg, Mitte, Friedrichshain and Treptow. Over the course of the years, the initial wall that had more or less been hastily jerry built was expanded to form an almost impenetrable barrier.

Escape attempts

More than 70 people were killed trying to escape. They were recalled by memorial crosses and stones put up on Bernauer Strasse, on the Reichstag building and on Zimmerstrasse among others. Over a hundred more people were injured by gunshots fired by East German border troops, and more than 3000 arrests were seen by observers on the western side. Many people nevertheless succeeded in making good their escape, sometimes involving desperately imaginative, inventive and courageous ideas, as can be seen from the photographs, documents and examples of the actual contraptions used that are on exhibit in the museum at **Haus am Checkpoint Charlie** (corner of Zimmerstrasse / Friedrichstrasse: 9am to 10pm daily).

The front of the Cold War

Checkpoint Charlie (»Allied Checkpoint Charlie« using the NATO international code for the letter »C«; »A, Alpha« was the border crossing at Helmstedt and »B, Bravo« was the checkpoint at Dreilinden.) became a

name known throughout the world as the sector crossing for foreigners, East German citizens, diplomats, agent exchanges and military personnel right in the heart of Berlin at the meeting place between the American and Soviet sectors. This was the one place that evoked the dread feeling of the Cold War like no other, where French, British and American soldiers' suspicious looks on one side were met with the equally grim gaze of the East German and Soviet border troops on the other. The security facilities on the eastern side were as complex as might be expected. There were several barrier gates, chicanes through which vehicles had to wend their way, and armed guards in watchtowers seeking to prevent any attempted escape. At the height of the **Berlin crisis** between 25 and 28 October 1961, American and Soviet tanks stood face to face with their engines running as the Americans asserted their right of uncontrolled access to the eastern sector of the city ▶(ill. p.24).

There is hardly any trace of any of this remaining today and the dread feeling is gone. One surviving watchtower skulks in the shadows of the American Business Center, a ribbon across the street marks where the border once ran and the actual checkpoint hut has been rebuilt.

The Wall on Zimmerstrasse in Spring 1990. Still attracting souvenir hunters

The Wall has gone

The end of the Wall was brought about by the opening of the East German border with West Berlin and the rest of West Germany on **9 November 1989**. As of 10pm that day and throughout the next, East Berliners flooded into the west of the city. On 11 November the orders to shoot were rescinded and various new border crossings were opened before the end of 14 November. It was on 28 November that the opening of the Brandenburg Gate made for a symbolic ending of Berlin's division. Even during that night between 9 and 10 November »Mauerspechte« (Mauer means wall; a Specht is a woodpecker) were chipping away at the concrete monstrosity with hammers and chisels. Later on, heavy machinery was brought in to tear it down and reduce it to concrete granules. By December 1990, 1 million tons of concrete had been disposed of. Many large sections, particularly those that had been painted with murals by well-known artists, were preserved, however, and sold off to all parts of the world.

Traces of the Wall

Finding traces of the Wall in modern-day Berlin is difficult. Often the former line of the wall can only be guessed at but it is being marked with a double row of paving stones. The first place to look for comprehensive information on the wall is the information centre at the **Gedenkstätte Berliner Mauer** memorial museum (Bernauer Strasse 111; S 1, S 2 to Nordbahnhof, U8 to Bernauer Strasse, Tue – Sun 10am – 6pm, Nov – Mar closes 5pm), where exhibitions relate the history of the construction and books and brochures are available. The actual memorial itself is opposite the information centre where there is 200m/220yd of the inner and outer walls with the gravel strip, access road and a line of floodlights between them. Other remnants can be found on the premises of the »Topographie des Terrors« exhibition on Niederkirchnerstrasse, at the Invalidenfriedhof cemetery, and in Prenzlauer Berg's Mauerpark; a 1300m/1420yd stretch of the Wall runs from the Oberbaumbrücke along the Spree, which was painted by artists often of considerable renown and has become known as the **East Side Gallery**, although few will realize that this is actually a strip of the inner wall or Hinterlandmauer rather than the outer wall (Vorderlandmauer) that actually faced the west. The documentation centre can also provide information on other remaining sections of the wall as well as the locations of the remaining three watchtowers and where memorials and museums are.

THE WALL

✳ ✳ **It is actually astonishing that there is practically no trace of the former Wall remaining in Berlin. That must surely be a good thing, though. In particular, there is nowhere where the full border facilities have survived. For the Wall was not just one wall; it was a complicated, multitiered installation that was practically impossible to cross. By 1988 the barrier was 155km/96mi long, of which 43.1km/27mi were within the city centre while the rest, 111.9km/69mi followed the border between West Berlin and the neighbouring East German regions.**

① Outer Wall (Vorderlandmauer)
The wall that faced West Berlin was 106km/66mi long and was made of concrete sheets, 3.6 – 4.1m/12 – 13.5ft high and 16cm/6in thick with a wide concrete tube along the top, which was replaced by metal fencing in places along the rural border.

② Vehicle traps
Intended to prevent crossing in vehicles. Total length 90km/56mi

③ Sentry strips
Continually raked and kept free of vegetation to make it easier to spot trails. Total length 165km/102.5mi

④ Access roads
6 – 7m/7 – 8yd-wide two-lane paved roads for vehicles and marching columns. Total length 172km/107mi

⑤ Lights
Rows of lampposts to flood 180km/112mi of the strip in bright light during the night

⑥ Watchtowers
190 watchtowers kept watch on the strip and served as control centres. In some sections the watchtowers were accompanied by dog runs.

⑦ Tank traps
Chevaux-de-frise (for 1km/0.6mi) or mats of nails (for 20km/12mi) to prevent penetration by vehicles.

⑧ Border signalling fence
Set off acoustic and visible alarms when touched. Total length 150km/93mi

⑨ Inner wall (Hinterlandmauer)
Initial barrier on the East German side, frequently only metal fencing. Total length 70km/43.5mi

August 1961: shortly before their windows were walled up, inhabitants of houses on Bernauer Strasse flee across the road to West Berlin. The pavement is already on the western side.

different.« At the southeastern corner of the group of blocks an **information point** provides information on victims and memorials in Germany and the rest of Europe (April-Sep daily except Mon 10am – 8pm, Oct – March 10am – 7pm).

On the other side of the road in the ► Tiergarten a memorial was dedicated in May 2008 to the homosexuals who were persecuted in the National Socialist period.

Bröhan Museum

K 11

Location: Schlossstr. 1a, Charlottenburg   **U-Bahn :** Richard-Wagner-Platz (U 7)
S-Bahn : Westend (S 41, S 42, S 46)   **Bus :** M 45, 109, 309

Opening hours:
Tue – Sun
10am – 6pm

The Bröhan Museum (Regional Museum for Art Nouveau, Art Deco and Functionalism) opened in a former infantry barracks next to the ► Museum Berggruen near Schloss ► Charlottenburg in 1983. It contains the private collection that Karl H. Bröhan bequeathed to the city of Berlin in 1982, and exhibits paintings, graphic and sculptural items, furniture, porcelain, ceramic, glass, tin and silver works of art from the period 1889 to 1939.

The ground floor features a sequence of rooms dedicated to specific artists and cataloguing their styles. They include myriad furniture items, art works and creations ranging from Art Nouveau to Art Deco. On the first floor there are paintings, silverwork and French Art Deco, including paintings by Walter Leistıkow, Hans Baluschek and Karl Hagemeister. The third floor includes two cabinets dedicated to Henry van de Velde and one of the founders of the Vienna studios, Josef Hoffmann.

Cemeteries

Many important figures are buried in Berlin's cemeteries. They bear witness to the history of the city itself.

A reflection of
the city's history

In the list of dignitaries below the actual locations of the graves are given in brackets wherever possible. Various tour operators (► Practicalities, Tours and Guides) offer guided walks through some of the cemeteries listed.

✱ Friedhof der Dorotheenstädtischen und Friedrichswerderschen Gemeinde

Chausseestr. 126,
city centre (J 16)

The small and romantic Dorotheenstadt and Friedrichswerden parish cemetery, located not far from the end of Friedrichstrasse,

Nine border crossings allowed westerners at least to pass across, although under severe restrictions. Checkpoint Charlie on Friedrichstrasse was limited to foreigners and diplomats from the West.

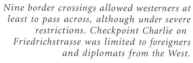

The best source of information about the Wall is the documentation centre at Bernauer Strasse 11 (Wed – Sun 10am – 5pm).

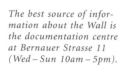

The »Vorderlandmauer« did not always follow the border precisely but was occasionally set back a little towards the eastern side, thus some areas that could be accessed by westerners were officially already in East Germany. Two of those places were near the Brandenburg Gate or in Wedding in the French sector, as seen above.

The »Vorderlandmauer« ran right behind the Reichstag. Security vessels patrolled the River Spree. A section of the »Hinterlandmauer« can be seen on the bank.

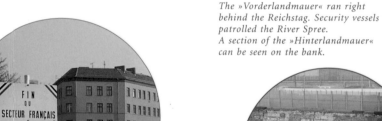

FIN DU SECTEUR FRANÇAIS

© Baedeker

was laid out in 1762 and many well-known figures from the worlds of art, culture, economics and politics are interred here, including the following (directions are given from the main path in front of the administration building):

◄ U-Bahn: Oranien-
burger Tor (U 6)
Tram: M 1, 12

Johann Gottlieb Fichte († 1814), philosopher (3rd path on the left, left-hand side)

Georg Wilhelm Friedrich Hegel († 1831), philosopher (3rd left, left-hand side)

Christoph Wilhelm Hufeland († 1832), doctor (1st left, left-hand side)

Karl Friedrich Schinkel († 1841), builder (5th left, left-hand side)

Johann Gottfried Schadow († 1850), sculptor (5th left, at the end)

August Borsig († 1854), industrialist (5th left, left-hand side)

Christian Daniel Rauch († 1857), sculptor (5th left, left-hand side)

Friedrich August Stüler († 1865), architect (5th left, at the end)

Ernst Litfass († 1874), printer and inventor of the advertising pillar (1st left, right-hand side)

Heinrich Mann († 1950), writer (1st left, left-hand side)

The twin grave of Bertolt Brecht and his wife Helene Weigel

Bertolt Brecht († 1956), writer, and Helene Weigel-Brecht († 1971), actress and theatre manager, (1st left, left-hand side)

Johannes R. Becher († 1958), writer, East German culture minister (1st left, left-hand side)

Hanns Eisler († 1962), composer (1st left, right-hand side)

John Heartfield († 1968), graphic designer (3rd left, right-hand side)

Arnold Zweig († 1968), writer (4th left, left-hand side)

Paul Dessau († 1979), composer (1st left, left-hand side)

Anna Seghers († 1983), writer (1st left, left-hand side)

Heiner Müller († 1995), dramatist

Bernhard Minetti († 1998), actor

Johannes Rau († 2006), state president

Französischer Friedhof (Hugenottenfriedhof)

Right next door (entrance on Liesenstr.) is the French Cemetery, which was opened in 1780. It includes:

Daniel Chodowiecki († 1801), engraver and illustrator

Madame Dutitre († 1827), a unique character in the city

Friedrich Ancillon († 1837), educator, foreign minister of Prussia in 1832 under Friedrich Wilhelm IV (headstone by Schinkel)

Ludwig Devrient († 1832), actor

Further north on Wöhlertstrasse (a side street off Chausseestrasse) lies another cemetery for the French community with the grave of Theodor Fontane († 1898) among others.

Invalidenfriedhof (Cemetery for the War Disabled)

Scharnhorststr. 33, Mitte (Y 15)
S/U-Bahn: Hauptbahnhof (S 5, S 7, S 75, S 9, U 55) ►

This cemetery beside the Berlin-Spandau ship canal was opened in 1748 to accommodate the deceased from the nearby invalids' home of the Prussian army. It is the final resting place of many officers of the Prussian and German armies. In 1972 the cemetery was partially levelled since it lay directly on the border between East and West Berlin. Its graves include:

Gerhard Johann David von Scharnhorst († 1813) – with its lion headstone designed by Schinkel and made by Christian Daniel Rauch with reliefs by Friedrich Tieck

General Graf Tauentzien von Wittenberg († 1824)

General Field Marshal Alfred Graf von Schlieffen († 1913)

Colonel-General Werner von Fritsch († 1939)

Manfred von Richthofen († 1918) was re-interred in Wiesbaden in 1972 where his sister and his brother are buried. The grave of Colonel-General Hans von Seeckt († 1936) was lost due to the levelling of 1972 but those of fighter pilots Ernst Udet († 1941) and Werner Mölders († 1941) have been reinstated.

Alter Garnison friedhof

The Alter Garnisonfriedhof on Linienstrasse in the centre of the city (U-Bahn: Rosenthaler Platz, U 8) was the cemetery of the old garrison and its graves include that of Adolf von Lützow († 1834), commander of the Lützow Freikorps, and poet Friedrich de la Motte Fouqué († 1843).

Dreifaltigkeitskirchhof (Cemetery of the Holy Trinity Church)

Bergmannstr. 39 – 41, Kreuzberg (O 17)
U-Bahn: Südstern (U 7) ►

Friedrich Daniel Schleiermacher († 1834), philosopher (B-OA-118)
Georg Andreas Reimer († 1842), book dealer (B-OA-72)
Charlotte von Kalb († 1843), friend of Schiller (B-HA-14)
Ludwig Tieck († 1853), poet (B top 3-3)
Martin Gropius († 1880), architect (C-W.S.-6)
J. G. Halske († 1890), co-founder of Siemens AG (M-HA-1-11)
Theodor Mommsen († 1903), historian (O-UA-36)
Adolph Menzel († 1905), painter (A-W.S.-48)
Georg Wertheim († 1940), store owner (H-HA-31-33)

Church Cemeteries near Hallesches Tor

From 1735 on, four cemeteries belonging to three different churches were set up near the Hallesches Tor. They are as follows:

Dreifaltigkeitskirchhof (Baruther Strasse):
Felix Mendelssohn-Bartholdy († 1847), composer (VI-6-7)
Fanny Hensel († 1847), composer, sister of Felix Mendelssohn-Bartholdy (VI-6-6)
Karl-August Varnhagen von Ense († 1858), writer, and Rahel Varnhagen von Ense († 1833; VII-2-38/39)
Heinrich von Stephan († 1897), general post office manager (VII-SA-10)

Jerusalems- und Neue Kirchengemeinde:
Cemetery I (Blücher-/Zossener Strasse):
memorial to Georg Wenzeslaus v. Knobelsdorff († 1753), builder for Friedrich II, and Antoine Pesne († 1757), court painter to Friedrich II (1/1 main avenue)
Cemetery II (Zossener/Baruther Strasse)
David Gilly († 1808), builder (3/2 Erbb)
August Wilhelm Iffland († 1814), actor (3/1 Erb.)
Henriette Herz († 1847), lady of letters (1/-3-9/10)
Cemetery III (Mehringdamm 21):
E.T.A. Hoffmann († 1822), poet and composer (1/1-32-6)
Adelbert von Chamisso († 1838), poet (3/1-38-1)
Carl Ferdinand Langhans († 1869), builder (2/2-12-16)
Adolf Glassbrenner († 1876), writer (1/2-17-20/21)
Ernst Christian Fr. Schering († 1889), chemist (4/3 Erb.)

Between ringdam Zossener Kreuzberg

◄ U-Bahn: Mehringdamm (U 6,

Zentralfriedhof Friedrichsfelde

This cemetery was laid out by Hermann Mächtig and bequeathed to the state in 1881. It was the preferred resting place of the SED's leading lights in East Germany. Its graves include:
Friedrich Archenhold († 1939), founder of the public observatory in Treptow (urn section at Feuerhalle no. 18)
Käthe Kollwitz († 1945), graphic artist and sculptor (8th urn section, niche 2)
Otto Nagel († 1967), painter (8th urn section, niche 3)
Arnold von Golssenau († 1979), who wrote under the pseudonym »Ludwig Renn« (8th urn section, niche 7)
Erich Mielke († 2000), former chief of the Stasi (anonymous urn)

Gudrunstrasse, Lichtenberg (east K 20)

◄ S-Bahn: Lichtenberg (S 5, S 7, S 75, U 5)

The **Socialist Memorial** was formerly situated on what is now Row 46. It was created by Mies van der Rohe in 1926 but was destroyed by the Nazis in 1935. In 1951 it was reinstated in an entirely different form near the front of the cemetery close to the administration building. Memorial plaques recall Karl Liebknecht († 1919), Rosa Luxemburg († 1919) and Rudolf Breitscheid († 1944). Among those interred there are Wilhelm Liebknecht († 1900), Franz Mehring († 1919), Karl Legien († 1920), Wilhelm Pieck († 1960) and Walter Ulbricht († 1973). The neighbouring graveyard on Pergolenweg has

Gedenkstätte der Sozialisten

the graves of Adolf Hennecke († 1975), a worker who became famous in East Germany for exceeding production quotas and was hailed as an example to the country, as well as film director Konrad Wolf († 1982).

Friedhof Heerstrasse

Trakehner Allee, Charlottenburg (L9 west)
U-Bahn: Olympiastadion (U 2) ►

The large cemetery on Heerstrasse was opened in 1924 and its grounds are among the loveliest in Berlin. Many artists and actors are buried here, including

Paul Cassirer († 1926), art publisher (5C no. 4)
Maximilian Harden († 1927), critic and publicist (8C no. 10)
Arno Holz († 1929), writer (3B nos. 29/30)
Helene Lange († 1930), women's rights campaigner
Joachim Ringelnatz (Hans Bötticher, † 1934), writer (12D no. 21)
Georg Kolbe († 1947), sculptor (2D)
Paul Wegener († 1948), actor (4B)
George Grosz († 1959), painter and draughtsman (16B no. 19)
Curt Goetz († 1960), dramatist and actor, with his wife Valerie von Martens († 1986), actress (16G nos. 11/12)
Grete Weiser († 1970), actress (18L nos. 228/229)
Tilla Durieux († 1971), actress (5C no. 4)
Victor de Kowa († 1973), actor (16G Nr. 29)
Hilde Hildebrand († 1976), actress (6F no. 12)
Käthe Haack († 1986), actress (16J no. 27)

Alter St. Matthäus-Kirchhof (Cemetery of the old St Matthew's Church)

Grossgörschenstr. 12, Schöneberg (N 15)
S-Bahn: Grossgörschen-/Yorckstrasse (S 1, S 2, S 25) ►

Jacob and Wilhelm Grimm († 1863 and † 1859; F-s-1/14)
Adolf Diesterweg († 1866), educator (I-s-1)
Friedrich Drake († 1882), sculptor (D-o-30)
Wilhelm Loewe († 1886), last president of the German national assembly (Erb 270 L-sI)
Ernst Robert Curtius († 1896), historian and philologist (D-17-16)
Heinrich von Treitschke († 1896), historian (Q-o-16)
Rudolf Virchow († 1902), doctor and social scientist (H-s-12)
Max Bruch († 1920), composer (Q-w-85)

There is also a memorial stone to the conspirators who were executed on 20 July 1944: Claus Schenk Graf von Stauffenberg, Ludwig Beck, Friedrich Olbricht, Albrecht Mertz von Quirnheim and Werner von Haeften, who were initially buried here but were later exhumed and cremated, their ashes being scattered.

? DID YOU KNOW ...?

■ Marlene Dietrich is buried in the small Stubenrauchstrasse cemetery in the Schöneberg suburb of Friedenau (U-Bahn: Friedrich-Wilhelm-Platz, U 9). Not far from her grave is that of photographer Helmut Newton.

Waldfriedhof Dahlem

Erich Mühsam († 1934), writer (2A 144)
Bernd Rosemeyer († 1938), racing driver (11-4a)
Henriette Hebel a.k.a. »La Jana« († 1940), actress (22B 97)
Gottfried Benn († 1956), doctor and lyricist (27W 32)
Hilde Körber († 1969), actress (20B 1/2)
Karl Schmidt-Rottluff († 1976), painter (10E 11/12)
O. E. Hasse († 1978), actor (23A 7)

**Hüttenweg 47,
Zehlendorf (Q 9)**
◄ U-Bahn: Oskar-
Helene-Heim (U 3),
then by 111 bus

Waldfriedhof Zehlendorf

Ernst Reuter († 1953), mayor (VI 18/19) and behind him:
Willy Brandt († 1992), chancellor
Otto Suhr († 1957), mayor (III U 49)
Jakob Kaiser († 1961), federal minister (XIV W 1-5)
Erwin Piscator († 1966), superintendent of the Volksbühne
(XX 688-91)
Paul Löbe († 1967), president of the Reichstag (III U 24)
Hans Scharoun († 1972), architect (I U 24)
Helmut Käutner († 1980), actor and director (III U 7)
Hildegard Knef († 2002), actress

**Potsdamer
Chaussee 75,
Zehlendorf
(S / T 7)**
◄ S-Bahn: Mexiko-
platz (S 1), then by
211 bus

On the other side of Potsdamer Chaussee east of the Rehwiese stands
the protestant church of Nikolassee designed by Erich Blunck in
1911. The small cemetery opposite the church (Kirchweg 18/420)
has the graves of
Hermann Muthesius († 1927), architect (family plot 83)
Jochen Klepper († 1942), writer who chose to die with his Jewish
wife and daughter (J 1/4)
Richard Friedenthal († 1979), writer (C II 49/50)
Axel Springer († 1985), publisher (family plot 98)

**Friedhof
Nikolassee**

Südwestfriedhof

The Südwestfriedhof belonging to the Berlin synod is near Pots-
damer Damm in Stahnsdorf (Rudolf-Breitscheid-Platz), which is part
of the Potsdam district. Its graves include
Werner von Siemens († 1892), industrialist
Gustav Langenscheidt († 1895), publisher
Engelbert Humperdinck († 1921), composer
Lovis Corinth († 1925), painter
Heinrich Zille († 1929), who drew scenes of the Berlin »milieu«
F. W. Murnau († 1931), film director
Erik Jan Hannussen (Hermann Steinschneider, † 1933), famous
spiritualist
Rudolf Breitscheid († 1944), SPD Reichstag member who was mur-
dered by Nazi stormtroopers

**Potsdam,
Stahnsdorf
(T 6 west)**
◄ S-Bahn: Babels-
berg (S 7), then by
601, 602 or 603 bus

Jewish Cemeteries

Note: When visiting Jewish cemeteries it is essential to cover your head (headwear can sometimes be hired from the administration buildings).

Alter Jüdischer Friedhof

Grosse Hamburger Str. 26, Mitte (K 17)
S-Bahn: Hackescher Markt (S 5, S 75, S 9) ►

Little remains of the oldest Jewish cemetery in Berlin, which was inaugurated in 1672. More than 3000 people were buried there before it closed in 1827. The cemetery was obliterated by the Nazis in 1943. There are now memorial stones commemorating:

Moses Mendelssohn († 1786), philosopher
Veitel Heine Ephraim († 1775), head of the royal mint under Friedrich II
Daniel Itzig († 1799), banker

Jüdischer Friedhof Schönhauser Allee

Schönhauser Allee 22/23, Prenzlauer Berg, (J 18)
U-Bahn: Senefelderplatz (U 2) ►

This cemetery was opened in 1827 to replace the aforementioned cemetery on Grosser Hamburger Strasse, which closed at the same time. People continued to be buried here until 1942 and among their number were:

Giacomo Meyerbeer († 1864), composer
Ludwig Löwe († 1886), factory owner and parliamentarian
Gerson von Bleichröder († 1893), banker and adviser to Bismarck
Leopold Ullstein († 1899), publisher
Max Liebermann († 1935), painter

Jüdischer Friedhof Weissensee

Herbert-Baum-Strasse, Weissensee (H 19)
Tram: M 4 ►

A Jewish cemetery that opened in 1880 and covers an area of some 40ha/100ac. The entrance and mourners hall with its yellow bricks were designed by Hugo Licht. It is the largest Jewish cemetery in western Europe and is the last resting place of some 115,000 people. There is a plaque at the gate listing the graves of:

Hermann Tietz († 1907), owner of the »Hertie« stores
Rudolf Mosse († 1920), newspaper publisher
Adolf Jandorf († 1931), founder of the »KaDeWe«
Lesser Ury († 1931), Impressionist painter
Samuel S. Fischer († 1934), publisher
Theodor Wolff († 1943), journalist
Stefan Heym († 2001), writer

Urns of 809 concentration camp victims are also kept in the cemetery and there are around 3000 graves of people who committed suicide during the time of Nazi rule. Jewish resistance fighter Herbert Baum († 1943) also has his grave here. Alex Tucholsky († 1905), the father of Kurt Tucholsky, is buried here, too. His mother died in Theresienstadt. This is a translation of Tucholsky's poem dedicated to the cemetery: »The clock is ticking. Your grave has time, three metres long, three metres wide. You see another three, four cities.

You see Grete, naked. Snow twenty or thirty times more – and then: field P – in Weissensee – in Weissensee«.

Friedhof der Adass-Jisroel-Gemeinde

The cemetery for the orthodox Jewish community of Adass Jisroel was closed in the mid-1970s and left in neglect. The Adassians have restored the site since 1986 and have reinstated it for use as a cemetery for their community. Between 1939 and 1942 a great many urns with the remains of Jews murdered in the concentration camps were brought here. There is a memorial to those victims of the fanatical racism of Nazi Germany (Wittlicher Str., Weissensee/east of H 19, Tram 12 from Friedhof Weissensee).

Jüdischer Friedhof Heerstrasse

A small Jewish cemetery was opened in Charlottenburg in 1955 to the west of Scholzplatz, between Heerstrasse and

In the Weissensee cemetery

Am Postfenn, and south of the neighbouring British military cemetery. Many headstones from the Spandau citadel are located here, including one from the 14th century. There is also a memorial to Jewish victims of the Nazis. Hans Rosenthal (► Famous People) is also buried here (Charlottenburg / M 9 west; U-Bahn: Theodor-Heuss-Platz (U 2, U 12), then by 149 bus).

◄ ★ Schloss Charlottenburg and Park

Location: Luisenplatz 1, Charlottenburg
Bus: M 45, 109, 309

U-Bahn: Richard-Wagner-Platz (U 7)

Since the demolition of Berlin's Stadtschloss (► Schlossplatz), Schloss Charlottenburg is now the finest example of the vigour and artistry of architecture under the kings of Prussia in Berlin.

In 1695 Brandenburg's royal director of building **Johann Arnold Nering** was commissioned to build a small summer residence for Elector Friedrich III's wife, Sophie Charlotte. Nering died before completion

Berlin's most exquisite Baroque palace

of this »Lietzenburg« palace (named after the district of Lützenburg). Thereafter Martin Grünberg took over supervision of the building work, adding the two side wings to house the palace retinue. Grünberg's successor, **Johann Eosander von Göthe**, a favourite of Sophie Charlotte, appended the central projection at the front in order to make space for a domed tower, 48m/157ft in height. After Sophie Charlotte died in 1705, the palace was given its present name in her honour. Between 1709 and 1712 Eosander von Göthe also erected an orangery on the western side. Under Frederick the Great **Georg Wenzeslaus von Knobelsdorff** made plans to supplement an orangery on the eastern side with a new wing (1740–46) and in the reign of Friedrich Wilhelm II a small theatre was built in addition to the orangery under the supervision of Carl Gotthard Langhans (1788). This brought the total length of the building to 505m/552yd. Both before and after Sophie Charlotte became the first queen of Prussia, the palace was the scene of many spectacular festivals and balls. In Frederick the Great's time it was used for large family gatherings. During the 19th century it became home to the Countess of Liegnitz, wife of Friedrich Wilhelm III, and Friedrich Wilhelm IV also lived there for a time. The entire complex suffered serious damage in an

Even if Charlottenburg lays claim to being Berlin's finest palace, Friedrich II preferred Potsdam's Sanssouci.

air raid on 23 November 1943 and the restoration took a great deal of time. It included replacing the statue of Fortuna on the dome with a copy made by Richard Scheibe.

Altes Schloss (Old Palace) (guided tours only): Apr – Oct Tue – Sun ⊙
10am – 4pm, Nov – March Tue – Sun 10am – 7pm, last tour 5pm
New wing (admission free): Apr – Oct daily except Tue 10am – 8pm,
Nov – Mar 10am – 5pm
Schinkel Pavilion: daily except Mon 10am – 5pm
Belvedere: Apr – Oct daily except Mon 10am – 8pm; Nov – March
daily except Mon noon – 4pm
Mausoleum of Queen Luise: March – May daily except Tue
10am – 4pm

An entrance flanked with two reproductions of the Borghese gladiator leads to a forecourt with a mounted statue of the Great Elector Friedrich Wilhelm in the centre. The statue is one of the most important equestrian monuments of the Baroque period (► ill. p.44). The design was commissioned by Friedrich III, son of the Great Elector, from **Andreas Schlüter**. Casting began in October 1700 and the statue was formally unveiled on 12 July 1703, the anniversary of the first Prussian monarch's birth. Friedrich Wilhelm is depicted in a mixture of Roman and contemporary garb featuring a brass breastplate and a flowing wig with his staff of command extended in authoritative fashion. The coat of arms on the marble pedestal has a Latin inscription expressing the gratitude of his son. The figures on chains at each end of the pedestal signify the elector's defeated enemies. The monument was originally situated at the Stadtschloss on the Long Bridge or Elector's Bridge, which is nowadays called the Rathausbrücke. In 1943 it was to be moved to safety by barge but the overloaded vessel sank in Tegel dock. The statue was salvaged in 1949 and erected in its current position three years later.

Ehrenhof ✱
◄ Statue of the Great Elector

The rooms used by Friedrich I (bedroom, study, the »braided room«, the audience chamber) and his second wife Sophie Charlotte (audience chamber, anteroom, living rooms) are on the western side of the Altes Schloss. The furnishings are mainly painted Chinese pieces, or European imitations, or carved and inlaid pieces dating from around 1700. Among the most remarkable of the rooms are the **Porzellankabinett (porcelain cabinet)** with its Far Eastern porcelain of the 17th and 18th centuries, the palace chapel where King Friedrich Wilhelm II entered into a morganatic marriage with Countess Julie von Ingenheim, and the tapestry room (Gobelinraum), which features two hangings from the *Grossmogul* series made in Jean Barraband II's Berlin studio at the beginning of the 18th century called *Die Teetrinker* (The Tea Drinker) and *Der mongolische Kaiser* (The Mongol Emperor). The large and fabulously carved and panelled oak gallery in the eastern wing of the palace was constructed in 1713.

Altes Schloss (Nering-Eosander Building)

Pure opulence: the porcelain cabinet

New wing (Knobelsdorff wing) In the adjoining »new wing« the ground floor houses the summer residence and the permanent residence of Friedrich Wilhelm III. On the first floor of the same wing are the apartments of Frederick the Great as well as two reception rooms. The walls of the great dining hall (Weisser Saal) are panelled with pink marble stucco and the 42m/46yd-long Golden Gallery leading away to the east, and taking up the entire width of the wing, contains some fabulous gilded stucco decoration. The former **apartments of Frederick the Great** – including the Yellow Atlas Chamber with its Rococo furnishings, specially created by Johann August Nahl in 1744 for the silver dining hall at Schloss Potsdam – include an important collection of paintings from the early 18th century French school, among them Nicolas Lancret's *Magic Lantern Man* and *Shop Sign of the Art Dealer Gersaint*, which is one of the most famous works by Antoine Watteau.

✱ Charlottenburg Park

The park was laid out as a French-style garden by Siméon Godeau in 1697 and was largely remodelled in English style by Peter Joseph Lenné at the beginning of the 19th century. The »Parterre«, however, has been restored as a Baroque garden in more recent times.

Schinkel Pavillon The Neue Pavillon (Schinkel Pavillon) at the eastern entrance was built in 1824/25 to designs drawn up by Karl Friedrich Schinkel and emulates a Neapolitan villa. Friedrich Wilhelm III commissioned the

Charlottenburg Plan

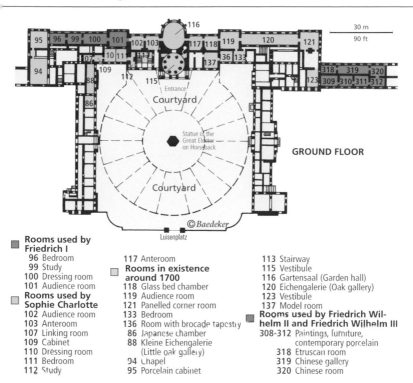

© Baedeker

Rooms used by Friedrich I
96 Bedroom
99 Study
100 Dressing room
101 Audience room

Rooms used by Sophie Charlotte
102 Audience room
103 Anteroom
107 Linking room
109 Cabinet
110 Dressing room
111 Bedroom
112 Study

117 Anteroom

Rooms in existence around 1700
118 Glass bed chamber
119 Audience room
121 Panelled corner room
133 Bedroom
136 Room with brocade tapestry
86 Japanese chamber
88 Kleine Eichengalerie (Little oak gallery)
94 Chapel
95 Porcelain cabinet

113 Stairway
115 Vestibule
116 Gartensaal (Garden hall)
120 Eichengalerie (Oak gallery)
123 Vestibule
137 Model room

Rooms used by Friedrich Wilhelm II and Friedrich Wilhelm III
308-312 Paintings, furniture, contemporary porcelain
318 Etruscan room
319 Chinese gallery
320 Chinese room

pavilion for himself and his second wife, Princess Liegnitz. It has several paintings on display, including some by C. D. Friedrich.

Belvedere

The Belvedere at the northern end of the park was built in 1788 by Carl Gotthard Langhans as a tea house. Nowadays it houses the Federal State of Berlin's collection of KPM (Königliche Porzellan Manufaktur or Royal Porcelain Factory) porcelain.

Mausoleum

At the end of an avenue of pines in the west of the park there is a small Doric temple with columns at the front made of erratic granite blocks found in the March of Brandenburg. This is the mausoleum that Friedrich Wilhelm III had built by Heinrich Gentz as the last resting place of Queen Luise (1776 – 1810). It was completed in 1812 and expanded in 1841 and 1889. The sarcophagus and the statue of the queen were created by **Christian Daniel Rauch**. The statue of the queen shows her asleep with her hands folded and dressed in a light dress that falls loosely from her reclining form. Thirty years after its construction her husband was also buried in the mausoleum. His sarcophagus was also designed by Rauch and shows the king in a simple greatcoat. Others were also interred here as time went by, including Prince Albert (1809–72), Kaiser Wilhelm I (1797–1888) and his wife Augusta (1811–90) as well as Princess Liegnitz, second wife of Friedrich Wilhelm III (1800–73). The heart of Friedrich Wilhelm IV (1795–1861) is kept in a special stone capsule.

Dahlem

P – Q 8 – 10

Borough: Steglitz-Zehlendorf   **U-Bahn:** Dahlem-Dorf (U 3)

Dahlem, in southwest Berlin, has long been one of the most affluent areas in the city. There is a good reason for this in that Kaiser Wilhelm II was particularly attracted to the area and inspired the institution of an academic quarter.

The results of this are still to be seen in the form of aristocratic villas, the university and some excellent museums accompanied by an almost rural idyll with plenty of green open spaces. The first mention of the locale dates from 1375 where it appears in the Land Book of Karl IV as »Dalm«. It remained as an estate or manor domain until the 19th century when the final owners surrendered it to the district tax authorities. In 1901 the area was divided up, part of it being used to build cottages and the rest being set aside for scientific establishments. Dahlem has considerable cultural and scientific importance within Berlin nowadays as the home of the Freie Universität (Free University), various institutes belonging to the Technische Universität (Technical University), the Max Planck Society and Dahlem's own museums.

★
Botanical gardens

The botanical gardens originated as a kitchen and herb garden for the elector's household at the Berlin Stadtschloss in the Lustgarten (▶Berliner Dom). The Great Elector decreed in 1679 that a »model garden« be laid out in Schöneberg – in what is now the Kleistpark. This developed into a real botanical garden. At the turn of the twentieth century it was relocated to Dahlem. Botanist Adolf Engler (1844–1930; his gravestone is to the left of the main avenue) fashioned this into one of the largest and most important botanical gardens in the world between 1899 and 1910. It covers an area of about 42ha/104ac and features more than 18,000 types of plant. There are fields laid out according to the geographical origins of the plants, a forestry section (with about 1800 types of tree and shrub), a section for cultivated and medicinal plants, 16 greenhouses (the largest hothouse is 60m/66yd long, 30m/33yd wide and 25m/82ft high), a biotope for water and marsh dwelling plants, the Elector's Garden with

Lily pond in the botanic gardens in Dahlem

plants dating from the 17th century as well as a special »touch and smell« garden for the blind and partially sighted.

From 2006 to 2009 the Grosses Tropenhaus (Great Tropical House), with a surface areas of 1750 sq m/19,000 sq ft and a height of 26.5m/ 87ft one of the world's largest hothouses without internal supports, was renovated and brought up to date in technical terms, halving its energy consumption. When it was built between 1905 and 1907 to a design by the royal architect Alfred Koerner the structure, consisting of a roof supported only from the exterior to which glass walls were added, was a sensation. This method of construction allows plant lovers to admire the tropical jungle without supports and pillars to spoil the view. With 1358 species and over 4000 tropical plants, the Tropenhaus also holds one the world's greatest varieties of plant life and is a veritable Noah's ark for endangered species.

★
◀ Grosses Tropenhaus

The Botanical Museum next to the entrance from Königin-Luise-Strasse has a herbarium with more than two million plants and a comprehensive botanical library. The Egyptian section is notable, as is a room that features various types of poisonous and edible mushrooms. There are **two entrances** to the botanical gardens: Königin-Luise-Str. 6 – 8 (near the Königin-Luise-Platz bus stop) and Unter den Eichen 5 – 10 (approached from the S-Bahn station).

◀ Botanisches Museum

Gardens: Nov – Jan daily 9am – 4pm, Feb closes 5pm, Mar and Oct closes 6pm, Sept open till 7pm, April and Aug till 8pm, May, June, July till 9pm; last admission 30 minutes before closing. Hothouses as gardens, at weekends from 10am; **Botanisches Museum**: 10am – 6pm daily.

◷

Dahlem-Dorf U-Bahn station

The picturesquely rustic underground railway station, Dahlem-Dorf is a half timbered, thatched building, erected in 1913 at the behest of Kaiser Wilhelm II.

Domäne Dahlem

🕐 Opening hours: 10am – 6pm daily except Tue

The Domäne Dahlem farm museum opposite the U-Bahn station is still farmed. The land covers 12 hectares/30 acres and the harvest is sold in the farm's own health food shop. The open-air museum, »the only farm in Berlin with its own U-Bahn station«, also hosts a varied programme of tours and events. Historic craft workshops including a blueprinting establishment and bee-keeping with a bee museum can also be viewed, and various other craft skills are regularly demonstrated. The **Gutshaus** or farmhouse is a Baroque building erected in 1680 by Cuno Hans of Willmerstorff and features the Willmerstorff Alliance crest on the gable. As part of the Domäne farm museum it now portrays the agricultural history of Berlin and Brandenburg, with its own nostalgic village shop. The Gothic chapel on the ground floor is also open to the public: its market days and craft festivals seem to attract half of Berlin. Further along Königin-Luise-Strasse is the **St.-Annen-Kirche** (St Anne's Church), built in 1220. Its late Gothic chancel dates from the 15th century while its Baroque pulpit and gallery were added in 1679. In the cemetery **the grave of the APO activist Rudi Dutschke** can be seen, and the theologian Helmut Gollwitzer (1908 – 93) is also buried here.

❓ DID YOU KNOW ...?

■ ... that the tower of Dahlem's village church was used from 1832 to 1892 as an intermediate station on the first optical telegraph line from Berlin to Koblenz?

✳ ✳ Dahlem Museums

🕐 Opening hours: Tue – Fri 10am – 6pm; Sat, Sun 11am – 6pm

The main attractions in Dahlem are the Berlin State Museums (run by the Prussian Cultural Heritage Foundation – Stiftung Preussischer Kulturbesitz), which have brought together their ethnographic collections in the village. The split-site locations are at Im Winkel (Museum Europäischer Kulturen – Museum of European Cultures) and the three-storey museum building on Lansstrasse, which was built between 1914 and 1923 by Bruno Paul. It was originally planned to house an Asian museum but has been extended at various times and now houses the Ethnologisches Museum as well as the Museen für Indische und Ostasiatische Kunst (Museums for Indian and Far Eastern Art).

Museum Europäischer Kulturen

The Museum of European Cultures (Arnimallee 25) was founded in 1999 to combine the ethnographic collections of the Museum für Volkskunde (Folklore Museum) founded by Rudolf Virchow and the European possessions of the former Völkerkundemuseum. It is divided into two sections, respectively covering the meaning of images in everyday life and the places where those images were perceived.

The museums formerly devoted to Indian art and Far Eastern art have now been amalgamated to form the Museum of Asian Art. The collections from South, Southeast and Central Asia on the ground floor in the left-hand wing include terra-cotta pieces, stone sculptures, bronze work, wood carvings and paintings from India, the countries of the Himalayas and Central and Southeast Asia. The oldest pieces date from the 2nd century BC while the most recent are from the 19th century. Nearly all the major Asian religions including Buddhism, Hinduism and Jainism are represented. The »Turfan« collection with its murals and sculptures from the 5th to the 12th centuries is the key highlight. They were brought to Berlin from Buddhist temples on the northern part of the Silk Road by four expeditions that took place between 1902 and 1914. The most impressive of the features is the reconstruction of a temple cave in Kizil with an original fresco, *The Ring-bearing Doves*, painted from 431 to 533. Two computer terminals are provided from which it is possible to learn about the life and works of Buddha. The Ostasiatische Kunstsammlung (Collection of Far Eastern Art) now bears once again the name it was given when founded in 1906 and since 1992 has united in Dahlem the »Far Eastern Collection« established in East Berlin with those pieces that were not transported to the Soviet Union after the war. Most of the collection that once existed nevertheless remains in the Hermitage of St Petersburg in Russia. The current sections – the core of which come from a collection belonging to art dealer Klaus Naumann – cover Chinese archaeology, Far Eastern Buddhist art, Japanese paintings and Chinese, Japanese or Korean arts and crafts including bronzes, ceramics, ink drawings, carvings, sculptures, paint and enamel works, screens, scrolls, jade carvings, grave items, tsuba pieces, miniature sculptures and furniture (including the throne of a Chinese emperor with screen from one of the emperor's provincial residences, dating from the second half of the 17th century), mother of pearl inlays, silk tapestries and embroidery. There is even a complete Japanese tea room.

★
Museum für Asiatische Kunst

◄ Collection from South, Southeast and Central Asia

◄ Ostasiatische Kunstsammlung

This is one of the best ethnological museums in the world and is far more extensive than the other two museums in the building. It possesses more than 500,000 exhibits and 60,000 musicological recordings from all over the world and presently features ancient American items (ground floor), exhibits from the South Seas (ground floor and upper floor), African items (upper floor) and Far Eastern works (attic). The African exhibition is particularly notable for its terra-cotta sculptures from Ife (western Nigeria, 10th–13th centuries), **bronze pieces from Benin** (16th century), a royal throne and a collection of masks from the grasslands of Cameroon as well as an initiation mask made by the Chokwe of southwest Congo. The Central and South American section features the »Golden Chamber« with pieces from Columbia, Costa Rica and Peru (including ancient Incan sacrifice dishes). The South Seas section includes an exhibition of

★ ★
Ethnologisches Museum

boats including an **ocean-going vessel from Luf** as well as original dwellings from New Guinea, the Palau Islands and New Zealand. On the ground floor there is an exhibition covering the North American Indians that has been recently refurbished. Among its most impressive items are some of the artefacts of the Prairie Indians, which include what is probably the oldest leather tepee still in existence (made by the Lakota tribe around 1820/30). Many of the exhibits were collected by Prince Maximilian of Wied, Duke Paul von Württemberg and Balduin of Möllnhausen on their various expeditions. Blind visitors to the museum have a hall of their own where they can touch and examine models of various buildings.

Juniormuseum ▶
⏱
The Juniormuseum is aimed at youngsters of eight and under who are interested in ethnology (entrance from Arnimallee 25; Tue – Fri 1pm to 6pm, Sat/Sun 11am – 6pm): they can go on safari here.

✱ Deutsches Technikmuseum
(German Museum of Technology)

N 15

Location: Trebbiner Str. 9, Kreuzberg   **U-Bahn:** Gleisdreieck (U 1, U 2, U 12, U 15), Möckernbrücke (U 7)

The German Museum of Technology, opened in 1983 as the Museum für Verkehr und Technik (Transport and Technology Museum) on premises used by the city markets and refrigerated storehouses, also includes the site of the Anhalter Bahnhof railway yard and the Anhalter goods yard.

⏱
Opening hours:
Tue – Fri
9am – 5.30pm,
Sat, Sun
10am – 6pm
For tours, telephone
90 25 41 24

The hall built for the horses of the market company in 1908 now accommodates the museum entrance, shop and cafeteria. The first floor is devoted to textile and communications technologies, the second floor to paper and printing, computing and automation. One of the highlights is a replica of the »Z 1«, the world's first computer, made by the Berliner Konrad Zuse in 1936.

New building

The themes in the new building, air, space and sea travel, are presented with the latest museum technology. Three whole floors are dedicated to water transport, subdivided into the inland waterways between the rivers Elbe and Oder on the ground floor, where there is a 33m/108ft-long barge dating from 1840, and sea shipping on the second floor. Above that the two floors of the air and space department contain a great many original items. The stand-out exhibits here are fully restored aircraft such as a Junkers 52, a Messerschmidt 109 and, on the terrace, one of the famous »raisin bombers« of the Berlin Airlift, as well as a fantastic collection of medals belonging to almost all the ace fighter pilots of the First World War. The evolution of German rocket science is also presented, with attention paid to

Landmark of the German Museum of Technology: a Douglas C47 »Skytrain«, one of the »Rosinenbomber« aircraft used in the Berlin Airlift

the appalling conditions of labour of the concentration camp inmates who worked in rocket production.

The two locomotive sheds of 1874 display »33 stages in railway history« with locomotives, wagons and station equipment, as original exhibits and models, including 40 wagons, some going back to 1840, and the Fürstenportal (Princes' Gate) of the Anhalter Bahnhof. A new exhibition examines the role played by the German state railways in the deportation of Jews to the death camps. In the railway offices behind the locomotive sheds departments for photography, films, scientific instruments, production technology and household technology can be seen. This includes the museum's own suitcase manufacture (a popular souvenir) and jewellery workshop In the park around the museum there are windmills and wind generators, a water wheel and a water tower.

Loco sheds and open-air museum

The principle of operation of many exhibits is illustrated by more than 250 experiments in the interactive **Spectrum** section in Möckernstrasse, which also features a double swing, a fog chamber and a Foucault pendulum in the atrium.

◀ Spectrum

Exhibition Grounds

Location: Hammarskjöldplatz, Charlottenburg
U-Bahn: Kaiserdamm (U 2)

S-Bahn: Messe Süd (S 7, S 75)
Messe Nord (S 41, S 42, S 46)

Major exhibitions and trade fairs such as the International Agricultural Exhibition or Green Week, the International Tourism Exchange and the International Radio Exhibition attract hundreds of thousands of visitors to the exhibition grounds at the base of the Funkturm (radio tower) every year.

Exhibition Centre Plan

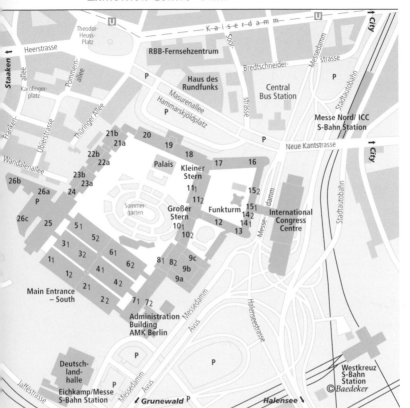

The first of the exhibition halls were erected at the beginning of the 1920s. The grounds were expanded to form a rectangular layout of halls in 1936 and after 1945. Finally Halls 1 to 7 were added in 1999. The oldest parts still standing include the Palais next to the Funkturm, which dates from the 1930s. To the south of the rectangle of halls is the Deutschlandhalle, built in 1957 and measuring 140m/460ft in length and 120m/394ft in width so that it can accommodate up to 8000 people (for sporting events, concerts etc). Between Halls 10 and 12 and along the Messedamm road visitors will find a Japanese garden and the Ursula Sax sculpture *Doppel-Looping*. Running along the south of the exhibition grounds parallel to the Messedamm road is the northern loop of the former Avus race track.

Avus ►

★
Funkturm

The Funkturm or radio tower is another of the city's major landmarks and has been affectionately dubbed »Langer Lulatsch« (beanpole) by Berliners. It was built in 1924 according to plans by Heinrich Straumer and features a steel girder construction mounted on ceramic piers. It first went into service at the third German Radio Exhibition in 1926. In 1930 it broadcast the world's first public television programmes; in 1945 a grenade destroyed one of the main girders but the tower did not collapse. It is 138m/453ft high (150m/492ft including the antennae) and has both a restaurant at 55m/180ft and an observation platform at a height of 126m/413ft, both of which offer fantastic views of the city.

◄ Viewing platform open 10am – 11pm daily

The International Congress Centre lies to the east of the exhibition grounds and is linked to them via a roofed bridge over the Messedamm. Before the new development at ►Potsdamer Platz, it was the largest building in Berlin built since the war (built 1970 – 79). The overall length of the complex is 320m/350yd, it is 80m/87yd wide and 40m/131ft high. The floor space covered by the building is some 800,000 cu m/1,050,000 cu yd. There are more than 80 rooms and halls for congresses and seminars. The largest hall, Saal 1, accommodates up to 5000 people.

International Congress Centre (ICC)

Another legacy of Germany's radio history lies to the north east just outside the exhibition grounds on Masurenallee. The five-storey Haus des Rundfunks (Broadcasting House) was built between 1929 and 1931 by Hans Poelzig and features a distinctive entrance hall. A television centre (1965 – 70) is situated to the north of it.

Broadcasting House

✱ Fernsehturm (Television Tower)

K 17

Location: Mitte
City centre map: B 14

S-Bahn and U-Bahn: Alexanderplatz
(S 3, S 5, S 7, S 75, S 9, U 2, U 5, U 8)

The TV Tower or Fernsehturm has become one of Berlin's most distinctive landmarks.

It came into existence because the East German republic needed a nationwide broadcasting facility, but its size and appearance arose from the GDR leaders' desire for a symbol to represent the socialist part of Germany to the world. It was inspired by Hermann Henselmann, the architect of the Karl-Marx-Allee development (► Friedrichshain), who envisioned a »dominating tower of socialism«. Construction began on 4 August 1965 using a design by architects Fritz Dieter and Günter Franke and a team of Swedish engineers. The tower was put into operation as early as 3 October 1969. At 368m/1207ft high (including antenna) it is the tallest building in the city. A viewing platform is placed at a height of 203m/666ft. 4m/13ft below that is the **Telecafé**, which makes a complete revolution every half

🕐
Viewing platform:
March – Oct
9am – 1pm daily,
Nov – Feb
10am – midnight
daily

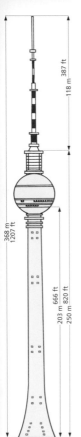

387 ft
118 m

368 m
1207 ft

203 m 666 ft
250 m 820 ft

© Baedeker

hour. In good weather it is possible to see for 40km/25mi. The Fernsehturm was hailed by the central organ of the ruling party, the SED, as a symbol of »New Germany«, the »Telespargel (TV asparagus)«, but the people themselves gave it several other playfully subversive nicknames including »Imponierkeule« (show-off's club), »Protzstengel« (swank stalk) or »St Walter« (since SED chief and state council leader Walter Ulbricht was said to have chosen the site). The GDR leadership were also mightily displeased the first time the sun shone on the mirrored ball since the reflection took the form of a cross, causing it to be dubbed the »Pope's revenge« on the atheist regime. The phenomenon is apparent every time the sun shines on Berlin.

Friedrichshain

K – M 18 – 20

Borough: Friedrichshain-Kreuzberg

S-U-Bahn: S 3, S 5, S 7, S 75, S 9, S 41, S 42, U 5

Like ► Prenzlauer Berg before Friedrichshain is undergoing a change from inconspicuous suburb to happening scene.

The traditionally rather dowdy working class district is increasingly being discovered by the well-to-do, sporting designer suits; artists, fashion gurus and young academics have also been moving in. The barbers and hairdressers are now hair stylists and busloads of tourists are descending on the fashionable new bars around Boxhagener Platz; Simon-Dach-Strasse, in particular, has become a mecca for pub-lovers and café-goers. What was formerly the smallest of Berlin's boroughs has now been amalgamated with neighbouring ► Kreuzberg on the other side of the Spree. It is not necessarily an essential item on the tourist itinerary in Berlin but it does have the former Stalinallee, the epitome of socialist architecture, and the park that gives the borough its name is one of the prettiest in the city.

Karl-Marx-Allee

Karl-Marx-Allee was built from 1952 as part of a »National Reconstruction Programme for Berlin«. Initially called **Stalinallee**, it was renamed in 1961; it was built on the site of a high-density rental district that had been utterly destroyed by bombs. The thoroughfare starts from the southeast corner of ► Alexanderplatz in the city centre and runs all the way to Strausberger Platz in Friedrichshain. Here begins the section of

? DID YOU KNOW ...?

■ Naturally Stalinallee had its obligatory memorial to the Soviet dictator. It stood at the southern edge between Andreasstrasse and Koppenstrasse and was not torn down until 1961.

Probably the most famous surviving piece of the Berlin Wall: East Side Gallery

the development that has gone down in German history: when the site was being built, the resentment of the workers against the excessive quotas boiled over into rebellion on 17 June 1953. The section between Strausberger Platz, dominated by the two skyscrapers »Haus Berlin« and »Haus des Kindes«, and Frankfurter Tor with its two tall domes is nevertheless that part of the site which most clearly exhibits the ambitions of the East German leadership. It is a »socialist magistral« with cheap but well appointed workers' apartments: giant housing blocks, tiled with Meissner ceramics, in the typical »confectionery style« of the Stalin era that had genuinely remarkable features such as central heating and waste disposal units. Karl-Marx-Allee is now a listed site. New tenants, a young and creative crowd, are starting to revive a street that had been declared dead with their chic offices and galleries.

Ostbahnhof

The Ostbahnhof to the south of Friedrichshain was called Schlesischer Bahnhof (Silesian station) until 1950 and was at one time the central terminus in Berlin. Until 2006 it was the main inter-city station in the east of Berlin. It was opened in 1842 as the Frankfurter Bahnhof for the line to Frankfurt an der Oder (extended to Breslau/Wroclaw in 1847).

East Side Gallery

A preserved section of the old Berlin Wall, 1.3km/1420yd long, leads away to the southeast of the station along Mühlenstrasse as far as the Oberbaumbrücke. Its design is that of the outer or Vorderland wall, although it was actually situated on the eastern side. It was intended to block off the view from the west, because Mühlenstrasse was on the motorcade route taken by dignitaries visiting the GDR from Schönefeld airport to the centre. After the fall of the Wall, 118 artists painted murals on this section and their works have achieved a kind of fame: the picture of that passionate embrace between Honecker and Brezhnev is known the world over. Thanks to a breach in the Wall and jetties for boats opposite the new O2-World Arena, the banks of the Spree are becoming a park and part of the new Mediaspree quarter.

Oberbaum City At the end of the East Side Gallery, beyond the Oberbaum bridge leading to ▶ Kreuzberg, the lights of Warschauer Strasse never went out as this was the site of the Osram factory and of VEB Narva bulbs after the war. The factory was closed in 1992 and Oberbaum City was built on the site as a service park and industrial estate. It includes the **International Design Centre Berlin**, which regularly puts on interesting exhibitions (information: www.idz.de).

On the Spree The Eierkühlhaus, once a refrigerated store for eggs built in 1928 by Oskar Pusch on the Allee am Spreeufer has also found creative new tenants. In the Spree the so-called Molecule Men stand for the districts of Kreuzberg, Friedrichshain and Treptow, which meet here (ill. p.50). Beyond them at Eichenstrasse lies the **Badeschiff** (bathing boat) – a barge for inland waterways whose hold has been converted to a swimming pool.

✳
Volkspark Friedrichshain
Between Landsberger Allee and Am Friedrichshain in the northern part of the borough is the Volkspark Friedrichshain. In 1840, on the hundredth anniversary of Friedrich II's ascent to the throne, the city magistracy decided to create a park in counterpoint to the ▶ Tiergarten. It was laid out during the latter part of the 19th century by Gustav Meyer but its 52ha/128ac had to be redesigned after the Second World War when hills with views were created from the rubble of two flak bunkers. The highest of them is 78m/256ft tall. Next to the Königstor at the western entrance is the Märchenbrunnen (fairy tale fountain) built in 1913, featuring figures from the Grimms' fairy tales. In the northern half of the park there is a leisure centre and in the east there is an open-air stage. There are also some political memorials including the »Friedhof der Märzgefallenen« (Cemetery of the March Revolutionaries) for victims of the fighting on the barricades of the March 1848 revolution. The west of the park also has a monument to anti-fascist Germans who fell fighting for the International Brigades during the Spanish Civil War.

> **! Baedeker TIP**
>
> **Krempelmarkt (flea market)**
>
> Even sceptics who prefer to avoid »fashionable districts« will find the Sunday flea markets at Boxhagener Platz worth a visit, if not for the produce on sale then for the atmosphere that frequently takes on the feel of a public festival.

Friedrichshain hospital Alongside the east of the park is the large hospital, the Städtisches Krankenhaus Friedrichshain. It was the first state hospital to be set up, being constructed between 1868 and 1877.

✴ Friedrichstrasse

Location: Mitte
City centre map: O – M 10 – 12

S-Bahn: Friedrichstrasse (S 1, S 2, S 5, S 7, S 75, S 9)
U-Bahn: U 6 between Hallescher Tor and Oranienburger Tor

The name still calls to mind the era when it was the centre of Berlin's entertainment district. It is also, however, a name forever associated with the partition of Berlin, since between 1961 and 1989 the street was divided in two by the Wall and the famous Checkpoint Charlie at Zimmerstrasse.

Friedrichstrasse runs for about 3.3km/2mi in a north-south alignment from Oranienburger Tor in the city centre to Mehringplatz by the Hallescher Tor in Kreuzberg. Few traces of the division can be seen nowadays, and the glitter of days past has not yet been recaptured by the somewhat soulless modern buildings on the site. Friedrichstrasse was constructed under Friedrich Wilhelm I to allow a direct march from the parade grounds on Tempelhofer Feld. Under Wilhelm II too, troops would regularly march along the route to the

In search of the old glamour

Berlin's »loveliest legs« dancing through the Friedrichstadtpalast

---

! *Baedeker* TIP

Am Schiffbauerdamm

Where should you go after a revue at the Friedrichstadtpalast or an evening of theatre at the Berliner Ensemble? The ideal places are just around the corner along Schiffbauerdamm. Lovers of Rhineland Sauerbraten can visit the Ständige Vertretung bar and restaurant (tel. 2 82 39 65), beer devotees can try Berliner Republik (tel. 30 87 22 93) and gourmets should go to Ganymed (tel. 28 59 90 46) – once the premier restaurant of the East German capital. If there are no tables there, they could move on to Brecht (tel. 28 59 85 85) or across the bridge to the trendy Grill Royal (tel. 28 87 92 88). The romantic, dimly-lit atmosphere under the S-Bahn bridge comes for free.

palace from their manoeuvres. With the founding of the German Empire, or Reich, the boulevard underwent a »colossal boom«, during which the famous Kaisergalerie was built, shortly to be followed by the Friedrichstrassenpassage, which was twice the size. This was the basis from which Friedrichstrasse developed into imperial Germany's foremost shopping street, and even more so to its premier entertainment centre. It had high-class hotels, opera houses, beer halls and revue palaces. Behrenstrasse, the first side street after Unter den Linden, became synonymous with the might of money – the headquarters of the Deutsche Bank and the Berlin branch of the Dresdner Bank both stood there. After the First World War, Friedrichstrasse lost its status as the premier shopping destination to an up-and-coming republican pretender, Kurfürstendamm, but for those seeking entertainment it still held top slot. A major US air raid on 3 February 1945 destroyed the centre of Berlin and hardly a building was left standing on Friedrichstrasse. The partition of Berlin meant the areas either side of the zone borders decayed to frontier wilderness. The East German leadership sought to recapture the flair of a boulevard in a world metropolis by creating such buildings as the Friedrichstadtpalast and the Grand Hotel but their plans were overtaken by events. Since 1989 the street has seen a positive swarm of investors. Between Friedrichstrasse station in the north and the former Checkpoint Charlie practically every block has been built up with new buildings. Building shells and older buildings dating from the GDR period have mostly been demolished. Architects have had to keep to the historic height limits, but they apparently lost track when it came to maintaining the small scale and thus the diversity on offer – bars and cafés are a rarity here.

Friedrichstrasse North of Unter den Linden

From the crossroads of ▶Unter den Linden and Friedrichstrasse and walking along Friedrichstrasse towards the north, practically the first thing you see is the Dussmann department store on the right. It offers books, videos, CDs and DVDs aplenty, and has its own internet café plus another café with US styling. Not far away the 25-storey Internationale Handelszentrum or International Trade Centre (1978) towers 93m/305ft over the street.

Diagonally opposite is the legendary Friedrichstrasse station, which opened on 1 May 1882 as a suburban station. It quickly became the most important station in the capital of the Reich. Between 1924 and 1926 it was completely refurbished, receiving two parallel train sheds, one for long distance services and the other for S-Bahn trains. After the building of the Wall in 1961 it was the only place in the city where there was a direct connection for inter-city, S-Bahn and U-Bahn services: long-distance travellers from the west and residents of West Berlin using the U6 underground service, which actually passed under East Berlin, were allowed to take S-Bahn trains to the west, albeit from just two ex-territorial and closely guarded platforms. Those travelling to the east were suspiciously assembled into narrow enclosures by East German border guards, and on their return they had to make their farewells to friends in the so-called »**Tränenpalast**« or Palace of Tears. This for a while became one of the most popular venues for concerts and performances of all kinds. It has now disappeared behind the dull architecture of the new Spreedreieck (Spree triangle) and awaits restoration as a memorial site, which is planned for 2011.

Bahnhof Friedrichstrasse

Beyond the S-Bahn bridge on the right is the former Haus der Presse (1910) with the cabaret theatre »Die Distel«. In the courtyard at the back stands the Admiralspalast, built in 1910 by Heinrich Schweitzer and Alexander Diepenbrock as a swimming baths and skating rink. After 1955 it became home to the Metropol theatre. This is the very building in which the merger of the socialist SPD and communist KPD parties of Eastern Germany was forced through in April 1946 to create the Socialist Unity Party (SED). The Admiralspalast was re-opened in August 2006

Admiralspalast

The Weidendammbrücke (1895/96), with Prussian eagles on its wrought iron balustrades, of which Wolf Biermann sang in *The Ballad of the Prussian Icarus* bridges the Spree. Down on the left is Schiffbauerdamm where the Berliner Ensemble was opened in 1892 under the name »Theater am Schiffbauerdamm«. Among other claims to fame it was the venue for the first performance of the *Threepenny Opera*. In 1954 Bertolt Brecht and Helene Weigel took it over. She was to remain its manager until 1971. Am Zirkus leads away from Bertolt-Brecht-Platz and provides a reminder of the **Friedrichstadtpalast**, built in 1869 as Berlin's first market hall, which

Berliner Ensemble

Wolf Biermann sang of the Prussian eagles on Weidendammbrücke.

was renamed the »Zirkus« in 1874 and was rebuilt as Germany's largest theatre, the Grosses Schauspielhaus (Great Theatre) in 1919. It had its heyday under Max Reinhardt. The »Palast« was reopened in 1984 on Friedrichstrasse itself opposite the junction with Reinhardtstrasse, where it became *the* temple of entertainment in East Germany. Even today its revues attract hordes of people. In front of it there is a memorial to Claire Waldoff (▶Famous People).

A short diversion to the Charité

Go past Reinhardtstrasse, Albrechtstrasse and Schumannstrasse – where Max Reinhardt built the fame of the Deutsches Theater – to reach a site that was established as a plague house by a decree of King Friedrich I on 13 May 1710. This was the original Charité. Since Berlin was fortunate enough to be spared the worst of plague, the site was re-dedicated as a hospital. When the Friedrich Wilhelm University was established in 1810 it was agreed that the manager of the Charité would be declared a professor. The first dean of the hospital was **Christoph Wilhelm Hufeland**, who introduced immunization against smallpox. Others that have succeeded him include **Rudolf Virchow, Robert Koch and Ferdinand Sauerbruch**. Although not for those of a queasy disposition, the Berlin Museum of Medical History, which was co-founded by Rudolf Virchow, invites visitors to view its pathological and anatomical collection. Exhibits include medicinal compounds, surgical instruments and various items that used to be personal possessions of Rudolf Virchow himself in the Pathology building; Tue–Sun 10am–5pm, Wed and Sat till 7pm).

Medizinhistorisches Museum ▶

A dizzying interior and equally dizzying prices at Quartier 206, centre of luxury and fashion

Friedrichstrasse South of Unter den Linden

To the south of Unter den Linden is the section of Friedrichstrasse that has seen the majority of the new building work. Right at the crossroads with Unter den Linden is the Lindencorso. This was originally intended as a French cultural centre but now houses a car showroom. Opposite, next to the Grand Hotel, a prestige project for the GDR when it opened in 1987, the main outlet of the legendary Café Kranzler once stood. History was made in the building at Friedrichstrasse 165 (on the corner of Behrenstrasse). This was the »**Haus der Demokratie**« (House of Democracy), where groups such as Neue Forum, who demanded the democratization of East Germany, had their headquarters. Before that, the SED council leadership for the Mitte (city centre) borough was based here and before the war the building housed a popular cellar pub serving the produce of Munich's Pschorr brewery. Further along the street is the Russisches Haus (Russia House), where the Soviet scientific and culture missions were once located.

The highlight of the new architecture on Friedrichstrasse – in terms of both size and cost – is the completely new Friedrichstadtpassagen, a complex of buildings that cost 1.4 billion deutschmarks. It consists of three blocks connected to each other underground and situated on the left-hand side of Französischerstrasse and Mohrenstrasse. The most northerly of the blocks (architect: Jean Nouvel of Paris), Quartier 207 (as per the old street numbering), rather stands out from the others as the only building made entirely of glass, with its elegantly curved corner. It has been occupied by the Berlin branch of the famous Paris store **Galeries Lafayette**. The spectacular 37m/ 120ft atrium with its two cones one above the other has often garnered more attention than the shop's own product lines. **Quartier 206** (architects: I. M. Pei, Cobb and Freed, New York) harks back to Art Deco architecture with its expressive façade featuring a myriad strips of lights. The floor of the inner courtyard enchants shoppers with Carrara marble. Beware though, the prices charged by the top-range shops in the building are just as breathtaking. **Quartier 205** (architect: O. M. Ungers, Cologne) is the most muted and formal of the buildings with the square geometry of its stark façade. Its array of stores and fashion boutiques is also on the conservative side.

Friedrichstadt-passagen

Who invented Germany's very own fast food, the curry sausage? Which ingredients make the sauce so spicy? Is Berlin's snack-bar culture thriving? To find the answer to these and other questions, visit the Deutsches Currywurstmuseum at Schützenstr. 70 (daily 10am – 10pm).

Deutsches Currywurst-museum

The border between the Soviet and the American sectors of post-war Berlin crossed Friedrichstrasse at Zimmerstrasse. The crossing was

Former Checkpoint Charlie

marked by the famous border post for foreign visitors, Checkpoint Charlie. Nowadays it is hard to believe that the site was once at the very crux of the Cold War. What was at this time a vast empty space has been filled by the American Business Center building. At the former border crossing, there is just a single sentry tower, a warning sign, a strip of paving, one outsized picture of a Soviet soldier and a GI plus a copy of the famous guard house. To find out how it once looked and how many desperate attempts were made to cross the border out of East Germany, visit the Museum at Checkpoint Charlie. The museum also highlights the human rights movement in the GDR and now possesses many historic artefacts including several whitewashed asphalt fragments, all that remains of the border line between East and West that was once painted across the street at Checkpoint Charlie (Friedrichstr. 43–45; opening hours: 9am–10pm daily).

Museum Haus am Checkpoint Charlie ►

Berlin's former **newspaper publishing district** around Kochstrasse/ Zimmerstrasse was once home to many large and important newspaper and book publishers. Kochstrasse as far as Axel-Springer-Strasse has been named Rudi-Dutschke-Strasse since April 2008, 40 years after the student leader Dutschke was shot, an attack for which the protest movement blamed Springer's publishing house. Right at the end of the street is the **Axel-Springer Tower**, which was quite intentionally built right next to the wall as early as 1966. In front of it stand the sculpture *Balancing Act* by Stephan Balkenhol. In Zimmerstrasse a new publishing and editing centre, the **Mosse-Zentrum** carries on the tradition. Here, as along Kochstrasse and Lindenstrasse, a new art gallery scene is springing up, away from the Spandauer Vorstadt, which is oversaturated with galleries.

Gedenkstätte Deutscher Widerstand

(Memorial to the German Resistance)

▌ M 14 ▐

Location: Stauffenbergstr. 13, Tiergarten
City centre map: C 8

U-Bahn: Kurfürstenstrasse (U 1)
Bus: 29, M 48

🕐
Opening hours:
Mon–Wed, Fri
9am–6pm,
Thu till 8pm,
Sat, Sun, holidays
10am–6pm;
Tours:
Sun 3pm

The so-called Bendlerblock (named after the road which was then called Bendlerstrasse, but is now Stauffenbergstrasse) was built between 1911 and 1914 at the southern edge of the ► Tiergarten and housed the Reichsmarineamt (admiralty) until 1918. Afterwards it was the headquarters of the army. Nowadays the German defence ministry's Berlin headquarters is here. It was in the Bendlerblock that Hitler gave his notorious speech to the army leaders laying claim to living space in the east on the 3 February 1933. Importantly, though, it was also the backdrop for the events of 20 July 1944: after the unsuccessful assassination attempt on the Führer at his head-quarters in eastern Prussia, generals Beck and Olbricht, colonels Graf von Stauffenberg and Mertz von Quirnheim and First Lieutenant von Haeften were shot by firing squad in the courtyard that same night. This event is commemorated by the Gedenkstätte Deutscher Widerstand or Memorial to the German Resistance, created in 1953 by Richard Scheibe. On the second floor a permanent exhibition shows the extent of resistance to National Socialism by communist and Christian groups in Germany. The tragic events of 20 July 1944 form the centre point of the display.

Stauffenberg

Gedenkstätte Plötzensee

(Plötzensee Memorial)

L 11

Location: Hüttigpfad, Charlottenburg

U-Bahn: Jakob-Kaiser-Platz (U 7), then by 123 bus

Plötzensee has become synonymous with resistance to the Nazi regime. Between 1933 and 1945 about 1800 people of various nationalities were executed for political crimes in the former Plötzensee penitentiary (now a borstal). In 1952 the Berlin Senate commissioned a memorial. It includes what was once the execution barracks in which it is still possible to see a ceiling beam with its eight hooks (a guillotine used to hang there), where victims of Nazi justice were hanged. Subsequent to the attempt to assassinate Adolf Hitler on 20 July 1944 no fewer than 89 of the conspirators (including the former mayor of Leipzig, Carl Friedrich Goerdeler, and Helmuth James Graf von Moltke) were executed here. In front of the barracks there is a memorial stone and a large stone urn filled with soil from Nazi concentration camps.

⊙
Opening hours:
Mar – Oct
9am – 5pm daily,
Nov – Feb
9am – 4pm daily

The unadorned cubic church of Maria Regina Martyrum at Heckerdamm 230/232 is another monument to the victims of the period 1933 to 1945. It was built between 1960 and 1963 according to designs by Würzburg architects Friedrich Ebert and Hans Schädel. The courtyard is lined with bronze sculptures depicting the Stations of the Cross by Otto H. Hajek. The sculpture of Our Lady on the outer wall was made by Fritz Koenig. The remembrance hall is dominated by a large altarpiece by Georg Meistermann, while the crypt-like underground chapel has a pietà by Fritz Koenig. There are sepulchres for Provost Lichtenberg (whose actual grave is in St. Hedwig's Cathedral in the city centre) and Erich Klausener, the leader of Catholic Action, as well as a symbolic grave for all Nazi victims who were denied a burial.

Maria Regina Martyrum

✶ ✶ Gendarmenmarkt

L 16

Location: Mitte
City centre map: C 12

U-Bahn: Französische Strasse (U 6),
city centre (U 2, U 6)

Gendarmenmarkt, the finest and most harmonious place in Berlin, is dominated by three monumental buildings that form a cohesive ensemble, the Schauspielhaus (theatre) and the churches known as the Französischer Dom and the Deutscher Dom.

From ►Friedrichstrasse it is just a stone's throw along Taubenstrasse or Jägerstrasse to Gendarmenmarkt, a square that has been in existence since the 17th century, when it was originally called the Esplanade. It then became Lindenmarkt, Mittelstädtischer and Friedrichstädtischer Markt and finally Gendarmenmarkt, because the **guards regiment, »Gens d'armes«** had their guardhouse and stables here between 1736 and 1782. As part of the 250th anniversary celebrations for the Akademie der Wissenschaften (Academy of Science) in 1950 the square, which had suffered serious damage during the Second World War, was briefly renamed »Platz der Akademie«. The square was still under East German control but years of reconstruction work had restored its former appearance, and when the two halves of Berlin were reunited, the square was given back its familiar name. Since then a lively restaurant district has built up around the square, which is fully in keeping with the tenor of the district. It includes the wine lodge **Lutter & Wegner** (Charlottenstr. 56). This is

Gendarmenmarkt: Berlin's prettiest square with the Deutscher Dom and the Schauspielhaus

very close to its historic site at the corner of Französische Strasse and Charlottenstrasse, where it stood upon its opening in 1811. E.T.A. Hoffmann, who lived on Gendarmenmarkt itself between 1815 and 1822, and the actor Ludwig Devrient were regulars at the establishment.

At the centre of the square at Gendarmenmarkt stands the Schauspielhaus, one of the finest of Schinkel's buildings. It was built between 1818 and 1821 atop the foundations of the old national theatre that had burned down in 1817. The latter had been constructed in 1802 as a successor to the Französische Komödie building, which was erected by Carl Gotthard Langhans and opened in 1774. The bas-reliefs on the gables and the muses on the roof were mostly made by Schinkel. Christian Daniel Rauch created the gables of the theatre hall itself and the figure of Apollo with a flight of griffins in harness on the top. Christian Friedrich Tieck added the spirits riding panthers and lions either side of the stairway. The opening play in 1821 was Goethe's *Iphigenie*, and Weber's *Freischütz* was also premiered here. The Schauspielhaus soon become one of the foremost theatres in Germany. Between 1934 and 1945 its superintendent was Gustaf Gründgens. After the war, though, its tradition as a theatre came to an end. In 1984 a reconstruction with an exterior true to the original was opened on the site under the name Konzerthaus Berlin.

★
Schauspielhaus (Konzerthaus Berlin)

> ! **Baedeker** TIP
>
> **World of chocolate**
> In 1863 Heinrich Fassbender opened a chocolate factory behind Gendarmenmarkt. Today **Fassbender & Rausch** is Europe's largest chocolate shop. Their biggest seller is the Diplomat assortment, and as a souvenir the little pieces of Plantagenschokolade (plantation chocolate) are popular (Charlottenstrasse 60, corner of Mohrenstrasse). A competitor has appeared: **Ritter Sport** has opened a flagship store close by with a chocolate trail, a chocolate workshop and a »Schokolateria« (Französische Strasse 24).

It was to be more than 50 years before the Schillerdenkmal (Schiller memorial), which had been erected in front of the Schauspielhaus by Reinhold Begas but removed by the Nazis in 1935, was returned to its accustomed place. In 1987, on the 750th anniversary of Berlin itself, the Senate of West Berlin handed the monument over to the East German authorities. The four female figures around the basin of the fountain are personifications of Lyric Poetry (with a harp), Drama (with a dagger), History (with tablets bearing the names of Goethe, Beethoven, Michelangelo and others) and Philosophy (parchment scroll inscribed »Discover Yourself«).

Schillerdenkmal

The Französischer Dom (French church) on the northern side of the square came into existence between 1701 and 1705 as the parish church for the Friedrichswerder and reformed French parishes and their Huguenots who had come to Berlin in 1685. The plans were by

★
Französischer Dom

Louis Cayart and Quesnay. The builders took the Huguenot church at Charenton, which had been destroyed in 1688, as their model. The pillared vestibule and domed tower – which also grace the Deutscher Dom or German church – were only added in front of the actual church in the time of Frederick the Great. An exhibition in the sanctuary documents the story of the cathedral's building and re-building. The tower is 70m/230ft tall with a religious allegory at the top and was constructed according to plans by Carl Friedrich von Gontard by Georg Christian Unger. In its interior is a carillon with 60 bells covering 5 octaves that can be played by means of a key-board. The balustrade 50m/164ft above the street offers a fine view over Gendarmenmarkt. The Hugenottenmuseum inside the tower relates the history of the Huguenots in France and Berlin-Branden-burg (opening hours: church 9am – 7pm daily; Huguenottenmuse-um: Tue – Sat noon – 5pm, Sun 11am – 5pm; carillon plays at noon, 4pm, 7pm daily)

Hugenotten-
museum ▸
🕐

Deutscher Dom ✳

The counterpoint to the French church is the German church, Deutscher Dom. Its builder Martin Grünberg initially created a sim-ple church for the German reformed community during the years 1701 to 1708. The dome is topped with a gilded sculpture 7m/23ft tall called *Tugend* or *Virtue*. Inside is the grave of Georg Wenzeslaus von Knobelsdorff. The democrats who died on the barricades in 1848, the »Märzgefallenen«, were laid out upon its steps. These events and others make up the theme of an exhibition inside the church called »Wege – Irrwege – Umwege« (ways, lost ways and di-versions), which catalogues the development of parliamentary de-mocracy in Germany (opening hours: Tue – Sun 10am – 6pm, June – Aug till 7pm; guided tours 11am and 1pm).

🕐

✳ Schloss Glienicke and Park

T 7 west

Location: Zehlendorf

S-Bahn: Wannsee (S 1, S 7), then by 316 bus

The palace and park of Schloss Glienicke have a wonderful location at the outer southwestern edge of Berlin on the eastern bank of the River Havel where a spit of land divides two lakes, the Jung-fernsee and Glienicker See.

A link with nearby Potsdam had already been built at the time of the Humboldts in the form of a bridge, the Glienicker Brücke, famous for its view of the Havel. The present iron bridge over the Havel (Jungfernsee/Tiefer See) was opened in 1907 to succeed a brick con-struction designed by Karl Friedrich Schinkel. During the GDR peri-od the **Glienicker Brücke** was renamed »Brücke der Einheit« (Bridge of Unity) and a border post was set up that was the exclusive domain of the allies, East German diplomats, exchanges of secret agents and the transfer of political prisoners. In 1962 American U2 pilot Gary Powers was exchanged here for the Soviet master spy Rudolf Abel. The bridge was the first border crossing to be opened on 12 November 1989 and since then it has once more become a major route to Potsdam. In the first building on the Potsdam side, Villa Schöningen, the Deutsch-Deutsches Museum records the history of the Glienicker Brücke and its role in the years when Germany was divided (Thu, Fri 11am – 6pm; Sat, Sun 10am – 6pm).

◄ Villa Schöningen

Schloss Glienicke was expanded into its current form during 1825 and 1826 by Karl Friedrich Schinkel. The design was based on the late classical, Italian style. At that time the building functioned as the summer residence of Carl of Prussia. The main building, the Cavalier wing added in 1832 and the ancillary buildings surround an Italian garden adorned with fountains. The antiquities let into the walls were brought back from his travels by Prince Carl. It is possible to visit the chambers of the prince and his wife as well as see an exhibition about the castles and palaces of Prussia. The restaurant in the palace offers the finest quality cuisine.

Schloss Glienicke

🕐
Opening hours:
Mid-May – Oct
Sat, Sun
10am – 5pm

The palace grounds cover 116ha/286ac and are open all year round. The park passed into possession of the city of Berlin in 1934, since which time it has officially – and somewhat confusingly – been called »Volkspark Kleinglienicke«. It was assembled in 1814 on the basis of an estate belonging to the Prussian chancellor Fürst Hardenberg. To convert the cultivated land, Hardenberg commissioned garden designer Peter Joseph Lenné in 1816. He was allowed to continue his work after Prince Carl took possession of the land in 1824. Lenné created a garden landscape around the Italian styled palace bordered by a so-called pleasure ground in the west and an English garden in the north. This design symbolized the passage from summery Italy across the Alps to the fields of northern Europe. The buildings that were added to the park on the prince's commission by Karl Friedrich Schinkel and Ludwig Persius between 1824 and 1840 took up this same theme. For example Schinkel's hunting lodge expresses an English styling, while the Alps are represented by Persius's Teufelsbrücke bridge. Persius also created the Matrosenhaus, the gardener's lodge and machine shed to pump water for the park from

Park Glienicke

Golden gryphons guard the door of Schloss Glienicke

! *Baedeker* TIP

A walk to Nikolskoe

A pretty route for a ramble: through Glienicker Park and along the riverside path to the Nikolskoe log cabin, which stands on a viewing platform created by Lenné, high above the Wannsee. Friedrich Wilhelm III had the place built for his daughter and named it after his son-in-law Czar Nikolaus. A restaurant and a beer garden attract day trippers who can also admire the Russian Church of St Peter and Paul, built by Friedrich August Stüler and Albert Dietrich Schadow between 1834 and 1837. By the way, the Pfaueninsel is only a 15-minute walk away. A bus can be used for the return journey (e.g. line 218 to Wannsee S-Bahn station).

the Havel, the greenhouse and orange house plus the Stibadium, a roofed bench built to a Roman pattern, situated to the south of the palace. Schinkel created the casino, the tea pavilion and the circular temple he called **»Grosse Neugierde«** (Great Curiosity) based on the 4th century BC Lysistrata monument in Athens, as well as the **»Kleine Neugierde«** (Small Curiosity), which is located in the southwest corner of the park on Königstrasse – both of which are excellent viewpoints, as their names are intended to suggest. The lions of the fountain outside the palace take the Villa Medici as their template. The art of gardening is elucidated by the newly opened **Hofgärtnermuseum** (Court Gardening Museum) (Sat, Sun, holidays, 10am – 5pm). The Klosterhof was built in 1850 by Ferdinand von Arnim based on Venetian models. What sets it apart are the more than 100 works of Byzantine art, collected by Carl of Prussia.

◀ Klosterhof

Jagdschloss Glienicke South of Königstrasse on the northeast bank of the Glienicker Lake stands Jagdschloss Glienicke, a hunting lodge built in 1682/83 for the Great Elector and remodelled in 1859. It is now a meeting place for young people from all over the world.

✶ Grunewald

O – Q 7 – 9

Location: Wilmersdorf/Zehlendorf   **S-Bahn :** Grunewald (S 7)

»Grunewald« means more to Berliners than just the name of one of their most popular local leisure spaces, it is also one of the plushest places to live in the city. The best proof of this is the collection of villas clustered around Grunewald S-Bahn station.

The forest covers 32 sq km/8000ac stretching from the east bank of the Havel between Heerstrasse and ▶Wannsee. The name dates back to 1542 when the elector Joachim II had a hunting lodge built here, which he called »Zum grünen Wald« (in the green wood). This appellation for the woodland was only officially adopted at the end of the 19th century, when it became a leisure destination; it had previously been known as the Spandau Forest. In the fierce winters that

The broad view over the Havel landscape from the Grunewaldturm

followed the end of the Second World War and during the blockade of Berlin, 70% of the trees were felled because no other fuel was available for heating. Nowadays the wood has been fully replanted and is home to game such as fallow deer and roe deer, wild boar (in the Saubucht) and European mouflon (allegedly the forerunner of the domestic sheep). There is a stream fed by the melting of ice age glaciers that runs through a landscape of moor and fen. In the east are innumerable lakes (Hundekehlesee, Grunewaldsee and Schlachtensee, Krumme Lanke) and 9km/5.5mi of river bank along the Havel in the west provides plenty of opportunity for bathing in both large and small havens, although Teufelsberg, Grunewaldturm, Schildhorn and Jagdschloss Grunewald are the places that attract most visitors. What was originally Germany's first race track, the Avus built in 1921, also runs between Nikolassee and Grunewald.

The S-Bahn station at Grunewald is among those places in Berlin that are tainted by an association with the Nazi terror. It was from here and the neighbouring Grunewald goods yard that tens of thousands of Berlin Jews were transported to death camps between 1941 and 1945. A memorial erected in front of the station in 1991 and one unveiled on platform 17 in 1998 testify to these terrible events. **Grunewald station (N/O 9)**
From the S-Bahn station pass under the Avus and turn left to reach the Waldmuseum (forest museum) of the Waldschule Grunewald, which is devoted to forests as a habitant and to their plants and animals (Königsweg 4; Tue – Fri 10am – 3pm, Sun noon – 5pm).

From the bus stop it is only a twenty-minute walk through the Grunewald to reach the hunting lodge on the lake known as Grunewald- **★ Jagdschloss Grunewald (P 9)**

U-Bahn station Dahlem-Dorf (U 3), then by X 83 and 183 bus to Königin-Luise-Str./Clayallee, the rest of the way on foot ►

see. It was commissioned by Joachim II, elector of Brandenburg, and built by the architect Caspar Theyss in 1542. Originally a simple Renaissance building, over the years it has seen many alterations. The gazebo was added to the rear façade in 1593 under Elector Johann Georg. Under King Friedrich I of Prussia (1657–1713), the palace was completely refurbished and altered before final modifications were made under Frederick the Great (1712–1786), when the service yard and barns for hunting gear were built. The Great Hall with its painted wooden ceiling remained in its Renaissance condition. The palace endured many troubled days: in 1814 the boxed components of the quadriga from the Brandenburg Gate were brought here when they were returned to Berlin, having been appropriated by Napoleon Bonaparte. They were kept here till they could be reassembled on top of the ►Brandenburg Gate. The attractions of the palace include not only the Great Hall but the collection of German and Dutch portraits from the 15th to the 19th centuries, including rare works by Barthel Bruyn, Lucas Cranach the Elder, Anton Graff, van Haarlem, Jacob Jordaens, Franz Krüger and Antoine Pesne. In the **Jagdzeugmagazin** (hunting stockroom) there is a collection of hunting weapons and trophies (May–Oct Tue–Sun 10am–6pm, Nov–March Sat, Sun and holidays 10am–4pm).

★
Brücke Museum
(P 10)

From the bus stop at Königin-Luise-Str./Clayallee it is not far northward along Clayallee to the Bussardsteig, where a bungalow built in a style reminiscent of the Bauhaus movement (no. 9, built 1967) houses the Werner Düttmann archive and an exhibition featuring the expressionist artists' collective »Die Brücke«, founded in Dresden in 1905. The museum was inspired by Berlin artist and former exponent of the Brücke group, Karl Schmidt-Rottluff, who donated most of the works. Among the Brücke artists represented are Erich Heckel, Ernst Ludwig Kirchner, Otto Mueller and Max Pechstein. The pieces are presented in ever-changing exhibitions (opening hours: 11am–5pm daily except Tuesdays).

Teufelsberg

It is about a half hour's walk from either of the S-Bahn stations at Grunewald or Heerstrasse to the leisure park around Teufelsberg at the northern edge of the Grunewald forest. The Teufelsberg is a mound 115m/377ft in height that consists of 25 million cu m/33 million cu yd of rubble, heaped between 1950 and 1972 from the ruins of a former defence faculty. By the mid-1960s a ski-lift and two ski-jumps had already been installed, but the fun didn't last long, as the Americans set up a listening post on top of the mound with five listening domes that could spy on

? DID YOU KNOW ...?

- The Maharishi Foundation for World Peace plans to build an esoteric university at the Teufelsberg, including a 12m/40ft-high Tower of Invincibility for German unity, at which 1000 students will meditate. Planning permission has been refused, but the foundation hopes to get its way through the law courts.

telephone and radio communications deep inside the Soviet Union. The mound was fenced off for military use but, even so, a world cup slalom event was still held here in 1986. With the ending of the Cold War the Americans abandoned the station and the Teufelsberg has reverted to leisure use, becoming a popular destination in both winter and summer.

The Grunewaldturm is a tower built on Havelchaussee that runs along the west bank of the Havel and was formerly known as the »Kaiser Wilhelm Tower« – quite properly as it was erected in honour of the Prussian king (later Kaiser) Wilhelm I. It is 56m/184ft tall and towers 104m/340ft above the Havel. 205 steps lead up to the top. It was built from red bricks in 1897 and 1898 by Franz Schwechten at the topographical mid-point between Berlin and Potsdam. Due to the poor condition of the stairs, the tower has been closed since 2007, and trippers have to be content with the view from the garden terrace of the restaurant. Boats on the Havel also dock at the jetty underneath the tower (opening hours: 10am to dusk every day).

Grunewaldturm

◄ 218 bus from Theodor-Heuss-Platz U-Bahn station (U 2)

★ Hamburger Bahnhof · Museum für Gegenwart (Museum of the Present Day)

J 13

Location: Invalidenstr. 50 – 51, Tiergarten

S-Bahn: Hauptbahnhof (S 3, S 5, S 7, S 75, S 9)

The Hamburger Bahnhof, the oldest surviving passenger railway station in Berlin, is a branch of the Neue Nationalgalerie (New National Gallery; ►Kulturforum)

North of the Spreebogen precinct on Invalidenstrasse the Neoclassical Hamburger Bahnhof was rebuilt by Josef Paul Kleihues and a new museum called the Museum für Gegenwart (Museum of the Present Day) established inside. It highlights contemporary art from the years after 1960, including works from the collections of Erich Marx, Egidio Marzona and Friedrich-Christian Flick, supplemented by pieces from the New National Gallery itself. The exhibits, which were rearranged in 2009, include works by artists such as Anselm Kiefer, Richard Serra the Junge Wilde in the main hall, Joseph Beuys in the west wing, as well as Andy Warhol, Cy Twombly and Robert Rauschenberg in the modern annexe make this venue **one of the most important museums of modern art in Europe**. The redesign of the exhibition has given the existing works some new company such as gigantic models of insects from the neighbouring ►Naturkundemuseum and copies of antique sculptures from the plaster-cast studio of the Staatliche Museen zu Berlin.

Opening hours:
Tue – Fri
10am – 6pm, Sat
11am – 8pm, Sun
11am – 6pm,

Hamburger Bahnhof was built between 1845 and 1847 according to plans by Friedrich Neuhaus and Ferdinand Wilhelm Holz. The concourse by Borsig was of purely iron construction and became a template for stations all over Germany. It has been many years, though, since trains passed through the station. After the new Lehrter Bahnhof opened right next door in 1879, Hamburger Bahnhof was closed to traffic by as soon as 1884. In 1906 Prussian minister of state Budde gave the site over to a building and transport museum. Its exhibits remained there after 1945 but under the control of the Reichsbahn and the GDR they remained inaccessible until 1984. Some of the items are now displayed at the ► Deutsches Technikmuseum.

Flick Collection The Friedrich Christian Flick Collection opened in the Rieck-Hallen at Hamburger Bahnhof in September 2004. The collection includes modern art, much of which is exhibited on the Documenta, including installations by Pipilotti Rist, Wolfgang Tilman's military series and Nam June Paik's Fluxus objects.

Hansaviertel

L/M 13

Location: South of Spreebogen, Tiergarten
U-Bahn: Hansaplatz (U 9)

S-Bahn: Tiergarten (S 5, S 7, S 75, S 9)

Today's Hansaviertel was built on terrain destroyed in the war by the most renowned architects of the time.

Already a popular upper-class housing district in the time of Wilhelm II, the district was almost completely destroyed during the Second World War. In 1953 it was decided to rebuilt the area as a model estate, a project that formed the centrepiece of the international building exhibition of 1957. 48 architects from 13 countries were involved in the planning and construction of the site. Among the most remarkable features are the eight-storey flats by Alvar Aalto near the Hansaplatz U-Bahn station (the square also has a memorial called »Denkmal der unbekannten Pulloverstrickerin« (memorial to the unknown knitter of jumpers) by Hans Uhlmann), the **Grips Theater** at Altonaer Str. 22, the four-storey block by Günther Gottwald at Klopstockstrasse (where the flats have movable walls), the large and curvaceous apartment block by Walter Gropius on Händelallee with the colourful block by Frenchman Pierre Vago next door, the blue-and-red panelled building by Fritz Jaenecke and Sten Samuelson on Altonaer Strasse, the building by Brazilian Oscar Niemeyer on its splayed pillars across and down the road, the seven-storey Punkthaus by Klaus Müller-Rehm and Gerhard Siegmann at the southern edge and the library by Werner Düttmann. At Hanseatenweg 10 there is

also one of two houses from the Berlin Akademie der Künste. Since ◀ Kaiser-Friedrich
1957 there has been a new building in place of the old neo-Gothic Gedächtniskirche
Kaiser-Friedrich Memorial Church, opened in 1895. Designed by
Ludwig Lemmer, the new church has a transparent 68m/223ft tower,
nicknamed the »Seelenbohrer« or »drill of souls«.

✴ Jüdisches Museum (Jewish Museum)

M 17

Location: Lindenstr. 9 – 14, Kreuzberg   **U-Bahn:** Hallesches Tor (U 1, U 15, U 6)
Bus: M 29, M 41, 248

Few of Berlin's new buildings have caused as much furore as Daniel Libeskind's Jewish Museum – it had hundreds of thousands of visitors before the actual museum even opened.

Striking architecture at the Jewish Museuem

🕐
Opening hours:
10am – 8pm daily
(Mon closes 10pm),
closed for Rosh
Hashanah and Yom
Kippur (Sept/Oct)
and Christmas Eve

This expressive building, built to a floor plan that zigzags like a lightning bolt, consciously differs from the mainstream of modern architecture. Thanks to its zinc façade with irregular, strip-like windows cut into it, the building has a highly abstract and objective character. The rooms inside are mostly delineated by ramps that guide visitors through the strikingly slanted and acute angles of the various halls. In some rooms it is only possible to see through narrow slits into nothingness, which seek to symbolize the absence of the people who were victims of the Holocaust. In September 2001 the exhibition finally opened, giving Berlin its first Jewish museum for more than 60 years: an earlier museum opened in January 1933 on Oranienburger Strasse but was closed down by the Gestapo in 1938.

The cellar of Libeskind's building is accessed by an underground passage from the Baroque Kollegienhaus. The passage is then crossed by three corridor axes lined with displays: the »Axis of Exile« leads out into the E.T.A. Hoffmann Garden, the »Axis of the Holocaust« leads to a steel door in front of the dark and empty Holocaust Tower. The »Axis of Historical Continuity« then leads to the actual exhibition, which is divided into 13 so-called epochal images depicting two thousand years of German-Jewish history by means of ceremonial items, documents, photographs, paintings, coins, arms, newspapers etc. This journey through the museum begins on the second floor with a copy of the first documentary mention of Jews in Germany in a decree made by the Roman Emperor Constantine in AD 321. It introduces important Jewish figures such as Moses Mendelssohn and Emil Rathenau and ends with developments subsequent to the Second World War. The Holocaust takes up comparatively little of the display, although the »voids« mentioned previously continually evoke it. Altogether some 4000 items are exhibited, often with multimedia background presentations – although, in conjunction with the asymmetric architecture, this makes it difficult to follow the thread of the museum's content.

Kollegienhaus

The entrance and service area incorporated into the Jewish Museum is composed of the former superior Court of Justice building, the »Kollegienhaus« built by Philipp Gerlach in 1734/35, which has the Prussian coat of arms on its gables with the goddesses Justicia and Veritas (Justice and Truth) above them. Since 2007 a glass roof borne by four free-standing steel supports has covered the 670 sq m/7200 sq ft, U-shaped inner courtyard. The support construction takes its inspiration from the form of a tree, which continues as a network of lines in the roof. With this design Daniel Libeskind makes reference to the Jewish Sukkot festival, or Feast of the Tabernacles, for which a hut is clothed in foliage.

Berlinische Galerie

The new Berlinische Galerie, the state of Berlin's museum of modern art, photography and architecture (Alte Jakobstrasse 124 – 128), is about ten minutes' walk from the Jüdisches Museum.

KaDeWe (Kaufhaus des Westens)

Location: Wittenbergplatz, Schöneberg   **U-Bahn:** Wittenbergplatz (U 1, U 2)
City centre map: D 6

Berlin's equivalent to London's Harrods is KaDeWe – the city's foremost consumer palace.

Berlin's most famous department store is the largest of its kind on the European continent. Adolf Jandorf founded the shop in 1907. 20 years later it passed into the hands of Hermann Tietz and now belongs to the Arcandor group. It has 60,000 sq m/15 acres of shop floor on eight storeys and provides practically anything the heart could possibly desire. The food department on the sixth floor remains a top attraction with its inconceivable range of produce, which can be sampled in-store at any of the counters or in the restaurant beneath the glass dome.

Kreuzberg

Borough: Friedrichshain-Kreuzberg   **U-Bahn:** U 1, U 6, U 8

For many years Kreuzberg was synonymous in Berlin with an alternative lifestyle, for its outstanding pub scene, where the nights never seem to end, and for its experiment in multi-cultural urban living.

Kreuzberg was also notorious for speculation in housing, squats and riots, which commonly took place on 1 May. All those aspects are becoming less and less apparent these days, for Kreuzberg itself has changed dramatically. With the fall of the Berlin Wall it is no longer frontier territory where many an alternative bloom could grow, sometimes supported by senate money. Now located right in the centre of the big city, Kreuzberg has been rediscovered, this time by higher earning individuals who have almost turned the old suburb into a chic city centre address that is booming as never before – and it still has the great pubs and bars for which it was known. The alternative and radical types have largely relocated to ► Prenzlauer Berg or ► Friedrichshain, leaving behind the large Turkish population, which represents the largest Turkish community in Germany. In Kreuzberg there is much to see and there is certainly plenty to do in the evenings, e.g. on Oranienstrasse between Oranienplatz and Heinrichplatz or along Adalbertstrasse. Top-quality chefs have opened restaurants on Paul-Lincke-Ufer, Fichtestrasse and round the Südstern.

A U-Bahn train rattles over the Spree on the Oberbaumbrücke between Kreuzberg and Friedrichshain

Kreuzberg's elevated railway

Kreuzberg came into being as a borough in 1920 in a merger of Friedrichstadt to the south, Luisenstadt and the suburb of Tempelhof. Its characteristic features are the U-Bahn, not underground here but running on elevated pillars above the streets, as well as the Landwehr canal, which bisects the district on a line from east to west. The major sights in Kreuzberg include ►Deutsches Technikmuseum or German Museum of Technology, the ►Martin-Gropius building, the cemeteries near the Hallescher Tor (►Cemeteries) and the ►Jüdisches Museum.

Kreuzberg (Viktoriapark) (O 15 / 16)

The name of the borough comes from the eponymous 66m/217ft hill, located towards the south near Berlin's Tempelhof airport (►Tempelhof). It was given to the Franciscans around 1300, when the hill was still known as Tempelhofer Berg. It was dubbed the »Runde« or »Götzesche Weinberg« due to the vineyards that existed on its slopes until 1740. Those slopes are now decked by the Viktoriapark laid out from 1888 to 1894 by director of gardens Hermann Mächtig and extended in 1913/14. It features the »wolf gorge« (Wolfsschlucht), a toboggan course and an artificial waterfall modelled on the Zackelfall in the Riesengebirge mountains. The vineyard tradition has also been reanimated in the park, although its red and white wines are only given to official guests of the senate. The summit of the Kreuzberg hill is topped with a 20m/66ft memorial to the wars of liberation from 1813–15, which was erected to a Schinkel design between 1818 and 1821. Twelve statues symbolize the major victories and carry a procession of the outstanding figures of the struggle. At the southern foot of the hill is the castle-like Schultheiss brewery, built in 1862 and now refurbished as luxury flats.

It is possible to experience a small chapter in the history of Berlin's domestic housing a little to the north of the Viktoriapark between Hagelberger, Grossbeerenstrasse and Yorckstrasse, where the atmosphere of old Kreuzberg can still be savoured beneath the gas lamps. Master bricklayer Riehmer had a three-winged housing estate built here between 1891 and 1899 that made a pleasant change from the barrack-like tenements of the time. The houses are grouped around a cobbled, tree-planted inner courtyard.

★
Riehmers Hofgarten

South of Gneisenaustrasse U-Bahn station (U 7) lies Bergmannstrasse. This authentic slice of Kreuzberg, a mix of young, multicultural, alternative and everyday, has now become an upmarket strip. The best parts are Chamissoplatz, a little further south, and Marheinekeplatz with one of the four remaining market halls of the 14 that once existed in Berlin.

Bergmannstrasse (O 16)

The 10.3km/6.5mi of the Landwehrkanal bisect Kreuzberg from east to west and connect the Upper Spree (at Schlesisches Tor) with the Lower Spree (at Charlottenburg). The canal was built between 1845 and 1850 according to plans by Peter Joseph Lenné in place of the existing Flossgraben and Schafgraben channels and was expanded from 1883 to 1889. The channels were originally border ditches and were mentioned as early as 1450. The canal has made a major contribution to Kreuzberg in the past but nowadays it is little used, at least in economic terms. It nevertheless remains an important leisure feature and the best walks along its banks and tow paths are on Fraenkelufer, which passes the buildings put up for the IBA event in 1987 and Paul-Lincke-Ufer, where there are several nice bars and cafés. Maybachufer across the canal hosts the famous »Türkenmarkt« on Tuesdays and Fridays. Next to the Turkish market, Neukölln with a few pubs and fashion boutiques is on the up and increasingly finding favour under the name **»Kreuzkölln«**.

Landwehrkanal (N 16–19)

► Friedrichstrasse comes to an end in Kreuzberg at Mehringplatz, which was formerly called Rondell, then Belle-Alliance-Platz. It was designed by Hans Scharoun as a ring-shaped housing estate although the results were not particularly inviting. The Friedenssäule or peace column in the middle is a memorial to the wars of liberation. At the corner to the west of Mehringplatz where Wilhelmstrasse and Stresemannstrasse form a sharp angle, Germany's social democratic political party, the SPD, commissioned architect Helge Bofinger to design them a spacious headquarters, now called the Willy-Brandt-Haus. Its atrium is dominated by a large image of Willy Brandt himself, created by Rainer Fetting (►ill. p.57).

Mehringplatz (N 16)

◄ Willy-Brandt-Haus

✴
Oberbaumbrücke
(M 20)

A little to the north of where the Landwehrkanal flows into the Spree stands the Oberbaumbrücke, a bridge that links Kreuzberg with Friedrichshain. The bridge is 30m/100ft wide with two massive towers designed in Gothic style using bricks from the March and erected in 1896. The name of the bridge dates from when a »Schwimmbaum«, a wooden barrier suspended under the bridge, was laid across the canal to prevent passage. When the Wall was erected, only pensioners in possession of appropriate passes were allowed to use the bridge. On 9 November 1989, shortly after the announcement that the border was to be opened, tens of thousands of East Berliners stormed the bridge. Five years later it was renovated and opened for traffic, including the reinstated underground railway line U 1.

Mariannenplatz
(M 18)

Mariannenplatz was designed in 1853 by Peter Joseph Lenné and is situated in the northern part of Kreuzberg between Adalbertstrasse and Waldemarstrasse (U-Bahn: Görlitzer Bahnhof; U 1). The former Bethanien hospital is situated on the western side of the square. Built between 1845 and 1847, it was the first large building in this area. From 1848 to 1849 Theodor Fontane worked there as an apothecary.

Künstlerhaus
Bethanien ►

Nowadays the building houses the Künstlerhaus Bethanien, an art centre with studios, exhibition halls and a theatre, as well as the Kreuzberg administrative office for art, the local archive and the Namik-Kemal-Bibliothek, the only Turkish library in Berlin. The northern side of the square is occupied by the neo-Romanesque Thomas-Kirche (Church of St Thomas).

✴ ✴ Kulturforum

M 15

Location: Tiergarten

Bus:: M 29, M 41, M 48, 200

S- and U-Bahn: Potsdamer Platz (S 1, S 2, S 25, U 2)

City centre map: N 8 / 9

The Kulturforum is the site for exhibiting the European art in the collection of the Staatliche Museen Preussischer Kulturbesitz (State Museums for Prussian Cultural Legacy).

The area between the southern edge of the ► Tiergarten, the Landwehrkanal and ► Potsdamer Platz forms one of the key sites of the state museums along with the ► Museumsinsel and the museums in ► Dahlem.

The idea of building a new cultural focus in the western part of the city is attributed to **Hans Scharoun** (1893 – 1972). The area where it is built was completely flattened during the Second World War, first to make way for the new capitol that Hitler was planning for the Third Reich, then by allied bombs. The initial cornerstone of the rebuilding work arose at the eastern corner of the site with the erection

Kulturforum Plan

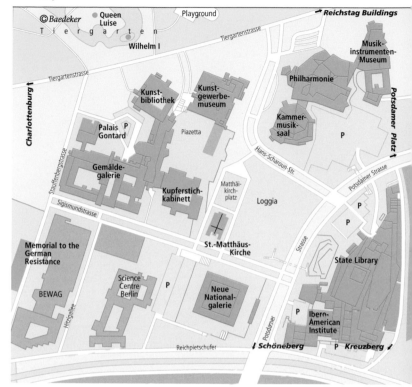

of the Philharmonie (1960–63) and the Staatsbibliothek (1966–78), the Neue Nationalgalerie (1965–68) appearing at the southern edge. The Staatliches Institut für Musikforschung (State Institute for Research into Music) with its museum of musical instruments then sprung up to the northeast of the Philharmonie between 1979 and 1984, to be joined by the Kunstgewerbemuseum (Museum of Decorative Arts) west of the Philharmonie and between 1984 and 1987 by the Kammermusiksaal (Hall for Chamber Music), adjoining to the south. Matthäikirchplatz had by 1994 gained Kupferstichkabinett (Copper Engraving Museum) and the Kunstbibliothek (Arts Library). The western side of the square has been completed by the buildings of the Gemälde- und Skulpturengalerie (Galleries of Painting and Sculpture) since 1998. The forum in the midst of all these buildings was designed by the Austrian Hans Hollein. St Matthew's Church) was built of brick in Italo-Romanesque style by August Stüler in 1846.

◄ St.-Matthäus-
Kirche

Gemäldegalerie *Plan*

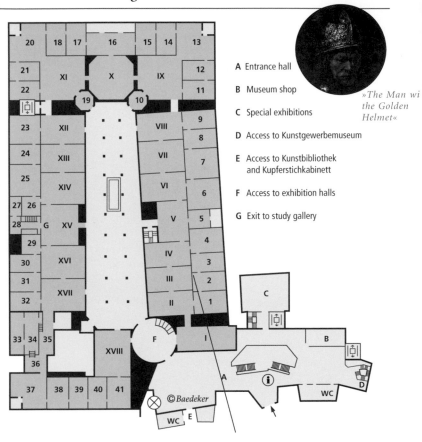

A Entrance hall

B Museum shop

C Special exhibitions

D Access to Kunstgewerbemuseum

E Access to Kunstbibliothek and Kupferstichkabinett

F Access to exhibition halls

G Exit to study gallery

»*The Man wi the Golden Helmet*«

©Baedeker

I-III / 1-4
German painters (Dürer, Cranach)

V-VI / 5-7
Dutch painters (Van Eyck, Bruegel)

VII-XI / 8-19
Flemish and Dutch painters (Rubens, Rembrandt)

20-22
English, French and German Painters of the 18th century

XII-XIV / 23-26, 28
Italian, French and Spanish painters

XV-XVII / 29-32
Italian painters (Raphael, Titian)
34
Miniatures

XVII / 35-41
Italian painters (Giotto, Botticelli)

27, 33, 42 (study gallery)
Digital gallery

Viewing Dürer's »*Madonna with Siskin*«

Gemäldegalerie (Picture Gallery)

The Gemäldegalerie (Picture Gallery) opened in the Altes Museum on the ►Museumsinsel in 1830. It emerged from the art collections of the Great Elector and of Frederick the Great. Wilhelm von Bode, its director between 1890 and 1929, expanded it into a museum of international renown and its exhibits were displayed from 1904 onwards in what is now the Bodemuseum (then Kaiser-Friedrich Museum. In spite of serious losses incurred during the Second World War, the gallery still counts as one of the finest collections of European art from the years up till the end of the 18th century. The works had been distributed after the war among the museums in Dahlem and on the Museumsinsel but have now been reunited at the Kulturforum. Art from the 19th century can be seen in the Alte Nationalgalerie on the ►Museumsinsel. The new gallery building, opened in 1998, is from a design by Rolf Gutbrod that proved highly controversial, so that the interior has been reconfigured by Munich architects Hilmer and Sattler. Its core is the three-winged lobby, which is completely empty apart from one installation by Walter de Maria but leads into the other halls in which 1000 works are displayed. Another 400 paintings are on show in the Studiengalerie in the basement.

Opening hours:
Tue – Sun
10am – 6pm,
Thu closes 10pm

✔ DON'T MISS

- Albrecht Dürer: *Madonna with a Siskin*
- Lucas Cranach the Elder: *Fountain of Youth*
- Pieter Bruegel the Elder: *Dutch Proverbs*
- Rembrandt: *Portrait of Hendrickje Stoffel*
- Rembrandt studio: *The Man with the Golden Helmet*

German paintings

The highlight of the collection of old German masters are the **eight works by Albrecht Dürer**, including *Madonna with a Siskin*, the *Young Venetian Girl* as well as the famous portraits of Hieronymus Holzschuher and Jacob Muffel. Martin Schongauer's *Birth of Christ* is one of his few altar pieces. Among the works of Lucas Cranach the Elder, *The Fountain of Youth* is clearly the outstanding piece. Almost as famous is Hans Holbein the Younger's *Portrait of the Merchant Georg Gisze*. German paintings of the 18th century, including those of Johann Heinrich Tischbein, can be seen later on in rooms 20, 21 and 22.

Dutch and Flemish painters

Paintings from Spain's Dutch territories as well as independent Holland form a core aspect of the collection. *Madonna in the Church* is one of the early oil paintings by Jan van Eyck. Other representatives of Dutch and Flemish painters from the 15th and 16th centuries include Hugo van der Goes, Hans Memling (*Mary with Child*), Gerard David, Rogier van der Weyden (*Woman with Wimple*), Hieronymus Bosch of course, and **Pieter Bruegel the Elder** with his wonderful depiction of *Dutch Proverbs*. The high-point of the entire collection is formed by the Dutch and Flemish masters of the 17th century, in particular the **works of Rembrandt and his studio** in room 10, including *Samson and Delilah*, *The Mennonite Preacher Anslo and his Wife*, *Susanna and the Elders*, *Portrait of Hendrickje Stoffel* and *The Man with the Golden Helmet*, even though it has now been proven that the latter was not painted by the master himself but was »only« a product of his studio. In addition there are portraits, genre paintings and landscapes Frans Hals (*Malle Babbe*), Thomas de Kayser, Jakob van Ruisdael, Salomon van Ruisdael (*Landscape with Thieves*), Jan Vermeer van Delft (*The Wine Glass*), Jan Steen and naturally Peter Paul Rubens.

Italian paintings

Apart from its Dutch and Flemish possessions the collection also concentrates on Italian paintings. All the most renowned names are represented, starting with religious scenes from the 13th century and taking in Botticelli's *Madonna with Child and Chorus of Angels*, Raphael's *Madonna Colonna*, Titian's *Venus and Organist* and Caravaggio's outstanding *Amor as Victor*, and extending into the 18th century with works by Tiepolo and Canaletto.

French paintings

French painting is much less well represented but there are still high-quality works including three paintings by Nicolas Poussin, a landscape by Claude Lorrain, works by Georges de La Tour, the Le Nain brothers and 18th-century artists such as Antoine Pesne, Jean Restout and Antoine Watteau (*The French Comedy*).

Spanish and English paintings

Among the works of Spanish painters are *Mater Dolorosa* by El Greco, Velázquez's *Portrait of a Woman*, Murillo's *Baptism of Christ* and Zurbarán's *Portrait of Alonso Verdugo*. English artists are mainly represented by fine portraiture such as Thomas Gainsborough's *Portrait of an Old Woman*) and Joshua Reynolds' *George Clive and Family*.

✳ Kupferstichkabinett and Kunstbibliothek (Copper Engraving Museum and Art Library)

🕐
Opening hours:
Tue – Fri
10am – 6pm, Sat
and Sun
11am – 6pm

The story of the Kupferstichkabinett or Copper Engraving Museum began in 1652, when the Great Elector obtained some 2500 drawings and watercolours that he had displayed in the court library at the Berlin Stadtschloss. In 1831 the Prussian Kupferstichkabinett opened as part of the Altes Museum. The archives presently hold more than 110,000 drawings, watercolours, gouaches and pastel paintings covering the 14th to the 20th centuries, as well as some 550,000 printed sheets from the late Middle Ages until the present day, printers' plates and books with original illustrations from the 15th to the 20th centuries, plus several hundred incunables. Early Italian, Old German and Dutch graphic work and drawings are all particularly well represented (including works by Botticelli, Dürer, Bruegel and Rembrandt) along with pieces by Schinkel and Adolph Menzel.

The Kunstbibliothek or Art Library was founded in 1867 from the guild museum of the Berlin craftsmen's guild, the Berliner Handwerkerverein. It currently possesses around 350,000 books, drawings and graphic works covering the history of art and culture of Europe in departments called Kunstwissenschaftliche Bibliothek (theory of art library), Lipperheidesche Kostümbibliothek (costume library), Plakat- und Reklamekunst (poster and advertising art), Ornamentstichsammlung (ornamental engraving collection) and Sammlung Grisebach (Grisebach collection of European books and typography from 15th to the 18th centuries) as well as a collection of illustrated book and press publications from the 19th and 20th centuries and photography.

Kunstgewerbemuseum (Museum of Decorative Arts)

The Kunstgewerbemuseum (Museum of Decorative Arts) opened in 1867 and was the first of its kind in Germany. Until 1921 it was incorporated into the ► Martin-Gropius-Bau and later moved to the Berlin Stadtschloss, where it remained until 1939. Part of the collection was reassembled after the war in Schloss Köpenick (► Alt-Köpenick) while the rest was housed in the palace of Schloss Charlottenburg until 1984 but moved to a new building at the Kulturforum designed by **Rolf Gutbrod** in 1985 (although this was of little benefit to the presentation of the collection). Schloss Köpenick and its 29 »epoch rooms« are still considered part of the museum. The building at the Kulturforum has four storeys displaying important examples of European decorative artwork from the early Middle Ages to the present day. Exhibits that should not be missed include the **»Welfenschatz«** (44 relics, monstrances and crucifixes from the

Opening hours:
Tue – Fri
10am – 6pm,
Sat and Sun
11am – 6pm

Relic dome from the »Welfenschatz« treasures

11th to the 15th centuries, formerly treasures of the St. Blasius Cathedral in Brunswick), the treasure trove of the former Dionysius trust of Enger/Herford (including the so-called purse relic, probably a baptismal gift from Charlemagne to the Saxon earl Widukind at the end of the 8th century), the collection of Spanish and Italian maiolica ceramics (16th century), the silver of the Lüneburg council (15th/16th century), the emperor's trophy by Wenzel Jamnitzer (1564), the celestial bowl of Jonas Silber (1589), a dressing table by Abraham Roentgen (18th century) and flashed glass designs by Emile Gallé (19th century). The »Neue Sammlung« (new collection) displays artwork and industrial design from the 20th century.

✴ Philharmonie

The Berlin Philharmonie is known not only to aficionados of classical music: the name also resonates in the world of architecture. The building was considered revolutionary when it was built between 1960 and 1963 (► ill. p. 48). **Hans Scharoun** designed the asymmetrically shaped building covered by a tent-like concrete roof. The concert hall has a stage ringed by groups of seats that rise up in the nature of an amphitheatre and seat some 2200 people. At the time this was a new and startling idea, although it has come to be accepted, not least because of its outstanding acoustics. Because of this unusual shape and the name of the chief conductor of the Philharmonic orchestra in those days, the hall was dubbed »Karajan's circus«. Adjoining it to the south is the Kammermusiksaal or Hall of Chamber Music (1984–87), which has come to be known as the »Little Philharmonie« and seats 1000 people.

> ## ! *Baedeker* TIP
>
> **The Mighty Wurlitzer**
> The sounds of grandad's generation, of the great cinema organs, can be heard in all their splendour as part of the regular Saturday guided tours of the Museum of Musical instruments. That's when »The Mighty Wurlitzer« gets played (around noon).

✴ Musikinstrumenten Museum (Museum of Musical Instruments)

🕐
Opening hours:
Tue, Wed, Fri
9am–5pm, Thu
until 10pm, Sat,
Sun10am–5pm;
Tours: Thu 6pm, Sat
11am

The Museum of Musical Instruments was founded in 1888 and its building adjoins the Philharmonie. Most of its 500 or so exhibits are exquisitely made European instruments from a period covering the 16th century into the 20th, including some unique pieces from the Renaissance and Baroque eras. The instruments are not solely for viewing, but can also be heard on the accompanying audio-guides. The main attraction is **the largest cinema or theatre organ in Europe, »The Mighty Wurlitzer«**, ordered from Siemens in 1929 by cinema organist Werner Ferdinand for his own private use.

Kunstgewerbemuseum *Plan*

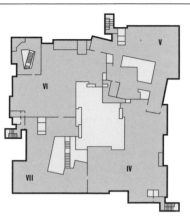

© *Baedeker*

INTERMEDIATE FLOOR
1 Metal
2 Glas, ceramics
3 Textiles, wood, furniture,
interior

GROUND FLOOR
I Middle Ages, treasures of Enger, Heinrichskreuz,
Operatio, Barbarossa's font, Welfenschatz treasures
II Southern European Renaissance, Venetian glasses,
maiolicas, bronzes, Limoges enamel, furniture, tapestry
III Northern European Renaissance, Lüneberg civic silver, series
of carpets after Petrarca, cabinet panes, hunting weapons

TOP FLOOR
IV Renaissance to Baroque: Pomeranian artist
cupboard, clocks, stonework, glass, silver.
V Baroque and Rococo: faience pottery, porcelain,
silver, furniture, Chinese items, Canton enamels
VI Rococo to Art Nouveau: 18th century French and
German furniture, classical porcelain and silver,
»Berliner Eisen«, costumes, Dugatti room
VII

BASEMENT
IX, X, XI The new collection, art and design from
1900 to the present

© *Baedeker*

✷ ✷ Neue Nationalgalerie (New National Gallery)

🕐
Opening hours:
Tue – Fri
10am – 6pm,
Thu closes 10pm,
Sat and Sun
11am – 6pm

The New National Gallery was erected between 1965 and 1968 according to a design by **Ludwig Mies van der Rohe**. The steel and glass building has a square hall constructed on a pedestal. Adjoining it to the west is a courtyard for sculptures featuring pieces by Alexander Calder, Henry Moore, Joannis Avramidis and George Rickey. The standing exhibition is often punctuated by special presentations but otherwise displays some 300 works of art from genres including Expressionism, Cubism, Bauhaus, Surrealism, Verismus and New Objectivity, plus a very fine collection of US paintings from the 1960s and 70s. Among the most important of the artists represented are Edvard Munch (*The Frieze of Life, Portrait of Graf Kessler*), Ernst Ludwig Kirchner (*Potsdamer Platz*), George Grosz (*Pillars of Society*), Max Beckmann (eleven works by him alone including *Portrait of the George Family*), Paul Klee, Max Ernst (*Capricorne*), Dalí, Miró, Penck and Baselitz. Cutting edge contemporary art is on display at the ►Hamburger Bahnhof.

Staatsbibliothek zu Berlin (Berlin State Library)

🕐
Opening hours:
Mon – Fri
9am – 9pm,
Sat 9am – 7pm

Berlin State Library (Staatsbibliothek zu Berlin) was constructed between 1967 and 1978 according to a design by Hans Scharoun. Originally the library was based on that part of the inventory of the Prussian state library that was stored in western Germany. The rest remained in East Berlin at the Deutsche Staatsbibliothek. Since the fall of the Wall, both sections have been reassembled as possessions of the »Staatsbibliothek zu Berlin – Preussischer Kulturbesitz«, although the two venues now have differing objectives. The library at the Kulturforum is a reference and lending library for literature published since 1956, while the former East German site on ► Unter den Linden is now a research library for literature produced up until 1955.

Kurfürstendamm

M/N 10/12

Location and course: In Charlottenburg and Wilmersdorf between Rathenauplatz and Breitscheidplatz
City centre map : C 1 – 5

S-Bahn : Zoologischer Garten (S 3, S 5, S 7, S 75, S 9)
U-Bahn : Kurfürstendamm (U 9, U 15), Uhlandstrasse, Adenauerplatz (U 7), Zoologischer Garten (U 2, U 9)

When West Berlin was an island of capitalism in the midst of the communist empire, Kurfürstendamm became *the* place to promenade and shop. It was, in a very real sense, the »shop window of the free world«.

Elegant stores and boutiques, hotels, restaurants, bars and cafés with outdoor seating, cinemas and theatres, and a bustling lifestyle that lasted well beyond midnight brought a taste of the big wide world to the Cold War front. Recently the gloss of »Ku'damm« has slightly faded, since the reunification has now allowed Friedrichstrasse, Unter den Linden and Potsdamer Platz to become genuine competitors once again.

Nevertheless the street is still able to persuade you to part with large amounts of your money and there are plenty of shops where the prices can make anyone earning an average wage dizzy just to look at them. Nevertheless, amid the Gucci and Versace, there are increasing numbers of discount stores creeping in and the closure of traditional establishments such as Café Möhring and some of the cinemas as well as the relegation of Café Kranzler to a rooftop restaurant above a fashion store is all indicative that the real world is putting its stamp on Kurfürstendamm. In spite of that no visit to Berlin should be without an expedition to the shops of Ku'damm.

The street is 3.5km/2mi long and over 53m/58yd wide. It already existed as early as the 16th century to allow Elector Joachim II to ride to his hunting lodge in ▶ Grunewald, but only after 1875 was it transformed into a prestigious boulevard on the orders of Bismarck. Almost half the buildings on the street had been utterly destroyed by the end of the Second World War and the rest were all damaged to a greater or lesser degree. The only survivors of the street as it once was are the **Iduna-Haus** (nos. 59/69, dating from 1905) and nos 201, 213 to 216 and 218, the latter built in 1896.

Various plaques are affixed to some of the buildings in memory of former inhabitants, including writers Max Hermann-Neisse (no. 215), Robert Musil (no. 217) and composer and cabaret performer Rudolf Nelson (no. 186). **Memorial plaques**

No. 68 was the site of the former Alhambra Lichtspiel cinema and a plaque records that this was where the world's first movie with sound was premiered in 1922.

In conjunction with Berlin's jubilee celebrations in 1987 a line of modern sculptures was erected as the »sculpture boulevard of Kurfürstendamm and Tauentzien Strasse«: on the central reservation of Tauentzien between Marburger and Nürnberger Strasse is the work *Berlin* by Brigitte and Martin Matschinsky-Denninghoff; at Breitscheidplatz stands *Two Lines Eccentric Joined With Six Angles* by George Rickey; on Joachimstaler Strasse is the *13. 4. 1981* installation by Olaf Metzel, a composition of outsized police barriers. Josef Erben's *Pyramide* adorns Bleibtreustrasse and the corner of Schlüterstrasse/Wielandstrasse boasts *Large Shadow on a Pedestal* by Frank Dornseif. Albrecht-Achilles-Strasse has *Large Figure of a Woman, Berlin* by Rolf Szymanski and *Concrete Cadillac* by Wolf Vostell is at Rathenauplatz. **Sculpture boulevard**

◀ Tauentzien/ Breitscheidstr.

◀ Kurfürstendamm

Across Kurfürstendamm to Kantstrasse

The best place to start a stroll down Kurfürstendamm is from Breitscheidplatz, where Kurfürstendamm meets Budapester Strasse, Kantstrasse and Tauentzienstrasse. Towering 63m/207ft over the square is
the ruined tower of the neo-Romanesque Kaiser-Wilhelm Memorial
Church, built from 1891 to 1895 in memory of Kaiser Wilhelm I using a design by Franz Schwechten. The church was hit in a bombing
raid on 23 November 1943 and for years after the war it was scheduled for demolition. In the intervening period, however, it developed
into a West Berlin landmark and a war memorial. For this reason, architect **Egon Eiermann** designed a new church building consisting of
a blue-glazed octagon with a flat roof and a hexagonal tower (built
from 1959 to 1961) alongside the ruin. This has now become a
monument opposing war and destruction and now houses mosaics,
architectural segments and photographs of the old church. The centrepiece of this collection is a statue of Christ from the old church
alongside a crucifix from Coventry Cathedral, which was obliterated
by German bombers during the war.

✷
Kaiser-Wilhelm-
Gedächtniskirche

Breitscheidplatz also has the Europa-Center, built from 1963 to 1965
on the site of a former Romanesque café to a design by K. H. Pepper
and rising to 86m/280ft in height (103m/338ft with the Mercedes
star on top). The Europa-Center remains a popular meeting place –
not least thanks to its fountain landmark featuring a globe of the
earth, popularly known as the »Wasserklops«.

Europa-Center

The »Bahnhof Zoo« railway station at Hardenbergerplatz was the
city's premier inter-city station until 2006 and remains an important
U-Bahn and S-Bahn interchange. It gained a sorry fame in the 1980s
with the release of the autobiographical *Wir Kinder vom Bahnhof
Zoo*, in which the 14-year-old Christiane F (the English version is
simply known under her shortened name) revealed her experiences
as a child involved in the Berlin drug scene. Jebensstr. 2, behind
Bahnhof Zoo, houses the newly established Museum of Photography.
The building was once a club for army officers. The museum takes
particular pride in a collection of more than 1000 pieces on permanent loan from the **Helmut Newton Foundation** (opening
hours: Tue – Sun 10am – 6pm, Thu closes 10pm). Helmut Newton
was a native of Berlin.

Zoologischer
Garten station

◄ Museum für
Fotografie

⊙

From Breitscheidplatz head westward along the Ku'damm. On the
right-hand side of the road, a glass building called the Neues Kranzler Eck by Helmut Jahn rises some 50m/164ft above the crossroads
with Joachimstaler Strasse. It completely dwarfs the once legendary

Neues Kranzler
Eck

← *A Berlin landmark and monument to the futility of war:*
the Kaiser-Wilhelm Gedächtniskirche

Café Kranzler building, which now houses two fashion boutiques. The original café was on Unter den Linden but this subsidiary outlet gained special fame. It still clings on in the round red and white building from the 1950s but only as a restaurant on the roof.

Fasanenstrasse The next street to cross the Ku'damm is Fasanenstrasse. Fasanenstrasse 23, to the south of Kurfürstendamm, is an apartment building from 1873 that has been home since 1986 to the **Literaturhaus Berlin**, which sponsors various exhibitions and readings; it includes the Wintergarten restaurant and a café in its splendid front garden. No. 24, the oldest dwelling on Fasanenstrasse, now houses the **Käthe-Kollwitz Museum**, which possesses some 200 works by the artist,

most of them from the collection of painter and art dealer Hans Pels-Leusden (opening hours: 11am – 6pm daily except Tue). Finally, no. 25 was built in 1891/92 as **Villa Grisebach**, and was once the abode of architect Hans Grisebach. It is now home to the Kunstgalerie Pels-Leusden.

To the north of Ku'damm it is worth going as far as the **Jüdisches Gemeindehaus** (no. 79/80), a meeting hall for the Jewish community that was built in 1959 on the site of the 1912-built synagogue, which was burned down by Nazis on the »Kristallnacht« of 9/10 November 1938. The façade incorporates surviving parts of the original building. The space in front of the site features a sculpture of a broken roll from the Torah and the pillared hall includes names of people incarcerated in concentration camps and Jewish ghettos.

Former Kurfürstendamm Karree Between the next two side streets, Uhlandstarsse and Knesebeckstrasse, the southern side of the road was until 2006 occupied as far as Lietzenburger Strasse by the Kurfürstendamm-Karree. The future of the Kudamm-Theater remains uncertain, but one feature that will definitely be retained is the multimedia show *The Story of Berlin*, which relates the history of the city (opening hours: 10am – 8pm daily, admission until 6pm).

Savignyplatz If the mood takes you, carry on as far as Olivaer Platz, turning right as far as Kantstrasse then right again onto Savignyplatz. An even nicer alternative is to turn off before Olivaer Platz onto Knesebeckstrasse (or Bleibtreustrasse with the Schrill department store) and go beneath the S-Bahn arches straight to the square. Though it is situated so close to busy Ku'damm and the heavy traffic on Kantstrasse, the spot still has the air of the old urbane Berlin as it once was, particularly at the time around 1968. It was and is still the heart of the

Charlottenburg scene that is so popular with students. It is surrounded by bars, including some smart new ones but including many traditional, almost legendary places such as Zwiebelfisch, Dicke Wirtin, Terzo Mondo, run by a pub landlord in a well-known TV soap opera, and Diener, where painter George Grosz, a proponent of New Objectivity, drank himself to death.

! *Baedeker* TIP

Open secret

This is no secret bar known only to insiders. On the contrary, it is known far and wide, yet anyone seeking an untrammelled pub, a glass of pils or a coffee at a price that is pretty reasonable by Charlottenburg standards need only try out the »Zwiebelfisch« on the corner of Savignyplatz and Grolmanstrasse.

Next, go back to Breitscheidplatz along Kantstrasse, which a large **Kantstrasse** number of Chinese restaurants, shops and snack-bars have turned into »Peking-Allee« – the first Chinese restaurant in Germany opened here in 1923 . At Fasanenstrasse the road passes the **Theater des Westens**, now a theatre for musicals, though when it was built in 1895/96 it was designed to house classical operetta and is reminiscent of some confectionery palace from a fairy-tale such as Cinderella. Next to the theatre stands another Berlin institution, the **Quasimodo** jazz bar. The **Kantdreieck** office block on the corner of Fasanenstrasse is most conspicuous for its giant silver weather vane, designed by architect J. P. Kleihues apparently in homage to Josephine Baker, who appeared at the Theater des Westens across the way in 1926. Along Fasanenstrasse in the direction of Hardenbergstrasse is the **Ludwig-Erhard-Haus** (headquarters of the Berlin chamber of commerce and the Berlin stock exchange, the Börse), one of the fascinating new building projects to have been undertaken in the west part of the city centre. The steel ribs of the building arch across the heavens like the scales of a giant armadillo, giving it a highly expressive, organic look.

Leipziger Strasse

M – L 15 – 17

Location and course: Mitte, between Spittelmarkt and Leipziger Platz
City centre map: C 10 – 13

U-Bahn: Stadtmitte (U 2, U 6), Spittelmarkt (U 2)

Leipziger Strasse, leading west from Spittelmarkt to Leipziger Platz, was a busy shopping street before the Second World War with many department stores and fashion boutiques.

Now it exhibits a quite different aspect with its 1970s housing blocks. **From west to** Since the fall of the Wall it has also become a key artery between the **east** east and west of the city once again. It starts at the eight-sided Leipziger Platz, which was once surrounded by large town houses and together with ► Potsdamer Platz was Berlin's principal hub of road traffic. At Leipziger Platz no. 7 an exhibition entitled Dali – Die Ausstellung displays 400 works by the Spanish Surrealist, including drawings, graphic work, sculptures and book illustrations (Mon – Sat noon – 8pm, Sun from 10am). An old guard tower from the Wall stands at Erna-Berger-Strasse, south of Leipziger Platz.

Bundesrat ► Further along on the right is the so-called Preussisches Herrenhaus, which was completed in 1904 and is now home to the Bundesrat, the house of representatives of the Bundesländer (federal states) and second chamber of the German parliament. Practically the whole length of the street opposite the building was formerly occupied by Kaufhaus Wertheim, in its day the largest department store in Europe. Also on the right, the building that stretches along Wilhelmstrasse towards Leipziger Platz was built from 1934 to 1936 as Goering's Reichsluftfahrtministerium or Ministry of Aviation. It was later used by the East German government as their »Haus der Ministerien«, when several ministries were housed there. It is now the headquarters of the Bundesministerium für Finanzen, the German Finance Ministry. A glass-covered memorial recessed into the ground in front of the building recalls the revolt of 17 June 1953.

Bundesministerium für Finanzen ►

✳
Museum für Kommunikation Berlin

Shortly afterwards comes the junction of Leipziger Strasse and Mauerstrasse with the former ministry for post and telephony, which is topped by a group of giant statues flanked by allegorical pieces representing science (left) and transport (right). It is now home to the Berlin Museum of Communication. This is the new name of the former Reichspostmuseum established in 1875 at the instigation of postmaster general Heinrich von Stephan (1831–1897). The museum began modestly but in 1898 moved to Leipziger Strasse with a grand opening. It counts as the oldest postal museum in the world. In the foyer there are three robots that relate the history of the building and the exhibition, which includes a range of exhibits from quaintly nostalgic items right through to the latest telecommunications technology. Much of the exhibition is interactive. Underneath the foyer is a treasure trove featuring the most valuable items, including the legendary red and blue Mauritius penny stamps (opening hours: Tue – Fri 9am – 5pm, Sat/Sun 11am – 7pm).

Information robots do the rounds in the foyer of the Museum für Kommunikation

As it approaches Spittelmarkt, Leipziger Strasse crosses Friedrichstrasse and Jerusalemer Strasse. This junction was once the site of
the famous Hermann Tietz department store. Just before reaching
Spittelmarkt, which gets its name from a hospital (Spital der hl.
Gertrude) that originally stood here, note part of the **Spittelkolon-
naden** built by von Gontard in 1776, which have been reconstructed
using parts of the original colonnades.

Spittelmarkt

Lichtenberg

L 20 east

Borough: Lichtenberg   **U-Bahn:** U 5

**Lichtenberg, a district dominated by industry since the early 20th
century, has relatively little to attract visitors – except for those
with an interest in history.**

What was once the borough of Lichtenberg extends on both sides of
Frankfurter Allee, which used to be the main road to Frankfurt
(Oder) and leads eastwards away from the city. It has now been
merged with the district of Hohenschönhausen, its neighbour to the
north, to form a new borough. Since the beginning of the 20th century, the area has largely been industrial in character and therefore
has relatively little to offer tourists, unless, that is, they take a special
interest in history.

Normannenstrasse was once synonomous with the Ministerium für
Staatssicherheit (MfS), the notorious and ubiquitous East German
»Stasi«. This was the site of the **Stasi headquarters.** On 15 January
1990 an angry mob of citizens stormed the complex. Only a week
later, the so-called central round table decided to re-establish the
building as the Normannenstrasse Research Centre and Memorial,
investigating human rights
breaches during the GDR era. Part
of the building is now home to the
»Bundesbeauftragter für die Unterlagen des Staatssicherheitsdienstes«
(Federal Office for the Documentation of the State Security Service), normally called the Gauck-
Behörde or nowadays the Birthler-
Behörde after its head. Haus 1,
where Erich Mielke was the last
minister to preside, accommodates
the research centre and place of
memorial that is better known as
the Stasi Museum. Visitors can in-

✱
**Forschungs- und
Gedenkstätte
Normannen-
strasse**

Erich Mielke gave orders from here

spect the former offices of Stasi chief Erich Mielke as well as conference rooms and secretariat offices. Exhibits reflect such aspects as bugging technology and include flags, medals, busts, a van for the transport of prisoners and various documents (U 5 to Magdalenenstrasse, entrance next to U-Bahn exit on Ruschestrasse; for guided tours of the archives and premises book at tel. 23 24 66 99 or www.bst.bund.de).

Museum Berlin-Karlshorst

In the former officers' club of the Wehrmacht's Pionierschule 1 (Zwieseler Str. 4 in Lichtenberg's Karlshorst district) a page of world history was written: on the night of 8 and 9 May 1945 army chief Keitel, General von Friedeburg and Colonel General Stumpff signed the unconditional surrender of German forces in the presence of the Soviet Marshall Shukov, British Air Marshal Tedder, US General Spaatz and French General de Lattre de Tassigny. For a period thereafter, the head of the Soviet military administration in Germany had his offices here and it was here that the Soviets granted full powers to the East German administration in 1949. During the GDR era, the building was made into a museum, literally entitled the »Museum of the Capitulation of Fascist Germany in the Great War of the Fatherland 1941 – 1945«. After the end of the East German regime, a German-Russian commission of experts devised a new concept. The museum was now to feature 16 rooms primarily covering Germany's campaign against the Soviet Union featuring countless documents, original items and films. The surrender room and Shukov's study are also open to visitors. Directions: S 3 to Karlshorst or U 5 to Tierpark, then by 396 bus (opening hours: Tue – Sun 10am – 6pm).

> ! **Baedeker TIP**
>
> **Little Vietnam – on a large scale**
>
> The language spoken in the Dong Xuan Center (Herzbergstr. 128 – 129) is Vietnamese. 200 traders in eight halls sell an overwhelming variety of jewellery, bling and artificial flowers, trousers with a traditional cut and other clothing, mountains of mangoes, bitter cucumbers, ladies' fingers, giant sacks of aromatic rice and spices. The locals meet in the food stores, and have their own restaurants and hairdressers, driving schools and lawyers.

Lübars

E 14 north

Borough: Reinickendorf	**S-Bahn:** Waidmannslust (S 1)
Bus: 222	

Rustic idyll

The old village of Lübars, which for many years belonged to the convent in Spandau, appeared in documents as early as 1247. Now listed as a protected site, it is the last practically complete village in the Berlin region and has managed to maintain all its rustic charm. Surrounded by fields, meadows and paddocks, Lübars used to be so well hidden that it was completely overlooked by passing soldiers during the entire duration of the Thirty Years' War. In winter, the village has its own sub-zero micro-climate and experiences the coldest temperatures in the Berlin region. Nowadays Lübars has become a very popular place for a day trip. The centrepiece of the hamlet is the village green with a parish church dating from 1793, a school and fire station. Various single-storey houses clustered around the green include the **Kossätenhaus** (Kossäten were landless but cottage-owning peasants from east of the Elbe), a few villas and the »Labsaal«, a historic tavern hall, now used for various events. The Alter Dorfkrug pub is just right for when you come back to the village after a walk. Footpaths lead from the centre of the village through the characteristic March landscape and along the Tegel valley.

✦ Marienkirche (Church of St Mary)

K 17 B 14

Location: Karl-Liebknecht-Str. 8, city centre

S-Bahn and U-Bahn: Alexanderplatz (S 3, S 5, S 7, S 75, S 9, U 2, U 5, U 8)

The Marienkirche or church of St Mary, seat of the bishops of the Lutheran diocese of Berlin-Brandenburg, is the second-oldest parish church in Berlin after the Nikolaikirche (►Nikolaiviertel).

The earliest written evidence of the church dates from 1294. By 1340 it had been expanded into a Gothic hall church with a five-sided choir to the east. This church burned down in 1380 but reconstruction was completed only a few years later. The pyramid tower that was added between 1790 and 1792 by Carl Gotthard Langhans is in a

Opening hours:
Oct – March daily
10am – 6pm,
April – Sep daily
10am – 9pm

Marienkirche Plan

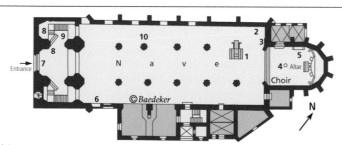

1 Pulpit
2 Memorial to the preacher Roloff
3 Epitaph to the Röbel family
4 Font stone
5 Epitaph to Field Marshall Spar

6 St Bernhardine of Siena
7 Organ
8 »Totentanz (Dance of Death)«
9 »Adoration of the Child«
10 Original site of pulpit

mixture of Gothic and classical styles. In front of the entrance there is a stone penitence cross erected in 1726 to recall the murder of church provost Nikolaus von Bernau in 1325. Inside, the first feature that demands attention is a 2m/6.5ft-tall and 22.60m/24yd 2ft-long fresco, the **»Totentanz«** or »Dance of Death« in the hall at the base of the tower. This was probably inspired by an outbreak of the plague that took place in 1484. There are fourteen groups depicted and verses in Middle Low German relate how death plucks all classes of society into his domain. The fresco was plastered over in 1730 but was rediscovered in 1860 by August Stüler. The bronze baptismal font of the Marienkirche dates from 1437 and has an inscription in Low German. The pulpit in the main aisle is a Baroque piece made in 1703 by Andreas Schlüter, while the organ front was added in 1722 (concerts during vespers from May to October on Saturdays at 4.30pm). Apart from the Protestant tombs, the carved image of St Bernhardino of Siena (15th century) and the bas-relief of the Holy Family attributed to Lucas Cranach the Elder are all worthy of attention, too.

Luther statue

Until 1975 a statue of Martin Luther stood next to the church, the remains of a large monument to the reformation, erected in 1895 and initially situated at Neuer Markt, although it was damaged during the Second World War. The original featured not only Luther but Johannes Reuchlin, Philipp Melanchthon and Ulrich von Hutten (and can now be seen at the Dorotheenstadt cemetery (►p.196).

Märkisches Ufer ·
✶ Märkisches Museum

L 17/18

Location: Mitte, southern bank of the Spree between the Inselbrücke and Jannowitzbrücke
City centre plan: C 14/15

S-Bahn: Jannowitzbrücke (S 3, S 5, S 7, S 75, S 9)
U-Bahn: Märkisches Museum (U 2)

The south bank of the Spree, now known as Märkisches Ufer, is one of the original settlements that gave birth to Berlin. It was first dubbed »Neu-Cölln on the water«, since it was actually part of Cölln, the oldest residential district of which was on the Fischerinsel island on the opposite shore.

An original nucleus of Berlin

Eight beautifully restored houses from the 18th century hint at the atmosphere of old Berlin. The prettiest of them spans numbers 10–12 and moved here in 1966 from Breite Strasse 11 on the Fischerinsel. The upper-class residence goes by the name of the **Ermelerhaus**. It originated at the end of the 17th century and underwent

The Ermelerhaus was moved from the Fischerinsel to Märkische Ufer and is the pride of its new location

restoration in 1724 before being rebuilt in Rococo style with a fine classical façade between 1760 and 1762. From 1824 to 1918 it was owned by the family of tobacco dealer Wilhelm Ferdinand Ermeler, who had it furnished most artistically; some of the furnishings can be admired in the café and the restaurant. Facing Wallstrasse is the Ermelerhaus hotel belonging to the art'otel group. The photographic archive of the Berlin State Museum is housed in the neo-Baroque houses at nos. 16 and 18. Two other buildings on Märkisches Ufer are also of historical interest: no. 48 near the Jannowitzbrücke is where the staff of the revolutionary peoples' navy had its headquarters during the revolution of 1918/19 (the site is now a restaurant); the German trades union congress, the Allgemeine Deutsche Gewerkschaftsbund, built its headquarters in 1922/23 on the corner of Wallstrasse and Inselstrasse.

★ **Historischer Hafen Berlin**

At Berlin's historic docks near the Inselbrücke and on the shores of the Fischerinsel, 21 old inland shipping vessels are moored, including a barge built in 1890, a tug from 1905, the rear-paddle-wheel tug *Jeseniky* with its beer garden and the *Renate-Angelika*, a barge from 1910 which features an exhibition covering 250 years of river shipping on the Spree and the Havel (opening hours: Tue–Fri 2pm–6pm, Sat/Sun 11am to 6pm).

★ Märkisches Museum (Am Köllnischen Park 5)

Opening hours:
Tue–Sun
noon–6pm, Wed
until 8pm

The Märkisches Museum is the main site for the Berlin City Museums Trust and covers the history of the city from its founding to the present day. The Märkisches Provinzialmuseum, the forerunner of the present Märkisches Museum, was founded in 1874. It moved into its distinctive building in Köllnischer Park in 1908. Architect Ludwig Hoffmann evoked the brick architecture of the March: the tower is based on the bishop's palace at Wittstock in the region of Ostprignitz/Ruppin; the southern gable with its fan tracery is reminiscent of St Katharine's in Brandenburg; the Roland statue in front of Wallstrasse is a copy of one created in 1474 for the Neustadt Rathaus in Brandenburg.

Permanent exhibition

The museum's permanent exhibition highlights various aspects of Berlin's history: the topography of the city, crafts and industry in Berlin, development of the community, Berlin as a royal residence and capital city, its influence on the Enlightenment and on modern science, Berlin's infrastructure, Berlin and modern art, work in the city, Berlin under the swastika, Berlin's division and reunification. A separate section is dedicated to the lives of Berliners themselves. Outstanding exhibits include a reconstruction of a hunter's cottage from the 6th and 7th centuries BC, a model of **Berlin as it was in 1750** that covers an area of 15 sq m/160 sq ft (the same hall also has two giant paintings by Anton von Werner and Ferdinand Keller), the **original head of one of the horses – the last remaining original piece – in Gottfried Schadow's quadriga** on the ► Brandenburg Gate, remains of the Berlin Stadtschloss after its demolition by explosives, a fabulously furnished parlour and a self-portrait by Lovis Corinth and a portrait of murder victim Walter Rathenau, also by Corinth. There are also numerous examples of Berlin arts and crafts and a unique collection of mechanical music devices (called automatophones), which are demonstrated every Sunday at 3pm. The cafeteria stands out, too, not necessarily because of the refreshments it offers, but rather for being furnished like an old chemist's shop.

Köllnischer Park and bear pit

Little Köllnischer Park to the south of the Märkisches Museum includes a lapidarium belonging to the museum and a bronze memorial to Heinrich Zille (►Famous People) by H. Drake (1965). One curiosity is the bear pit dating from 1939, which is still home to two brown bears.

Martin-Gropius-Bau

M 16

Location: Stresemannstr. 110, Kreuzberg
City centre plan: D 10

S-Bahn and U-Bahn : Potsdamer Platz
(S 1, S 2, S 25, S 26, U 2)

The Martin-Gropius-Bau, a huge brick building, is a pillar of Berlin's cultural life, as it is regularly the venue for exhibitions of the highest calibre.

Exhibition centre
🕐
Opening hours:
April – Sep daily
10am – 6pm, Oct –
March closed Tue

The Martin-Gropius-Bau was built in Hellenic Renaissance style from 1877 to 1881 by Martin Gropius – great uncle of Walter Gropius, one of the founders of the Bauhaus movement – along with Heino Schmieden, was home to the Prussian Museum of Decorative Arts until 1921. It was badly damaged in the Second World War and restoration only began in 1979, faithfully recreating the rich decoration on the west, east and south façades.

The northern side facing Niederkirchnerstrasse, right next to the course of the Berlin Wall, was only restored after reunification, though the soot-blackened and damaged figures around the portal were retained as a war memorial. The interior is impressive with its encircling gallery and imposing proportions, and the building is regularly used for various and very attractive exhibitions.

Around the Martin-Gropius-Bau

The Martin-Gropius-Bau lies in a city block bounded by four streets: Niederkirchnerstrasse (formerly Prinz-Albrecht-Strasse), Wilhelmstrasse to the south, Anhalter Strasse and Stresemannstrasse (formerly Saarlandstrasse). During the Third Reich the SS and Gestapo headquarters were located in this block: it was indeed the **control centre of Nazi terror**. The most important buildings included Prinz-Albrecht-Strasse no. 8, a former academy of commercial arts called the Kunstgewerbeschule (1901 – 05), as of 1934, the Gestapo headquarters; Prinz-Albrecht-Strasse 9, built in 1887/88 as Hotel Prinz Albrecht but renamed »SS-

Prinz Albrecht area

! **Baedeker** TIP

Remains of the Wall

A 200m/220yd length of the last remains of the Wall runs along Niederkirchnerstrasse.

Haus« and given over to the »Reichsführung SS«. Wilhelmstrasse 102 was the Prinz-Albrecht-Palais, built in 1737 as a palace for Baron Vernezobre and purchased by Prince Albert of Prussia, son of King Friedrich Wilhelm III, in 1830. This was initially used as the base for the security service (Sicherheitsdienst, SD) of the SS but from 1939 it was the headquarters for the main security authority »Reichssicherheitshauptamt«. Excavations unearthed cellar walls along Niederkirchnerstrasse in 1986 and exposed the floors of cells used for the Gestapo's internal prison. In a new building opened in May 2010 the exhibition »Topografie des Terrors« documents the history of the site and the activities of the Nazi authorities that were based here (opening hours: May – Sept 10am – 8pm daily, Oct – April closes 6pm).

◄ Topography of terror

The former seat of Prussian government, the Prussian Landtag building, built from 1892 – 1897, and the current Bundesrat (► Leipziger Strasse), sit practically back to back on Niederkirchnerstrasse opposite the Martin-Gropius-Bau. The former is presently the headquarters of the current Berlin state council and is now called the Berliner Abgeordnetenhaus (Berlin House of Representatives). It also has the **memorial to the baron of the Reich, Karl vom und zum Stein** created by Hermann Schievelbein. It was unveiled in 1870 a little further east along Leipziger Strasse in front of what was then the Prussian Abgeordnetenhaus. The memorial was badly damaged during the Second World War, but was erected once again in 1981 by East German authorities at the top of Unter den Linden. It has now been returned to somewhere at least close to its original site.

Berliner Abgeordneten-haus

Anhalter Bahnhof was once a magnificent railway station, Berlin's gateway to the south. Nowadays only a section of the façade and the portico on Askanischer Platz testify to its former glory. The first station to be called Anhalter Bahnhof was opened in 1839 and in 1841

Anhalter Bahnhof

August Borsig's first locomotive steamed out of the station, pulling a train to Jüterbog. The commission for the building of a much larger station was given to architect Franz Schwechten, who had designed buildings including the Kaiser-Wilhelm-Gedächtniskirche and the AEG factory, along with engineer Heinrich Seidel, who had also made a name for himself in the world of literature with his autobiographical novel *Leberecht Hühnchen*. The train shed was 170m/186yd long and 60m/66yd wide, its iron roof covering an area of some 10,200 sq m/2.5ac. Along with the brick, terra-cotta and dressed stone adorned entrance hall, it was considered to be the exemplary railway station. The first train left for Lichterfelde on 15 June 1880. The golden age of the station was after 1900, with 58 trains running in and out every day, and 40,000 people embarking and disembarking. The station was so badly hit by an air raid on 23 November 1943 that all long-distance traffic had to be abandoned. The building fell into decay after the war and it was demolished in 1961. After reunification, the long neglected site was redefined as a sports facility. Since December 2001 life has returned to the location with the legendary Tempodrom finding a new home here in its tent-like new building. This is a venue for concerts, circus performances, theatre and musicals. On the station site facing Schöneberger Strasse, an air-raid bunker remains in existence. Its history and various items that have been found there are exhibited in its basement. On the floors above, Berlin's Gruselkabinett or Cabinet of Horrors contains a full complement of mannequins, skeletons and artificial blood to strike terror into the heart of even the bravest visitor (opening hours: 10am – 7pm every day except Wed, Fri closes 8pm, Sat opens noon).

Tempodrom ►

Cabinet of Horrors ►
⊘

Marzahn

F 20 east

Borough: Marzahn-Hellersdorf

S-Bahn : Marzahn (S 7, S 75), then by 195 bus to Erholungspark Marzahn

What was to become the 19th Berlin borough of Marzahn was raised on the sandy soil of Brandenburg from 1977. Marzahn was a prestige project for East Germany, intended to realize an ideal of »socialist living conditions«.

New estate with a historic centre

Since then the hamlet of Alt-Marzahn has been encircled by eleven-storey towers with a total of 57,000 apartments – the largest prefabricated housing estate in Europe. The suburb's main landmark is the windmill built in 1719 at the corner of Landsberger Allee and Allee der Kosmonauten. In the midst of this monotonous architectural landscape **Alt-Marzahn**, with its brick church, village tavern and a school building from 1911 all clustered around a village green, seems a tad forlorn. Nevertheless, in addition to the local museum for Mar-

The largest Chinese garden outside China: the »Garten des wiedergewonnenen Mondes« in Marzahn

zahn-Hellersdorf in the old school, it does have a historic farmyard ensemble with rare domestic animals, paddocks for horses and donkeys, goats, turkeys, geese and sheep, a yard with small animals and poultry, an educational cereal garden and old rustic equipment at the foot of the hill on which the mill stands.

Gärten der Welt (Gardens of the World) started out as a garden show in the Wuhle valley around the Kienberg hill that was laid out in 1987 for Berlin's 750th anniversary celebrations. Among its attractions is a fairy-tale garden for children. One authentic highlight is the Garten des wiedergewonnenen Mondes (Garden of the Regained Moon), the largest Chinese garden outside China. It was created by experts from the Beijing Institute for classical garden architecture in a northern Chinese style. The garden has since been supplemented by a Japanese Garden of Confluent Waters, a Balinese Garden of the Three Harmonies, an oriental Garden of Four Rivers and the Korean Seoul Garden. In 2007 a maze was added, based on that at Hampton Court in London. Since 2008 an Italian Renaissance garden has demonstrated European garden styles form the 14th to the 16th century, and the remodelled Karl-Foerster-Garten presents contemporary horticulture (daily from 9am).

Gärten der Welt
✴
◀ Entrance:
Eisenacher Strasse

In Hellersdorf, neighbouring Marzahn to the east, from 1960 Charlotte von Mahlsdorf a.k.a. Lothar Berfelde collected furniture and household goods of the Gründerzeit, the period from 1870, in the manor house Gutshaus Mahlsdorf. Charlotte (1928 – 2002) was awarded the Federal Republic of Germany's major honour, the Bundesverdienstkreuz, and revealed to have been a Stasi informer shortly before her death. She left behind nine fully furnished rooms in Mahlsdorf, the most impressive of which is the **»Mulackritze«** room from 1890, taken from the last of Berlin's taverns from the milieu of Heinrich Zille (opening hours: Wed, Sun 10am – 6pm).

Gründerzeit-
museum
Mahlsdorf

🕐

★ Müggelsee

O 20 southeast

Location: Köpenick · · · · · **S-Bahn:** Friedrichshagen (S 3), then by 60 or 61 tram

When West Berlin had the Wannsee, the East Berliners were well served by the Müggelsee. It is not only a place for swimming, since about 160km/100mi of paths range through its woods.

Berlin's biggest lake Covering an area 7.5 sq km/1850ac and reaching a depth of some 8m/26ft, the lake east of ►Alt-Köpenick is the largest in the metropolitan district. Its woods were among the most best-stocked hunting grounds between the Elbe and the Oder until well into the 18th century. It goes without saying that boat trips round the lake are on offer (►Practicalities, Tours and Guides).

Friedrichshagen From the S-Bahn the tram passes through the suburb of Friedrichshagen on **Bölschestrasse** to the lake. Friedrich II had 1200 mulberry trees planted here in a gap in the forest in the year 1753 and built workers' dwellings for employees of his planned silk spinning factory, although the latter did not actually get off the ground. What remains is the broad Bölschestrasse avenue, flanked with limes. It is a lovely place for a walk because the route has plenty of nice shops, bars and restaurants, many in attractive single storey cottages. A memorial to Friedrich II that disappeared has now been restored and erected once again on Bölschestrasse. The avenue ends at the Berliner Bürgerbräu

Weekend idyll in Neu Venedig (New Venice) with greenery, water and a boat of your own to be the envy of all

building, from where a left turn followed by another quick right leads to the approach road for the 120m/130yd-long **Spree tunnel**, which dips underneath the Müggelspree river spur to come out on the eastern shore of the Müggelsee lake. Friedrichshagen also has its own museum: it is situated a little out of town towards the east (Müggelseedamm 307). Its exhibition, in an old watermill at the **Friedrichshagen waterworks**, tells the story of supplying water to Berlin from the Middle Ages to the present day. The museum is particularly proud of its machine hall from 1893 (tram 60; opening ☺ hours: April – Oct Wed – Fri 10am – 4pm, Sat, Sun closes 5pm, Nov – March closes 3pm or 4pm).

Further along, the Müggelseedamm leads past the Müggelsee beach, Strandbad Müggelsee, to Rahnsdorf, part of which is called Neu-Venedig or New Venice. This is an allotment site, criss-crossed by drainage channels where many a Berliner has bought an idyllic weekend home. The highly picturesque spot came into existence in the 1920s during the building of a ship canal.

✱
Neu-Venedig

There are many ways of getting to the southern shore of the lake: on foot from Friedrichshagen, by 169 bus from Köpenick S-Bahn station, by car via Müggelheimer Damm or by steamship right across the lake to the »Rübezahl« jetties or Hotel Müggelsee. From there, various paths lead up to the Müggelberge hills, which reach a height of 115m/377ft. Routes lead over the moors around the Teufelssee and come to an end at the **Müggelturm**, an old tower that is a popular destination for Berliners taking a day trip, although it is now somewhat in need of repair. Originally there was a wooden tower at the site, built in 1899, but when it burned down in 1958 it was replaced by a modern building. Between 1928 and 1933 there was a tented camp for workers not far away from the Müggelseeperle hotel, which gained fame with the release of the eponymous film *Kuhle Wampe*, with a screenplay written by Bertolt Brecht.

✱
Müggelberge

! *Baedeker* TIP

A boat trip with sunshine

Glide across Müggelsee without noise, pollution or a skipper's licence. The starting point is Köpenick, and the trip via the Müggelspree is done by electric, solar-charged boat. Afterwards take refreshments at the floating Solarcafé (Köpenick, Müggelheimer Str. / Schlossplatz; tel. 303 94 11 38; Mon – Fri noon – 8pm, Sat/Sun from 10am; www.solarwaterworld.de).

? DID YOU KNOW ...?

■ Long before the Fernsehturm was erected at Alexanderplatz there was a plan to build a tower on the Müggelberge hills. It was to be 130m/430ft high. Construction work began in May 1954, but was called off in November 1956 – the planners had overlooked the fact that it would have stood right in the approach path for Schönefeld Airport. The stump of the tower, today a directional radio station, is visible a few hundred metres from the Müggelturm.

✳ Museum Berggruen

K 11

Location: Schlossstr. 1, Charlottenburg   **U-Bahn:** Richard-Wagner-Platz (U 7)
Bus: M 45, 109, 309

With the help of government funds, what began as a loan from an émigré to the city of his birth has become a major institution: one of the most important private collections of modern art in November 2000.

🕐
Opening hours:
Tue – Sun
10am – 6pm

The collection was assembled by **Heinz Berggruen**, who was compelled to emigrate to the USA in 1936, remaining there until 1996. Under the theme »**Picasso and his times**« it exhibits no fewer than 70 paintings by Pablo Picasso, a personal friend of Berggruen. They include *Seated Harlequin* from 1905, *The Painter and His Model* and *The Yellow Pullover*, 1939. In addition, there are 27 pieces by **Paul Klee** alongside works by Cézanne, van Gogh, Seurat, Braque and Giacometti. The collection is exhibited in the west wing of Friedrich August Stüler's »cavalier building« opposite ▶ Schloss Charlottenburg, which features a wonderfully light stairway designed by Stüler. There are plans to build an extension. Heinz Berggruen himself occupied an apartment on the top floor until his death in 2007.

Scharf/Gerstenberg collection

The eastern part of Stüler's building has hitherto been the home of the Egyptian museum, which has now moved to the refurbished

Almost modern art in its own right: the stairway in the Museum Berggruen

Neues Museum (►Museumsinsel). Since 2008, instead of Egyptian art, the Scharf/Gerstenberg collection has been on show. This too is a major collection of modern art and includes more than 200 works concentrating on graphic art, for example by Goya, Klee and Max Ernst, as well as Picasso, Giacometti, de Chirico and Miró. With this and the Berggruen Museum, Charlottenburg now possesses a unique repository of modern art.

✶ Museum für Naturkunde

(Natural History Museum)

H 15/16

Location: Invalidenstr. 43, Mitte   **U-Bahn:** Museum für Naturkunde (U 6)
Tram: M 6, M 8, 12

The director of the British Museum in London praised the Museum für Naturkunde in 1893, as »a remarkable illustration of the absolute revolution in ideas for the design of museums«.

The collection of the Museum für Naturkunde, the Natural History Museum of Humboldt University, possesses more than 25 million items, based initially on a teaching collection started by the Berliner Bergakademie (mountaineering school) in the 18th century. As of 1810 the museum was located in the university's main building on Unter den Linden. Expedition finds and donations by Alexander von Humboldt and Adelbert von Chamisso, among others, caused the collection to expand immensely, so that a new museum building was conceived in 1875. The new site on Invalidenstrasse opened in 1889. Large parts of the building were damaged by air raids during the Second World War and many truly valuable pieces were destroyed, including the Hall of Anatomy with all its skeletons and the Whale Hall, containing skeletons of great whales and other marine mammals. Having now been reconstructed, it is once again among the world's premier natural history museums. Its newly designed sec-

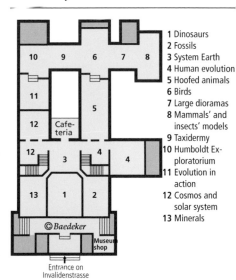

Museum für Naturkunde

1 Dinosaurs
2 Fossils
3 System Earth
4 Human evolution
5 Hoofed animals
6 Birds
7 Large dioramas
8 Mammals' and insects' models
9 Taxidermy
10 Humboldt Exploratorium
11 Evolution in action
12 Cosmos and solar system
13 Minerals

© Baedeker

Museum shop

Entrance on Invalidenstrasse

The pride of the Museum für Naturkunde are its dinosaur skeletons.

⏱
Opening hours:
Tue – Fri
9.30am – 5pm, Sat/
Sun 10am – 6pm

tions provide a tour through the history of nature on earth. The main attraction is the Dinosaur Hall with original fossil skeletons from Upper Jurassic strata in Tanzania (*c*150 million years old), including the **largest authentic dinosaur skeleton on display in any museum on the globe, a brachiosaurus brancai** 23m/75ft long and 12m/39ft high. So-called »Jurascopes« bring the world of the dinosaurs to life. Another highlight is the original fossil of the ancient bird-like dinosaur **archaeopteryx** from the Solnhofen slates, the best example of the seven fossils of the species found to date. The zoological collections use dioramas and taxidermy to provide an insight into the animal world. One particularly interesting diorama – one of the first in the world – concerns the »Bavarian Alps«. Ano-ther fascinating exhibit is the stuffed model of the gorilla »Bobby«, who was a popular inhabitant of Berlin's ►Zoologischer Garten between 1928 and 1935. The art of taxidermy is given its own section; there is a new section entitled »Evolution in Action«, which explains, among other things, why the zebra has stripes. The Hall of Minerals exhibits the third largest collection of meteorites in Germany. It has largely been maintained in its 19th-century state and includes pieces collected by people such as Alexander von Humboldt himself.

✶ ✶ Museumsinsel (Museum Island)

K 16/17

Location: Am Kupfergraben, Mitte
City centre plan: B 12/13
Tram: M 1, M 4, M 5, M 6, 12
Bus: 100, 200

S-Bahn: Friedrichstrasse (S 1, S 2, S 25, S 26, S 5, S 7, S 75, S 9), Hackescher Markt (S 5, S 7, S 75, S 9)
U-Bahn: Friedrichstrasse (U 6)

The world-famous Museumsinsel or Museum Island, situated between Kupfergraben and the Spree, was declared a World Cultural Heritage Site by UNESCO in 2000. It is the oldest of Berlin's centres of art.

It originated in 1830 with the opening of the Altes Museum (Old Museum), endowed by King Friedrich Wilhelm III in order to give the public at large access to the art treasures of the royal palaces. Friedrich Wilhelm IV declared in 1841 that the whole of the site beyond the museum would be given over to forming a **»district dedicated to the study of art and the science of antiquity«**. Between 1843 and 1855 the Neues Museum (New Museum) was erected on the other side of Bodestrasse. The Nationalgalerie or National Gallery, slightly set back on the right, was opened in 1876 and in 1904 the Kaiser-Friedrich Museum, now the Bodemuseum, opened on the other side of the railway line. In 1909 work started on construction of the Pergamonmuseum, although it was not opened until 1930.

www.smb.spk-berlin.de

Under the aegis of **Wilhelm von Bode** (1845 – 1929), who managed the museums between 1872 and 1920 and was named as General Director of Museums in 1905, the collections were to become world class, comparable with those of the Louvre in Paris, the Hermitage of St. Petersburg or London's British Museum and Victoria and Albert Museum. During the Second World War, though, the buildings on the Museum Island were 70% destroyed. The art treasures had earlier been shipped to safety and largely survived the war, but they were distributed throughout various parts of the now divided Berlin. The concept of reorganizing the Museumsinsel to reclaim its pre-war status as a comprehensive display of high culture from all parts of the world, from the ancient Sumerians to Expressionist painters, can now at least partially be achieved. The Museum Island is benefiting from a good deal of architectural change, too. A master plan passed in 1999 foresees a new central entrance building built by the British architect David Chipperfield, a graceful and transparent temple-like structure with slender columns that fits the existing ensemble.

✶ Altes Museum (Old Museum)

The Altes Museum or Old Museum was designed by **Karl Friedrich Schinkel** and opened in 1830. Alongside the Fridericianum in Kassel (1779) and Klenzes Glyptothek in Munich (1816 – 30), it counts among the oldest museum buildings in Germany and is certainly **the oldest museum in Berlin**. Two sculptures flank the stairs to the foyer

Entrance:
🕐
Opening hours:
Daily 10am – 6pm,
Tue until 10pm

MUSEUMSINSEL

✱✱ This unique and fabulous cultural landscape has been declared a UNESCO World Heritage site. The Museumsinsel or Museum Island, one of the largest museum complexes in the world, is wholly dedicated to art and archaeology. One day is not enough to take it all in, but the Pergamon altar, the bust of Nefertiti and the Alte Nationalgalerie (Old National Gallery) are not to be missed. An entrance ticket is valid for all the museums. One curious thing is that railway trains and S-Bahn units constantly rattle through the middle of the island.

🕐 Opening hours for all museums:
Tue – Sun 10am – 6pm, Thu closes 10pm

① Bode-Museum

The Bode-Museum opened as the Kaiser-Friedrich-Museum in 1904 but was renamed after its founder, Wilhelm von Bode, when it reopened in 1956. It includes the coin collection in the Münzkabinett as well as ancient and Byzantine artefacts in the Museum für Spätantike und Byzantinische Kunst.

② Pergamonmuseum

The Pergamonmuseum was completed in 1930 and actually comprises three museums: the Antikensammlung (Collection of Antiquities), Vorderasiatisches Museum (Near East Museum) and the Museum für Islamische Kunst (Museum of Islamic Art). There is a new fourth wing facing Kupferstrasse by O.M. Ungers.

③ Alte Nationalgalerie

The Old National Gallery (built from 1866 to 1876 according to plans by Friedrich August Stüler and Johann Heinrich Strack) was originally intended as a teaching and entertainment venue for German art. It is designed in the form of a Corinthian temple on a high base. After a long rebuilding period, the gallery now displays brilliant paintings and sculpture from the 19th century.

Rotunda in the Altes Museum

④ Neues Museum

Friedrich August Stüler built the »new« museum from 1843 to 1847. It has now been fully restored and presents the collections of the Egyptian Museum and the Museum for Pre-History and Early History, including Heinrich Schliemann's collection of Trojan antiquities.

⑤ Altes Museum

The Altes Museum came into existence on the northern edge of the Lustgarten between 1824 and 1830 under the aegis of Karl Friedrich Schinkel and takes the form of a Greek temple with the Royal Museum. It is considered Schinkel's finest work. Since summer 2009 it has displayed a trial run of how the collections of non-European art and cultural artefacts from Dahlem could be shown in the Humboldt-Forum, the planned reconstruction of the old royal palace (Stadtschloss).

⑥ Neues Eingangsgebäude

Designed by David Chipperfield

⑦ Archäologische Promenade

The »Archaeological Promenade« is to link the Bode-Museum and Pergamonmuseum with the Altes and Neues Museums via underground passages to allow rapid transit between the key exhibits of all four.

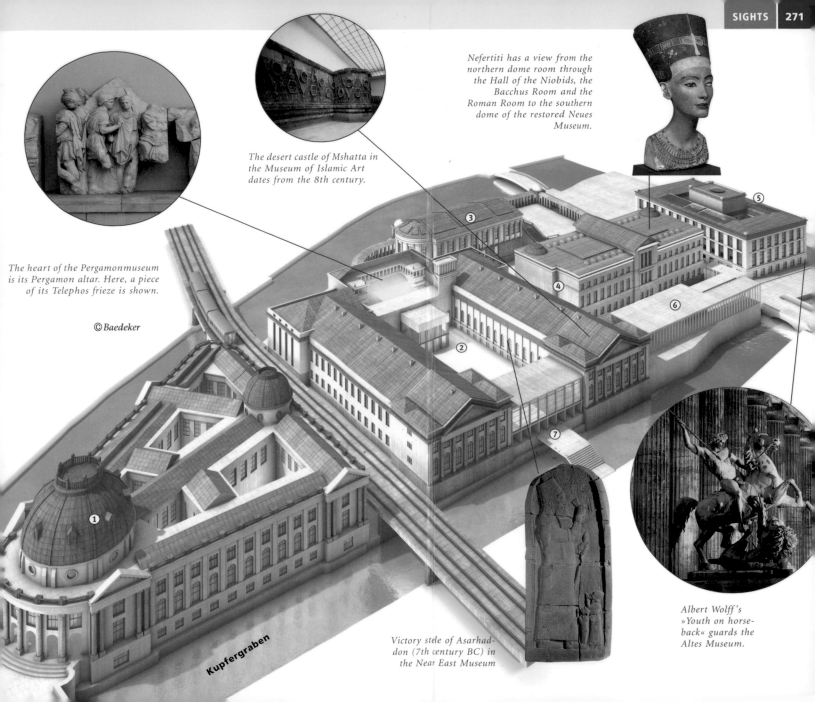

The heart of the Pergamonmuseum is its Pergamon altar. Here, a piece of its Telephos frieze is shown.

©Baedeker

The desert castle of Mshatta in the Museum of Islamic Art dates from the 8th century.

Nefertiti has a view from the northern dome room through the Hall of the Niobids, the Bacchus Room and the Roman Room to the southern dome of the restored Neues Museum.

Kupfergraben

Victory stele of Asarhaddon (7th century BC) in the Near East Museum

Albert Wolff's »Youth on horseback« guards the Altes Museum.

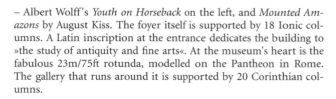

– Albert Wolff's *Youth on Horseback* on the left, and *Mounted Amazons* by August Kiss. The foyer itself is supported by 18 Ionic columns. A Latin inscription at the entrance dedicates the building to »the study of antiquity and fine arts«. At the museum's heart is the fabulous 23m/75ft rotunda, modelled on the Pantheon in Rome. The gallery that runs around it is supported by 20 Corinthian columns.

✳ Antiken-sammlung

The **Collection of Antiquities** largely goes back to the Antiquarium founded in 1830 and has been divided between the Pergamonmuseum and, as of May 1998, the Altes Museum, where art and sculpture of the Greeks and Romans is displayed. The present tour of the main floor encompasses 30 so-called »compartments«, starting with a set of idols from the Cyclades from the 3rd century BC. Antiquity is represented by pieces from Olympia and city states such as Athens, Sparta and Corinth. The classical period features heroes and gods such as the Attic cup by the Sosias painter, featuring Achilles binding the wounds of his friend Patroclus. Other compartments display sculptures, vases and everyday items on the themes of sport, festivals and revelry, gods, Greek cities, the lives of women and finally examples of Roman art. There are also treasure troves with gold in compartment 8 and silverwork in no. 20.

Neues Museum (New Museum)

**Entrance:
Bodestrasse** ⏱

**Opening hours:
Daily 10am–6pm,
Thu–Sun until
8pm, admission
only with timed
ticket!**

The Neues Museum or New Museum was erected between 1843 and 1847 according to designs by **Friedrich August Stüler**. Its interior, including a towering and grandiose staircase, was not completed until 1855, however. The building was badly hit during the Second World War, and attempts at repairing the damage did not begin until 1986. When it was first opened, the Neues Museum was regarded as a universal museum, a composition of architecture, interior decoration and exhibits, the most modern museum of the day. Today, after a long process of restoration, it is at one and the same time **a historical gem and a modern museum space**. Restored colourful frescoes from the original decoration can be seen alongside coolly monumental exhibition halls of freestone. The re-opening of the museum after 70 years of closure was preceded by years of debate, and David Chipperfield's concept of archaeological restoration, which did not exclude new designs, as in the case of the famous stair hall, has not met with unanimous approval.

✳✳ Ägyptisches Museum and Papyrus Collection

The opening in October 2009 brought the Egyptian Museum back to its original location. The limestone bust of Queen **Nefertiti** (from around 1350 BC), wife of the pharaoh Akhnaton. The bust was discovered in 1912 and its presence here has led to Nefertiti herself being described as Berlin's most famous daughter. She is now on display in the perfectly lit north domed room, looking to-

wards monumental statues of the late Roman imperial period from Alexandria under the south dome. Other outstanding pieces are the so-called family stele, depicting Nefertiti and Akhnaton with three of their six daughters, as well as »A Walk in the Garden« (a painted relief showing the royal couple in their youth), portrait masks from the sculptors' workshops of Thutmos in Amarna, a small ebony head of Queen Tiy, mother of Akhnaton (from around 1370 BC), an almost perfectly preserved but incomplete statue of Pharaoh Akhnaton plus the »Green Head of Berlin« (c300 BC).

The Museum for Pre-History and Early History surveys the **civilizations of the ancient world** from the Stone Age until the Middle Ages. The exhibits range from hand-axes to the famous **Berlin Golden Hat**, and from the beginnings of human settlement in Europe through Roman time to the Middle Ages. Silver vessels, weapons, ceramic figures and skeletons are arranged in a chronological circuit; the highlights apart from the golden hat include the Le Moustier Neanderthal and above all **Heinrich Schliemann's renowned collection of Trojan antiquities**.

★
Museum für Vor- und Frühgeschichte

★ ★ Alte Nationalgalerie (Old National Gallery)

The Old National Gallery building was designed by Friedrich August Stüler und Johann Heinrich Strack and built during the period 1866 to 1876. Above the entrance is an equestrian statue of King Friedrich Wilhelm IV fashioned from bronze in 1886 by Alexander Calandrelli. The Nationalgalerie suffered during the war, but also under the Nazi regime itself. A large part of its collection of German Expressionists was shipped to Munich to be shown at a notorious exhibition entitled »Entartete Kunst«, or »Degenerate Art«. Afterwards the pieces were sold at give-away prices. Another part of the collection was incinerated while in storage at a bunker in Friedrichshain.

Entrance: Bodestrasse
⏲
Opening hours: Tue – Sun 10am – 6pm, Thu until 10pm

A tour begins in the Sculpture Hall, in the middle of which is Schadow's famous statue of the two princesses, Crown Princess Luise and Princess Friederike (►ill. p.46). To the left, the museum takes up the topic of realism and the highlights of this section are works by Adolph Menzel, starting with his *Flute Concert in Sanssouci* (► ill. p.367) and including *The Balcony Room*, then finally *Iron Mill* from 1875. Next come paintings from the 19th-century period under the rule of Wilhelm II, where the outstanding pieces are those of Max Klinger. The two rooms after that are concerned with the Secession group and the turn of the 20th century and include Franz von Stuck's *The Sin* and *Tilla Durieux as Circe* as well as Max Beckmann's *Death Bed*. Around the staircase leading to the first floor there is a frieze featuring figures from German history, art and science. This floor starts with the so-called Germano-Romans Arnold Böcklin (*Island of Death*), Anselm Feuerbach, Hans von Marées and Adolph von

Museum tour

✓ **DON'T MISS**

■ Johann Gottfried Schadow: Crown Princess Luise and Princess Friederike
■ Adolph Menzel: *Flute Concert in Sanssouci* and *Iron Rolling Mill*
■ Arnold Böcklin *Isle of the Dead*
■ Paul Cézanne: *Mill on the Couleuve near Pontoise*
■ Caspar David Friedrich: *Abbey in the Oak Wood*

Hildebrand, leading on to a room of French impressionists that includes masterpieces such as Manet's *Winter Garden* or Cézanne's *Mill on the Couleuve near Pontoise*, which was the first of his works ever to hang in a museum. Other rooms cover Wilhelm Leibl, realism in Germany and Austria (Hans Thoma, Spitzweg), Max Liebermann, the Munich school, historic paintings and salon idealism. The second floor takes the visitor through the times of Goethe, Romanticism and Biedermeier. Most of these rooms include some of Schinkel's fine landscape paintings or works by Caspar David Friedrich (among them *Abbey in the Oak Wood*). Three rooms feature views of Berlin by such figures as Eduard Gaertner and J. E. Hummel. Finally come the boards for the frescoes in the Göttessaal at the Munich Glyptothek by Peter Cornelius.

✷ ✷ Pergamonmuseum

Entrance:
Kupfergraben
🕐
Opening hours:
Daily 10am – 6pm,
Thu until 10pm

Alfred Messel and Ludwig Hoffmann's Pergamonmuseum took shape between 1909 and 1930. It too is one of the oldest museums of its kind in the world. It combines the Antikensammlung (Collection of Antiquities) with the Vorderasiatisches Museum (Museum of the Near East) and Museum für Islamische Kunst (Museum of Islamic Art).

✷ ✷
Antiken-
sammlung

The **Collection of Antiquities** covers most of the Pergamonmuseum's main floor. The centrepiece is the reconstruction of the altar to Zeus from Pergamon in Asia Minor (now Bergama in Turkey). This was probably a votive offering to Zeus and Pergamon's patron god Athena by King Eumenes. Made during a period from 180 to 160 BC, the altar was brought to Berlin by Carl Humann in 1902. The artistry of its Greek masons is most apparent in the frieze showing the battle between gods and titans that once ran around the whole altar. Other important exhibits include valuable examples of early Hellenic architecture from Priene, Magnesia and Miletos as well as sculptures from Milet, Samos, Naxos and Attica on display in the hall to the left of the Pergamon Altar. The magnificent market gate from Milet dates from Roman times (165 BC) but clearly displays Hellenic influences. Another wonderful item is the Roman floor mosaic from Gerasa in modern-day Jordan (3rd century BC).

✷ ✷
Vorderasiatisches
Museum

The Pergamon's Vorderasiatisches Museum (**Museum of the Near East**), located in the right-hand wing on the main floor, provides a comprehensive insight into 4000 years of history, art and culture in the Near East. Its items are mainly archaeological finds from digs

Pergamonmuseum Plan

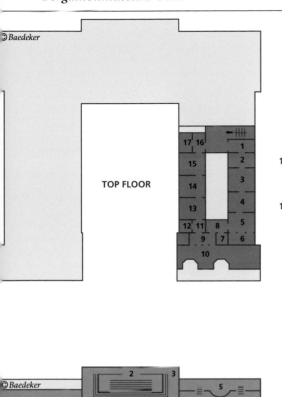

■ **Museum of Islamic Art**

1 Umayyad dynasty
2/3 Abbasids and Fatimids
4 Seljuqs (Iran)
5 Seljuks (Asia Minor) and Ayyubids
6 Mameluks
7 Dome from the Alhambra
8 Khanids and Timurids
9 Spanish Moorish carpets
10 Mschatta façade
11/12 Book art
13 Early Ottomans
14 Safavids and Moghuls
15 High Ottomans
16/17 Aleppo room

■ **Collection of Antiquities**

1 Pergamon altar
2 Telephos frieze
3 Pergamon documentation
4 Roman architecture
5 Trajaneum
6 Hellenic architecture
7/8 Archaic sculpture
9/10 Classical Greece
11 Late classical sculptures
12 Antique copies of Greek masterpieces
13 Antique portrait copies
14 Hellenic sculpture
15 Roman art

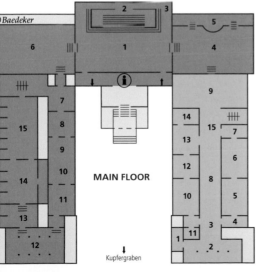

■ **Museum of the Near East**

1 Rock carvings from Yazilikaya
2 Syria, Anatolia, Mesopotomia
3 Stele of Asarhaddon
4 Graves of Assyrian kings
5 Sumeria
6 Babylon
7 Ancient Iran
8 Processional Way from Babylon
9 Ishtar Gate
10 Assyria
11 Assyrian graves
12 Assyrian royal palace
13 Assyria
14 Original Aryans
15 Steles from Assyria

undertaken by the German Oriental Society (Deutsche Orientgesell-schaft) from 1898 to 1917. Its most fabulous and monumental pieces are the Ishtar Gate (▶ill. p. 272) and Processional Way as well as parts of the royal palace façade from Babylon at the time of Nebuchadnez-zar II (603 – 562 BC). Other examples of ancient monumental archi-tecture from the Near East include a cone mosaic wall (from c3000 BC) and a brick façade (c1415 BC) from the Inanna shrine in Uruk. Another unique item is the giant bird statue from Tell Halaf (c900 BC): Also featured are the victory stele of Assyria's King Asarhaddon (680 – 669 BC) and the great Lion Gate from the fortress at Zincirli.

✴ Museum für Islamische Kunst

The **Museum of Islamic Art** on the top floor was founded by Wil-helm von Bode (1904) after the donation of what is still its finest treasure, the façade of the desert castle of Mshatta in Jordan (8th century), gifted to Kaiser Wilhelm II by the Sultan of Turkey. It also features the Aleppo room from the early 17th century, a prayer niche from the Maidan mosque in Kashan (13th century), a decorated Qur'an and prayer niche of the Safavid dynasty (16th century), Irani-an stone stair pillars from the 14th century, Persian and Indian mini-atures, plus carpets and carvings.

✴ Bode-Museum

Entrance: Kupfergraben / Monbijoubrücke

The domed Bode-Museum, designed by Ernst von Ihne, projects out into the Spree. After a lengthy period of renovation, it opened again in autumn 2006. Daylight shines down onto the equestrian statue of the Great Elector in the great hall beneath the dome and onto the five medallions depicting Prussian queens and emperors, who were recognized for their sponsorship of the arts. The marble inlays in the floor of the basilica-shaped building have been reconstructed, as has the Tiepolo cabinet, around which is a collection of **some 1700 sculptures** belonging to the Museum für Byzantinische Kunst (Museum of Byzantine Art) and the Gemäldegalerie (Picture Gallery). The sculptures date from late antiquity right up to the end of the 18th century. There are also about **150 paintings**, as well as the **Münzkabinett** (coin cabinet) and a very nice café in the rotunda.

Neukölln

T – V 17 – 20

Borough: Neukölln   **U-Bahn:** U 7, U 8

The Neukölln borough in the south of Berlin was called Rixdorf un-til 1912. It comprises the areas of Neukölln itself in the north plus Buckow, Britz und Rudow in the south. Its rustic, almost village character makes it attractive for trippers.

The park on Columbiadamm (U 7, U 8 to Hermannplatz) covers some 56ha/140ac. It was an enclosure for breeding hares at the time of the electors but in 1838 Peter Joseph Lenné laid the area out as a park. As of 1878, though, its function changed again and it became a garrison shooting range until it was converted back into a park between 1936 and 1939. In Berlin the name of the Hasenheide park is inseparable from that of the »father of gymnastics«, Friedrich Ludwig Jahn, who founded **Germany's first open-air gymnastic arena** here in 1810. A memorial erected at the northern edge of the park by Erdmann Encke in 1872 recalls the fact. There are plans to construct a Buddhist temple opposite. Berlin's most handsome mosque has been built to the south on Columbiadamm. The papal nunciature lies on its eastern margin, just inside Kreuzberg.

Hasenheide Volkspark (O 18/17)

! *Baedeker* TIP

Knight of the Black Pudding

Marcus Benser was awarded this title by the French fraternity Confrérie des Chevaliers du Goûte Boudin. This means good business for his Berlin black pudding factory, including orders from top chefs (Karl-Marx-Platz 9 – 11).

The Bohemian village (Böhmisches Dorf) around Richardplatz (U 7 to Karl-Marx-Strasse) is an unexpected oasis of seclusion in the midst of Berlin. The village still has its 18th century smithy, the oldest in Berlin, and it is possible to rent horse-drawn carriages for a nostalgic ride. King Friedrich Wilhelm I allowed the village to be built in 1737 for the settlement of Bohemian religious refugees. »Bohemian Rixdorf« remained independent until 1873. Nowadays its community still carries on customs such as the Easter walk to the Bohemian cemetery. The most idyllic spot in this idyll is the **Comenius Garden**, which recalls the teachings of the Bohemian brotherhood's last bishop, Johann Amos Comenius (1592 – 1670).

✶ Böhmisches Dorf (P 20)

Britz is bounded to the north by the Teltowkanal (U 7 to Parchimer Allee). This is where Bruno Taut and Martin Wagner built their **Hufeisensiedlung** (horseshoe estate), one of the most famous major housing projects from the time of the Weimar Republic. The nucleus of the 1024 dwellings on the estate is formed by the buildings on Louise-Reuter-Ring, built between 1924 and 1927. The centre of the old village between Britzer Damm and the street called Alt-Britz is dominated by the **Britzer Dorfkirche** or village church, which picturesquely overlooks the scene from a small hill that rises away from the village pond. The stone building dates from the 13th century, though a crypt (now the sacristy) was added in 1766. Among the church's possessions is an altar donated in 1720 and a late medieval font made from Nuremberg brass. To the west of the village centre on Fulhamer Allee is Britz park and its palace, Schloss Britz. The latter dates from 1547, although it gained its present appearance in 1706 at the instigation of the then lord of the manor, Field Marshall von Erlach (Tue – Sun 11am – 6pm; tours first Sun in the month

Britz (Q 20)

✶ ◀ Schloss Britz and park

2pm). To the south of Britz, the broad parkland of the **Britzer Garten** extends between Buckower Damm and Mohriner Allee (U 7 to Britz-Süd, then by 144 bus). It is a popular leisure destination and has some unique features, such as the »Katastrophenbrunnen« (Catastrophe Fountain) or the »Rhizomatischen Brücke« (Rhizome Bridge). On Buckower Damm at the eastern edge of the park stands the Britzer Mühle, a Dutch windmill dating from 1865.

The **parish church of Buckow village** (U 7 to Johannisthaler Chaussee, then by X 11, 172 or 736 bus) was built between 1220 and 1250. The early Gothic stone blocks of the present gabled building date to the 19th-century period of Wilhelm II, although the late Gothic cross vault is 15th century. The west tower is the only one in Berlin which has remained unaltered since the 13th century. It also has a bell dating from the time it was built. A second bell has been dated to 1322. An impressive epitaph to Johann von Hohenlohe, who was killed in the battle of Kremmener Damm in 1412, is considered the **oldest panel painting in Berlin**.

> ## ! *Baedeker* TIP
>
> ### Neuköllner Opera
>
> Real opera aficionados go to the Staatsoper Unter den Linden as well, but the name »Neuköllner Oper« makes their eyes sparkle. The stage at Karl-Marx-Straße 131-133 is among the most experimental of the German opera scene – to be experienced every year at the Neuköllner opera competition, among other occasions (U 7 to Karl-Marx-Straße; tel. 68890777).

✳ Nikolaiviertel

L 17

Location: Mitte	**S-Bahn and U-Bahn:** Alexanderplatz
City centre plan: C 13/14	(S 3, S 5, S 7, S 75, S 9, U 8)

The Nikolai Quarter, which now exudes the atmosphere of old Berlin, with all kinds of shops and taverns to attract tourists, is indeed a historic nucleus of the city.

Distilled idyll — In the area around where the Nikolaikirche later came into existence, the eastern part of the twin settlement of Cölln-Berlin grew up alongside a ford on the Spree. In 1981 the site southwest of the Rotes Rathaus (▶Rathaus Buildings), bounded by Spandauer Strasse, Molkenmarkt, Mühlendamm, Rathausstrasse and the Spree, was selected by the East German government for the building of an »Island of Old Berliner Milieu« that was to be completed in time for Berlin's 750th anniversary celebrations in 1987. The project was to assemble various historic features, some of which had originally been situated at other sites in the city. Where no suitable original was available, a modern equivalent was to be built to emulate its historic predecessor.

The Nikolaikirche or Church of St Nicholas, **the oldest ecclesiastical building in Berlin**, is aligned in an east-west direction at an angle to the street grid of the original settlement. The original church was a Romanesque stone basilica dedicated in 1230 to St Nicholas, patron saint of mariners and merchants. The western part of this building remains in existence. A new building was begun in 1380 and completed in 1470. It comprised a late-Gothic brick hall with an overarching gabled roof and twin towers standing in close proximity to one another. The interior was rebuilt in 1817 by F. W. Langhans and the building was renovated again from 1876 to 1878, at which time the towers took on their present form. The building suffered serious damage during the Second World War. A lady chapel with a stepped gable roof abutting the front of the towers on the right hand side dates from 1452.

A mixture of nostalgia and genuine history in the Nikolaiviertel

Air raids destroyed much of the interior. Some remnants of late medieval murals have been exposed in the choir. The present furnishings are partially made up of reconstructed elements such as the Kötteritz Chapel, a masterpiece of the late Renaissance, or the Krautsch gravestone, one of Berlin's finest 18th-century grave pieces. Other interesting features include the grave of Daniel Männlich by Andreas Schlüter and the Renaissance epitaphs for Paul Schultheiss and Johann Zeideler. Several other notables are buried here including the teacher of natural law Samuel Pufendorf (1632 to 1694; his grave is on the outside of the choir) and the pietist Philipp Jakob Spener (1635–1705). Paul Gerhardt (1607–76), composer of several Lutheran hymns, was vicar of the Nikolaikirche from 1657 to 1666. There is an exhibition by the Stadtmuseum Berlin up in the gallery that features him and various other personalities that have been associated with the church.

★ Nikolaikirche

⊙ Opening hours:
Tue, Thu–Sun
10am–6pm, Wed
noon–8pm

Nikolaikirchplatz no. 10 was the home of Gotthold Ephraim Lessing from 1752 to 1755. It has been reconstructed and is now no. 7.

Lessinghaus

Hearty Berlin specialities, such as Eisbein (knuckle of pork), sauerkraut and mashed potatoes are all available in the »Zum Nussbaum« restaurant, situated in a gabled house at the corner of Nikolaikirchplatz and Propststrasse. One of the tavern's appreciative guests in former times was Heinrich Zille, although in those days the building was located on the Fischerinsel, where it is known to have stood since about 1570.

»Zum Nussbaum«

Nikolai Quarter *Map*

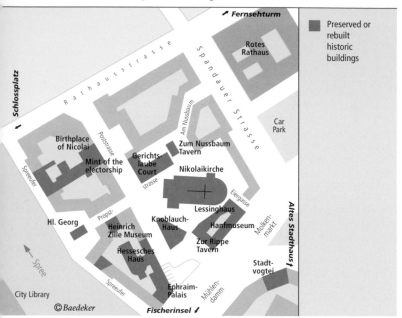

▶ *Fernsehturm*

Rotes
Rathaus

Rathausstrasse

Spandauer Strasse

Schlossplatz

Car
Park

Birthplace
of Nicolai

Poststrasse

Am Nussbaum

Zum Nussbaum
Tavern

Mint of the
electorship

Gerichts-
laube
Court

Nikolaikirche

strasse

Spreeufer

Eiergasse

Lessinghaus

Propst-

HI. Georg

Knoblauch-
Haus

Hanfmuseum

Altes Stadthaus

*Molken-
markt*

Heinrich
Zille Museum

Zur Rippe
Tavern

Hessesches
Haus

Stadt-
vogtei

Spree

Spreeufer

Ephraim-
Palais

*Mühlen-
damm*

City Library

©*Baedeker*

▶ *Fischerinsel* ◀

■ Preserved or
rebuilt
historic
buildings

Propststrasse The life and works of Heinrich Zille are illustrated in the **Heinrich-Zille Museum** at Propststr. 11 (opening hours: 11am – 6pm daily, April – Oct closes 7pm). At the end of Propststrasse stands the bronze **Drachentöter** statue of St George killing the dragon, created by August Kiss in 1856. As of 1865 the statue stood in the first court-yard of the Berlin Stadtschloss. It was moved to the Volkspark in Friedrichshain after the Second World War. For connoisseurs of beer brewed on-site, the Georgs-Brauerei is a delight.

Poststrasse Some of the buildings on Poststrasse have been at their current loca-tions throughout their history. No. 4 was the birthplace of the book-seller and publisher Friedrich Nicolai (1733 – 1811), no. 5 was the city's mint at the time of the electors and no. 12 is an original too, going by the name of the Hessesche Haus. Diagonally across from the entrance to the church is the **Gerichtslaube**, the old town hall or Rathaus in the Middle Ages (now a restaurant). Its original location was 200m/220yd further to the north but the building was demol-ished in 1870. Afterwards a reconstruction was built in the park at Schloss Babelsberg, which is still in existence. As such the Gerichts-laube building in the Nikolaiviertel is actually a copy of a copy.

✳
Knoblauchhaus ▶ The Knoblauchhaus at the corner of Nikolaikirchplatz and Post-strasse was reconstructed in 1989 but this actually is its original site.

The building was initially commissioned by Johann Christian Knoblauch and was built between 1754 and 1760. The well-to-do family – Eduard Knoblauch, architect of the new synagogue on Oranienburger Strasse is a more recent descendant – received many prominent visitors in the house, including Lessing, Mendelssohn, Wilhelm von Humboldt, Scharnhorst and Baron vom Stein. An exhibition focuses on the history of the family during the 19th century and is located in rooms furnished in the original style of the times (opening hours: Tue, Thu – Sun 10am – 6pm, Wed noon – 8pm).

✶
Ephraim Palais

At the corner of Poststrasse and Mühlendammbrücke the Ephraim Palais, which was demolished in 1935, has been reconstructed some 16m/50ft from its original location. Originally known as the »Tonnenbindersche Haus«, it was modified and expanded in 1763/64 for Nathan Veitel Heine Ephraim (1703 – 75), master of the mint in the time of Friedrich the Great. The result was a four-storey city mansion in fine Rococo style with a façade that was rounded at the corners, as well as some magnificent balconies. It was dubbed **»the prettiest corner in Berlin«**. The interior is no less beautiful, particularly the stairway and a copy of Schlüter's ceiling from the Wartenberg Palais. It is owned by the Stadtmuseum Berlin (opening hours: Tue, Thu – Sun 10am – 6pm, Wed noon – 8pm).

Hanfmuseum

Mühlendamm leads along the front of the Ephraim Palais past a reconstruction of the »Zur Rippe« tavern, originally established in 1665, to another reconstructed town house (no. 5). This contains the Hanfmuseum or **Museum of Hemp**, which tells visitors all there is to know about this inestimably useful yet oft ignored plant (opening hours: Tue – Fri 10am – 8pm, Sat/Sun noon – 8pm).

Molkenmarkt

Molkenmarkt

Molkenmarkt, which once bore the name Alter Markt, was perhaps the original core of Berlin. The name comes from the Low German word »Mollen«, referring to the mills (German: Mühlen) of Mühlendamm. This was where Berlin's earliest settlement was situated, along with its first town hall or Rathaus. From here the original river crossing, Mühlendamm itself, linked the two settlements Berlin and Cölln on either side of the Spree. There is nothing of this to be seen nowadays. Berlin's earliest core is submerged beneath the massive interchange between Mühlendamm and Spandauer Strasse. Rising 80m/260ft above the drone of traffic is the tower of the **Altes Stadthaus**. The administrative building was built between 1902 and 1911 according to a design by Ludwig Hoffmann for the city's local services. It later became the base for the East German Council of Ministers and is now the headquarters of the internal senate. Molkenmarkt was previously the site of a building known as Alter Krögel and the city bailiwick, but they were demolished in 1935 to make way for the

Reichsmünze (National Mint). This later became the headquarters of the East German culture ministry. The front of the building has a copy of a frieze Gottfried von Schadow made from sketches by Friedrich Gilly and modelled on murals that were made for the earliest mint building on Werderscher Markt. The original is now situated in Charlottenburg on the building at Spandauer Damm 42 – 44. The mint building also incorporates Palais Schwerin, designed by de Bodt in 1704.

Parochialkirche Parochialstrasse leads through the gap between the Altes Stadthaus and the Neues Stadthaus down towards the Parochialkirche (parish church). This was begun by court builder Grünberg in 1695 using plans by Johann Arnold Nering and was completed by Philipp Gerlach in 1714. It was **Berlin's first Baroque church**. It suffered serious damage during the Second World War but the tower was preserved. The tower once contained a Dutch glockenspiel with 37 bells, installed there for Friedrich Wilhelm I. It played for the first time in 1715 but since 1944 it has not been heard again. The church cemetery contains the grave of Kaspar Wegely († 1764), founder of the Königliche Porzellan-Manufaktur (Royal Porcelain Factory).

Remnants of city wall, »Zur letzten Instanz« Behind the church on Waisenstrasse there are some remnants of Berlin's medieval city walls from the 13th/14th century. Waisenstr no. 16 is allegedly the **oldest tavern in Berlin**. Its name, »Zur letzten Instanz«, a reference to the court of ultimate resort, is explained by the tavern's proximity to Berlin's municipal court. Now, as then, hearty Berlin specialities are on the menu.

Franziskaner-klosterkirche The 13th-century church on Klosterstrasse was part of the Franciscan monastery founded in 1254, which stood on land belonging to a neighbouring park. In 1574 it became a school called the »Gymnasium im Grauen Kloster«. Its alumni included Gottfried Schadow, Friedrich Schleiermacher, Karl Friedrich Schinkel and Otto von Bismarck. Friedrich Ludwig Jahn was not only a pupil but became a teacher as well. Its ruins are now a memorial repudiating war; there is an exhibition of sculptures here by Berlin artists.

★ Olympic Site

M 9 west

Location: Charlottenburg

S-Bahn and U-Bahn: Olympiastadion (S 5, S 75, U 2)

The XIth Olympic Games took place in Berlin in 1936. For the ruling Nazis it was a welcome opportunity to portray the Third Reich as a peaceful and tolerant nation.

Most of the events were held at the so called Reichssportfeld in the western part of Charlottenburg. It comprised the Harbig Sporthalle, the Sportforum built between 1926 and 1928 and the Haus des Deutschen Sports (House of German Sport) from 1932. The swimming stadium was situated to the north of the site with the hockey stadium and the equestrian arena to the south. The site as a whole still exudes the monumental character implicit in the art and architecture of the Third Reich, from its sculptures fashioned by prominent Nazi artists to the massive Olympic arena beyond the Olympic Gate. The centrepiece of the site is the Olympic stadium itself, built between 1934 and 1936 according to plans by Werner March, although Hitler himself and his favourite architect, Albert Speer, both had considerable input. It was built as a replacement for the Deutsches Stadion, which had been built in 1913 by Werner March's father Otto on the same site. The new stadium was designed to accommodate 100,000 spectators (it seats 76,000 today). The stadium oval rises to only 16.5m/ 52.5ft as seen from the outside, as the actual playing fields were sunk by some 12m/39ft. The Marathontor, the gate at the west of the site, bears the names of all the Olympic champions from 1936. After the Second World War the Sportforum was used as a headquarters by the British and the Maifeld playing fields were given over to polo and cricket. Nowadays the stadium has been newly renovated, roofed and equipped with a blue tartan track. It hosts both athletics events and concerts and is the home ground of Hertha BSC Berlin football club. Each May it also serves as the venue for Germany's football cup final.

🕐
Opening hours:
Mid-March – May
and mid-Sep – Oct
daily 9am – 7pm;
June – mid-Sep until
8pm; Nov – mid-
March until 4pm.
Tours: tel.
25 00 23 22

A blue tartan running track, naturally in the renovated Olympic stadium

Maifeld The Maifeld playing fields were used for equestrian dressage and polo matches, though it was later employed as a parade ground. To the west of the fields stands a bell tower some 77m/253ft high that was originally called the »Führerturm«. It was destroyed during the war but was rebuilt in 1962. The old bell is now situated in front of the southern entrance to the stadium. Its observation platform provides a fabulous view that stretches as far as Potsdam and the Müggelberge hills (opening hours: April–Oct 10am–6pm daily). The Langemarckhalle under the stands was intended as a tribute to the dead at the battle of Langemarck (1914), primarily school scholars and students who had joined volunteer regiments. Nazi propaganda heralded the battle as an »example of selfless courage and sacrifice«. Nowadays an exhibition recounts the history of the stadium and screens a film about the development of the Olympic Games.

Waldbühne To the north of the Maifeld in the Murellenberge hills, Werner March built the Waldbühne, an open-air theatre in the form of an amphitheatre seating 20,000 people. It was completed in 1936 and used by the Nazis for their so-called »Thing plays«. Nowadays it is a popular venue for open-air concerts. Bob Dylan and the Rolling Stones are among those who have played there and contributed to the fact that the site is no longer associated with the evil sentiments of its builders.

✶✶ Parliament and Government Precinct

J/K 15

Location: Tiergarten, Mitte
S-Bahn: Unter den Linden (S 1, S 2, S 25, S 26)

Bus: 85, 100
City centre plan: A/B 9/10

Germany's parliament, its ministries and offices are scattered across the city centre, mainly in the districts Tiergarten and Mitte, and are accommodated in various buildings, old and new.

The government quarter extends from the Bundesinnenministerium (interior ministry) at the Moabiter Spreebogen Center in the west as far as the Auswärtiges Amt (foreign office) on Werderscher Markt in the east, and from the Bundesfinanzministerium (finance ministry/treasury) in the south at Leipziger Strasse to the Bundeswirtschaftsministerium (economics ministry) on Invalidenstrasse in the north. The place where power in the land is really concentrated is on the site between the Reichstag building and the Spree, known as the **Spreebogen**. Until the Second World War this was a middle class housing district called the Alsenviertel. However, during the Nazi

The plenary hall of the Reichstag building is airy and light

dictatorship, Hitler's architect Albert Speer devised plans to build his Grosse Volkshalle here, a gigantic domed building 290m/950ft in height. By 1942, before Berlin had suffered from its really major air raids, most of the area had already been demolished. The only building that has survived from that time is the Swiss embassy. The land remained desolate after the war until a general plan for the site by architects Axel Schultes and Charlotte Frank – incorporating the so-called **»Band des Bundes«**, a strip of land running from east to west across the Spreebogen site – conceived the new chancellery (Bundeskanzleramt) and offices for members of parliament. Beyond the Spree stands the glittering train shed of Berlin's first ever central station, the Hauptbahnhof designed by the architects' bureau Gerkan, Marg und Partner, although the agency later fell out with its client, the German railway company the Deutsche Bahn, because a third of the project had to be abandoned. Nevertheless the huge, airy, steel and glass design provides splendid views both inside and out. The only difficult part is finding the right platform.

◀ Hauptbahnhof

✱ ✱ Reichstag Building · Bundestag

When the establishment of the German Empire or »Reich« was proclaimed on 18 January 1871, Prussian capital Berlin was declared capital of the new German state. Its new parliamentary body, the Reichstag, needed a prestigious building to replace its temporary home at Leipziger Strasse 74 in the Royal Porcelain Factory. **Paul Wallot** was commissioned to realize the new building, which he built between 1884 and 1894 in the style of a squat neo-Renaissance palace. The Kaiser himself laid the foundation stone. 30 million Reichs-

History of the Reichstag

REICHSTAG BUILDING

✴ ✴ **Inaugurated in 1894 and burned down in 1933. Bombarded in 1945 but since 1990 the seat of parliament for all of Germany. The history of the Reichstag building has been rich and varied. Its new dome has become a Berlin landmark.**

🕐 Opening hours (dome):
8am – 12 midnight daily (last admission 10pm)

① Dome
The glass dome is 23.5m/77ft high and its base has a diameter of some 40m/131ft. Two ramps wind up the inside in different directions as far as an observation platform (and back down again). The objective of the dome is to allow entry of air into the building and its mirrored design directs light into the plenary hall.

② Roof terrace
In the roof garden restaurant you can take a break (reservation recommended, tel. 22 62 99 33)

③ Plenary hall
The plenary hall houses parliamentary sessions. Seen from where the members sit, the seats occupied by the government are on the left of the lectern and the parliament's president, while officials of the Bundesrat (house of the Bundesländer) sit on the right.

④ Party meeting rooms
The north and the south wing contain rooms for party meetings; the office of the parliament's president is in the south wing..

⑤ Modern art
Contemporary artists have donated works of art

After WW II the Reichstag Building was renovated without a dome

to the Reichstag, including the colours of the German flag in the entrance hall in a work by Gerhard Richter as well as a floor relief by Ulrich Rückriem in the atrium.

⑥ Graffitti
Some inscriptions carved into the newly conquered walls by Soviet troops have been preserved.

⑦ Security gates
Everyone has to pass through a security gate before going up to the dome in glass lifts.

The Reichstag in 1930 with the original dome by Paul Wallot

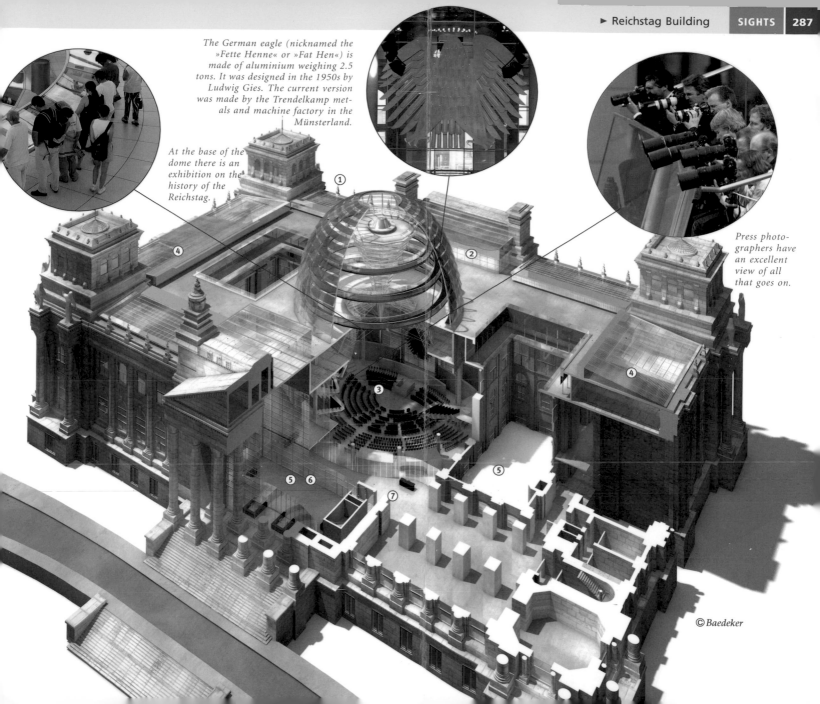

The German eagle (nicknamed the »Fette Henne« or »Fat Hen«) is made of aluminium weighing 2.5 tons. It was designed in the 1950s by Ludwig Gies. The current version was made by the Trendelkamp metals and machine factory in the Münsterland.

At the base of the dome there is an exhibition on the history of the Reichstag.

Press photographers have an excellent view of all that goes on.

© Baedeker

marks were diverted from the war reparations paid by France in 1871. It was not until 1916, though, that the famous inscription was added to the gable: »Dem Deutschen Volke«, »For the German People«. On 9 November 1918, power really did accede in a sense to the German people when, from the Reichstag building itself, Philipp Scheidemann declared Germany a republic.

Reichstag fire ► On the evening of 27 February 1933 the Reichstag caught fire. The »Reichstag fire« entered the pages of history but the cause of the fire has never been indisputably established. The Nazis suggested that the blaze was the result of a plot by the German communist party, the KPD. However, this was called into question when two of the suspects, **Georgij Dimitroff and Ernst Torgler**, were cleared of arson by a Leipzig court in December 1933, even though one other suspect, **Marinus van der Lubbe** was convicted and sentenced to death by the same court. The alternative theory, championed most loudly by the KPD, was that the Nazis started the fire themselves in order to use it against their political opponents, though this too has never been proven. Nevertheless, the political consequences of the Reichstag fire were drastic. The crime was used as an excuse to declare the **»Notverordnung zum Schutz von Volk und Staat«** on 28 February 1933, which suspended German citizens' basic rights and gave the National Socialists the opportunity to persecute and eliminate their opponents shortly before the Reichstag elections took place on 5 March 1933. Subsequent to the fire, the building fell into disuse and was not renovated. The Reichstag's elected officials moved into the **Krolloper** building in the Tiergarten (where the Kongresshalle now stands) – although under the Nazis parliament lost all semblance of importance anyway. On 30 April 1945 two soldiers of the Soviet Red Army hoisted the Soviet flag over the ruins of the Reichstag building. That same day, Hitler committed suicide in his »Führerbunker« just a few hundred metres away (information board on Vossstrasse).

Reconstruction Reconstruction of the building was not finished until 1970. Even then it was decided not to rebuild the dome blown up by a demolition team in 1957. For symbolic reasons the West German parliament, the Bundestag, held regular sittings in the Reichstag, evoking equally regular protests from the Soviet Union and the East Germans. On 4 October 1990, a body comprising members of both the Bundestag and East Germany's Volkskammer held its very first sitting in the plenary hall and 17 January 1991 saw the first constitutional meeting of a pan-German parliament voted for by the reunited German people in the election held on 2 December 1990. The Bundestag held its first sitting in the newly reconstructed Reichstag building, an inaugural ceremony for the new edifice, on 19 April 1999. During the latest rebuilding, an event took place that would draw the eyes of the entire international art world to Berlin. In June and July 1995 the whole building disappeared for

Perhaps a little over-proportioned: the new chancellery (Bundeskanzleramt)

two weeks under 100,000 sq m/25ac of glittering silvery fabric. The American-Bulgarian artist Christo and his wife Jeanne-Claude had doggedly pursued their **»Wrapped Reichstag«** idea since 1971, and on 20 June 1994 the Bundestag finally voted that it could take place. The outstanding success of the project was a thorough vindication of the artists' vision.

The latest version of the Reichstag building was designed by the British architect **Norman Foster**. Keeping only the exterior walls, the resulting edifice is now a highly functional, modern parliament building, and there are few places where the original fabric peeks through. The finest architectural feature is undoubtedly the dome. Illuminated at night, it has become a landmark, a symbol of the new Berlin and one of its biggest tourist attractions: a spiral ramp leads up the inside of the structure to an observation platform with excellent views of the city (dome opening hours: 8am – midnight daily, last admission 10pm; long waits are likely).

The new design

★ ★

◀ Dome

🕐

Other Buildings in and around the Spreebogen

The Bundeskanzleramt, the new chancellery opposite the Reichstag building, forms an intriguing architectural counterpoint. Axel Schultes and Charlotte Frank designed a structure with two long rows of offices, some 18m/60ft high and 335m/366yd long in the case of the southern wing, linked by a nine-storey cube rising to 36m/120ft. This is where the power behind the German government is really concentrated. On the sixth floor is the cabinet room with the office of the chancellor above it. To the east there is a courtyard adorned with Eduardo Chilida's »Berlin« sculpture. Towards the west the office wings reach all the way to the Spree, although a bridge then leads across the river to the Kanzlergarten or Chancellor's Gardens on the opposite bank. The monumental character of the building has come in for some rough criticism. The populace themselves,

★
Bundeskanzler-amt

though, have treated it with rather more humour, dubbing the chancellery with nicknames such as the »Bundeswaschmaschine«, (federal washing machine) due to the circular windows in the central cube, or the »Kohlosseum«, a reference to former chancellor Helmut Kohl, who was the building's prime champion.

Swiss embassy
The most exclusive address for any diplomat, at least in terms of proximity to the seat of power in Germany, can be claimed by the Swiss. Their building was the only one to survive the destruction during the war and is now the immediate neighbour of the Bundeskanzleramt, although the great slab-like presence of the new building hardly sets off the neighbouring palais from 1870 to best effect.

Paul-Löbe-Haus
North of the Reichstag building stands the massive but seemingly transparent Paul-Löbe building, designed by Stephan Braunfels and named after formed social democratic president of the pre-war Reichstag Paul Löbe (1875 – 1967). The eight-storey building with its high, turned up canopy accommodates nearly 1000 offices, meeting rooms and the Bundestag's visitor services.

Marie-Elisabeth-Lüders-Haus
A catwalk leads from the Paul-Löbe-Haus across the Spree to the Marie-Elisabeth-Lüders-Haus. This is another Braunfels-designed building that houses the Bundestag's library and its research services. The name of the building recalls the liberal politician Marie Elisabeth Lüders (1878 – 1966).

Jakob-Kaiser-Haus
The largest of the new buildings on the Bundestag site, at least in terms of area covered, is named after a co-founder of Germany's conservative CDU party, Jakob Kaiser (1888 – 1961). The building was conceived by a group of architects' bureaux and stretches beyond the Reichstag down both sides of Dorotheenstrasse, providing direct access to Pariser Platz alongside the ►Brandenburg Gate. Among the offices in the building is that of the Bundestag president.

Bundespresseamt
Wherever power is assembled, the media is never far away. Germany's national broadcaster **ARD** has its main studio here (tours: Wed, Sat 3pm by appointment, tel. 22 88 11 10), which directly adjoins the Jakob-Kaiser-Haus on the river bank next to the Reichstag. Further east, directly below Friedrichstrasse station, is the Bundespresseamt or national press office, while Germany's second public TV channel **ZDF** is based at Unter den Linden 36 – 38. The **Bundespressekonferenz** or press conference service has its headquarters to the north of the Lüders building on Schiffbauerdamm.

★ Pfaueninsel

Location: Zehlendorf   **S-Bahn:** Wannsee (S 1, S 7), then by 218 bus and ferry

The »pearl of the Havel lakes is one of the Berliners' favourite destinations for a day trip and a World Heritage site.

The Pfaueninsel is an island some 1.5km/1mi in length and 500m/550yd wide, situated midstream in the river Havel at the southwestern tip of Berlin. It is now a protected nature reserve with centuries-old trees and rich bird-life. The 98ha/242-acre islet was dubbed Pfaueninsel in the 17th century, but unexpectedly the name does not derive from the modern German word for a peacock, »Pfau«, but from the Middle Low German word »page« meaning »horse«. Before being so named, the island was used by the Great Elector for breeding hares, at which time it was known as the Kaninchenwerder or

Pfaueninsel Map

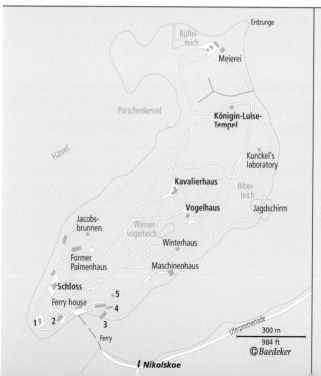

1 Schweizer Haus
2 Kastellanshaus
3 Fregattenhafen
4 Greenhouses
5 Slide

© Baedeker

»rabbit eyot«. Also under the Great Elector, a spot on the eastern side of the island was used by alchemist **Johann Kunckel von Löwenstern**, who produced his highly coveted ruby water here in 1685. Remains of his laboratory were discovered in 1972.

Palace
⊙
Opening hours:
April – Oct Tue – Sun
10am – 5pm

In 1793 Prussia's King Friedrich Wilhelm II rediscovered the island and commissioned master carpenter Alfred Brendel to fashion a love nest for himself and his mistress Wilhelmine Encke, later to be known as the Countess Lichtenau. The small **palace**, which can still be seen today, was built during the period 1794 to 1797 and was allegedly based on a sketch by the countess herself. Friedrich Wilhelm III and his wife Queen Luise were also fond of the building. It was during their time that the island actually was populated with peacocks, and the descendants of these birds inhabit the eyot today. The little pleasure palace is constructed in the style of a romantic ruin. Its two towers are connected by a bridge that was originally made of wood, but was replaced with an iron structure in 1807: the ironwork is an early example of the skill of Berlin's ironsmiths. The splendid interior of the palace shows exquisite taste and testifies to the craftsmanship that was a hallmark of Berlin and Potsdam in the late 18th century and early 19th centuries. The most beautiful examples are the classical Great Hall on the upper floor and the iron spiral staircase.

❓ DID YOU KNOW …?

■ … why there is also a dairy on the Pfaueninsel? The noble lords wanted to enjoy an idyllic setting, complete with cows and cowherds. So master carpenter Brendel was obliged to build a dairy farm in 1795 in the same romantic-ruin style as the pleasure palace.

As the royals and their cohorts wished to enjoy a rural idyll, surrounded by cows and servants, Alfred Brendel built a **dairy** in 1795, designed of course in the form of a romantic ruin like the palace.

Park

⊙
Opening hours:
Nov – Feb
10am – 4pm daily,
March, April, Sep
and Oct 9am – 6pm,
May – Aug
8am – 9pm

Peter Joseph Lenné designed the park between 1821 and 1834. A menagerie that was set up by Friedrich Wilhelm III but abandoned in 1842 was to form the basis for the collection at the ▶ Zoologischer Garten. Schinkel's Palmenhaus burned down at the end of the 19th century and a rose garden was moved from here to the park at Sanssouci. What did remain were such unusual trees as Weymouth and Swiss pines, giant sequoia, ginkgos and cedars as well as native plants. There are other buildings as well as the little palace. The southern part of the island has Schinkel's Schweizerhaus (1830), the Russian slide and the Fregattenhafen while another Schinkel building, the Kavaliershaus, graces the centre of the island. The latter was rebuilt between 1824 and 1826 with the façade of a Gothic town house, the Patrizierhaus from Danzig (Gdansk). A memorial temple

Horses gave the island its name, not peacocks. An especially beautiful one is strolling past the palace here. →

for Queen Luise in the northern part of the island has the original sandstone portico from the mausoleum in the park around Schloss ►Charlottenburg (1829).

★ ★ Potsdamer Platz

M 15

Location: Tiergarten
City centre plan: C 9 / 10

S-Bahn and U-Bahn: Potsdamer Platz
(S 1, S 2, S 25, U 2)

None of the building work undertaken in the »new Berlin« has caused as much interest as the reconstruction of Potsdamer Platz, at least in terms of the extent of the project. The plan was to re-design from scratch a prime slice of inner city that had lain deso-late for decades between the Berlin Wall and the »death strip« parallel to the Wall, and to restore it to its former status as the vibrant heart of one of the world's great cities.

Centre of the new Berlin
Potsdamer Platz was laid out in the 18th century under the name »Platz vor dem Potsdamer Thor« (Thor = gate), receiving its current shortened name in July 1831. Before the Second World War it was the **busiest square in Europe** and, along with neighbouring Leipziger Platz, it formed a hinge between the eastern and western parts of Berlin. Its most memorable landmark was its Verkehrsturm or traffic watchtower, from which a policeman would supervise the vehicles being controlled by the traffic lights that had been installed in 1924, the first such installation in Germany. All around the square there were popular hotels and restaurants such as the **Haus Vaterland**, which was the biggest restaurant in Europe, seating 2000 people, or

Potsdamer Platz as it was in 1933 with its traffic lights in the centre

Hotel Esplanade, where Greta Garbo and Charlie Chaplin would stay and where Wilhelm II hosted men-only sessions in the Kaisersaal. During the Nazi era the notorious Volksgerichtshof or people's court was based next to the hotel. Second World War bombs entirely obliterated the whole square. Practically nothing remained of the earlier buildings, including the Potsdamer Bahnhof station that had been built in 1872 but had to be ripped down after the war. Only **Weinhaus Huth** on the old Potsdamer Strasse and the **Kaisersaal** of the Esplanade hotel testified to the Berlin that had been there before. Some of the square was honeycombed with underground rooms and passages. This subterranean labyrinth was the reason that the East German government drew the double lines of its Wall so far apart at this point, when they were erecting it in August 1961, so that no one could use the tunnels to escape to the west. The same thinking was behind the decision to withdraw train services to Potsdamer Platz S-Bahn station overnight and wall up its entrances. The Wall had made the square a **no-man's-land** between the twin lines of wall leading south to the Brandenburg Gate. Tank traps, barbed wire, watchtowers and death zones were the features that dominated this desolate space.

The senate sought investors and instigated an architectural contest. **New life** The competition was won by Munich architects Hilmer and Sattler, who presented a design based on Berlin's previous street grid. On the basis of this plan, the main investors – Daimler, Sony, Hertie, ABB and Haus Vaterland AG – commissioned internationally renowned architects to create their new buildings on the site. Daimler chose Renzo Piano, Richard Rogers, Arata Isozaki and Hans Kollhoff; Sony went for Helmut Jahn, and ABB for Giorgio Grassi. For years the area was dubbed **Europe's biggest building site** and became a top attraction for the public. The construction work required some major actions, such as the temporary diversion of the Spree. The site became into a completely new district where, amongst primarily commercial buildings, 20% of the new structures are given over to housing, albeit of the most luxurious sort. The main axis of the development is the Neue Potsdamer Strasse, which divides the Daimler premises from the Sony Center and which finishes at Potsdamer Platz itself. Here the roofs of the U-Bahn and S-Bahn stations rise up and there is even a replica of the old traffic light installation. The **Park Kolonnaden** arcades by Giorgio Grass stretch away to the south although, to an extent, they are overshadowed by the Daimler and Sony buildings. At the northern end the decidedly bulky **Beisheim Center** with the Ritz Carlton luxury hotel dominates the scene.

Quartier Daimler

The first of the major developments to be opened was the Quartier **Marlene-** Daimler (previously DaimlerChrysler) site, which was unveiled in **Dietrich-Platz**

Light, airy and impressive: the tent roof over the Sony Center has been a great success for architect Helmut Jahn. At night, the colours even change.

October 1998. Its focus is Marlene-Dietrich-Platz at the end of Alte Potsdamer Strasse. Various public buildings are concentrated in this area, such as the Grand Hyatt hotel (architect: Rafael Moneo), the spherical Bluemax Theatre, Spielbank Berlin and the cinema used for the Berlinale film festival (architect: Renzo Piano), its kinked structure abutting against the back of the Staatsbibliothek library by Hans Scharoun at the ▶ Kulturforum. Towards the river bank, the Reichpietschufer, is the debis-Zentrale, a tower rising to some 83m/272ft and panelled in ochre terra-cotta with a fluorescent green cube on top. Piano's debis building features a massive atrium reminiscent of a cathedral (▶ill. p.10/11).

debis-Zentrale

Potsdamer Platz Arkaden

The Potsdamer Platz Arkaden building, a three-storey shopping mall, largely featuring rather expensive shops, runs from Eichhornstrasse behind the Bluemax Theatre to Fontaneplatz. In its middle level there are two models that show the plans of the area from 1993 and the results of the development from 1999.

Haus Huth

Looking a little forlorn on Fontaneplatz, but still here in its traditional location, is Haus (formerly Weinhaus) Huth. Nowadays it contains the offices of Daimler with the Galerie Daimler Contemporary (daily 11am–6pm), Diekmanns restaurant and a wine dealer, as before. Hans Kollhoff designed the building that stretches from here to Neue Potsdamer Strasse and includes the Cinemaxx cinema (with its 19 screens) and the Daimler Tower, in which there is a **panorama platform at a height of 96m/315ft** (opening hours: Tue–Sun 11am–8pm).

Various sculptures and installations are spread all over the Daimler **Sculptures**
site: *Riding Bikes* by Robert Rauschenberg, *Méta-Maxi* by Jean
Tinguely, *Galileo* by Marc di Suevo, *Light Blue* by François Morellets,
Nam Sat by Nam June Paik, *Boxer* by Keith Haring and *Balloon Flow-
er* by Robert Rauschenberg.

Sony Center

In contrast to the Daimler site's conscious reference to traditional ur- **Forum**
ban forms, the buildings in Sony's plan, completed in 2000, can
evoke awe in a way that the Daimler Quarter's polished dullness does
not really achieve. The landmark building here is a 103m/338ft-high
glass tower which is now occupied by Deutsche Bahn AG (though
possibly not for long, as Sony has sold the site). The Sony Center's
seven buildings, as devised by Jahn, cluster around an oval forum
covering 4000 sq m/43,000 sq ft and covered by a light, tent-like sail
suspended at a height of 40m/130ft. The roof is particularly impressive under its nightly illumination. Underneath there are cafés, restaurants, Sony's own store, the Cinemaxx multiplex and much more.

Part of the Esplanade Hotel with its famous Kaisersaal meeting room **Kaisersaal**
was spared destruction from the bombs of the Second World War
and this too is now part of the Sony development. It was floated in
its entirety on an air bag foundation and, using a scheme that involved a terrific level of technical complexity, it was moved by some
75m/82yd to its new site from its previous location in March 1996.
Enclosed in steel and glass and completed by the addition of rebuilt
breakfast and silver dining rooms, it now forms part of a new hotel,
the Esplanade Residenz.

Berlin's Filmhaus Mediathek is situated in the direction of the new **★**
Potsdamer Strasse. The development includes the **Fernsehmuseum** **Filmmuseum**
or TV Museum about the history of German television , the German **Berlin**
Film and Television Academy and the Arsenal cinema for independent art films. But the highlight of the complex is the new Filmmuseum Berlin. Anybody taking an interest in film will find this outstandingly designed museum unmissable. It utilizes clever computer
and video technology, more than 200 film clips are shown on 84
monitors, and the history of German film is illustrated in a building
whose architecture is as fascinating as its contents. Yet even the technology takes second place to the exhibits from the life of Marlene
Dietrich: film costumes, her feather boa, a cigarette holder, her own
make-up case, even love letters from Jean Gabin, Erich Maria Re-
marque and Ernest Hemingway. It is almost enough to make you
forget that the museum also features other original items, such as the
set designs for the first and famous expressionistic film *The Cabinet
of Dr. Caligari* and a costume worn by Romy Schneider as »Sissi«
(opening hours: Tue – Sun 10am – 6pm, Thu closes 8pm). ⏲

Prenzlauer Berg

H – J 17 – 20

Borough: Pankow

U-Bahn: Senefelderplatz, Eberswalder Strasse, Schönhauser Allee (U 2)

»Prenzl. Berg« has been transformed; first of all from a working-class quarter to a centre of alternative sub-culture, is now on the way to becoming an upmarket residential area.

From workers' suburb to in- quarter

Prenzlauer Berg is one of the most densely populated areas of Berlin. Its five-storey rented apartment buildings are characteristic of what was once a typical working class suburb. It came into existence at the start of the 19th century and was incorporated into Berlin in 1920. During the Second World War the borough suffered little from the bombing apart from at its eastern side, but what the bombs and grenades failed to achieve was soon accomplished by the »Magistrat« of East Berlin. Other than a few carefully maintained prestige buildings such as those on Husemannstrasse, little was spent on the upkeep of the buildings and, even now, many houses remain in atrocious condition. On the other hand, even in the dying days of East Germany and certainly in the years since reunification, many of the flats were occupied by young people. In the era of the East German regime of Erich Honecker, any kind of alternative culture was strictly proscribed and suppressed, particularly the nascent scene in Prenzlauer Berg, which became a centre of opposition to the GDR government. Nevertheless the autonomously alternative era of »Prenzl. Berg« is already starting to meet its end. The chic ambience of newly renovated housing is attracting prosperous young people from the west, driving the truly alternative out to ►Friedrichshain. The changes are evident on **Kastanienallee** with its shops and cafés, many offering a hearty breakfast until well into the afternoon: the street has now earned the nickname »Castingallee«. There is still an appealing beer garden, Prater, and Konnopke's snack bar beneath Eberswalder Strasse U-Bahn station holds out as before.

!

Baedeker TIP

Dial A for art

If you would like to have your portrait painted, an agency called Berliner Sippschaften can provide artists who will do it in almost any style, from classical painting to a caricature (Kollwitzstr. 52, tel. 69 58 23 70, www.berliner-sippschaften.de).

Schönhauser Allee

The elevated railway rattling across its steel arches dominates the main thoroughfare of Prenzlauer Berg, Schönhauser Allee. It starts at Senefelderplatz, where there is a monument to **Alois Senefelder** (1771 – 1834), inventor of lithography. The new **Kulturzentrum Pfefferberg** is located here in a former brewery, the beer garden of

Café Schwarz Sauer, a popular meeting place on Kastanienallee

which is listed for protection. A little further to the north there is a Jewish cemetery on the right (►Cemeteries), which was laid waste by the national socialists in 1943. Opposite the right turn down Wörther Strasse is the Segenskirche (Church of Blessings, 1905/1906), which is fully incorporated into the terraced front of the street. Next comes Sredzkistrasse, with the entrance to the Kultur-Brauerei. This was built by Franz Schwechten for the Schultheiss beer brewers in 1892, at which time it was the biggest lager brewery in the world. The architect was the same man who had designed and built the Kaiser-Wilhelm-Gedächtniskirche. The KulturBrauerei is now one of Berlin's best venues and includes stages, restaurants and a multiplex cinema as well as being a fine testament to the industrial architecture of the period of Wilhelm II's reign. Under the elevated railway at the intersection of Schönhauser Allee, Danziger Strasse and Kastanienallee it is possible to get a bite to eat at **Konnopke**, a snack bar which is a veritable Berlin institution. It has been owned by the same family since 1930 and its »Currywurst« (►Baedeker Special p.110) is really well worth trying, although there are plenty more dishes on offer. A little further to the west along Eberswalder Strasse is the **Mauerpark**, formerly occupied by a section of the Berlin Wall but now a park linking east and west and including a few remnants of the Wall itself.

★
◄ KulturBrauerei

The Gethsemane-Kirche (Gethsemane Church) was opened on Stargarder Strasse near the S-Bahn/U-Bahn station at Schönhauser Allee in 1893. In the final years of the GDR, opponents of the government representing all political viewpoints would meet there.

Gethsemane-Kirche

Wörther Strasse leads from Schönhauser Allee to Kollwitzplatz. A monument erected there by Gustav Seitz in 1959 is in memory of

Kollwitzplatz

Käthe Kollwitz. She lived in what was then Weissenburger Strasse 25 (now Kollwitzstrasse) from 1891 till the destruction of her house in 1943. On the other side there is a copy of her statue *The Mother*. Kollwitzplatz is now the centre of Prenzlauer's more up-market scene and is appropriately ringed by bars and cafés, of which Restauration 1900 and Trattoria Lappreggi are among the very best, and Pasternak among the most unusual. Husemannstrasse leads north from Kollwitzplatz. During the GDR period, the street was expensively renovated for Berlin's 750th anniversary celebrations, but now the ravages of time are beginning to make their presence felt once more. **Dunckerstrasse** is a continuation of Husemannstrasse. At no. 77, it is possible to visit a rental apartment constructed in around 1900 (Mon – Sat 11am – 5pm).

Husemannstrasse ▶

🕐

Rykestrasse   Rykestrasse runs parallel to Husemannstrasse. No. 53 contains the
Synagogue ▶   only synagogue in all of Germany that was not destroyed by the Nazis on »Kristallnacht« or Pogrom Night in 1938. Nevertheless it was later misused as a camp by the Wehrmacht. It was reconstructed be-
Wasserturm ▶   tween 1976 and 1978. Rykestrasse leads southwards to the premier landmark of Prenzlauer Berg, the tower of the water works built in 1856. The thick round tower itself was added to the plant in 1873. Nazi stormtroopers converted the machine house into a torture chamber in 1933. The slopes of the hill, a popular meeting place in the summer months, was planted with vines in 2005.

Zeiss-   To the east, beyond the heart of the Prenzlauer Berg scene, the for-
Gross-   mer site of a city gas works that closed in 1981 stretches between
planetarium   Danziger Strasse and Greifswalder Strasse. The area has now been made into the **Ernst-Thälmann-Park**, named after the leader of the communist party who was born in 1886 and murdered at Buchenwald concentration camp in 1944. A bronze memorial to him, created by Soviet sculptor Lew Kerbel and verging on the monumental, has managed to survive reunification. At the northern edge of the park is the spherical dome of the Zeiss-Grossplanetarium. To find out about the many tours available in the planetarium, phone the automatic hotline on 4 25 16 52.

Rathaus Buildings

As the city has grown from many smaller settlements, Berlin has many town halls. Each district is governed from its own town hall (»Rathaus« in German).

One city, many   The oldest Rathaus for the government of Berlin is said to have been
town halls   situated at the location of the present-day Rotes Rathaus back in the 13th century. The building was rebuilt several times after fires in

1380, 1448 and 1581. The square in front of its court building, the Gerichtslaube, which was demolished in 1868, was used for executions until 1694. Between 1307 and 1442, when the administrations of Cölln and Berlin were combined, both towns were ruled from a Rathaus next to the bridge, the Lange Brücke (now called the Rathausbrücke). The building was knocked down in 1514. Cölln Rathaus was located on Breite Strasse and was chosen as the seat of a common administration in 1709 when Berlin, Kölln, Friedrichswerder, Friedrichstadt and Dorotheenstadt were combined. Berlin's Rathaus became the base for the city's law authorities. The Rotes Rathaus was used as the seat of the Magistrat and the mayor or Oberbürgermeister of greater Berlin until the end of the Second World War. When the city was divided, East Berlin laid claim to the use of these historical appellations. On 1 October 1991 the administration of the reunited Berlin – the senate – moved back to the Rotes Rathaus, which has been considered the official city hall of Berlin ever since.

When the city was booming between 1885 and the start of the First World War, many of the boroughs erected their own prestigious Rathaus buildings, like the Art Nouveau structure at Charlottenburg, which has the highest Rathaus tower in Berlin (88m/289ft), or those in Köpenick (►Alt-Köpenick) and Steglitz, both fine examples of the neo-Gothic style.

The Rotes Rathaus was built between 1861 and 1869 to a neo-Renaissance design by Hermann Friedrich Waesemann that featured a tower rising up to 74m/243ft. King Wilhelm I took part in the laying of the foundation stone on 11 June 1861. The first sitting of the Magistrat was held at the end of 1865. The name of the Rotes Rathaus literally means »Red City Hall«, the name not being bestowed on the

✷
Rotes Rathaus
(L 17 B 14)

The tower of the Rotes Rathaus stands proudly even in the shadow of the Fernsehturm

S- und U-Bahn:
Alexanderplatz (S 5,
S 7, S 75, S 9, U 2,
U 5, U 8) ▶

basis of any particular democratic ideal, but simply because of the red colour of its brick façade. The so-called **Steinerne Chronik** runs around the building at about first floor height. This is a frieze of 36 terra-cotta reliefs with scenes from the history of Berlin. In front of the Rotes Rathaus as far as the ▶ Fernsehturm and the ▶ Marien-kirche there is a park that features two sculptures by Fritz Cremer – *Trümmerfrau* and *Aufbauhelfer* (*Woman Searching in the Rubble* and *Reconstruction Helper*). Furthermore there is a major landmark in Reinhold Begas's **Neptunbrunnen** or Neptune fountain from 1891, which originally stood between the Stadtschloss and the Marstall or royal stud. Its statues represent the sea god Neptune and his court, including four female figures representing the rivers Elbe, Oder, Rhine and Vistula. On the other side of Spandauer Strasse by what was the rear wall of the Palast der Republik (▶ Schlossplatz) stands the **Marx-Engels Forum**, which opened in 1986 and features a statue with Karl Marx (seated) and Friedrich Engels (standing) cast in bronze as well as various metal pillars with etched photographs depicting the »History of Class War«. Shortly after the fall of the Wall one wit added a slogan to the base, declaring »Wir sind unschuldig« – »it's not our fault.«

Rathaus Schöneberg (O 13)

U-Bahn: Rathaus
Schöneberg (U 4) ▶

The Rathaus for the borough of Schöneberg was built between 1911 and 1914 and served between 1949 and 1990 as the headquarters for West Berlin's mayor and the seat of its council meetings. It thus has great symbolic importance in terms of the history of West Berlin. To the left of the main entrance there is a **plaque recalling the visit of US President John F. Kennedy**, who in 1963 delivered his famous

speech from these steps, in which he declared he too could proudly utter the words, »**Ich bin ein Berliner**« (▶ ill. p.38). The 70m/230ft tower of the Rathaus contains a »freedom bell« paid for by the USA and modelled on the Liberty Bell in Philadelphia. It was handed over on United Nations Day (24 October 1950) by General Lucius D. Clay. It is inscribed with the words »Möge diese Welt mit Gottes Hilfe die Wiedergeburt der Freiheit erleben« – a variation on Abraham Lincoln's theme in his Gettysburg Address: »… this nation, under God, shall have a new birth of freedom«.

✷ Schlossplatz · Werderscher Markt

L 18

Location: Mitte
City centre plan: B/C 12/13

S-Bahn: Hackescher Markt (S 5, S 7, S 75, S 9)
Bus: 100, 200

The Palast der Republik, demolished in 2007, and the entire site around it was until 1950 occupied by the Berliner Stadtschloss, the City Palace, of which reconstruction is planned.

The Stadtschloss originated under Elector Friedrich II as a castle, built between 1443 and 1451. The massive building was 200m/220yd in length and 120m/130yd wide; it also had a dome 70m/230ft high. The Baroque design of the palace was widely praised and its magnificent interior was the result of a re-furbishment conducted in around 1700 under Andreas Schlüter. After 1945 all that was left of the palace was a burnt-out ruin, although there were plenty of good reasons for it to be rebuilt. However, the East German government viewed the building as a symbol of a »feudalistic and imperialist« past and ordered that the ruin be blown up. That order was carried out in 1950. There remained a broad, empty space used for parades and demonstrations. It was appropriately called Marx-Engels-Platz.

Schlossplatz in around 1905 with the Stadtschloss city palace and the Schlossbrücke bridge

The **Palast der Republik** (Palace of the Republic) was erected from 1973 to 1976 according to a design by Heinz Graffunder. It was a prestige building for the GDR and, perhaps for that very reason the public response was not as fulsome, evoking nicknames such as »Palazzo Prozzo« or »Erichs Lampenladen« (Erich Honecker's lamp shop). The building measured 180 x 85m (200 x 93yd) and was the seat of East Germany's parliament (Volkskammer) as well as being a popular venue for events. After the fall of the Wall it was intended that the palace be used as a cultural centre, but in 1990 it became necessary to close the building due to the asbestos used in its construction. After the asbestos was removed various artists' groups were able to use the building before it was finally demolished in 2009.

Reconstruction of the Stadtschloss

The debate about what should be built in place of the Palast der Republik, and in particular whether the Stadtschloss should be recreated, raged for years. A commission of experts recommended the reconstruction in a report at the beginning of 2002. They suggested calling the building the **Humboldt Forum**, a new structure behind a façade recreating the appearance of the Stadtschloss to accommodate the non-European parts of the collections now held by the city's museums in ▶Dahlem. The Italian architect Franco Stella won the competition to built the new Stadtschloss, which is scheduled for completion in 2013 − at least according to the optimists.

Former Staatsrat building

The southern side of the square is occupied by the building of the East German Staatsrat (Council of State). Its façade includes the only surviving piece of the Stadtschloss (»Portal IV«), from which Karl Liebknecht declared Germany a socialist republic in 1918.

Marstall

On Breite Strasse, which runs past the left of the former Staatsrat building, there is a building called the Neue Marstall (1896 – 1901), both wings of which incorporate sections of an older Marstall building from 1670. Marstall refers to the royal stud or court stables and the building is the only remaining example of the early Baroque period in Berlin.

✱ Ribbeckhaus

Further along is a four-gabled building called the Ribbeckhaus, which was built in 1624 for the aristocratic Brandenburg family of von Ribbeck, immortalized in the literature of Theodor Fontane. This is the only remaining Renaissance dwelling in Berlin and now hosts the **Zentrum für Berlin-Studien** , a centre for the study of Berlin and the first port of call for anyone interested in all aspects of the city. Rubbing shoulders with the Ribbeckhaus is the **Stadtbibliothek** (City Library). Its door is decorated with 117 different versions of the letter A, a design by Fritz Kühn.

Brüderstrasse

Neumannsgasse leads from Breite Strasse toBrüderstrasse, where Andreas Schlüter once lived at no. 33. No. 10 is the so-called **Galgenhaus**, built in 1688 for von Happe, a councillor of the Board of Domains. It is one of the few buildings in Berlin itself that still has a Baroque town house at its core. There is a story that one of the councillor's maids was hanged outside the building for the alleged theft of a silver spoon, which she had not taken (thus the name Galgenhaus, meaning gallows house). No. 13 was built in 1709 but modified in 1787 by Carl Friedrich Zelter for writer, critic and publisher **Christoph Friedrich Nicolai** (1733 – 1811), who also had a bookshop in the building. This was also the meeting point for the intellectual elite of the time and a centre of the Enlightenment. It attracted such figures as the aforementioned master builder, musician and intimate of Goethe, Zelter, as well as Moses Mendelssohn, Gottfried Schadow and Daniel Chodowiecki. In 1892 the bookshop was relocated to Dorotheenstrasse. The Berlin City Museums Trust puts on rotating exhibitions in both the Nicolaihaus (including one featuring the history of theatre in Berlin) and the Galgenhaus (opening ⏱ hours: Tue – Sun 10am – 6pm).

Werderscher Markt

From Brüderstrasse, Sperlingsgasse leads away to the Jungfern-brücke, **Berlin's last remaining lifting bridge**, which was built in 1798. The bridge crosses the Spree canal and then a right turn leads on to Werderscher Markt. The route also passes the Reichsbank building, erected between 1934 and 1938, which was occupied by the central committee of East Germany's ruling SED party as of 1958. After reunification, it played a key role as the »Haus der Parlamentarier« (house of parliamentarians) and now houses the Auswärtiges Amt or German foreign office. In front of the old building between here and Werderscher Markt itself, a new building by Thomas Müller and Ivan Reimann has been constructed. The old East German foreign ministry was on the site between here and Unter den Linden. One corner of the façade and some printed plans mark the location of Schinkel's former **Bauakademie** (1832 – 35) or College of Building.

Auswärtiges Amt

The two towers of the neo-Gothic Friedrichswerdersche Kirche, the church opposite the Auswärtiges Amt, mark a building that was erected between 1824 to 1830 according to plans by Karl Friedrich Schinkel and which now contains the Schinkelmuseum. The building is a simple hall construction with stellar vaulting. Inside is an exhibition of selected classical sculptures that illustrate Karl Friedrich Schinkel's works in Berlin. In addition, some lovely new-year plaques made by the Berliner Eisengiesserei or iron casting works are also on ⏱ display (opening hours: Tue – Sun 10am – 6pm).

Friedrichswerder-sche Kirche (Schinkel-museum)

Schloss Schönhausen

E 18

Location: Ossietzkystrasse, Pankow   **S-Bahn:** Pankow (S 4, S 8)

Schloss Schönhausen was built in 1664 as a manor for the Countess von Dohna. Johann Arnold Nering (as of 1691) and Eosander von Göthe (as of 1704) modified the building on behalf of Elector Friedrich III. From 1740 to 1797 Elisabeth Christine, wife of King Friedrich II, lived in the palace at the behest of her royal spouse, although the building was ravaged by Russian troops in 1760 and had to be rebuilt by Johann Boumann the Elder. After the death of Friedrich Wilhelm III, Countess Liegnitz moved into the palace. When the new East German state was established in 1949, the palace served as the residence of the nation's first president, Wilhelm Pieck, until

⏱
Opening hours:
Opening hours:-
Tue – Sun
10am – 5pm

1960 when it was used to accommodate guests of the government. In the dying days of the GDR, the state and its people met at a round table discussion in the building and it was also here that the decisive »Two plus Four« talks took place. It was reopened for visitors in 2009. Some of the apartments of Queen Elisabeth Christine on the ground floor have been furnished in authentic period style. On the upper floor Wilhelm Pieck's study, which has been preserved fully intact, and a guest apartment occupied by Fidel Castro and Indira Gandhi among others, can also be viewed.

Spandau

U 7 west

Borough: Spandau
Bus: X 33 (to the Zitadelle)

U-Bahn: Altstadt Spandau, Rathaus Spandau, Zitadelle (U 7)

Spandau developed thanks to its position in the Middle Ages on the eastern border of the German Reich.

Former border post
The old fortress town of Spandau, which was independent of Berlin until 1920, is situated at the confluence of the Spree and Havel rivers. Between 1160 and about 1200, the Havel formed the border of the German Holy Empire. As the border was moved eastward, the town of Spandau, which receives its first known mention in 1197, became a rearward base and was granted a town charter in 1232. The town arose on the island where the present Altstadt or old town is located. The fortress was on the island where the citadel stands. The rise of Berlin rather passed Spandau by, and by the end of the 19th century it was still only a middle-sized town. Spandau had a certain notoriety on account of its prison, which was located in the Altstadt until the end of the 19th century. The jail for war criminals some way outside the town, where the four powers oversaw the imprisonment of the one remaining inmate, **Rudolf Hess**, until he committed suicide in 1987, has now been torn down and replaced by a shopping centre.

! *Baedeker* TIP

Florida, nice and cold
When Berliners hear the word »Florida«, they think of ice cream and come from all quarters of the city to Klosterstrasse in Spandau to get a scoop or two. Ice cream-maker Olaf Höhn also welcomes his customers in a second ice cream parlour in the Ellipse, and now in the government quarter behind the Marie-Elisabeth-Lüders-Haus.

Old town
Spandau's old town is located on the western bank of the Havel river. Air raids and the construction of an underground railway have left little trace of its earlier buildings, but around Reformationsplatz, in particular, the small scale has at least been retained. Reformations-

platz in the centre is the site of the St. Nikolai church, a brick hall ◄ St. Nikolai
church dating from the first half of the 15th century that was built
over an earlier 13th-century building. The hall is most conspicuous
for its altar, which is 8m/26ft high and made of limestone and stucco
with rich decoration in the form of paintings and sculptures. This
masterpiece of the late Renaissance was financed in 1582 by the
master builder of the town's fortifications, Rochus Graf zu Lynar,
who is buried beneath the altar. Other noteworthy features include
the baptismal font from 1398 and the Baroque pulpit, originally fashioned for the chapel of the Potsdam City Palace, the Stadtschloss, in
around 1700. The house opposite the church is occupied by the **Museum Spandovia Sacra**, which has an exhibition on the history of
the church community and the town (opening hours: Thu, Fri, Sat ◷
3pm – 6pm, Sat 1pm – 6pm). The **Gotisches Haus** (Gothic House) at
Breite Str. 32 is considered to be the oldest non-ecclesiastical building in the Berlin region. Remains of Gothic brickwork suggest that it
may have been constructed in the 15th century; a room on the upper
floor holds an exhibition on the history of Spandau (opening times
Mo – Fr 10am – 6pm, Sat until 5pm). The so-called **Wendenschloss**
(Jüdenstr. 35), an elaborate house for a city-dwelling farmer, was
built in around 1700. The original building was broken up in 1966
and replaced by a new building, but its façade was designed to match
that of its historical predecessor. The river embankment at Viktoria-
Ufer still has a 116m/127yd remnant of the 14th-century **town walls**.

In the village of Gatow lying to the south of the Altstadt on the west- **Luftwaffen-**
ern bank of the Havel a military airfield, Militärflugplatz Gatow, **museum**
came into existence in 1935. After the war it was taken over by the
British. It is now the site for the German forces' **Luftwaffenmuseum**
(German Air Force Museum) and
includes 100 military aircraft of var
ious origins dating from the First
World War until the present day.
Among them are many that formerly belonged to East Germany's
military forces, the Nationale Volks-
sarmee (opening hours: Apr – Oct
Tue – Sun   10am – 6pm,   Nov –
March 9am – 4pm; 135 bus from
Rathaus Spandau, then change at
Alt-Kladow to a 334 or X34 bus to
the Kurpromenade stop).

A Fokker D VII in the Luftwaffenmuseum

Zitadelle Spandau

The Spandau Citadel is the **only remaining Renaissance fort in Germany** and testifies to early Italian fortress building skills. The Italians
were the first to design their forts as sharply angled bastions rather

🕐
Opening hours:
Daily 10am – 5pm

than in the rounded bastion style that had been common until then. The earliest building on the site was an island fortress built by the Ascanians (12th century). Elector Joachim II had the Spandau Citadel erected as of 1560 for the defence of Berlin. Christoph Römer and the Venetian Chiaramella di Gandino were in charge of the building, while Rochus Graf zu Lynar took over in 1584 and completed construction in 1594. The basic form has remained unchanged since then. It is a square protected by moats on every side, each side being approximately 200m/220yd long with bastions at each corner that bear the names King, Prince, Crown Prince and Brandenburg. The citadel was considered impregnable. During the Thirty Years' War it was occupied without a fight by Swedish troops after negotiations between Sweden's King Gustaf Adolf and Brandenburg's Minister Adam Graf Schwarzenberg. When the Austrians invaded Brandenburg in 1757, the king and his court sought refuge here. In 1806 the fortress was surrendered without bloodshed to Napoleon's French forces. It continued to be used for military purposes until 1945 but is now used as a museum and venue for various events.

Spandau *Citadel*

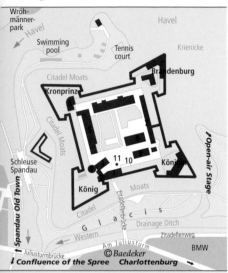

© Baedeker

1 Kommandantenhaus
   (gatehouse, ticket office)
2 Casemates
3 Palace
4 Juliusturm (tower)
5 Administration and
   officers' building
6 Kanonenturm

7 Magazine
8 Exercise sheds
9 Neues Zeughaus (museum)
10 Remains of Altes Zeughaus
    (former arsenal replaced
    by Neues Zeughaus)
11 Statue of Albert the Bear

A narrow bridge leads to the so-called **Kommandantenhaus** (the 16th-century gatehouse). It was furnished with a new façade in 1839. Its segmented gable end features a coat of arms depicted in relief with symbols of all the constituent parts of Prussia at the beginning of the 18th century, encircled by the British Order of the Garter. The castle commandant lived on the upper floor, where nowadays an exhibition describes the history of the citadel.

Zitadellenhof   Straight ahead of the entrance is the Zitadellenhof, where the army's »Heeresgasversuchsanstalt« (gas experimentation station) has left an unpleasant legacy. At the end of the war remains of its weaponry were thrown into the wells. To the right there is a monument to the Lord of the March, Albrecht the Bear (▶ill. p.25).

The Kommodantenhaus and the Juliusturm reflected in the moat of the Spandau Citadel

Diagonally opposite the Kommandantenhaus is the Palas, the living **Palas** quarters of the fortress, built in around 1350 but remodelled at the beginning of the 16th century as well as in 1821, then altered into an officers' casino in 1936. The newly renovated Gothic hall is used as a venue for a variety of events. At the base of the building on the southern side it is possible to see gravestones (13th/14th century) with inscriptions in Hebrew. They date from Spandau's Jewish cemetery that was ravaged around 1510 and its stones used, as here, for building materials. The tower known as the **Juliusturm** is the oldest part of the citadel. It was built as early as the beginning of the 14th century as a watchtower and refuge. Its name is probably a corruption of »Judenturm« or »Jewish Tower«. This goes back to 1356 when Margrave Ludwig gave the lucrative job of running the tower to his servant »Frizen the Jew«. The tower became a byword as the **repository of the German Reich's war treasury**. In 1874 Chancellor Otto von Bismarck deposited gold to the value of 120 million marks here, money that had been received as war reparations from the French after their defeat in the Franco-German war of 1870/71.

The Neues Zeughaus (1856–1858) contains the **Stadtgeschichtliche** **Other buildings** **Museum Spandau** (Museum of the History of Spandau), displaying various historic finds from Spandau. The casemates in the King bastion are open to visitors. The north western boundary of the citadel is formed by the Crown Prince bastion with its »Kavalier« defence, a massive semi-circle intended for defence against heavy artillery bombardment. To the north is the Brandenburg bastion. The ruins of the **Heeresgasversuchsanstalt** from 1940 can still be seen here.

It is possible to walk along the moat around the citadel, offering excellent views of the Havel. Such a walk passes the **Schleuse Spandau** (Spandau lock), which was opened for traffic in 1910. An original lock had already been built here as early as 1723.

! *Baedeker* TIP

Nocturnal flyers

The Spandau citadel is one of the major hibernation habitats for bats in Germany. For those interested in observing the creatures, tours are held from mid-August until the end of September every Friday and Saturday at 8pm and 9pm. These are by appointment only, which can be made by calling 79 70 82 67. The cellar of building 4, where exotic bats are kept, is opened on Fridays and Saturdays.

Fort Hahneberg It is less well known that the Spandau district also has a second fortress. Fort Hahneberg was constructed between 1882 and 1888 and was the **last German artillery fort**. After the division of Germany, it spent more than 40 years in a kind of *Sleeping Beauty* slumber, because it was directly on the border strip between the villages of Staaken-West (East Germany) and Staaken-Ost (West Berlin). Nowadays it is rather overgrown and derelict, and rather spooky (tours: Sat/Sun 10am – 4pm; approach via Heerstrasse/B 5 and Reimerweg/ Weinmeisterhornweg).

✴ Spandauer Vorstadt · Scheunenviertel

K 15 – 17

Location: Mitte
S-Bahn: Oranienburger Str. (S 1, S 2), Hackescher Markt (S 5, S 7, S 75, S 9)

U-Bahn: Oranienburger Tor (U 6), Weinmeisterstrasse, Rosenthaler Platz (U 8), Rosa-Luxemburg-Platz (U 2)
City centre plan: A 9 – 15

Now an attractive district with the highest concentration of bars in Berlin, the Scheunenviertel was once a ghetto of poverty and criminality: the area was home to low-skilled workers, the proletariat, Jewish refugees from the East, prostitutes and pimps, petty criminals and grafters. Alfred Döblin's novel *Berlin Alexanderplatz* describes it all.

A fixture of the Spandauer Vorstadt scene, the Hackesche Höfe

The region to the northwest of modern-day Alexanderplatz and north of the River Spree was called Spandauer Vorstadt when it was first settled around 1700. As early as 1672 a fire prevention decree by the Great Elector had already stipulated the building of 27 barns for the storage of flammable materials: the name »Scheunenviertel« comes from the German word for a barn. With the coming of industrialization, the area was given over to low-rent, barrack-like dwellings, squalid housing with entire families in a single room and a shared privy for each floor. To this **»backyard of Berlin«** came floods of eastern European Jews taking flight from the pogroms of the 19th century. A uniquely fascinating mixture of eastern Jewish culture, proletarian poverty and big-city crime was the result. Around the main thoroughfares of Dragonerstrasse (now Max-Beer Strasse) and Grenadierstrasse (now Almstadtstrasse), Yiddish was spoken as often as German, matzo bread and rissoles were on sale and the beer flowed in bars like the »Mulackritze«. The Nazis brought an end to all this with their destruction of the Jewish culture, which simultaneously meant lumping the whole area up to the edge of the Spandauer Vorstadt district around Oranienburger Strasse with the notorious »Scheunenviertel«, in order to bring discredit on the Jews living there. Finally the Jews were transported and taken to death camps from an assembly point on Grosse Hamburger Strasse. Anything that still remained at the end of the Nazi era disappeared during the GDR epoch. After reunification, the area did experience a brief alternative

The home of Franz Biberkopf

spring until it was refurbished with costlier flats and became a haven for celebrities, the nouveau riche and tourists spoilt for choice by the plethora of bars.

A Walk through Spandauer Vorstadt

Oranienburger Strasse
Jewish culture has indeed made a return, and a walk through the district should not miss the memorial sites or the reawakened Jewishness of Berlin. A good place to start is the junction of Friedrichstrasse and Oranienburger Strasse, full to bursting with restaurants and bars.

Tacheles
Almost immediately on the right comes the ruin that houses the art centre called Tacheles. The building was constructed from 1907 to 1909, when it was a large shopping arcade. Its ruins were occupied as of 1990 by artists and denizens of the alternative society. New owners took over for a symbolic rent of 1 € per year, but the contract expired in 2008 and the owner is insolvent, so it is unclear whether the artists' studios, theatre and the grungy Zapata bar can stay there. For the time being, they remain.

Tucholskystrasse
A little further on is the junction with Tucholskystrasse (formerly Artilleriestrasse). On the corner stands the former **Postfuhramt**, built by Carl Schwatlo as a central post office and parcel delivery centre between 1875 and 1881. The magnificent clinker-built edifice is decorated with terra-cotta. C/O Berlin puts on outstanding photo exhibitions here. Two other buildings on Tucholskystrasse are of interest: two cornucopiae and the head of the Lion of Judah mark the fact that no. 9 once housed the College for the Study of Judaism, where lessons were still being given by the last of its teachers, **Leo Baeck**, until 1942. No. 40 is the community centre for the Israeli synagogue community, **Adass Jisroel**. A few steps away on Oranienburger Strasse is the entrance to the **Heckmann-Höfe**, a beautifully renovated shopping parade that goes as far as Sophienstrasse. There are some interesting and unusual shops and a **sweet factory** where it is possible to watch the sweets being made (opening hours: Wed – Sat noon – 8pm).

> ! **Baedeker TIP**
>
> **Beth-Café**
>
> Not a place to go in the evening (it closes at 8pm), but well known for its authentic kosher dishes: the orthodox Adass Jisroel community's Beth-Café at Tucholskystrasse 40 (closed Fri and Sat).

★
Neue Synagoge
The magnificent gold dome of the New Synagogue glitters some 50m/164ft above the street and is visible from quite a distance away. The building was designed in a Moorish/Byzantine style by Eduard Knobloch between 1857 and 1859 and completed in 1866 by

Friedrich August Stüler. It was the place of worship for what was at that time Germany's largest Jewish community. When it was inaugurated on 5 September 1866, even the Prussian king numbered among the 3000 people gathered in its main prayer hall. The synagogue was plundered and desecrated during the pogrom of 9 November 1938 but a courageous intervention by a policeman called **Wilhelm Krützfeld** prevented the Nazi stormtroopers from setting the building ablaze. It did burn, though, four years later, but this time on account of an allied bomb. In 1958 the prayer room had to be detonated due to the threat of collapse. Rebuilding efforts began in 1988 with the foyer, the male vestibule, the main stairway, room of representation and the upper ladies' gallery. The main prayer room was however not reconstructed. Its former location is now marked by white gravel paving in the present-day courtyard. The synagogue is now known as the Centrum Judaicum and functions not only as a place of prayer but also as a memorial, museum, community hall, scientific study centre, library and archive for the Jewish community. An exhibition entitled »Tuet auf die Pforte« relates the history of the New Synagogue and Berlin's Jewish community as a whole (opening hours: May–Aug Mon, Sun 10am–8pm, Tue–Thu closes 6pm, Fri closes 5pm; Sep–April Tue–Thu and Sun 10am–6pm, Fri closes 2pm).

◄ Centrum Judaicum

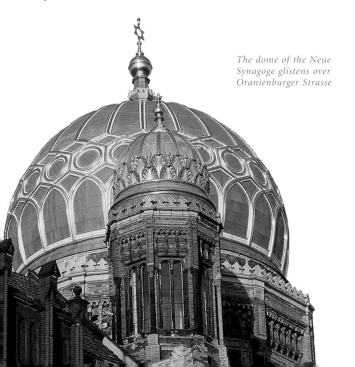

The dome of the Neue Synagoge glistens over Oranienburger Strasse

Grosse Hamburger Strasse

Beyond the new Jewish Communication Center and the Kunsthof art establishment lies Grosse Hamburger Strasse. On the right is a piece of land dotted with trees. This is all that remains of the first Jewish cemetery that was ravaged by the Nazis. **Moses Mendelssohn** is one of the figures who was buried here. A memorial plaque and a bronze sculpture at the front of the site are in memory of the persecution and murder of Jews. This was previously the location of the Jewish Old Folks Home, which became an **internment camp for Berlin's Jewish population** as of 1941. It was from here that people were transported to the death camps. No. 27 was once the site of the Jewish boys' school, of which Moses Mendelssohn was among the founders (his gravestone and others have been preserved by the wall). On the other side of the road an installation by Christian Boltanski entitled *The Missing House* evokes the inhabitants of a house that no longer exists. At the end of the road is St Hedwig's hospital, which became Berlin's first Catholic hospital when it opened in 1844.

★
Sophienkirche

Shortly before there, a drive leads off to the right up to the Sophienkirche, a church that was endowed by Queen Sophie in 1712. Its Baroque tower is probably one of the finest in Berlin, although it was not finished until 1734. The cemetery has the graves of builder and composer Carl Friedrich Zelter († 1832; on the left-hand side of the church) and historian Leopold von Ranke († 1886; gravestone in the wall on the right) among others.

The fluorescent colours of the Sophie-Gips Höfe

Sophienstrasse is a turning off Grosse Hamburger Strasse. The **Sophie-Gips-Höfe** at no. 21 is the name of an art centre decorated in bright, fluorescent colours that leads through to Gipsstrasse. Here, visitors can peruse the **Hoffmann collection** of contemporary Western European and North American art (opening hours: Sat 11am – 4pm, appointments by telephone: 28 49 91 21). Between 1864 and 1905 the house at Sophienstrasse no. 15 was the meeting hall of the craftsmen's union that was founded in 1844. When the union had to leave to make way for the new Wertheim store in 1905, it purchased nos. 17/18. It was in the meeting rooms of this building, known as the Sophiensäle, that the communist movement made its mark in history with Karl Liebknecht's declaration of a **proletarian revolution** in October 1918. In November 1918 the Spartacus league was constituted here and in 1920 the KPD and USPD parties were merged. The building is now used as a theatre.

Sophienstrasse

! *Baedeker* TIP

Tea to go

Chaja is Berlin's first tea-to-go shop. Water at temperatures of 70°C/160°F and 95°C/200°F in green to golden-brown boilers is poured over black tea, green tea, herb teas and fruit teas, and even lovers of oolong, matcha and white tea will find what they are looking for (Chaja, 1st Tea to go, Oranienburger Str. 27).

Sophienstrasse opens into Rosenthaler Strasse. On the right is the entrance to the Hackesche Höfe, once the largest combined work and housing complex in Europe. The development was completed in 1908 (decoration by August Endell) and consists of eight courtyards (Höfe), of which the first, still retaining its Art Nouveau design, has now become one of the most happening places on the Berlin scene. The other courtyards extend as far as Sophienstrasse and contain many shops (bookshops, jewellers, various fashion labels and such amusing establishments as a shop devoted to the »Ampelmännchen«, the hat-wearing figure of a walking man that lit up on pedestrian crossings in East Germany), as well as workshops.

★
Hackesche Höfe

Right next door in the courtyard of Rosenthaler Str. 39 – the only unrestored court, and it is planned to leave it that way – there was once a small brush factory that Otto Weidt founded in the early 1940s. He employed deaf and blind people, Jews and non-Jews, and, since the business was recognized as »vital to the war effort«, it was often a last place of refuge for persecuted individuals and their dependents (opening hours: Mon – Fri noon – 8pm, Sat/Sun from 11am).

Otto Weidt's blind workshop

The restaurant and pub-lined streets of Neue und Alte Schönhauser Strasse lead into what counts as the »bona fide« Scheunenviertel around Rosa-Luxemburg-Platz. The **Volksbühne** theatre opened here in 1914. It was where director Erwin Piscator was to create a theatri-

Rosa-Luxemburg-Platz

cal furore (as Frank Castorff does there today). Another building on the square is the Karl-Liebknecht-Haus, the former headquarters of the German communist party.

Auguststrasse The last of the really »trendy« streets, Auguststrasse, runs from Rosenthaler Strasse back to Oranienburger Strasse. It too features plenty in the way of art, shopping and bars. The primary art venue goes by the name of **Kunst-Werke Berlin** (no. 69). Another place that has become popular, not with the older generation but with modern youngsters, is the old ballroom of **Clärchens Ballhaus**.

Tegel

F–G 9–12

Borough: Reinickendorf   **U-Bahn:** Alt-Tegel (U 6)

Two names are associated with Tegel, those of Humboldt and Borsig. The Humboldt brothers grew up here and August Borsig laid the foundations of an engineering empire, to which the Borsigturm, the double tower of his factory gates from 1898, bears witness.

Schloss Tegel (Humboldt-schlösschen) North of the Tegeler Hafen docks on Adelheid-Allee stands Schloss Tegel. In 1550 this was a manor in the possession of Elector Joachim II. Later it became a hunting lodge for the Great Elector and since 1765 it has been owned by the Humboldt family. Wilhelm von Humboldt had it rebuilt in Classical style by **Karl Friedrich Schinkel** between 1822 and 1824. The latter is also responsible for the painting in the vestibule, the blue salon and the library. The four towers at the corners were designed by **Christian Daniel Rauch**. They feature bas-reliefs of the eight wind gods of antiquity. The collection of originals and casts of ancient sculptures that Wilhelm von Humboldt put together during his time as ambassador in Rome are a fascinating part of any guided tour (tours: May–Sept, Mon only 10am, 11am, 3pm, 4pm). The park was laid out as a Baroque garden in 1792 and modified by Schinkel 32 years later. An avenue of lime trees leads past a pond called the Humboldteich to a mausoleum that Wilhelm von Humboldt had built for his family by Schinkel after the death of his wife Caroline († 1829). In the middle there is a granite Ionic column with a copy of *Hope* by the Danish sculptor Bertel Thorvaldsen (opening hours: May–Sept, Mon only 10am–6pm).

! *Baedeker* TIP

Dicke Marie

Berlin's largest tree can be seen by wandering northward along the riverbank from the Tegel docks. In a bay called Grosse Malche grows a 900-year-old oak, now 26m/85ft tall and popularly known as »Dicke Marie«.

★
Mausoleum of the Humboldt family ▶

⏱

The site of the present-day airport had once been used as a shooting range for the fusiliers in around 1870. In 1909 Graf Zeppelin landed here with his Z 3 airship. It then became an exercise ground for the Berlin airship battalion. In 1931 it was used for the first rocket test experiments of **Hermann Oberth and Wernher von Braun**. The area was first used as an airfield during the blockade of Berlin and the Berlin Airlift of 1948/49. It involved building a runway and apron 2400m/2625yd long, the longest in Europe at the time. The site was then used by the French as a military airfield, but opened for passenger services in 1960. The present airport took shape in 1969 using designs by architects von Gerkan, Marg and Nickels. It was official opening on 1 September 1975.

Berlin Tegel Airport (Flughafen Otto Lilienthal)

Tempelhof

O – Q 16 – 18

Borough: Tempelhof-Schöneberg　　　**U-Bahn:** U 6

Tempelhof gets its name from the Knights Templar, who founded the settlement in 1247. The borough stretches a considerable distance towards the south and its buildings, ranging from airport to farmhouse, run the full gamut of architectural forms, for both commerce and transport.

One of its landmarks is the **Ullsteinhaus** on the other side of the Teltow canal. Built in 1927 and measuring 72m/236ft in height, it was the first steel reinforced concrete skyscraper in Berlin. Culture is represented not least by the **ufa-Fabrik** events venue at the end of Tempelhofer Damm.

Ullsteinhaus

Tempelhofer Feld was another former exercise ground for troops that attracted pioneers of aviation: in 1883 the painter **Arnold Böcklin** sought to get airborne with two unpowered biplane-type structures that he had built himself, but gusting winds put paid to the attempt. In 1908 the Wright brothers themselves managed a 19-minute powered flight from the field. By 1923, the site was in business as a commercial airport and during 1936 to 1939 **one of the largest linked buildings on the planet** was constructed in the typical monumental style of the Third Reich, using designs by Ernst Sagebiel: the building shaped in the form of a 90° circle arc measures as much as 1.2km/1300yd and the terminal itself is 400m/450yd long.

Berlin Tempelhof Airport

？ DID YOU KNOW ...?

■ During the eleven-month blockade, 250,000 flights delivered 2,324,257 tons of goods to West Berliners. 222 American, 110 British and 48 other aircraft were used in the airlift, and 41 Britons, 31 Americans and five Germans died while taking part. Freight planes landed not only in Tempelhof but also in Tegel and Gatow, while flying boats even made use of the Wannsee.

The days of Tempelhof Airport are numbered, but its monumental architecture will remain

After the Second World War, the Americans took over the airport. Civil flights were not reinstated until 1950 with Tempelhof's central airport service opening for business again a year later. However, after 1975, commercial flights were redirected to Tegel airport. Tempelhof remained a military airfield until the fall of the Berlin Wall. After that it was a regional airport until the extensions to Schönefeld were completed. The last plane took off here on 30 September 2008.

Tempelhof's monument to the Berlin Airlift

The concourse in front of the main entrance to the airport is nowadays called the Platz der Luftbrücke in memory of the Berlin Airlift. Since 1951 a monument has recalled the blockade of 1948/49 and its consequences. Between June 1948 and May 1949 US generals Clay and Wedemeyer organized an air lift of supplies to provide the citizens of West Berlin with the essential food and goods they needed and thus managed to defeat the Soviet blockade. Eduard Ludwig's 20m/66ft sculpture, called ***Hungerkralle*** (Claws of Hunger), symbolizes the three air corridors that linked Berlin with the western-controlled sectors of Germany.

★ Tiergarten

L/M 13 – 15

Location: Both sides of Strasse des 17. Juni
City centre plan: A – C 5 – 10
Bus: 100, 106

S-Bahn: Tiergarten, Bellevue (S 5, S 7, S 75, S 9)
U-Bahn: Hansaplatz (U 9)

The Tiergarten is to Berlin what Hyde Park and Regent's Park are to London's: a green oasis at the heart of the city.

The Tiergaren in bloom

It was formerly a hunting enclosure for the electors, located at that time beyond the city gates. Elector Friedrich III initiated its transformation into a park as of 1700 and had the avenue of Unter den Linden extended through the park towards Charlottenburg along what is now Strasse des 17. Juni. Friedrich the Great commissioned the park to be laid out along French lines but his successor Friedrich Wilhelm II had it altered to an English pattern. Nevertheless large parts of the Tiergarten still fall into the category of a natural park. It was between 1833 and 1838 that the famous landscape designer **Peter Joseph Lenné** redesigned it as a public park. Although it was badly hit during the Second World War, and then felled bare by Berliners seeking firewood to keep warm in the winters that followed, the park was reconstituted from 1949, many of its new trees being donated by towns elsewhere in Germany, as commemorated by a memorial stone on Grosser Weg. It now has 25km/16mi of rambling paths and offers boat rides on the Neue See plus one of the biggest beer gardens in the city alongside the lake, both of which are major attractions that regularly tempt Berliners out of their homes on summer weekends, often with a barbecue grill in tow.

Monuments and Memorials

The Tiergarten has a great many memorials. The trend began in 1901 when Kaiser Wilhelm II presented the Siegesallee to his capital. It features 32 emotionally depicted groups of figures with crowned heads and was intended to demonstrate the magnificence of the Prussian empire along a route from Königsplatz (Platz der Republik) to what is now Kemperplatz. The marble parade – dubbed by one contemporary a »snow-white open-air panopticon« – was mocked and scorned abroad, and even the Berliners themselves made jokes about it. »Going down to the dollies« became their way of describing

Siegesallee

The Mexican Embassy has opted for lighting effects

MORE BOLD THAN DIPLOMATIC?

While the construction of the government quarter, Potsdamer Platz, the Jewish Museum and new buildings on Pariser Platz was transforming Berlin into a prestigious capital city, it also gained, unnoticed by some, a world-class architectural exhibition.

120 countries and the 16 states of the Federal Republic of Germany have built their embassies and representative offices, and in doing so have set their stamp on Berlin. These buildings can be interpreted as an expression of the true or desired importance of the state concerned. They are proclamations of wealth or modesty, even of architectural boldness, and in some cases seem more avant-garde than diplomatic.

Striking and new

The **British Embassy** (architect: Michael Wilford & Partners) wittily gets around the demands of Berlin's urban planners in respect of height and the use of stone: everything is as desired, with a sandstone façade and sloping roof, and above the plain entrance there is a hole through which pale blue and violet architectural elements thrust into the street façade. An English oak grows in the paved courtyard, steps lead to the second courtyard and the viewer sees the historic entrance of the old embassy, which stood on this site and was destroyed in the war. Many embassies hide their greatest charms behind inhospitable walls: the **French Embassy** (by Christian de Portzamparc and Steffen Lehmann), for example, gives its occupants a view of the Brandenburg Gate from every office through windows that look like arrow-slits. Those who enter it from Wilhelmstrasse pass sequestered courtyards with beautiful sculptures on the lawns.

To see the diplomatic quarter, take a walk in the southern part of Tiergarten, which had this role before the Second World War. The marks of war have been obliterated almost everywhere, except where they have been integrated into the new buildings as stone witnesses to history. The **Nordic Embassies** (Berger and Parrkinen), which share a complex of buildings behind the blades of a band of green copper, amount to a little diplomatic village. In this way Denmark, Norway, Finland, Iceland and Sweden aim to express their geographical, historical and political connections in the so-called Felleshus, which catches the eye

on busy Klingelhöferstrasse at the corner of Rauchstrasse. However, the **Mexican Embassy** (González de Leon) steals the show, especially at night, when the illuminated concrete strips of the façade tilt mysteriously in varying directions according to the angle of view. Curious passers-by can look inside through the glass wall behind the concrete supports, and the cylindrical atrium with a roof entirely of glass allows a view out from some 400 bull's-eye windows.

Return to tradition

The old diplomatic quarter also extends along Tiergartenstrasse. Lovely, shady paths have been laid, but the built-up side of the street opposite, which rose out of more or less romantic ruins after the fall of the Wall, is more interesting. The **pink palace of the Italian Embassy** in the monumental style characteristic of its period (1939–41) has a ground floor clad in travertine stone from Rome; the **Indian Embassy** displays glowing red sandstone from Rajasthan, which has been cast into the slabs of the façade in rough, broken chunks; the

Austrian Embassy by Hans Hollein on the corner of Stauffenbergstrasse looks like an architectural exclamation mark behind its skin of green copper, as its colourful red volume rises two storeys with large windows facing the Tiergarten next to austere cubes. The **base of the Japanese diplomats** in Hiroshimastrasse, by contrast, rebuilt in the 1980s, resembles a fortress: the main entrance, with traditional Japanese design features, gilded grilles with Buddhist motifs and stone vases, presents the imperial seal in the form of a stylized chrysanthemum, but the garden in the courtyard, one of the most beautiful Japanese gardens in Berlin, remains invisible, as visitors are not welcome.

Fairy-tale realm by the Tiergarten

Take just a few steps, as far as Hiroshimastrasse no. 18–20, and you are in a different world. With its conspicuous corner and central blocks, the **Embassy of the United Arab Emirates** (Krause Bohne) is a palace from 1001 Arabian Nights

*A break with convention:
the British Embassy*

between the delegations of the federal states of North Rhine-Westphalia and Bremen. Columns with gilded capitals bear halls that are adorned with palm trees. Guests in the banqueting hall on the garden side, which is surrounded by galleries and has a glazed garden front, tread an enormous, colourful carpet as if walking on velvet.

Southern refinement

For a truly enjoyable trip around the world, don't miss the refinement of southern lands. At Auguste-Viktoria-Strasse 74–76, at the border of Schmargendorf and Grunewald, the copper roof of the **Israeli Embassy** (Samuel Willenberg) glows from afar through the trees above an exterior of shell limestone. This monumental structure is divided inside by an ochre-coloured wall of so-called Jerusalem stone. Six cubic elements in the façade are a reminder of the six million Jews who died in the Holocaust. **Thailand**, by contrast, has given itself an urban look in Lepsiusstrasse in Steglitz, though with a Buddhist shrine in the front garden, while **Ethiopia** has opted for a site on the other side of the Teltow Canal in Lichtenberg. **Macedonia** has settled in without much ado between Königsallee and Hubertusstrasse, and the **Embassy of the Polish Republic** hunkers down in a forbidding castle-like

structure in Furtwänglerstrasse. At Hagenstrasse 56, on the corner of Teplitzer Strasse, this architectural walk has returned to the orient: the magnificent and theatrical **palace of the Emirate of Qatar** (John S. Bonnington) hides behind high smooth walls with arched openings and white crenellations. The complex is built of concrete and steel but imitates marble thanks to the use of polished white granite from Spain. In Dahlem, at Clayallee 82, the **Embassy of the Sultanate of Oman** (Hierholzer) lies behind a European façade of dark brick, but opens a dialogue of the cultures by means of traditional elements taken from Arab architecture: a classic three-part front and the arrangement of the rooms around an atrium as in an Omani dwelling. The **Embassy of the Islamic Republic of Iran** (Diba and Sfavardi) at Podbielskiallee 65–67 also builds bridges between cultures and nations, employing such characteristics of Iranian architecture as geometry, transparency and simplicity. Built like its neighbour of light-coloured limestone, this elongated structure fits into the surroundings in terms of its height and volume. A concave concrete wall emphasizes the entrance and is intended to convey hospitality, but the barriers in front of it have not yet been removed.

a saunter along the avenue. After the war, the statues, even the undamaged remnants, were taken away. Some fine sculptures remain in the Tiergarten, though, among them the **Goethe Monument** by Fritz Schaper (1880), which stands at the east end of the park, its base depicting allegorical figures of Lyric Poetry (and Amor), Drama (spirit with a symbol of death) and Science. Then there is the **Monument to Queen Luise** by Erdmann Encke (1880). The relief on its base shows scenes from the life of a soldier and women tending to the

! **Baedeker TIP**

In the open air and free!
A museum open all year round and 24 hours a day, and admission is free? Where on earth could you find such a thing? In Berlin of course – or to be more precise, in the Tiergarten. Along the route through the park from the Berlin Pavillon to the Schleusenbrücke, as well as on Joseph-Haydn-Weg, a hundred gas lamps from the whole of Europe – dating from 1826 to the 1950s – can be examined in the **Gaslaternen-Freilichtmuseum** (Gas Lamp Museum).

wounded, representing Queen Luise's own deeds during the war of 1806/07. The **Monument to Friedrich Wilhelm III**, created by Friedrich Drake, was unveiled on 3 August 1849, making it one of the oldest statues in the Tiergarten.

Two other monuments refer to an entirely different time of history. Right under the Lichtensteinbrücke bridge on the right-hand bank of the Landwehrkanal stands a sculpture dedicated to Rosa Luxemburg who, together with Karl Liebknecht, founded Germany's communist party KPD. After the failure of the Spartacus uprising of 15 January 1919, she was murdered by soldiers of the Freikorps and her body was thrown into the canal from the bridge. Karl Liebknecht was also shot on the same day by the Neue See, and his memorial, the counterpart to Rosa Luxemburg's, is located at the lake.

Monuments to Karl Liebknecht and Rosa Luxemburg

Grosser Stern and Siegessäule

Grosser Stern is not precisely in the middle of the Tiergarten, but it is the focus of all the routes through the park. In its midst, surrounded by the roar of traffic, stands the Siegessäule or Victory Column. It is some 69m/226ft tall and was erected in memory of the three victorious campaigns against Denmark in 1864, Austria in 1866 and France in 1870/71. Its unveiling was on the 3rd anniversary of the battle of Sedan, on 2 September 1873, accompanied by a military parade in the presence of Kaiser Wilhelm I. At that time it was located on Königsplatz, where it remained until 1938, when it was moved to make way for Speer's designs for

★
Siegessäule

»Germania«, his planned capital of the Third Reich. The shaft of the Siegessäule incorporates rifles that were seized as spoils of war and stands on a tall granite base with bronze bas-reliefs showing scenes from the three wars. The lower part includes a mosaic designed by Anton von Werner that symbolizes the unification of the various parts of the German Empire or »Reich« in 1870/71. At the top, the statue known as **»Goldelse«** surveys Berlin. The 8m/26ft figure of Victoria, goddess of victory, was fashioned by Friedrich Drake. The Siegessäule can be climbed: a staircase of 285 steps leads to an ⏱ **observation platform at 48m/157ft** (opening hours: April – Oct Mon – Thu 9.30am – 6.30pm, Fri – Sun closes 7pm, Nov – March closes 5.30pm or 6pm).

Monuments on the roundabout

The roundabout at Grosser Stern also features the national monument to Bismarck, created in 1901 by Reinhold Begas. Alongside him are General Field Marshall Moltke (by Joseph Uphues, 1905) and war minister von Roon (by Harro Magnussen, 1904). These three statues were also originally located in front of the Reichstag.

The South of the Tiergarten

Diplomats' quarter (M 16 C 6 – 8)

To the south of Tiergartenstrasse between Stauffenbergstrasse and Klingelhöferstrasse is an area that was called the **Diplomatenviertel** or diplomats' quarter at the time of the Third Reich. After the war, which only the Italian and Japanese embassies survived, the latter severely damaged, the site was a wasteland, and now further embassy buildings (Austria, India) and the representation of the federal state of Baden-Württemberg, which is anything but modest, have been built there. The so-called Tiergarten Triangle between Stülerstrasse, Klingelhöferstrasse and the Landwehrkanal has also gained new embassies (Scandinavia, Mexico). Here the federal headquarters of the Christian Democratic Union political party sails into the intersection like a glass ship's bows.

The Northern Part of the Tiergarten

Königliche Porzellan-Manufaktur (KPM)

The Königliche Porzellan-Manufaktur or Royal Porcelain Factory of Berlin has been situated at Wegelystr. 1 since 1868. Its origins go back to 1751 when Wilhelm Kaspar Wegely founded Berlin's first porcelain factory, which was taken over by Frederick the Great himself in 1763. It was the great king who introduced the still-extant trademark showing the blue sceptre of the Brandenburg electorship. Among the older buildings, some turning and forming mills, dating from 1871, have survived alongside the Spree. The factory is still producing high-quality porcelain for domestic use or for decoration. It has indeed been increasingly successful since the present designer, Enzo Mari, was appointed in 1993. The full range of products and the history of the factory are celebrated in an exhibition at Wegelystrasse no. 1 (opening times: daily 10am – 6pm); there are salesrooms at Wegelystrasse, Kurfürstendamm 27 and Unter den Linden 35.

Haus der Kulturen der Welt (Kongresshalle)

Haus der Kulturen der Welt literally means »house of the world's cultures«. The building in the northeast corner of the Tiergarten is seen as a forum for the countries of the Third World and promotes regular exhibitions and concerts. The perfect backdrop is provided by the former Kongresshalle, a milestone in modern architecture. It was designed by Hugh A. Stubbins with the assistance of Werner Düttmann and Franz Mocken to be the US-contribution to the International Building Exhibition of 1957, and built on the site of the former Kroll opera house, where the German parliament sat after the burning of the Reichstag building in 1933. The startling curved roof of the building has led to the Kongresshalle being nicknamed the **»Schwangere Auster«** or »Pregnant Oyster«. A sculpture entitled *Two Forms* that stands in the pool in front of the hall stems unmistakably from Henry Moore. In the summer of 1980, the Kongresshalle's roof collapsed. It was rebuilt and reopened in time for the city's jubilee celebrations in 1987. The Haus der Kulturen der Welt Museum moved in to the building in 1989 (programme of events at www.hkw.de). Next to the Kongresshalle stands a bell tower 42m/138ft high, which contains the fourth biggest **carillon** in the world (the biggest in Europe). The carillon chimes every day at noon and 6pm.

The view takes in the Soviet Memorial and the Brandenburg Gate

Soviet memorial

The Soviet memorial on the northern side of Strasse des 17. Juni, not far from the ►Brandenburg Gate, was built in 1945/46. It has a bronze casting of a Red Army soldier in full combat dress. Two Soviet tanks that took part in the conquest of Berlin in 1945 flank the monument on either side. There is another Soviet monument in ► Treptower Park, and one more on the Schönholzer Heide in Pankow.

»Der Rufer«

On the central reservation of Strasse des 17. Juni, in between the Brandenburg Gate and the Soviet monument, there is a 3m/10ft-high bronze sculpture by Gerhard Marcks that is goes by the name of *Der Rufer*, meaning the Caller. Its granite base has an inscription quoting the Italian poet Petrarch (1304 – 74): »I walk through the world and call: ›Peace, peace, peace.‹«

★ Tierpark Friedrichsfelde

L 20 east

Location: Lichtenberg
Tram: M 17

U-Bahn: Tierpark (U 5)

⊙ Opening hours: Daily from 9am; Jan – mid-March, Nov, Dec until 4pm, mid-Sep – Oct until 5pm, mid-March – mid-Sep until 6pm)

The Friedrichsfelde zoo was opened in the grounds around Schloss Friedrichsfelde on 2 July 1955 as East Berlin's answer to the ►Zoologischer Garten in the west. The buildings and enclosures were designed by the man who was director of the park for many years, Heinrich Dathe. Compared to the western zoo, the Tierpark grounds are much more expansive and much less cramped in terms of both the outdoor enclosures and the animals' stables and hutches. The Alfred-Brehm-Haus tropical house, for example, has a huge hall where almost 100 species of birds can fly, alongside an extraordinarily large house for large feline predators with extensive enclosures inside the hall where the animals can wander freely. The pride of the collection of big cats is its breeding programme for **Indian lions and Siberian tigers**. Its elephant house contains not only pachyderms but also rhinoceroses and hippopotamuses. It also contains a large viewing pool with rare West Indian **manatees** (sea cows) from the Caribbean. The Tierpark has been particularly successful with breeding programmes for rare

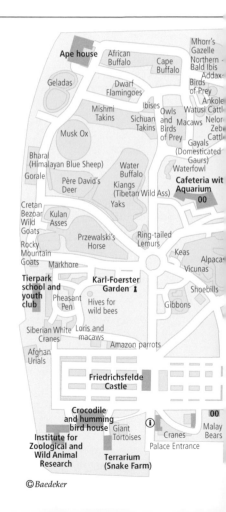

© Baedeker

hoofed animals, such as the Takin from Burma, sometimes called the beestung moose. The snake farm boasts the largest selection of poisonous snakes in Europe.

The park around Schloss Friedrichsfelde was laid out by Benjamin Raulé at the end of the 17th century. He had been in charge of the navy under the Great Elector. The palace itself was built in around 1695 according to plans by Johann Arnold Nering and extended in 1719. It is now used by the zoo offices.

Schloss Friedrichsfelde

Tierpark Friedrichsfelde Map

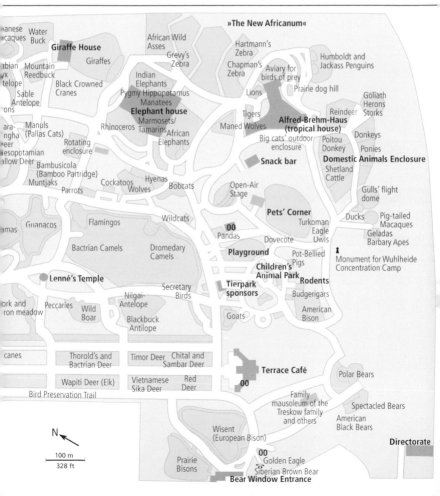

✳ Treptower Park

Location: Puschkinallee, Treptow

S-Bahn: Treptower Park (S 4, S 6, S 8, S 85, S 9)

The Treptower Park is a long stretch of open woodland with a rose garden and extensive lawns by the river Spree.

The Soviet memorial to its heroes in Treptower Park

The Treptower Park and the Plänterwald forest that neighbours it to the east were created by Berlin's municipal director of gardens, Gustav Meyer, a pupil of Peter Joseph Lenné. Meyer created the park between 1876 and 1882 and in 1896 the »Great Berlin Exhibition of Commerce« was held at the site. Towards the end of the rule of the Kaisers and during the period of the Weimar Republic, Treptower Park often hosted large workers' rallies. Treptower Park itself is a long, slightly wooded green space alongside the Spree, with rose gardens and broad lawns. Close to the S-Bahn station there is a dock for the Spree steamboats. The **Plänterwald** forest was laid out in 1876 and where it adjoins the park there is a nice beer garden belonging to the popular »**Zenner**« tavern, which is popular with day trippers. The tavern took the place of the »Neues Gasthaus an der Spree« built here in 1821/22 by Carl Ferdinand Langhans. On the opposite bank is the Abteiinsel, an island that belonged to the local abbey but which is now termed the Insel der Jugend or Island of Youth. Behind the S-Bahn station, it is impossible to miss the two 125m/419ft-high Allianz Treptowers, built in 1997/98.

✳ **Soviet monument**

The main attraction in Treptower Park is its huge Soviet monument, built between 1947 and 1949 according to a design by Yevgeny V. Vuchetich and Yakov B. Belopolsky to provide a central monument for the Soviet soldiers killed in the struggle for Berlin in 1945. The main part of the installation is made from Swedish granite that had been stored by the Nazis, in order for it to be used to construct a triumphal arch in Moscow. The figure of a woman on the access avenue is known as *Mother Homeland* and is sculpted from a single 50-ton granite block. A wide promenade planted with weeping birches leads to the Ehrenhain (honour grove), where two red granite walls symbolize flags lowered in mourning. The main section of the grove, which is the last resting place of 5000 Soviet soldiers, is made up of five lawns bounded by cast laurel wreaths. On both sides of the grove stand eight walls featuring bas-reliefs. The central feature of the monument is a hill of honour with a cylindrical mausoleum that emulates the ancient warrior tombs of the Don plains and includes the main monument to the Soviet soldiers. A figure of a soldier 11.6m/38ft high carries a child in its left arm while the right holds a lowered sword that has split a swastika asunder. The domed hall under the 70-ton monument is decorated with mosaic pictures by the painter Gorpenko on the theme »the representatives of all the republics of the union remember their dead«. The roof also bears the emblem of the Soviet Union's Order of Victory. There are other Soviet memorials in the ►Tiergarten and on the Schönholzer Heide in Pankow.

In the southeastern part of Treptower Park there is a short stretch of road called Alt-Treptow that leads to the Archenhold Observatory. It was built in 1896 and named after its founder, astronomer Friedrich Simon Archenhold. Its main attraction is the **largest refracting telescope in the world**, 21m/69ft long and weighing 130 tons, with a lens 68cm/27in in diameter. The accompanying Himmelskundliche Museum relates the history of the observatory as well as covering other astronomical themes (opening hours: Thu 8pm, Sat/Sun 3pm; stargazing through the large telescope: Oct – March every 2nd Fri at 8pm; telephone for further information at 5 34 80 80). Next to the observatory is a spot called the **Hain der Kosmonauten** or »Cosmonauts' Copse« that recalls the Soviet space missions. It includes busts of Yuri Gagarin, the first man in space, and East German cosmonaut Sigmund Jähn, the first German in space.

Archenhold Observatory

◄ Hain der Kosmonauten

✦ ✦ Unter den Linden

L 16/17

Location: Mitte, between Schlossbrücke and Pariser Platz
City centre plan: B 11 – 13
Bus: 100, 147, 200, TXL

S-Bahn: Western end: Brandenburger Tor (S 1, S 2, S 25, U 55); eastern end: Hackescher Markt (S 5, S 7, S 75, S 9)

1400m/1550yd long and 60m/65yd wide, the most famous street in Berlin, if not in all Germany, runs between the Schlossbrücke bridge and Pariser Platz. A place for both Berliners and tourists to promenade, it is the prestigious avenue of the high and mighty: Unter den Linden.

 It succeeds an equestrian thoroughfare established during the era of the electors in 1573, which led through the sand of the March to the hunting grounds beyond the city gates. It was the Great Elector who

Berlin's most famous thoroughfare

instructed his court gardener Hanff and architects Dressler and Grünberg to plant the stretch leading from the castle to the Tiergarten with six rows of walnut trees and limes in 1647. The walnuts later disappeared but the limes remain. The first buildings along the road were domiciles, commercial buildings and state offices alongside a couple of palatial mansions, but the Zeughaus or arsenal that was built under Friedrich I was to hint of greater magnificence to follow. Until 1734 the road only went as far as what is now Schadowstrasse, but was extended to Pariser Platz in that year. Friedrich II finally commissioned **Georg Wenzeslaus von Knobelsdorff** to create a prestigious forum, the Forum Fridericianum. However, the architect was soon to lose favour with the king and was only able to complete the opera house, now the Staatsoper on Unter den Linden. Others, though, continued the work he had begun. St Hedwig's Cathedral was built between 1747 and 1773 and the library that came to be known as the Alte Bibliothek was built by Georg Christian Unger. Between 1789 and 1791, Langhans gave Unter den Linden the prime architectural feature that provides a fitting culmination to the road, the ▶ Brandenburg Gate. Karl Friedrich Schinkel's Neue Wache was to follow between 1816 and 1818. In the 1920s Unter den Linden and Friedrichstrasse made up the key arteries of republican Berlin.

The Second World War ruined Unter den Linden. However, new trees were replanted as early as 1946. In 1958 reconstruction work began on the Forum Fridericianum and many new buildings were erected, particularly to the west of Charlottenstrasse. The object was to make Unter den Linden the prestigious boulevard of the GDR, an evocation of history featuring embassies and ministries. After reunification, the cranes and diggers were back again, building new banks, parliamentary offices, embassies, hotels, company headquarters and, not least, plenty of quality restaurants.

From Schlossbrücke to Bebelplatz

✳
Schlossbrücke

Starting from ▶ Schlossplatz, first the Kupfergraben is bridged by **Karl Friedrich Schinkel's** Schlossbrücke, planned in 1819 and built between 1822 and 1824. It was preceded by a wooden bridge, known to have existed in the 16th century, by the name of the Hundebrücke, so-named because hunters would gather there with their hounds before riding into the game reserves around the city. The eight sculptures that look down from their white Carrara marble plinths were created between 1845 and 1857 by eight different sculptors using designs by Schinkel himself. Facing towards Unter den Linden they are as follows:

✳ ✳
Statues on the bridge ▶

Right-hand side: Iris, bearing the fallen hero to Olympus (August Wredow, 1841–57); thronging youths under the guardianship of Athena (Gustav Bläser, 1854); Minerva accompanies a soldier off to war (Albert Wolff, 1853); Nike, supporting a wounded warrior (Ludwig Wichmann, before 1857).

View from the Schlossbrücke to the Zeughaus

Left-hand side: Nike crowns the victor (Friedrich Drake, 1857); Athena arms a warrior for his first battle (Heinrich Möller, 1846 – 50); Pallas Athena teaches a boy to throw the javelin (Hermann Schievelbein, 1853); Nike teaches the history of heroism (Emil Wolff, 1847). The sculptures were all taken down during the Second World War and were only returned to the East Berlin senate from West Berlin in 1981.

On the right hand side straight after the bridge stands the former Zeughaus or arsenal, **the largest and most impressive Baroque building in Berlin**. Building began in 1695 using designs by Johann Arnold Nering but it was only completed by Martin Grünberg, Andreas Schlüter and Jean de Bodt. The building was temporarily authorized for use as early as 1706 although it was not completely finished until 1730. From then until 1877 the ground floor was used as an arsenal for heavy artillery, while the top floor stored infantry weapons and trophies of war. For this reason, the Berlin revolutionaries elected to attack the building on 14 June 1848. After the new »Reich« was established in 1870, Kaiser Wilhelm I had the building made into a war and armaments museum for the Brandenburg-Prussian army. The building was badly damaged in the Second World War and rebuilding was not completed until 1965.

★ ★
Zeughaus

The façade is 90m/100yd long with a clearly delineated structure; projections and recesses break the uniformity. Its designer was de

Mars, god of war, enthroned on the roof of the Zeughaus

Bodt. The outstandingly sculpted decoration was mainly provided by Andreas Schlüter, as were the ancient helmets on the cap stones over the windows outside. The allegorical figures on the plinths that project from the front entrance are by Guillaume Hulot and represent the art of making fireworks along with arithmetic, geometry and mechanics. Hulot also made the trophy sculptures on the roof and the group featuring Mars to designs by Jean de Bodt. Nevertheless, it is the heads of the **22 dying warriors** in the courtyard, the so-called Schlüterhof, which are considered the outstanding example of Baroque architectural sculpture in Germany.

✳
Deutsches Histori-
sches Museum ▶

🕑
Opening hours:
10am – 6pm daily

Until September 1990 the Zeughaus was home to the German History Museum, the Museum für Deutsche Geschichte, which had been the leading historical museum in East Germany since being established in 1952. This has now been included in the Deutsches Historisches Museum. Although for many years the set-up was rather temporary in nature, the museum reopened in a new form in 2006. Its chronology begins in the west wing of the upper floors with the early ages of antiquity up until about 1500. The tour then passes through a second set of selections leading up to 1918/19 in the south wing of the upper floor. It continues in the east wing on the ground floor with the period from the Weimar Republic until the Second World War, then covers the post-war period up until reunification and the withdrawal of the allies in 1994 in the west wing. The annex, designed by I. M. Pei with a spectacular spiral glass stairway outside it, is intended to accommodate rotating exhibitions.

✳
Neue Wache

Beyond the Zeughaus stands the Neue Wache or new guardhouse. This was created between 1816 and 1818, with **Karl Friedrich Schinkel** once more the designer. It replaced the earlier Königswache. In front of the castle-like brick building, Schinkel designed a portico of

Doric columns, reminiscent of a Greek temple; the bas-relief on the gable is by August Kiss. The German president Paul von Hindenburg declared that the Neue Wache was to be used as a war memorial for the fallen of the First World War, and the redesign that this entailed was completed in 1931 according to plans fashioned by Heinrich Tessenow: the walls of the halls were lined with limestone panels around a tall black granite block under a skylight. On the block there was a silver and gold wreath in the shape of oak-leaf laurels. The East German leadership had the building remodelled again, this time as a memorial to the victims of fascism and militarism. It included an eternal flame over the urns of an unknown concentration camp victim and an unknown soldier. At the end of 1993, it was inaugurated as the central memorial for the whole of the German Federal Republic and it now contains a more than life-sized bronze pietà by Käthe Kollwitz to recall the victims of war and totalitarianism. The original smaller figure by Hermann Haacke was recreated in four times its original size (opening hours: 10am – 6pm daily).

Behind the Neue Wache there is a wood of chestnut trees, the »Kastanienwäldchen«. The Palais am Festungsgraben (palace by the moat), built in 1753 and redesigned in 1860, is situated amid the trees. Until 1945 it was the residence of the Prussian finance ministers. It now houses the Museum des Heimatvereins Berlin-Mitte, the local museum for the centre of Berlin. The classical building style of the neighbouring Maxim-Gorki Theater was designed by Schinkel's pupil Ottmer and built in 1827 as the vocal academy of Carl Friedrich Zelter. Its concert hall was famed for its acoustics at the time and it was used in 1829 for the performance by Felix Mendelssohn-Bartholdy of the St Matthew Passion that had been thought lost after the death of Johann Sebastian Bach (1750), but which had been rediscovered by Zelter.

Kastanienwäldchen

Opposite the Zeughaus there used to be a tower block that housed the East German foreign ministry. The tower was built from 1964 to 1967 on the site of the former house of Berlin's city commandant from 1653, which had been badly damaged during the war. Its external design is now reflected in the new Bertelsmann-Stiftung building that replaced the skyscraper after its demolition in 1995. Beyond it, stretching as far as Werderscher Markt (▶Schlossplatz), is Schinkelplatz, now decorated once again with all its old familiar monuments, including one to Karl Friedrich Schinkel himself, as well as one for agricultural reformer Albrecht Thaer (1752 – 1828) and one for industrialist Christian Wilhelm Beuth (1781 – 1853). Some masonry and a printed textile sheet simulate Schinkel's Bauakademie (Academy of Architecture), which a sponsor is planning to rebuild.

Schinkelplatz

To the right of the Kommandantenhaus is the palace of the crown prince, the Kronprinzenpalais, built by Johann Arnold Nering (1663/

Kronprinzenpalais

64). It passed into the possession of Friedrich Wilhelm I in 1732 and he had it rebuilt by Philipp Gerlach. It was the home of Prince August Wilhelm, brother of Frederick the Great, who became Crown Prince Friedrich Wilhelm after 1793. He lived here with his wife Luise. In 1856 the man who was to become Kaiser Friedrich III moved in with his wife Viktoria. Wilhelm II, the last of the German »Kaisers«, was born here on 27 January 1859. During the Second World War, the building was badly damaged and nowadays there are no longer any copies of the original plans in existence. Thus Richard Paulick's reconstruction of 1968/69 was forced to use only old engravings as its source. The result was a cultural centre and a guesthouse for dignitaries visiting East Germany that was renamed »Palais Unter den Linden«. It was here that the reunification treaty between East and West Germany was signed on 31 August 1990.

Prinzessinnen-palais (Operncafé)

The neighbouring Prinzessinnenpalais, another faithful reconstruction by Paulick, was originally built between 1733 and 1737 according to plans by Friedrich Wilhelm Dietrich and was linked to the crown prince's palace by Heinrich Gentz's gatehouse in 1811. It was the home of Friedrich Wilhelm III's three daughters until they were all married and this is where it gets its name. Nowadays it houses the Operncafé, whose coffee and cakes can be enjoyed on the terrace during the summer months, where there is a splendid view of the **Prinzessinnengarten**. The garden includes statues of Generals Blücher, Gneisenau, Scharnhorst and Yorck, created by Christian Daniel Rauch.

Forum Fridericianum

The Forum Fridericianum begins with the Staatsoper Unter den Linden. It was initially planned that the area around what is now Bebelplatz (formerly Opernplatz) was to be laid out according to Frederick the Great's concept of a cultural focal point for the Prussian capital.

✱
Deutsche Staatsoper Unter den Linden

In building the opera house or Staatsoper between 1741 and 1743, Georg Wenzeslaus von Knobelsdorff opened up the way for classicism in Germany. It was **the first theatre in Germany outside a palace of the nobility** and was also the largest theatre in Europe at the time, although all of its 2000 seats were reserved for invited guests only. An inscription on the gable portico leaves no doubt as to the ambitions of the commissioning monarch: FRIDERICUS REX APOLLINI ET MUSIS (Friedrich, king over Apollo and the muses). In 1789 the opera house was opened to the general public but on the night of 18 – 19 August 1843 the building burned down, only to be resurrected just a year later by Carl Ferdinand Langhans. Meyerbeer, Lortzing and Richard Strauss all had major successes here. During the Second World War an incendiary device reduced the building to a shell and, although it was quickly restored, it was finally obliterated

The present-day Staatsoper was the earliest theatre in Germany that was not appended to an aristocratic palace

in February 1945. Another reconstruction was started in 1951 under the aegis of Richard Paulick and Kurt Hemmerling, and on 4 September 1955 the building was officially reopened with a performance of Richard Wagner's *Meistersinger.*

The Baroque Cathedral of St Hedwig at the southeast corner of Bebelplatz is modelled on the Pantheon in Rome and is the seat of the Catholic bishop of Berlin. Building started in 1747 using designs by Georg Wenzeslaus von Knobelsdorff. The necessary money for the project was collected by the Carmelite monk Mecenati from predominantly Catholic countries and the land was donated by Frederick the Great. St. Hedwig's is the only one of Berlin's churches that was built during his reign. After the Seven Years' War, building continued under Johann Boumann the Elder from 1772 onwards, and the church was inaugurated on 1 November 1773. It was named after Hedwig (1174 – 1243), wife of Duke Heinrich of Silesia, who was well revered in that region. When Silesia was conquered by Frederick, it was the first area with a consolidated Catholic population to fall into Prussian hands. St Hedwig's Cathedral burned to a shell during 1943 and its reconstruction lasted from 1952 to 1963. The newly designed interior may seem a little naked but the historical reconstruction of the dome is faithful.

✸
Sankt-Hedwigs-Kathedrale

The western side of the square is occupied by the Alte Bibliothek or Old Library, built between 1775 and 1780 as a royal library using a design Fischer von Erlach had originally intended for the Michaelertrakt wing of Vienna's Hofburg palace. Its effectively curvaceous

Alte Bibliothek

Baroque façade led to it being dubbed the »Kommode«. By 1914 it had served its purpose as a library and was being used as a university. It burned down in 1945 and restoration was not begun until 1967, being completed only in 1969. It is now occupied by the law faculty of Humboldt University.

Adjoining the Alte Bibliothek is another reconstructed building in the form of the Altes Palais, which is nowadays also part of Humboldt University. It was formerly the home of Wilhelm I, who lived here for 50 years – throughout his time as crown prince, king of Prussia, and emperor of Germany – till his death in 1888. The last window on the left-hand side of the ground floor is the so-called »historic window« from which Wilhelm I is said to have observed the changing of the guard every day at noon. He himself gave the following reason for sticking to this routine: **»The people await my greeting – it says so in Baedeker.«** **Altes Palais**

A monument by artist Micha Ullmann was unveiled in the centre of Bebelplatz during 1995 to recall the burning of books that was perpetrated here by the Nazis on 10 May 1933. It portrays the vacuum left by the exodus of artists who were dubbed »degenerate« in the form of an underground library with empty shelves. The room can be seen through a glass pane in the ground. **Memorial to the burning of books**

A huge mounted statue of Frederick the Great, which including its pedestal towers rises 13.5m/44ft above the central reservation of Unter den Linden, was designed by **Christian Daniel Rauch** and dates from 1851. In 1950 it was taken to the park at Sanssouci and it was only restored to something like its original location in 1980. Rauch's masterpiece shows the king of Prussia in his coronation vestments and jackboots, carrying a trident and cane, while mounted upon his favourite horse, »Condé«. Four panels on the plinth beneath bear the names of 60 leading contemporaries of the king. The central section shows Prussia's generals, the western end under the horse's tail covers men of politics, art and science, while the corners feature other mounted figures including Prince Heinrich of Prussia, Duke Ferdinand of Brunswick and Generals Friedrich Wilhelm von Seydlitz and Hans Joachim von Ziethen. The upper section is decorated with bas-reliefs depicting scenes from Friedrich's life. **★ Equestrian statue of Frederick the Great**

Humboldt University is marked by the rare ginkgo trees in its front garden and the marble statues of the brothers Alexander und Wilhelm von Humboldt in front of the entrance. The university dates from an endowment of King Friedrich Wilhelm III that enabled Wilhelm von Humboldt to establish it as an educational institution. The **Humboldt University**

← Friedrich II on his steed in Unter den Linden – a masterpiece by Rauch

building was originally intended to be a palace for Prince Heinrich, the brother of Frederick the Great, and had been built between 1748 and 1766 by Johann Boumann using plans by von Knobelsdorff. In 2006 a monument to Max Planck by Bernd Heiliger was placed in the courtyard.

From Bebelplatz to Pariser Platz

Staatsbibliothek zu Berlin Beyond Humboldt University the avenue passes the Staatsbibliothek or State Library. The original »Churfürstliche Bibliothek zu Cölln an der Spree« dates back to the electorship days of 1661 when the library was housed in the Apotheken wing of the Berliner Stadtschloss. It was renamed the Royal Library in 1701. In 1780 the library of that name relocated to the Alte Bibliothek building (see above). Until 1902 the present Platz der Bibliothek was occupied by the Marstall or royal stud, built between 1687 and 1700 by Johann Arnold Nering und Martin Grünberg. This later housed the Akademie der Wissenschaften (Academy of the Sciences) and Akademie der Künste (Academy of the Arts). The Rotes Saal or Red Hall is known as the venue of **Johann Gottlieb Fichte's** *Lectures to the German nation* in 1807 and 1808. The present building was built between 1903 and 1914 by Ernst von Ihne in neo-Baroque style and gained the name »Preussische Staatsbibliothek« or Prussian State Library after the First World War. Subsequent to the Second World War, Berlin was divided and its library collections along with it. The building on Unter den Linden was now given over to East Berlin's »Deutsche Staatsbibliothek«, while in West Berlin the »Staatsbibliothek Preussischer Kulturbesitz« was established (▶Kulturforum). The two libraries were merged after reunification to form the »Staatsbibliothek zu Berlin – Preussischer Kulturbesitz« (Berlin State Libraries – Prussian Cultural Heritage). The building on Unter den Linden is now used as a research library for pre-1955 literature.

Neues Gouverneurshaus Opposite the library and next to the Alte Palais there is a plot that was formerly occupied by the Niederländische Palais or Dutch Palace, which was completely destroyed in the Second World War. The Neue Gouverneurshaus or New Governor's House that replaced it features decoration on its façade originating from the old Kommandantenhaus, which once stood on the corner of Rathausstrasse and Jüdenstrasse.

! ## *Baedeker* TIP

Berlin Story

This may look like an enormous souvenir shop, but those who take a closer look will discover a rich source of Berlin literature, city maps, illustrated books, CDs etc – and plenty of souvenirs and kitsch, too (Unter den Linden 40, daily 10am–7pm).

Next door, on the corner of Charlottenstrasse, there is a branch of the Deutsche Bank that not only handles financial affairs but also hosts the **German branch of the Guggenheim Museum**, which features exhibitions of outstanding modern art (opening hours: ⊙ 11am – 8pm daily, Thu closes 10pm).

The crossroads between Unter den Linden and Friedrichstrasse was one of the liveliest places in Berlin before the Second World War. The southeast corner was occupied by the famous and traditional Café Bauer, which was supplanted by the Lindencorso during the GDR era. Since reunification, a new Lindencorso building has been erected. The northeast corner was once the site of the Hotel Victoria and its café; later on Café König stood here. The **Haus der Schweiz** (1936) is one of the few buildings in this area that survived the war almost intact. At the southwest corner of the crossroads, urbanites used to flock to the world famous **Café Kranzler**. This too was destroyed in the war and has been replaced by a new building.

Crossroads with Friedrichstrasse

The crossroads with Friedrichstrasse also marks the end of the regal section of Unter den Linden. During the 19th century the stretch between Friedrichstrasse and Pariser Platz developed into a boulevard flanked by shops, cafés, restaurants and hotels, and the pedestrian path along the central reservation really did pass under an avenue of linden (lime) trees. Nothing remains from this period of history. On the northern side of the road, there has been a huge amount of building work in recent years, with new offices including German broadcaster ZDF's headquarters in the capital (nos. 36 – 38) and the long façade of the Bundestag offices. At the corner of Schadowstrasse the Willy Brandt Foundation has moved from the Schöneberger Rathaus into considerably more spacious premises. An exhibition there outlines the political career of Brandt, who was ruling mayor of Berlin for many years, and later federal chancellor and chairman of the Social Democratic Party. Among the items on display are the official document of his Nobel Peace Prize and the watch of party founder August Bebel, which Brandt possessed (opening times: Tue – Sun 9am – 6pm). Next door, in what was the Polish embassy, the German branch of Madame Tussaud's waxworks has opened up (opening times: daily 10am – 7pm).

Towards Pariser Platz

One building that harks back to a historic forerunner is the **Russian embassy** (no. 65). Its site was previously occupied by the palace of Princess Amalie, Frederick the Great's sister. In 1832 the Russian ambassador moved into the palace and after the October revolution the Soviet ambassador took his place until 1941. The building was bombed into oblivion during the Second World War. In the post-war years it was the first building to be restored on Unter den Linden (1950 – 53) and it then continued in its role as the Soviet embassy to East Germany. It is still used as an embassy by the present-day Russian Federation. From here it is only a stone's throw across Wilhelmstrasse and past **Hotel Adlon** to Pariser Platz and the ►Brandenburg Gate.

✶ Wannsee

Location: Zehlendorf　　　　　　　**S-Bahn:** Wannsee (S 1, S 7)

A popular song of the 1950s praised the Wannsee and captured the attitude of the isolated people of West Berlin to »their« lake.

The name »Wannsee« refers to both the village of Wannsee, part of Zehlendorf, with its magnificent old villas in large and well-tended grounds one of the poshest parts of Berlin, and of course to the natural landscape around the two lakes, Grosser and Kleiner Wannsee. Berliners still regard this as their most popular leisure destination and indeed the area has it all: the beach, Strandbad Wannsee, opened in 1907 and extended in 1930 to make it the largest open-air bathing facility in Berlin; other beaches featuring sailing, rowing and other water sports clubs; and the Wannseeterrassen and many other similar taverns on the banks of the lake or nearby. There are plenty of walks too. The Wannsee area, a relic of the ice age, covers 260ha/640ac where the Havel forms a broad bay. Around the main Wannsee lake, the Grosser Wannsee, there are a number of smaller linked watercourses: Kleiner Wannsee, Pohlesee, Stölpchensee (with beach), the Prinz-Friedrich-Leopold-Kanal and Griebnitzsee, where the Teltowkanal begins.

Summer in Berlin has to include a trip to the lake of Wannsee

The village of Wannsee is one of the longest settled areas in Berlin and was formed in 1899 from the amalgamation of three other villages: Stolpe on Lake Stölpchensee, which is first documented in 1299, the colony around the railway station and the Alsen colony of villas established on the west bank in 1863 by a member of the Chamber of Commerce, a certain Herr Conrad.

Wannsee village

The road Am Grossen Wannsee runs along the west bank of the lake. The house on the corner of Colomierstr. (no. 3) played host to Max Liebermann for 25 summers starting in 1910. 400 of his paintings and drawings were produced there. It is now a museum (opening hours: 11am – 6pm every except Tue, Thu closes 8pm).

Lakeside road
◄ Liebermann Villa

The large villa at nos. 56 – 58 dating from 1914/15 was the scene of a notorious event on 20 January 1942. It hosted a conference for which the theme was »The Final Solution to the Jewish Question«. Under the chairmanship of Reinhard Heydrich, leading Nazis gave official sanction to the extermination of Europe's Jews that had already been under way since mid-1941. The meeting and its consequences are documented in an exhibition entitled »Die Wannsee-Konferenz und der Völkermord an den europäischen Juden« (The Wannsee Conference and the Genocide of the European Jews). In the accompanying Mediathek facility, it is possible to view reports including videos of survivors relating their experiences (opening hours: 10am – 6pm daily; 114 bus from Wannsee S-Bahn station).

✷
◄ Site of the Wannsee Conference

🕐

On Bismarckstr. 3, between some boathouses on the shores of the Kleiner Wannsee, is the **grave of Heinrich von Kleist**, who committed suicide here on 21 November 1811 along with Henriette Vogel.

Kleist's grave

✷ ✷ Zoologischer Garten (Zoological gardens)

M / L 13

Location: Tiergarten
City centre plan: B/C 5/6

S-Bahn and U-Bahn: Zoologischer Garten (S 5, S 7, S 75, S 9; U 2, U 9)

The famous zoological gardens lie in the western part of the inner city, right next to Bahnhof Zoo and bounded by the railway, by Budapester Strasse and the Landwehrkanal.

Hardenbergplatz 8 (Löwentor), Budapester Str. 34 (Elefantentor) March daily 9am – 5.30pm, end of March – end of Sept until 6.30pm, end of Sep – end of Oct until 6pm, end of Oct – end of Feb until 5pm; aquarium all year daily 9am – 6pm.
Building of the zoo began in 1841 when King Friedrich Wilhelm IV donated to the city all of the animals from his pheasant pens in the Tiergarten as well as all the animals that had been housed on the ► Pfaueninsel. The gardens opened on 1 August 1844 and were

Entrances and opening times

Zoological Gardens Map

the first zoological gardens in Germany. However, it was not until 1 October 1869 that Heinrich Bodinus was appointed to be the zoo's first proper scientific director. The job was taken on by Ludwig Heck from 1888 and he considerably increased the variety of animals, making Berlin Zoo one of the most varied zoos in the world. Under his son and successor Lutz Heck, the first large enclosures with no bars or fences between animals and visitors were established. By

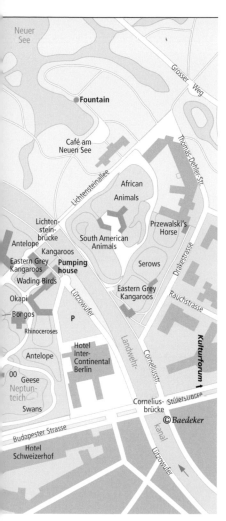

Neuer See

Grosser Weg

● Fountain

Café am Neuen See

Thomas-Dehler-Str.

Lichtensteinallee

African Animals

Lichten-
stein-
brücke

Przewalski's Horse

Antelope

South American Animals

Kangaroos

Drakestrasse

Eastern Grey Kangaroos

Pumping house

Serows

Wading Birds

Lützowufer

Eastern Grey Kangaroos

Rauchstrasse

Okapi

Bongos

P

Rhinoceroses

Hotel Inter-Continental Berlin

Landwehr-

Antelope

Corneliusstr.

Kulturforum ↑

00 Geese

Neptun-
teich

Swans

Cornelius- Stülerstrasse
brücke

© Baedeker

Budapester Strasse

kanal

Hotel Schweizerhof

Lützowufer ↑

1939 the zoo owned more than 4000 mammals and birds with a total of over 1400 species. Air raids and battles during the Second World War destroyed much of the zoo and killed many animals, and rebuilding work was not begun until long after the end of the conflict. Even the Elefanten-tor, the elephant-shaped gatehouse from 1899 that had been destroyed in the war, was reconstructed. A counterpart to this zoo, ▶ Tierpark Friedrichsfelde, was also opened in 1955 in East Berlin's Lichtenberg district during the division of the city.

Animals

The zoo currently has some 13,700 animals of about 1390 species. The main attractions are the apes, the lion enclosure, the elephant herd, the hippo house and, of course, the very rare **giant panda**, now the only panda in any German zoo since the death of his female companion. The **aquarium** (with its crocodile hall and insectarium) boasts about 500 species on three floors.

Potsdam
from A to Z

JUST HALF AN HOUR'S
S-BAHN RIDE AWAY
FROM THE CENTRE OF
BERLIN, VISITORS TO
POTSDAM ENTER
A WORLD OF
PRUSSIAN GLORY.

PALACES AND GARDENS

Nowadays 129,000 people live in Potsdam home, a town on the Havel river at the point where it broadens into various lakes and canals. The Prussian kings established a summer residence here, a tradition that was continued by the German emperors, and the king most associated with Potsdam is Frederick the Great. The place still conveys undertones of »old Prussia«.

Potsdam's array of palaces and gardens is what led it to be adopted onto UNESCO's list of World Heritage Sites in 1990. The bombardment of April 1945 did do serious damage to the historic town centre and East Germany's town planners chose to tear down many of the ruins rather than restore them, but there are still many charming corners, such as the Dutch quarter. However, it is Potsdam's **unique collection of great parks and palaces** created by the finest landscape gardeners, architects, painters and sculptors that make the town special. Since it also has the Volkspark, Babelsberg and the Filmmuseum, an excursion to Potsdam is not to be missed.

How to get there: S 7 or regional service RE 1 to Potsdam Hauptbahnhof, RE 1 also stops at Charlottenhof and Sanssouci

Potsdam was first documented in 993, when it was called Poztupimi. It is described as a town from 1317 onwards. The small country town only really expanded, though, when Elector Friedrich Wilhelm selected it as the site of a second residence after his palace in Berlin. The Stadtschloss (Potsdam City Palace) was built to his commission between 1664 and 1670. Under the strict regime of Friedrich Wilhelm I, the »Soldier King«, Potsdam began a transformation that was to make it an administrative centre and garrison town. Friedrich II continued the building work. The Stadtschloss was expanded, and work began on the palace of Schloss Sanssouci and the Neue Palais (New Palace). Whole suburbs were demolished and reconstructed. During Friedrich's reign, Potsdam attracted many writers, musicians and philosophers, in particular Voltaire. In 1838 Prussia's first railway line opened between Berlin and Potsdam. 21 March 1933 became known as

History

Potsdam Programme

- The town centre and Schloss Sanssouci should definitely be on the itinerary: both are easily reached on foot. Those wishing to walk across the entire park to the Neue Palais will need to be a bit fitter – or jump on the bus. The same applies to the Neue Garten and Schloss Cecilienhof. The coordinates given in the following section refer to the map of Potsdam's town centre printed on the back of the enclosed Berlin city map.

»Tag von Potsdam« or **»The Day of Potsdam«**, when Hindenburg and Hitler signified a symbolic bond between the German nation and the National Socialist party at the garrison church, an event seen

← *Prussia's former elite troops have been reformed for the benefit of tourists. The »Langen Kerls« are on the march again.*

by many as the beginning of the Third Reich. But Potsdam is also closely associated with its ending: in August 1945 allied leaders Truman, Churchill (and later Attlee after his election in Britain) and Stalin met at Schloss Cecilienhof to sign the **Potsdam Agreement**, which sealed the fate of Germany. Since reunification, Potsdam has been the capital of the federal state of Brandenburg and has experienced a cultural, political and economic boom period, helped not least by its proximity to the national capital.

Alexandrowka · Russian Colony

B 4

Location: Between Jägerstr. and Puschkinallee

Tram: Puschkinallee (90, 92, 95)

The 13 houses in the colony of Alexandrowka with their wooden balconies and carved gables remain unique to this day as an example of Russian architecture outside the Russian homeland.

A piece of Russia inside Prussia The colony was founded as the result of a »top priority cabinet order« decreed by Friedrich Wilhelm III on 10 April 1826 on behalf of twelve Russian singers, who had been brought to Potsdam as prisoners of war in 1812 by General Yorck, who had captured them while they were fighting for Napoleon. They later sang in the local choir and remained in Potsdam after the defeat of Napoleon, officially designated as a »gift from Tsar Alexander«. The royal decree that the colony should be designed in the form of the Russian saltire of St Andrew was implemented by Peter Joseph Lenné: he populated the two lines of the cross with four opposing pairs of houses, each of which was aligned to four other houses built on the arcs of the oval site. The **foreman's house (no. 8)** was built at the intersection of the cross. The homes were not to be sold. Instead, they were passed on to the next generation as long as the oldest child was a boy, and the name plates thus describe the history of the families to this day. White writing on a black background denotes the deceased family heads, while the names of the present-day descendants of the original Russian singers are written black on white. At house no. 2, originally built in 1826, the lower floor has been converted into a **site museum** (opening hours: Tue–Sun 10am–6pm).

! *Baedeker* TIP

Truly wonderful

This is how the painter Carl Ludwig Häberlin described the view of the palaces and gardens of Potsdam from the Belvedere on the Pfingstberg (reached from Puschkinallee; daily 10am–6pm, in summer until 8pm). The Belvedere was built between 1847 and 1863, based on sketches by Friedrich Wilhelm IV. Don't be so distracted by the view that you miss the small Pomonatempel by Schinkel (1801), located north of the Kapellenberg (opening times: mid-April–Oct Sat, Sun and holidays 3pm–6pm).

The orthodox Church of St Alexander Nevski on the chapel hill was dedicated in 1829 in the presence of Tsar Nicholas I. Karl Friedrich Schinkel designed the chapel using the Desiatin Church in Kiev as his model. To the north of the Russian colony, in the area of fine villas between the Pfingstberg and Neuer Garten, the Soviet secret service made itself a home in the so-called Forbidden City until 1994. The wall that closed it off still stands at the corner of Langhansstrasse. In the imperial period aristocrats, army officers and bankers lived here, well out of sight of proletarian Berlin. Some of these villas are dilapidated, but others, such as Villa Lepsius, built on the Grosse Weinmeisterstrasse for Frederick the Great's chamberlain, have been carefully restored. It takes its name from the theologian Johannes Lepsius (1858–1926), who lived their until his death and supported the cause of Armenians persecuted in Turkey. The establishment of a Lepsius archive here is planned. Villa Quandt next door houses an archive relating to the writer Fontane (Grosse Weinmeisterstr. 46/47, Mon–Thu 9am–4pm, Fri until 3pm)

Church of St Alexander Nevski

Fine residences

◀ Villa Lepsius

◀ Fontane-Archiv

Babelsberg

S-Bahn : Babelsberg (S 7)

Babelsberg, which lies to the east and is Potsdam's largest suburb in terms of area, has gained renown as a centre for film and the media.

Its main attractions are the palace of Schloss Babelsberg amid its beautiful parkland as well as the former site of the UFA film studios. For those with time to linger, it is still possible to see the villas of Neu-Babelsberg (Griebnitzsee S-Bahn station) on the banks of the Griebnitzsee where UFA's stars once had their homes, or the relatively modest Stern hunting lodge (Jagdschloss Stern), built for the »Soldier King« Friedrich Wilhelm I between 1730 and 1732.

Home of UFA

The area of Babelsberg to the north of the present-day town centre was leased in 1833 by Friedrich Wilhelm III to his son, the future Kaiser Wilhelm I, who commissioned Schinkel to design a palace for him and his wife Augusta von Sachsen-Weimar, an admirer of the English Tudor style. The decidedly modest building was finished by the end of 1835. Schinkel was soon commissioned again for extension work, which would be carried on after his death by Persius, Strack and Gottgetreu. Schinkel's original plan, based on Windsor Castle, was partially realized by Persius in the east wing. Between 1844 and 1849 Strack completed the western section in the form of a neo-Roman fort. Little of Schinkel's initial interior design can be seen today. The palace provides a magnificent view over the bowling

Schloss Babelsberg
◀ 694 bus from Babelsberg S-Bahn station

green that descends down to the Havel and as far as Glienicker Brücke bridge and Glienicker Park itself (opening hours: March – Oct Tue – Sun 9am – 5pm).

Babelsberg Park ▶

130ha/321ac of parkland stretch away to the west of the palace between Tiefer See and Glienicker Lake. The Babelsberg Park was laid out by Lenné and later by Fürst Pückler-Muskau. Take a stroll to Glienicker Lake where there is a **steam engine shed** built by Persius between 1843 and 1845. The walk leads further west, past the **Kleines Schloss**, built for the court ladies in waiting in 1841/42, all the way to the **Matrosenhaus**, which was erected in 1842 for the crews of the boats and gondolas belonging to the palace. On the hill is the landmark of the Babelsberg Park, the 40m/130ft **Flatowturm** or Flatow Tower, built between 1853 and 1856 and modelled on the tower of the Eschenheimer Tor in Frankfurt am Main. The Bismarck Bridge beneath it is said to be where Wilhelm I named Bismarck as Prussian prime minister. Northeast of the Flatow Tower is the medieval **Gerichtslaube** or Court Arbour, which was moved here from Berlin in 1872 to make way for the building of the Rotes Rathaus. The lower floor dates from about 1280 and includes the Schöffenstuhl or seat of the lay judges. Above it is the Ratsstube or council hall, added in 1485.

Medienstadt Babelsberg

German film history was made at Grossbeerenstrasse (buses 602, 690, 698) from 1912 on the 45ha/111 acres of studio grounds belonging to the former UFA production company. Nowadays it is home to the Medienstadt Babelsberg estate, where countless film companies and TV broadcasters produce movies and TV series. Filmpark Babelsberg is a key highlight for tourists. It offers a look behind the scenes of Janosch's dream land or a visit to the garden of Little Mook, followed by a stunt show in a volcano; alternatively you can even risk a peek inside the cabinet of Doctor Caligari (opening hours: mid-March – Oct 10am – 6pm daily). The Exploratorium is a new feature at the Medienstadt station. It offers a hands-on look at science for children (opening hours: Tue – Thu 8.30am – 6pm, Fri until 7pm, Sat/Sun from 10am).

Filmpark Babelsberg ▶

✶ ✶ City Centre

C/D 3/4

The following description is a walking tour around Potsdam's city centre. From the main station Potsdam Hauptbahnhof, which has now been incorporated into the gigantic Potsdam Center, it only takes a few minutes to cross the Lange Brücke (Long Bridge) to Alter Markt (Old Marketplace).

Alter Markt

Until the 1930s Alter Markt was the centre of Potsdam. This is where the Great Elector had the Stadtschloss built between 1664 and 1670 (although it saw many alterations in subsequent years). As of 1750

This view of the Nikolaikirche has now been partly blocked by construction work for the Stadtschloss palace

the square was refurbished in Baroque style by Georg Wenzeslaus von Knobelsdorff and others. An allied air raid on 14 April 1945 hit the Stadtschloss and it was gutted by fire. In spite of vociferous protests, the ruins were demolished in 1960/61. Rows of poplars now mark where the walls once stood. The Fortuna-Tor, the gate that was first built by Jean de Bodt in 1701 when Prussia was first made a kingdom, has been rebuilt. Reconstruction of the palace to make it the seat of parliament of the federal state has begun, turning the centre into a building site.

Today the Nikolaikirche or Church of St Nicholas towers over the square. It dates back to a hall church built between 1721 and 1724 by Philipp Gerlach, although that church burned down in 1795. It was 1830 before a new church was built on the site. The selected design for a domed church reminiscent of St Paul's Cathedral in London was suggested by Karl Friedrich Schinkel. Ludwig Persius undertook the actual construction work and the church was dedicated in 1837, although at that time it only had a flat roof. The 78m/256ft dome was only added after Schinkel's death in a subsequent phase of building that took place from 1843 to 1849 at the behest of Friedrich Wilhelm IV. The interior was redesigned in 1849, partly using the existing decoration and partly the Schinkel designs.

★
◄ Nikolaikirche

The obelisk in the square is from an original design by von Knobelsdorff that was destroyed during the Second World War. It was reconstructed in 1979, although the original depictions of Prussian rulers were replaced with others of the kind by authentic Prussian masons.

◄ Obelisk

The Altes Rathaus or Old Town Hall was the fourth of its kind to stand upon Alter Markt, having been built from 1753 to 1755 by Johann Boumann the Elder in Palladian classic style with richly ornate façades. The gilded Atlas carrying the globe of the world on the tower is visible from far and wide.

◄ Altes Rathaus

The three-storey town house next door to the Rathaus on the right was designed by von Knobelsdorff and reflects the architecture of the Alter Markt as it was in the years before it was destroyed in 1945.

◄ Knobelsdorffhaus

Opposite Alter Markt the Marstall or royal stud can be seen stretching into the distance. This is all that remains of the original palace complex that formerly consisted of the Stadtschloss and its Lustgarten park. The stud was originally built as an orangery in 1685 to plans by Johann Arnold Nehring but it was converted to stables in

Marstall

Potsdam Map

Where to stay
① Hotel am Luisenplatz

Where to eat
① Speckers Landhaus
② Drachenhaus
③ Meierei im Neuen Garten
④ Zum Fliegenden Holländer

Café
⑨ Café Heider

- - - - Shipping traffic

▨▨▨ Pedestrian zone

500 m
0,25 mi
© Baedeker

BORNSTEDT

Schloss
Lindstedt

Am Raubfang
Thaerstr.
Zum Lausebusch
Amtsstr.
Thaerstr.
Potsdamer Straße
Thaerstr.
Habichtweg
Fliederw.
Meisenweg
Rosenweg
Birnenweg
Apfelweg
Kirschallee
Paul-Engelhard-Str.
Hermann-Materm-Promenade
E.-Mendelsohn-Allee
E.-Barth-Str.
A.-Klein-Str.
L.-Boltzmann-Str.
Kirchallee
Pappel Allee

Katharinenholzstr.

Am Teufelsgraben
Grabenstr.
Eichenallee
Amundsen Straße

Drachenberg

+ + + + + +
+ + + + **Krongut
Bornstedt**

Ribbeckstraße
Bornstedter See
Bornstedter Straße

Ruinenberg

Belvedere ② **Drachenhaus**

Maulbeerallee

Lindstetter Weg

**Botanical
Gardens**

Orangery

Maulbeerallee

**Neue
Kammern**

Z. Hist. Mühle

**Historic
Windmill**

**Picture
Gallery**

Voltaire

PH

**Am
Neuen**

Communs

PH

Palais

**Neues
Palais**

**Schloss-
theater**

Am Neuen Palais

Lindenavenue

**Temple of
Antiquity**

Hauptallee

**Temple of
Friendship**

Ökonomieweg

R e h g a r t e n

**Sicilian
Garden**

**Bell
Fountain**

**Schloss
Sanssouci**

L u s t g a r t e n

**Great
Fountain**

**Neptu
Grotto**

**Small
Fountai**

**Frieden
kirch**

S a n s s o u c i

**Chinese
House**

Ökonomieweg

Am Grünen
Gitter

BRANDENBURGER

Wildpark

P a r k

C h a r l o t t e n h o f

**Roman
Baths**

**Schloss
Charlottenhof**

Lenne straße

Feuerbachstraße

**Park Sanssouci
Station**

Am
Wildpark

Hippodrom

Pheasant pen

Geschwister-Scholl-Straße

Schafgraben

H.-Sachs-Str.

Meistersinger-
str.

VORSTADT

**Erlöser-
kirche**

Zeppelinstraße

**Charlottenhof
Station**

Forststr.

Werderscher Weg

Zeppelinstr.

Schiller-
platz

*Caputh, Werder,
Brandenburg* ✎ **Kunstspeicher**

Berlin

Jungfernsee

NAUENER

Belvedere

Schloss Cecilienhof

Green House

VORSTADT

Alexander-Newski-Kirche

Neuer

Red House

BUGA-PARK

Park Gate Entrance

Kieperheuer Allee

C.-C.-Horvath-Str.

Potsdam Technical College

Alexandrowka

Russian Colony

Garten

Heiliger

Marmor-palais

BERLINER

VORSTADT

H.-Kasack-Str.

Am Pfingstberg

G.-Hermann-Allee

Neditzel Str.

Puschkin Allee

Hesse Str.

Weinmeisterstraße

Am Neuen Garten

Orangery
③

See

Seestraße

L.-Richter-Str.

Rubensstr.

Glienicker Brücke

Tizianstr.

JÄGER-VORSTADT

Pappel Allee

G.-Hermann-Allee

weg

Brentano-weg

Gregor-Mendel-Straße

Weinbergstr.

H.-Lange-Str.

Fr.-Ebert-Straße

Eisenhartstraße

Am Neuen Garten

Gothic Library

Mangerstr.

Helmholtzstr.

Berliner Str.

Schloss Babelsberg

①

Regional Council Office

Behlertstraße

Behlertstraße

Tiefer See

Jägerallee

Law Court

Nauener Tor
④

Kulturstraße

Leibelstr.

Am Jägertor

Hegelallee

Mittelstr.
⑨

Dutch Quarter

Hospital (Klinikum)

Berliner Straße

Museum Fluxus+

Hans-Otto-Theater

obelisk

Schopenhauer

Jägerstr.

Gutenbergstraße

Museum gegen politische Gewalt

Peter- u. Paulskirche

Humboldt-brücke

①

Luisen-platz

Luisen-str.

Straße

Brandenburger Tor
ℹ

Brandenburger Str.

Charlottenstr.

Lindenstraße

Dorfstr.

Yorckstr.

Alte Wache

Franz. Kirche

Posthofstr.

Am Kanal

Nuthestr.

Humboldtring

Breite Str.

Steam Engine Shed

Neustädter Havelbucht

Kiezstr.

Potsdam-Museum

Film Museum

Marstall

Lange Brücke

Library

Nikolai-kirche

Alter Markt

Theater

Altes Rathaus

Alte Fahrt

Neuefahrt

Exhibition Pavilion

Freundschafts-Insel

Babelsberger Straße

L.-Pulewka-Str.

Humboldtring

Babelsberg, UFA

ℹ

Potsdam Center/ Potsdam Station

Untere Planitz

Obere Planitz

Havel

Lustgarten

Caputh, Einsteinturm

Beelitz

TELTOWER VORSTADT

Straße

★ ★
Filmmuseum ►

1714. It gained its present form in 1746 at the hands of Georg Wenzeslaus von Knobelsdorff. Since 1981 the Marstall building has been the home of Potsdam's Filmmuseum. Although it is not as pepped up with high technology as its rival on Potsdamer Platz in Berlin, it can still show off eight decades of Babelsberg's film history with no less impressive original items once owned by such figures as Zarah Leander, Lilian Harvey and, in particular, Hans Albers. Both emigration and the Nazi era are dealt with in detail, but the main theme is the GDR era, including the topic of state censorship (opening hours: 10am – 6pm daily).

★
Neuer Markt

Beyond the Marstall is the so-called Neuer Markt, a new marketplace that was laid out in 1680. Its centrepiece is the Kutschstall or coaching stables, built in 1671 and then furnished with its splendidly decorated portico by Andreas Ludwig Krüger between 1787 and 1789. It now includes the **Haus der brandenburgisch-preussischen Geschichte** or Museum of Brandenburg and Prussian History (opening hours: Tue – Fri 10am – 5pm, Sat/Sun until 6pm). The house at Neuer Markt 1 (1753) is said to be the birthplace of Wilhelm von Humboldt. More certain is the fact that the future King Friedrich Wilhelm II lived here in 1786. The Königliche Ratswaage (council scales) has been on Neuer Markt since 1735, though the present building dates from 1836.

Yorckstrasse

The tour now leads from Neuer Markt to Yorckstrasse. This former prestige boulevard was originally called Am Kanal, since it followed the course of a former canal link through the town that gave the spot the air of a Dutch canal-side. The canal itself was filled in during the 1960s, although one section of it has since been reopened. Some of the old houses still remain at no. 2 (1783), the Happe-Röhrichtschen houses at nos. 3 and 4 (1822 to 1833) and no. 19/20, which was completed in 1776 according to a design by von Gontard for the Brocke glass polishing company.

Bassinplatz

Bassinplatz to the east of Friedrich-Ebert-Strasse was constructed at the same time as the Dutch quarter. Its name dates from the time when a basin was constructed during the reign of Friedrich Wilhelm I between 1737 and 1739, which was linked with the Heiliger See by a canal. It was filled in during 1863. Nowadays it is the site of a daily market, which takes place in the shadow of the Peter-und-Pauls-Kirche (Church of Saints Peter and Paul) built in 1870. A more remarkable sight, though, is the French Church or Französische Kirche at the southeastern corner, which is reminiscent of the Pantheon in Rome and was probably designed by von Knobelsdorff and built by von Boumann the Elder in 1752/53.

Just looking at this gable makes it clear where the Dutch quarter got its name →

✶✶
Dutch Quarter

Not far from Bassinplatz is the Dutch Quarter, 134 truly exquisite houses built between 1732 and 1742 to accommodate an expected wave of Dutch immigrants. Johann Boumann the Elder's plans mainly featured five-storey buildings with eaves or brick gabled houses with a triple axis and adorned with white and green decorations on the porticos and window shutters. They have now been lovingly restored and are occupied by all kinds of shops (many of them craft shops), bars and cafés. Only the front gardens once possessed by each of the houses are no longer in existence.

There are plenty of nice shops in the Dutch quarter

To the east of the Dutch Quarter, at the **Tiefer See** (the name means »deep lake«), a lively cultural scene and high-tech companies have taken over an area formerly used for military and industrial purposes around Schiffbauergasse. Along with the Waschhaus, a popular venue for films, concerts, dances and readings since 1992, art events take place in protected buildings such as the Schinkelhalle and Husaren-Pferdeställe (Hussar stables). Above all the new waterside Hans-Otto-Theater designed by Gottfried Böhm has pulled in crowds since 2006 (tram 93 from Potsdam Hauptbahnhof).

Brandenburger Strasse

Brandenburger Strasse, which dates from 1735, leads away from the Peter-und-Pauls-Kirche to Luisenplatz. Since the end of the 19th century it has been Potsdam's main shopping street and is now a pedestrian zone. Theodor Storm lived at no. 70 while he was training to be an assessor at the Potsdam law courts (1853–56). More recent residents of Potsdam are recalled by the memorial at no. 54 on Lindenstrasse, one of the streets that cross Brandenburgerstrasse. The large Dutch house that was built here in 1737 later became the interrogation headquarters of East Germany's notorious secret police, the Stasi. They were not the first organization to use the building for this purpose since it was also used by the Soviet secret service and the Nazis to interrogate those who voiced their opposing views too loudly.

Luisenplatz

✶
Brandenburg Gate ▶

Luisenplatz is the starting point for many a visitor to Potsdam wishing to view the park and palace of Schloss Sanssouci since an avenue leads to Sanssouci from the northeast corner of the square. Potsdam's own Brandenburg Gate dominates the eponymously named square (Brandenburger-Tor-Platz) having been erected in 1770 in memory of the Seven Years' War. The façade towards Brandenburger Strasse is by von Gontard, while the one facing the square was designed by Unger. Enthroned on the parapet are Mars and Hercules.

Back along Brandenburger Strasse, turn right onto Dortustrasse to get to Breite Strasse. Constructed in 1668 under Elector Friedrich Wilhelm in 1668, the road led from the Stadtschloss to the village of Golm in the northeast. The boulevard was destroyed in 1945 and there are few buildings remaining that can testify to its former splendour. Until the 1970s, the town canal that was also built under Friedrich Wilhelm also passed by the intersection of Dortustrasse and Breite Strasse.

Breite Strasse

Another feature at the intersection of Dortustrasse and Breite Strasse is the four-storey Militärwaisenhaus building, which was formerly a military orphanage. It was established in 1722 by Friedrich Wilhelm I. During the Seven Years' War more than 2000 orphans of soldiers were housed here. Karl Ludwig von Gontard remodelled it into its present form between 1771 and 1778. The pair of buildings opposite, the so-called Hiller-Brandtschen Häuser, were built in 1769 by Georg Christian and form part of the Potsdam Museum, featuring exhibitions of history and art. On Breite Strasse 13 there is another museum building where the exhibits concentrate on nature and the environment and also include an aquarium. The exhibition »Potsdam und der 20. Juli 1944« at the Ministerium für Stadtentwicklung (Ministry for Urban Development), Henning-von-Tresckow-Str. 2 – 8 also belongs to the museum (opening hours: Tue – Sun 10am – 6pm).

◄ Former military orphanage

◄ Potsdam Museum

Potsdam also has its own Brandenburg Gate

Connected to the Hiller-Brandtschen Häuser is the so called Predigerwitwenhaus, the oldest dwelling in Potsdam, built in 1664. Passing by there, heading out of town on Breite Strasse, you come to the Neustädter Havelbucht, a bay on the river, directly alongside which is the town's **mosque**. It is housed in what is none other than the steam engine shed erected in 1842 according to plans by Persius for the Sanssouci waterworks. From here water was pumped up to the Ruinenberg in order to supply the fountains in the gardens (opening hours: mid-May – mid-Oct Sat/Sun 10am – 5pm).

Back along Breite Strasse towards Lange Brücke the road passes the Rechenzentrum (computing centre, built 1969–72). This was formerly the site of the Garnisonkirche or Garrison Church, built from 1732 to 1735 by Philipp Gerlach, which housed the sarcophagi of Friedrich Wilhelm I and Friedrich II until the autumn of 1943. History was made here on 21 March 1933, the »Day of Potsdam« when Hitler opened the sitting of the Reichstag in the presence of German president von Hindenburg. The church was demolished in 1968.

◄ Garnisonkirche

Since 1991 a reconstruction of the church's bell tower has stood behind the Rechenzentrum. One of the door grilles can still be seen at the Predigerwitwenhaus.

✳
Langer Stall ► A bit further on, a late Baroque/classical façade faces the street. This is a remnant of the so-called Langer Stall, which was opened in 1734 as an exercise shed for winter manoeuvres by the Potsdam garrison and was later modified in 1781 by Unger.

Neuer Lustgarten The route has now arrived back at Lange Brücke, where Havel steamers dock at Neuer Lustgarten, a park laid out around the »Ringerkolonnaden«, which once connected the Stadtschloss and the Marstall.

✳ Neuer Garten (New garden)

A/B 4/5

Location: Northeast of the town centre   **Bus:** 692

The Neuer Garten is a wonderful example of a »sentimental« landscape park of the late 18th century.

At the foot of Pfingstberg hill lies the Neuer Garten (New Garden), which stretches over 74ha/183 acres on the west bank of the Heilige See as far as the Jungfernsee. The land is mentioned as early as the 18th century when it is described as the king's vineyard. In 1783 the crown prince, who was later to become King Friedrich Wilhelm II, built a vineyard here with its own pleasure house. Between 1787 and 1791, inspired by Wörlitzer Park near Dessau, the prince had Johann August Eyserbeck the Younger, son of the Wörlitzer garden's architect, lay out a »sentimental« landscape garden.

A Walk through the Neuer Garten

Holländisches Etablissement The Hauptallee or main avenue starts from the front entrance. From here the southern end of the Heilige See can be seen with its Gothic library, completed in 1794 by Langhans. On the left-hand side of the avenue is the Holländisches Etablissement (Dutch establishment) with its ladies rooms, stables and carriage sheds, built in 1789/90 according to plans by von Gontard and Andreas L. Krüger.

Orangery Two years later Carl Gotthard Langhans' Orangery between the Holländisches Etablissement and the Marble Palace was completed. Its sphinx by Michael Christian Wohler, two black guards by Gottfried Schadow and the statue of Isis near the lake all took up its Egyptian theme. Here Friedrich Wilhelm III received the message about the Convention of Tauroggen, which started the process to wrest Prussia from Napoleon's hands in 1812.

The main building in the Neuer Garten was built between 1787 and 1791 as a summer residence for King Friedrich Wilhelm II and goes by the name of the Marmorpalais or Marble Palace. This early classical palace with a red-brick façade decorated by grey Silesian granite was started by Karl von Gontard and completed by Langhans, who also added the wing at the side in 1797. Since the building's restoration, it is possible to enjoy a tour including the concert hall and the Gesellschaftszimmer (parlour) on the upper floor with some lovely views of the lakes and gardens, just as Langhans conceived it (opening hours: Mai – Oct Tue – Sun 10am – 6pm; Nov – April Sat/Sun only 10am – 5pm). The pyramid north of the marble palace, also by Langhans, was used as an ice cellar and for refrigerating food.

★
Marmorpalais
(Marble Palace)

Right behind the northern entrance to the Neuer Garten is the Gothic-looking Meierei, built in 1791 by Langhans and modified by Persius in 1844 with the addition of a pumping house for watering the gardens and given a new look in the style of a Norman castle.

Meierei

At the northern edge of the Neuer Garten, hidden behind some trees, stands Schloss Cecilienhof, the last palace to be built for the Hohenzollern dynasty in Prussia. It was built from 1913 to 1917 at the instigation of Crown Prince Wilhelm by Paul Schultze-Naumburg and takes the form of an English country mansion with its picturesque buildings grouped around five inner courtyards. In 1918 the crown prince fled into exile in Holland. When he returned in 1923, the Hohenzollern family was given the right of abode in Schloss Cecilienhof. In February 1945, before Potsdam was bombed, the family fled the town and their right of abode was abandoned.

★
Schloss
Cecilienhof

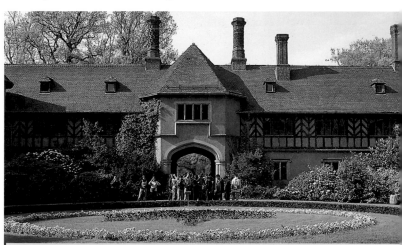

The victorious powers of the Second World War cemented the shape of post-war Europe at Schloss Cecilienhof with the Potsdam Agreement

Potsdam conference ▶ Between 17 July and 2 August 1945 the heads of the allied forces met together at Schloss Cecilienhof – Stalin for the USSR, Truman for the USA and Churchill representing Britain, although having lost Britain's 1945 election he was to be replaced by his successor Clement Attlee. The conference led to the Potsdam Agreement, which was to cement the political regime in Europe after the end of the Second World War. For the conference 36 rooms of the palace plus its audience chamber were furnished with items from various different Potsdam palaces. Those rooms have been left in their 1945 condition. One major attraction is the audience chamber with its round table, around which the conference negotiations took place (opening hours: April–Oct Tue–Sun 9am–5pm, Nov–Mar closes 4pm). Most of the other parts of the palace now belong to an international hotel chain.

Ruinenberg

D 2/3

Location: North of the town centre **Bus:** 691

The Ruinenberg gets its name from the ruins that are scattered over the summit at a height of 74m/243ft.

Friedrich II had a 4000 cu m/900,000 gallon water cistern dug out here to supply the fountains, springs and greenhouses in the park at Sanssouci, and commissioned von Knobelsdorff to surround it with a ring of architectural follies made to look like ruins. Von Knobelsdorff and the decorative painter at Berlin's Italian opera house, one Innocente Bellavita, set up one piece to represent part of the round terrace of an amphitheatre, another in the form of a circular temple with a collapsed dome and three Ionic columns with a fourth toppled to the ground. In 1845 Friedrich Wilhelm IV had a watchtower added, which in 1945 was itself reduced to the ruin that now remains. The cistern never fulfilled its intended purpose, however. Its sluices were only opened once, on Good Friday in 1754, when the cistern was only half full. The fountain in front of the Bildergalerie (picture gallery) spurted forth a gush of water but it quickly subsided. It was not until a pumping shed was built next to the Havel in 1841 (▶ Breite Strasse, mosque) that the reservoir was able to be used. Nevertheless, there is a fabulous view from the Ruinenberg.

»No cares« are what Friedrich II was seeking from his vine encircled palace

✶✶ Sanssouci

Entrances: Obelisk Portal (Schopenhauerstrasse), Grünes Portal (Avenue to Sanssouci), Historic windmill

The area once known as the »Desolate Hill« is now an incomparable landscape of palaces and gardens, which was declared a World Heritage site by UNESCO in 1990.

The fabulous assemblage of palaces and gardens at Sanssouci was born on 5 April 1744, when Friedrich II decreed that the barren hill northwest of the town, where Friedrich Wilhelm I had already laid out a kitchen garden in 1725, was now to be redeployed as a hillside vineyard. The building of the summer palace was started as early as 1745, with the orangery following in 1747 followed by the Neptune Grotto in 1751 and the picture gallery in 1753. All the buildings were designed by Georg Wenzeslaus von Knobelsdorff, who was probably also responsible for laying out the gardens. In the 19th century Friedrich Wilhelm IV had large areas of the grounds redesigned or newly laid out – as at Charlottenhof Park and the Marlygarten – in the form of a landscape park by Peter Joseph Lenné. On the northern side of the east-west avenue that runs for 2.3km/1.5mi lies the Lustgarten or pleasure park. To the south (as far as Ökonomieweg) is the Rehgarten or deer park and Charlottenhof Park. Some 60km/37mi of paths run through the park.

Sanssouci Park Map

Schloss Lindstedt

BORNSTEDT

Royal Gardeners's Graves

Bornstedt Cemetery

Klausberg (Drachenberg) ▲ 58

Belvedere

Former Vineyard

Drachenhaus
Winzerhaus

Potentestück

Former Park Bandstand

Krimlindenallee

Prinzenspielburg

Orangery

Paradiesgarten

Nordic Garden

Botanical Gardens

Villa Persius

Court Gardener's Lodge

Jubiläums-terrasse

Sicilian Garden

Court Gardener's Lodge

Potsdam University

Heckentheater

Hopfengarten

Temple of Antiquity

Commun

Neues Palais

Pomona
Hauptallee
Flora

Rehgarten

Hauptallee

Kolonnade

Mopke

Temple of Friendship

Chinesisches Haus

Commun

Schlosstheater

Ökonomleweg

Potsdam University

Kastellanhaus

Ökonomleweg

Schafgraben

Meierei

Lennéstrasse

Park Charlottenhof

Friedrichsicht

Court Gardener's Lodge

Roman Baths

Theaterweg

Tiroler Berg

Tea Pavilion

Lenné

Schloss Charlottenhof

BRANDENBURGER

Lindenavenue

Maschinenteich

Kaiserbahnhof

Hippodrom

Poets' Arbour

VORSTADT

Pheasant Pen

Geschwister-

Park Sanssouci Station

Scholl-

Strasse

Weg

Wildpark

Werderscher

Schloss Sanssouci

The palace itself is accessed either through the park or by 695 bus or car to the car park at the Historische Mühle (historic windmill). Georg Wenzeslaus von Knobelsdorff incorporated into his plans for the palace numerous sketches that had been made by the king himself. The palace was ready for its inauguration as early as May 1747. The palace and its ancillary buildings and gardens are considered to be the architect's masterpiece and the defining epitome of Prussian Rococo. The name »sans souci« is French for »no cares« and indicates the fact that Friedrich II planned to move here, even though it has just twelve rooms, a remarkably small number for a royal palace. Persius added some short and slightly set-back wings along the lengthways axis of the building in 1841/42. The frontage of the palace looks out over the park, to which an outdoor staircase leads down, taking in six curving vineyard terraces. The decoration of the façade – herm pilasters with bacchantes – stems from Friedrich Christian Glume. On the eastern side of the terrace is the grave of Frederick the Great: as early as 1744 he had requested that he be buried in Sanssouci next to his wind chimes. On the 205th anniversary of his death, 17

🕐
Opening hours:
Tours: April – Oct
Tue – Sun
10am – 6pm,
Nov – Mar
closes 7pm

★
◄ Grave of Frederick the Great

August 1991, his well-travelled mortal remains were finally laid to rest here under a modest gravestone.

The **design of the rooms** inside the palace is considered to be among the most successful examples of the Rococo style. Apart from von Knobelsdorff, the main participants in the achievement were Johann August Nahl and Johann Hoppenhaupt the Elder. Above the vestibule is the Kleine Galerie (Small Gallery), which displays antiques from the collection of Cardinal Polignac, purchased in 1742, along with paintings by Watteau. The royal chambers start with the audience chamber. Its roof painting *Zephyr Crowning Flora* was created by Antoine Pesne. The most important room in terms of art history is also the most intimate room in the building, the cedar-panelled circular library with its four wall cupboards containing 2000 of the king's books. After Frederick died, the adjoining study, bedroom and living room were redecorated in classical style in 1786 by his nephew and successor, Friedrich Wilhelm II. The chair in which Frederick died and his work desk were only recently put on display here. The concert room is a symphony of playful Rococo. The artistically minded king, himself a talented flute player and com-

The Marble Hall at Schloss Sanssouci

poser, gave many a concert in this room. The pictures on the walls hark back to Ovid's poem *Metamorphoses* and were also painted by Pesne. The centrepiece of the palace is the oval Marmorsaal (Marble Hall), which among other things was the site of Frederick's famous round table meetings. The west wing contains some uniform guest rooms. A bust in the fourth of them is a reminder of one of the Prussian court's most distinguished guests – although he never actually slept in these chambers – the French philosopher Voltaire.

Neue Kammern (New Chambers)

Two similar buildings flank the palace. The Neue Kammern to the west were built as of 1747 in the form of an orangery designed by von Knobelsdorff. In 1771 they were reconfigured by Unger for use as a guest house by turning the seven large rooms into four richly decorated banqueting halls and seven smaller »cavalier« apartments. Among the finest are the Jaspissaal (Jasper Hall) and the Ovid Gallery (opening hours: April Sat/Sun 10am – 6pm, May – Oct Tue – Sun 10am – 6pm).

★
◄ Bildergalerie (Picture Gallery)

The Bildergalerie on the eastern side was built between 1755 and 1764 according to plans by Johann Gottfried Büring in order to accommodate Friedrich II's art collection. It is the oldest surviving museum building in Germany. Even if the collection as displayed today is not as extensive as in former times, its paintings by Rubens, van Dyck, Vasari, Reni, Tintoretto and Caravaggio clearly reflect Friedrich's excellent taste (opening hours: April – Oct Tue – Sun 10am – 6pm). In the Holländischer Garten (Dutch Garden) in front of the gallery there are eight massive busts representing the rulers of the House of Orange.

Sanssouci windmill

The historic windmill behind the palace is a reconstruction of an original that was obliterated down to its base in 1945. This mill was itself built in 1790 to succeed a post mill that had been in operation since 1739. Legend has it that Friedrich II was irritated by the rattling of the windmill, but the miller managed to plead against its demolition. However it has been shown that this story really is no more than hearsay (opening hours: April – Oct 10am – 6pm daily, Nov – March Sat/Sun only till 4pm).

✴ ✴ Sanssouci Park

Obeliskportal

An obelisk and the Obeliskportal, both by von Knobelsdorff, mark the eastern end of the Hauptallee. The hieroglyphics on the obelisk are just simple decoration and make no sense, while the busts on the portal and alongside it represent Roman gods and emperors.

★
Marlygarten

To the south of the Obeliskportal Friedrich Wilhelm I commissioned the construction of the Marlygarten, originally a kitchen garden that would later be laid out as a magical landscape garden by Lenné in 1850.

PARK AND PALACE OF SANSSOUCI

✱✱ **Frederick II commanded construction of a place of refuge, a palace that is positively modest in scale. Sanssouci is not just a palace, however: many more delights are to be found in and around the park.**

① Neues Palais

Right at the western end of the park there is a palace by the name of the Neues Palais that seems a little out of place here with its gigantic scale. Friedrich II spent little time there.

② Hauptallee

The main avenue of the park measures some 2.3km/1.5mi in length and links the Obelisk gate to the Neues Palais.

③ Historic windmill

Just a legend: the miller of the mill behind the palace stood up to the king who had complained about the noise.

④ Bornstedter See

Outside the park but well worth going out of your way to see. Bornstedter See features the Italian-style Krongut building.

⑤ Ruinenberg

Also beyond the park but in fact intended to provide water for the palace and park, even if the only time that ever worked was on Good Friday in 1754.

⑥ Weinbergterrasse

Six terraces planted with cherries, apricots and plum trees. In its glass-covered niches, vines and figs also thrive.

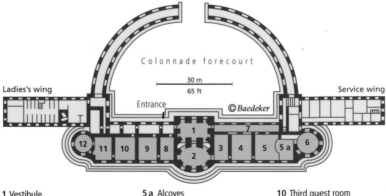

1 Vestibule
2 Marble Hall
3 Audience room
4 Concert room
5 Study- and living room
   (Frederick the Great died here)

5 a Alcoves
6 Library
7 Small Gallery
8 First guest room
9 Second guest room
   (»Blue and White Room«)

10 Third guest room
   (»Red and White Room«)
11 Fourth guest room
   (»Voltaire Room«)
12 Fifth guest room
   (»Rotenburg Room«)

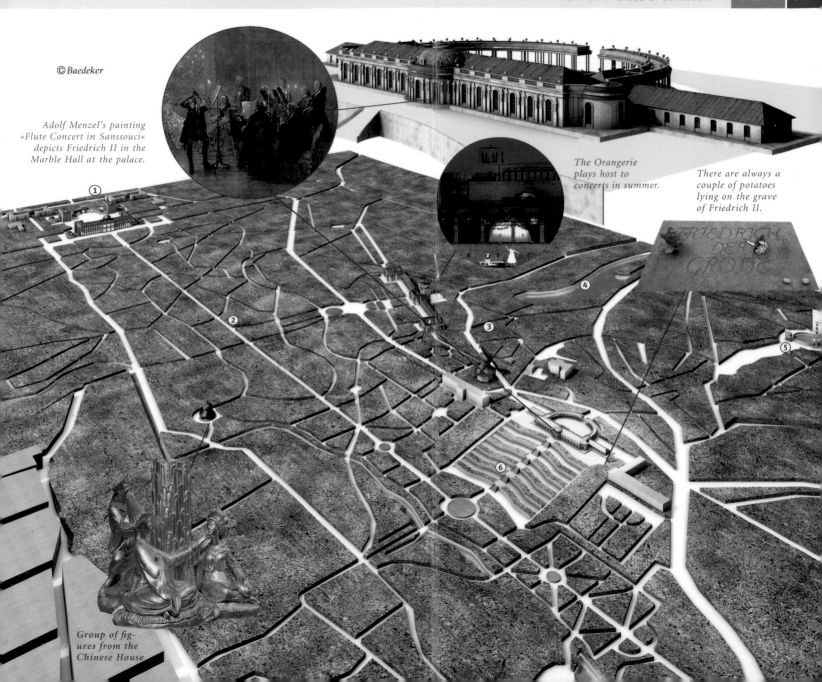

©Baedeker

Adolf Menzel's painting
»Flute Concert in Sanssouci«
depicts Friedrich II in the
Marble Hall at the palace.

The Orangerie
plays host to
concerts in summer.

There are always a
couple of potatoes
lying on the grave
of Friedrich II.

FRIEDRICH
DER
GROSSE

Group of fig-
ures from the
Chinese House

Friedenskirche ▶ The garden encircles the Friedenskirche or Peace Church, which was built between 1845 and 1848 by the combined efforts of Persius, Hesse and Stüler. It is modelled on the basilica of San Clemente in Rome. Its most valuable feature is the late 12th-century mosaic from the Church of San Cypriano on the island of Murano near Venice that has been incorporated into the apse. It was purchased by Friedrich IV in 1834 and is one of only two original Italo-Byzantine mosaics to be found north of the Alps. Underneath the altar is the grave of Friedrich Wilhelm IV and his wife Elisabeth. To the north of the atriums is the mausoleum of Emperor Friedrich III and his wife Victoria, where the sarcophagus of Friedrich Wilhelm I was also kept until 1991. Next to the Marlygarten is the second main entrance to the park, the Grüne Gitter or Green Grille, which can be reached from Luisenplatz.

Neptungrotte (Neptune Grotto) The Neptungrotte is not far north of the Obeliskportal and was constructed between 1751 and 1754 according to a design by von Knobelsdorff. The giant clam in the centre is made from a huge number of real shells.

Grosse Fontäne (Great Fountain) At the foot of the Weinberg is a roundel that includes the Grosse Fontäne with its depiction of the four elements and figures from ancient mythology. Passing the Glockenfontäne (Bell Fountain) from 1750 and the Musenrondell (Roundel of the Muses) with its eight marble statues sculpted according to a von Knobelsdorff design by Glume in around 1752, you reach the Entführungsrondell (Abduction Roundel), which has four groups of marble figures (from about 1750) by Georg Franz Ebenhech representing »abductions« in ancient mythology. These include the Romans' abduction of the Sabine women, Paris' seduction of Helen, Pluto and Persephone, Bacchus and Ariadne.

★★ Chinesisches Haus (Chinese House) Southwards from here is the Chinese House, emblematic of the playfulness of Rococo and the fashion for China at that time. The house was constructed between 1754 and 1756 to plans by Johann Gottfried Bühring using the Turkish trèfle from the palace gardens at Lunéville as his model. It imitates a sweeping tent supported by posts in the form of palm trees, beneath which three cabinets are clustered around a central hall. Life-size gilded Chinese figures made of sandstone – in particular the tea drinkers and musicians – by Johann Peter Benckert and Johann Gottlieb Heymüller bring the scene to life. Also to be admired here are porcelain exhibits from the 18th century (opening hours: May–Oct Tue–Sun 10am–6pm).

Orangerie A path leads from the Glockenfontäne up to the Neue Kammern, and from there through the Felsentor (Stone Portal) and along Maulbeerallee (Mulberry Avenue) to the patio in front of the Orangerie or Orangery Palace. The mounted marble statue of Friedrich II is an 1865 copy of Rauch's bronze figure on Unter den Linden in Berlin. The upper terraces were added in 1855, while the lower one, the Jubiläumsterrasse (Jubilee Terrace), was built in 1913 for the 25th jubilee of Kaiser Wilhelm II. Friedrich Wilhelm IV had planned a major »Höhenstrassenprojekt« (»main road« project), but between 1851 and 1860 all that came to pass of this idea was the Orangery Palace. 300m/330yd long and linking motifs from the later part of the Italian Renaissance and Baroque periods, the building was constructed by Stüler using the king's own sketches and a design put together by Persius. In the Raffaelsaal (Raphael Hall) in the middle, which is modelled on the Sala Regia in the Vatican, there are copies of paintings by masters of the Italian Renaissance and sculptures by Germano-Roman masons. Both towers offer a fabulous view of the parks and of Potsdam itself (tours: April Sat/Sun only, May–mid-Oct Tue–Sat 10am–6pm; Sun free access).

Statue of Friedrich Wilhelm IV in front of the orangery

Botanical Garden

To the west below the Orangerie is the Botanical Garden belonging to Potsdam University, laid out in 1844 by Persius and designed as a paradise garden using a northern Italian model.

Drachenhaus (Dragon House)

From the Orangerie it is not far to the Drachenhaus (Dragon House), built in 1770 by von Gontard for storing wine and modelled on London's Kew Gardens pagoda.

Belvedere on Klausberg hill

Belvedere, built atop Klausberg hill between 1770 and 1772, is the last of Sanssouci's 18th-century buildings. Unger patterned the building on a painting by Francesco Biarchini that was in Friedrich II's collection and depicted Nero's macellum or meat market in Rome.

✹ ✹ Neues Palais

The Neue Palais or New Palace was built at the western end of the Hauptallee. It is the most recent and most magnificent of the palace buildings in the park. It was conceived as a »fanfaronade« or ostenta-

One of 292 sandstone figures around the New Palace

⏱ Opening hours:

Opening hours:
April – Oct daily
except Tue
9am – 6pm,
Nov – March closes
5pm

tious boast after the end of the Seven Years' War to express the might and glory of Prussia and to realize Friedrich II's notion of a prestigious summer residence. Building work began in 1763 under Büring and he was succeeded by von Gontard in 1765. After just seven years of building work, a three-storey palace covering some 240m/260yd with single-storey pavilions at the corners had come into existence. The façades are decorated with an allegorical and mythological set of figures, there are 292 sandstone sculptures in front of the pilasters and parapet alone. The king stubbornly insisted on using forms of the late Baroque period, making the Neues Palais the last important late Baroque palace building in Prussia; it is considered the epitome of Prussian Baroque architecture. The New Palace was mainly used as a court guest house although members of the royal family also lived there.

Interior

The design for the rooms inside was handled by von Gontard. One conspicuous feature is the large number of motifs taken from other Prussian palaces. About 60 of the rooms are open to visitors and contain furniture and porcelain by local craftsmen and artists as well as paintings that mainly come from the demolished Stadtschloss. The original furniture is kept in the palace of Doorn in the Netherlands, where Kaiser Wilhelm II fled into exile in 1918. The highlights include the rooms of Friedrich II, the cabinet of paintings in the lower nobles' quarters, the oval cabinet, the concert room in the upper nobles' quarters, the Marmorsaal (Marble Hall), which extends across two storeys and the Schlosstheater or Palace Theatre, which opened in 1768 and still stages plays.

The splendid pair of buildings opposite the Neues Palais are not another set of palaces but are service buildings known by the name Communs. They were built between 1766 and 1769 according to plans by Jean Laurent Le Geay and von Gontard. The southerly of the two buildings contained a kitchen and service rooms that were connected to the Neues Palais by means of an underground tunnel. The northern building contained the servants' quarters.

Communs

North of the Hauptallee away from the roundel that opens up at the side of the gardens is the Antikentempel or Temple of Antiquities, built in 1768 by von Gontard using sketches by Friedrich II. It once contained numerous statues from Friedrich II's collection, although most of them were passed on to the Altes Museum in Berlin in 1829. The grave of Auguste Victoria, wife of the last German emperor, Wilhelm II, is here.The Freundschaftstempel or Friendship Temple south of the Hauptallee is also the work of von Gontard in 1768 with a major contribution to the design from Friedrich II himself. The building is dedicated to the memory of the king's sister Countess Wilhelmine von Bayreuth, who died in 1757.

Antikentempel (Temple of Antiquities)

◀ Freundschafts-tempel

✱ Schloss Charlottenhof and Park

The area to the south of the Freundschaftstempel was only added to Sanssouci's park in 1826. In 1825 Friedrich Wilhelm III obtained lands belonging to Charlotte von Gentzkow and gifted them to his son Crown Prince Friedrich Wilhelm. Karl Friedrich Schinkel and Peter Joseph Lenné realized his ideas for a palace and gardens between 1826 and 1829 and created in the process one of the most consummate ensembles of romantic classicism.

The palace of Schloss Charlottenhof is a single storey building, the central section of which has a gabled roof that projects out from the building. In front of the entrance there is a fountain with a statue of Neptune (1850) and a poets' arbour created in 1851. At the rear there is a Doric gabled portico leading to an artificially gritted terrace. The interior of the miniature palace was abundantly furnished by Schinkel in the style of unprepossessing bourgeois classicism. One of the most comfortable rooms is the living room, coloured uniformly in light blue and featuring landscape water colours from Italy and Switzerland. The most surprising room, though, is the tent room with its striped wallpaper and tent-like ceiling. It was originally a bedroom for ladies-in-waiting but later became the living room of Alexander von Humboldt when he was staying at Sanssouci (tours May – Oct Tue – Sun 10am – 6pm).

Schloss Charlottenhof

In the gardens Lenné, along with Schinkel and Persius who designed its buildings, was able to realize his concept of an English landscape garden. To the west of the palace he added a Hippodrome in 1836, a

Charlottenhof Park

Roman baths ▶ garden in the shape of an ancient horse racing circuit. The pheasant hutch and paddock to the west were built between 1841 and 1844. Next to the machine pond east of the palace, Persius spent from 1829 to 1840 realizing Schinkel's plans for Roman baths. Its eight buildings are modelled on Italian country houses. They comprise the Hofgärtnerhaus (1829), built as a guest-house, a tea pavilion in the style of a Roman podium temple (1830), various apartment buildings, and the Roman bath itself (1834 – 40), with its large jasper basin, a gift from Tsar Nicholas I. The bath is now used as a venue for art exhibitions (opening hours: as above).

Telegrafenberg

E 4 south

Location: Albert-Einstein-Strasse   **Bus:** 693

Telegrafenberg hill, 94m/308ft above sea level, gets its name from the optical telegraph system that was installed there in 1832.

Science hill   It was the fourth of 61 stations forming a route from Berlin to Koblenz. After the establishment of the German Empire in 1871 the hill was made the site of various scientific institutes: the Astrophysics Institute from 1879, the Meteorological Observatory in 1890 and the Geodetic Institute in 1892. Nowadays it is the site of the »Albert Einstein Science Park« and is mainly used by Potsdam's geological research institute.

The functional yet artistic architecture of the Einsteinturm

The Astrophysics Institute remains the principal building with its three observatory domes and a building housing a refracting telescope which boasts the fourth largest lens in the world (visiting times: May – Oct Sat/Sun 11am – 6pm). The main attraction among the buildings, though, is the extraordinary 18m/59ft-high **Einsteinturm** (Einstein Tower). The solid, brick-built tower came into existence between 1919 and 1924 having been designed by Erich Mendelsohn for research into Einstein's prediction that light might be bent by the gravitational field of the sun. Einstein himself never actually worked here. The tower is still in use (tours are permitted in the six winter months: contact Urania Verein, tel. 03 31 / 29 17 41).

Volkspark

A 1 – 3

Location: North of the city centre   **Tram:** 96

Bornstedter Field was an army training ground in Prussian days and remained so until Soviet troops left at the end of the last century. The site was reanimated as a leisure park for the 2001 German national garden show (BUGA).

Its broad meadows and ancient trees have been supplemented by lines of roses, kitchens, a giant slide, playgrounds, a skating rink and the **Potsdam Biosphere (Biosphäre Potsdam)**, which at the time of the BUGA garden show was a hyper-modern, 200m/220yd-long greenhouse but has now been made into a »Naturerlebniswelt« or nature experience, a mixture of high-tech museum and tropical greenhouse (opening hours: Mon – Fri 9am – 6pm; Sat, Sun and holidays 10am – 7pm).   ⊕

The suburb of Bornstedt lies to the west and south of the Volkspark. The cemetery on Ribbeckstrasse includes the graves of Ludwig Persius (1803 – 45), the family of court gardener Johann Samuel Sello (1715 – 87) and Peter Joseph Lenné (1789 – 1866). Memorial stones recall the conspirators of the attempt to assassinate Hitler on 20 July 1944, Henning von Tresckow and Ulrich Freiherr von Sell. Alongside the lake, Bornstedter See, the palace of Krongut Bornstedt was reconstructed in Italian style by Johann Heinrich Haeberlin in 1846 after a fire. The garden was laid out by Lenné. The model home of Friedrich Wilhelm and his wife Victoria has been restored and apart from allowing a visit to the royal chambers, it also provides a glimpse into a cross section of Brandenburg's tradition of arts and crafts with attractions such as a brewery and beer garden, a schnaps distillery, a glass-blowing workshop, a pottery, and a tin-casting shed.

Bornstedt

◄ Krongut Bornstedt Tram 92

INDEX

LIST OF MAPS AND ILLUSTRATIONS

PHOTO CREDITS

PUBLISHER'S INFORMATION

Illustrations etc: 214 illustrations, 27 maps and diagrams, one large city plan
Text: Rainer Eisenschmid, Isolde Bacher, Gisela Buddée
Editing: Baedeker editorial team (Robert Taylor, John Sykes)
Translation: Simon Clay
Cartography: Franz Huber, München; Falk Verlag, Ostfildern (city plan)
3D illustrations: jangled nerves, Stuttgart
Design: independent Medien-Design, Munich; Kathrin Schemel

Editor-in-chief: Rainer Eisenschmid, Baedeker Ostfildern

2nd edition 2011
Based on Baedeker Allianz Reiseführer »Berlin«, 20th ed. 2010

Copyright: Karl Baedeker Verlag, Ostfildern
Publication rights: MAIRDUMONT GmbH & Co; Ostfildern

Printed in China

BAEDEKER GUIDE BOOKS AT A GLANCE
Guiding the World since 1827

- ▶ Andalusia
- ▶ Australia
- ▶ Austria
- ▶ Bali
- ▶ Barcelona
- ▶ Berlin
- ▶ Brazil
- ▶ Budapest
- ▶ Cape Town • Garden Route
- ▶ China
- ▶ Cologne
- ▶ Dresden
- ▶ Dubai
- ▶ Egypt
- ▶ Florence
- ▶ Florida

- ▶ France
- ▶ Gran Canaria
- ▶ Greek Islands
- ▶ Greece
- ▶ Iceland
- ▶ India
- ▶ Ireland
- ▶ Italian Lakes
- ▶ Italy
- ▶ Japan
- ▶ London
- ▶ Madeira
- ▶ Mexico
- ▶ Morocco
- ▶ Naples • Capri • Amalfi Coast
- ▶ New York

- ▶ New Zealand
- ▶ Norway
- ▶ Paris
- ▶ Portugal
- ▶ Prague
- ▶ Rome
- ▶ South Africa
- ▶ Spain
- ▶ Thailand
- ▶ Turkish Coast
- ▶ Tuscany
- ▶ Venice
- ▶ Vienna
- ▶ Vietnam

DEAR READER,

We would like to thank you for choosing this Baedeker travel guide. It will be a reliable companion on your travels and will not disappoint you.
This book describes the major sights, of course, but it also recommends the best »Berliner Kneipen« (pubs), as well as hotels in the luxury and budget categories, and includes tips about where to eat or go shopping and much more, helping to make your trip an enjoyable experience. Our author Rainer Eisenschmid ensures the quality of this information by making regular journeys to Berlin and putting all his know-how into this book.

Nevertheless, experience shows us that it is impossible to rule out errors and changes made after the book goes to press, for which Baedeker accepts no liability. Please send us your criticisms, corrections and suggestions for improvement: we appreciate your contribution. Contact us by post or e-mail, or phone us:

► **Verlag Karl Baedeker GmbH**
Editorial department
Postfach 3162
73751 Ostfildern
Germany
Tel. 49-711-4502-262, fax -343
www.baedeker.com
www.baedeker.co.uk
E-Mail: baedeker@mairdumont.com